M000206687

Normalizing an American Right to Health

Normalizing an American Right to Health

CHRISTINA S. HO

OXFORD
UNIVERSITY PRESS

OXFORD
UNIVERSITY PRESS

Oxford University Press is a department of the University of Oxford. It furthers the University's objective of excellence in research, scholarship, and education by publishing worldwide. Oxford is a registered trade mark of Oxford University Press in the UK and certain other countries.

Published in the United States of America by Oxford University Press
198 Madison Avenue, New York, NY 10016, United States of America.

© Christina S. Ho 2023

All rights reserved. No part of this publication may be reproduced, stored in a retrieval system, or transmitted, in any form or by any means, without the prior permission in writing of Oxford University Press, or as expressly permitted by law, by license, or under terms agreed with the appropriate reproduction rights organization. Inquiries concerning reproduction outside the scope of the above should be sent to the Rights Department, Oxford University Press, at the address above.

You must not circulate this work in any other form
and you must impose this same condition on any acquirer.

Library of Congress Cataloging-in-Publication Data
Names: Ho, Christina S, author.
Title: Normalizing an American right to health / Christina S. Ho
Description: New York, NY : Oxford University Press, [2023] |
Includes bibliographical references and index.
Identifiers: LCCN 2022062189 (print) | LCCN 2022062190 (ebook) |
ISBN 9780197650592 (hardback) | ISBN 9780197650608 (updf) |
ISBN 9780197650615 (epub) | ISBN 9780197650622 (digital-online)
Subjects: LCSH: Right to health—United States. |
Medical care—Finance—Law and legislation—United States.
Classification: LCC KF3822 .H6 2023 (print) | LCC KF3822 (ebook) |
DDC 362.10973—dc23/eng/20230130
LC record available at https://lccn.loc.gov/2022062189
LC ebook record available at https://lccn.loc.gov/2022062190

DOI: 10.1093/oso/9780197650592.001.0001

Printed by Sheridan Books, Inc., United States of America

Note to Readers
This publication is designed to provide accurate and authoritative information in regard to the subject matter covered. It is based upon sources believed to be accurate and reliable and is intended to be current as of the time it was written. It is sold with the understanding that the publisher is not engaged in rendering legal, accounting, or other professional services. If legal advice or other expert assistance is required, the services of a competent professional person should be sought. Also, to confirm that the information has not been affected or changed by recent developments, traditional legal research techniques should be used, including checking primary sources where appropriate.

(Based on the Declaration of Principles jointly adopted by a Committee of the American Bar Association and a Committee of Publishers and Associations.)

You may order this or any other Oxford University Press publication by visiting the Oxford University Press website at www.oup.com.

For Ting and Lily Ho

Contents

Acknowledgments

Any book, especially a first book, memorializes the lifetime of debt one has accumulated to her community. A number of folks gave early encouragement, perhaps without even realizing it at the time, so my heartfelt thanks go to Bernie Bell, Mark Hall, Nan Hunter, John Jacobi, Robin West, Larry Gostin, John Monahan, Jeanne Lambrew, and Wendy Parmet. Colleen Flood, Aeyal Gross, Bill Alford, Kim Mutcherson, and Phil Harvey all nudged me along the path to thinking about health rights in comparative contexts; I am lucky to have been the beneficiary of their breadth of vision. My love always to Duncan Kennedy, Christopher Edley Jr., Scott Moss, Heather Hughes, and Vikas Arora who have provided intellectual friendship over nigh two decades.

I am so grateful to those who generously pointed me in the right direction as I pulled together the project proposal. Thank you so much, Allison Hoffman, Stuart Green, Peter D. Jacobsen, Eugene Mazo, George Thomas, Carlos Ball, Suzanne Kim, and Adil Haque.

So many have helped me refine these ideas through various workshops that I cannot thank them all here. They include Alicia Yamin, Nicole Huberfeld, Carl Coleman, Gwendolyn Majette, Craig Konnoth, M. Gregg Bloche, David Orentlicher, Lisa Forman, Victoria Nourse, Alan Morrison, Bijal Shah, Glenn Cohen, and the community at ClassCrits.

On reinsurance, I have benefited so much from Katherine Swartz, Govind Persad, Erin Fuse Brown, Elizabeth Weeks, Chloe Reichel, Margarida Lima Regos, Birgit Kuchke, J. Gabriel McGlamery, and the community of critical finance scholars.

My Rutgers Law colleagues have influenced this book over the years through conversation, workshopping, and through their own scholarship. My fondest to, among many others, Bernie Bell, John Leubsdorf, David Frankford, Reid Weisbord, Stuart Green, Jorge Contesse, Chrystin Ondersma, Jean-Marc Coicaud, David Noll, Rick Swedloff, Ann Freedman, Rand Rosenblatt, Kati Kovacs, and Kim Mutcherson.

Elizabeth Popp Berman, I couldn't have done it without the wonderful writing community you brought together—you all know who you are! I was blessed with wonderful research assistants over many years, each of whom contributed to various parts of this project: my deepest gratitude to Hansi Men, James Stone, Robert Evans, Chinsu Sajan, Christine H. Lee, Isaac Lee, David

Shafiei, and Hudson Cleveland. Oxford University Press gave excellent guidance throughout.

Finally, thank you to my family: my mother and father who gave me all the runway, my sister Barbara who ever inspires me, and my husband, Tom, who is my rock. He, with the boys, Mack and Dominic, keep us true.

1

Introduction

The US healthcare system is, for good reason, a punching bag and a cautionary tale, a bogeyman of late capitalism to scare the world straight. The United States is one of a small minority of countries where health is as yet not enshrined in the constitution.[1] I remember a moment in the deep midnight of the COVID-19 pandemic when darkly comic videos began to circulate showing how people in other countries react when learning about seemingly basic health services that are provided only conditionally at significant cost under the US healthcare system. In reaction to an invoice showing that an American hospital charged 35 USD for "skin-to-skin" care for an infant post–C-section, a Japanese woman gasps, "You have to pay to hold your baby?!"[2] Meanwhile, the British man-on-the-street, when asked how much he thinks the ambulance charge would be in the United States, shakes off his confusion ("Is there a price for that?") and guesses 100 USD—less than a tenth of the actual average cost.[3]

In some sense, we in the United States have taken the burden of our health failings on board. For some it is a source of shame. Yet others seem almost to embrace our healthcare exceptionalism with belligerence. We now almost numbly recite the couplet that the United States spends more per capita on health than any other developed country, only to achieve worse outcomes than our peers.[4] Reform-minded Americans invoke ritual outrage that the United States remains impervious to the claims of health as a human right. Yet for all these self-critiques, what might have been a goad to action strangely also threatens to encrust into nihilistic identity. Our comparative failure to recognize the right to health has somehow turned into a way of defining down who we are and who we can be.

With permission, Chapter 1 adapts minor material from Christina S. Ho, *With Liberty and Reinsurance for All: The Deep Case for a Government Backstop in Health Care*, 100 Denv. L. Rev. ____ (forthcoming 2023), and from Christina S. Ho, *Health Impact Assessments: A Negative Procedural Health Right?* 50 Seton Hall L. Rev. 643 (2020).

[1] Eleanor D. Kinney & Brian A. Clark, *Provisions for Health and Health Care in the Constitutions of the Countries of the World*, 37 Cornell Int'l L.J. 285, 291 (2004) (finding that 67.5 percent of the world's constitutions address health or healthcare).

[2] Chai Dingari, "What Does U.S. Health Care Look Like Abroad?" N. Y. Times, Opinion (April 21, 2021), https://www.nytimes.com/2021/04/28/opinion/healthcare-us.html.

[3] True Cost of US Healthcare Shocks the British Public (December 3, 2019), https://www.youtube.com/watch?v=Kll-yYQwmuM.

[4] *See, e.g.,* Ezekiel J. Emanuel et al., *Comparing Health Outcomes of Privileged US Citizens With Those of Average Residents of Other Developed Countries*, 181 JAMA Internal Med. 339 (December 28, 2020).

This book has a mission: to push back on this conventional wisdom that the right to health is too pie-in-the-sky, quixotic, and somehow meant only for other communities and other times, that it is simply not a serious pursuit for the re-formist and policy-active citizenry of the United States.

For as long as I can remember, claims for health rights have met with a routine discursive deflection that brackets them outside legitimate policy consideration, requiring some constitutional or superpolitical transformation far beyond the frontier of political possibility. This de-normalization is doing a lot of work to keep health rights off the agenda, but why is it deemed self-evident? In fact, this book will use ordinary legal and policy examples, many well-known, to show that this de-normalization is eminently contestable.

The US health rights project is evergreen in its importance. But it is particu-larly urgent now. We are witness in our times to increasingly stark competition between human health and other material values. Lifespans in the United States are shrinking, "deaths of despair" continue to mount, and in these past few years of pandemic, climate hazard, and military escalation, there seems no place to rest our gaze from the spectacle of human bodies heedlessly shredded in the service of some other gain or preference.

Despite our horror over the human toll of our current arrangements, there is pact of silence—a dead space—where we might otherwise be discussing our right to protection, our right to rescue, our right to care, and our right to flourish despite the depredations of our time. The "right to health" slogan is everywhere, to be sure. Yet I find myself in this book trying desperately to fill in the visioning gap, which slogans cannot replenish. Bless the stalwarts who have done the spadework to draft, strategize, prod, and protest in the service of Medicare for All. Without them, no one would be talking at a level of policy or doctrinal detail about what health rights we have or ought to have.

Yet they are regularly dismissed and marginalized as not serious, naïve, overreaching, and poised to squander all their hard-earned political capital. How strange these accusations are when our past successes stare us in the face, showing how we have indeed entrenched near-universal statutory health rights at least for those over the age of sixty-five, and now arguably for the populations addressed in the Affordable Care Act (ACA).[5] Yet any further claims to health rights meet routinely with the same exhausted discursive gesture.

Many have sought to advance head-on by fighting for that transforma-tion. And as we mobilize, I propose a coordinated flanking offense, one that gives us space to maneuver. My book presses back against the idea that a US right to health is out of reach by showing that the change we need is not always

---

[5] Erin C. Fuse Brown, *Developing a Durable Right to Health Care*, 14 MINN. J. OF L. SCI. & TECH. 439 (2013).

extraordinary, but familiar; that we have already laid considerable ground-work in ordinary cases and policies, but have simply yet to acknowledge these examples as rights-building. I seek, as the project title announces, to *normalize* American health rights discourse and bring a right to health, including a right to healthcare, within the domain of ordinary policy debate. A right to health is already growing in our midst if we know where to look and what to nurture. We could use a fresh framing of health rights as bite-size legislative measures with long-standing parallels in other fields. My hope is that this tactic can side-step the stagnant arguments over how we recognize "costly" or "quixotic" economic and social rights in the US system.

This book is an act of resistance. It counters that dismissal of whether the rights-building work is worth doing by just going ahead and doing it, showing that it can be and indeed is being done. The dream is that we can stop talking about whether it's worth talking about rights and just talk about what health rights we already have and how they connect up with those we could and should have. The book proceeds with this task both as a descriptive project and as a pre-scriptive one, conceiving the two as continuous rather than cleaved. After all, rights themselves, as matters of principle that must apply in each like case, con-tain their own expansionary potential.

The following describes how the book will proceed.

Chapter 2 sets forth the models of rights that tell us how to recognize the rights-building that is already taking place. Our pluralist society is capacious enough to exhibit more than one conception of rights, so I detail the three main frameworks that I lean on throughout the book. These models I later use as litmus tests to de-tect the presence of health and health-adjacent rights in our midst. For instance, Ronald Dworkin offers a relatively deontological portrait of rights as a special type of norm that works by simply ruling out certain competing claims as valid reasons to compromise the right. Dworkin describes rights thus: if we recognize a value as important enough to constitute a right, say speech, for instance, then restricting speech in the interest of those who are offended by hearing the speech is presumptively ruled out as illegitimate.[6] After all, the whole point of making free speech a right is internally undermined if it is not protected from compro-mise in the face of the countervailing values of those who disagree with the views expressed. Health law is often characterized by this line of reasoning. Indeed, one might travel far and wide before finding a better example of Dworkinian rights-thinking than the emerging norm that we should not deny health coverage to those with preexisting conditions. Denying someone healthcare because they are sick and therefore *need* costly healthcare displays exactly the kind of logic that

[6] This capsule reading of Dworkin draws not only from his own writings, but also on Jeremy Waldron's account of Dworkin. *See* Jeremy Waldron, *Rights in Conflict*, 99 ETHICS 503 (1989).

Dworkin believes rights are designed to rule out, or to "trump." Meeting the *need* for healthcare is the whole purpose of valuing the right in the first place. Thus using someone's health need as a reason to compromise the right should be unacceptable *should* we choose to treat *health* as a right. This model sets up the later descriptive chapters of the book where I trace examples of this and related kinds of distinctive rights-grammar throughout our existing health-related case law, as well as our statutory enactments.

Another theoretical account that I utilize to test for health rights is the view of rights as proportionality. This type of right differs from a Dworkinian right inasmuch as it allows for the balancing of competing considerations against rights, albeit with heavy weighting toward the right. This is the category of right that we see at work in the constitutional tests that require (1) a sufficiently weighty countervailing purpose and (2) some measure of "fit." I proceed in Chapter 5 of the book to show that a certain category of legislation, encompassing various regulatory impact assessments, imposes showings of sufficiency of purpose and considerations of fit, upon any action that would injure the value designated in the legislation. Enacting a health impact assessment would establish a right to health along the lines of these existing impact assessments that have been legislated in other domains.

The final framework I introduce in Chapter 2 is David Super's model of American statutory entitlements. Because the fight for affirmative government provision in the United States has transpired almost exclusively through statutory enactment rather than constitutional law, we are better equipped to recognize potential socioeconomic rights here if armed not with abstract theories of affirmative rights, but with accounts of the common US legal and political usage of the term "entitlement." Super sets out a list of characteristics that signify when a program qualifies as an entitlement in the US political-legal vernacular. I will show that we routinely confer these characteristics—positive entitlement, budgetary entitlement, responsive entitlement, and even functional and subjective entitlement—on a category of program that I call "state-sponsored reinsurance." Yet these entitlements, which abound in areas from flood insurance to banking, are not often recognized as rights to affirmative state provision. I go on to propose that such an entitlement to state-sponsored reinsurance should be extended to health coverage.

In the meantime, Chapters 3 and 4 comprise the descriptive portion of my argument. This section seeks to persuade that a health right is closer at hand than we credit. I show that we have already laid considerable groundwork in ordinary cases and policies, but have simply yet to acknowledge these examples as rights-building. These chapters in effect identify the scope of positive law in the health domain as the "preinterpretive" practice to be "fit" and "justified" by my hypothesized right to health.[7] The methodology, as I explain in Chapter 2, draws

---

[7] Ronald Dworkin, Law's Empire, 225–75 (1996).

more than a little from Ronald Dworkin. Dworkin himself offers this usefully condensed description of the approach of constructive interpretation which I undertake here:

> [There are] three stages of an interpretation. . . . First there must be a "preinterpretive" stage in which the rules and standards taken to provide the tentative content of the practices are identified. . . . Second, there must be an interpretive stage at which the interpreter settles on some general justification for the main elements of the practice identified at the pre-interpretive stage. This will consist of an argument why a practice of that general shape is worth pursuing if it is. The justification need not fit every aspect or feature of the standing practice, but it must fit enough for the interpreter to be able to see himself as interpreting that practices, not inventing a new one.[8]

Dworkin goes on to say of the third step: "Finally, there must be a postinterpretive or reforming stage, at which [the interpreter] adjusts his sense of what the practice 'really' requires so as better to serve the justification he accepts at the interpretive stage."[9]

This brings us to my prescriptive story, told in Chapters 5 through 7, where I move from showing where a right to health might already lodge in our legal corpus to showing how we could incrementally build out the right from where we sit. I identify a few next steps that we can take to advance a right to health in the United States, and show that they are not naïve, vain, or idle. We know they are feasible because we employ similar measures all the time for material interests other than human health. Yet if pressed, I doubt we could say that we prioritize these other interests over health as a value.

As I propose in Chapter 5, there is a "shovel-ready" way to recognize a "negative" liberty from health harms, and that measure would take the form of a Health Impact Assessment (HIA). As I noted in the preview of Chapter 2, we have already established a set of legislative and regulatory impact assessments that impose claimable demands for the articulation of (1) sufficiency of purpose and (2) sufficiently tailored fit with respect to government actions that threaten to burden various other designated values. This description is enough to suggest that the structural features of impact assessments plausibly map onto the model of rights as proportionality. We currently require such impact assessments as a result of statutes like the National Environmental Policy Act (NEPA), the Small Business Enforcement and Regulatory Flexibility Act (SBERFA), the Unfunded Mandates Reform Act (UMRA), and the Paperwork Reduction Act. I argue that

---

[8] *Id.* at 65–6.
[9] *Id.* 65–6.

these impact assessments are de facto elevations of specific subconstitutional values (including the environment, small business interests, economic freedom for state and local governments, and freedom from paperwork) to the status of rights. We therefore ought to require impact assessments for any government action that injures health as well. This extra scrutiny should be applied, for instance, to penal measures that harm the health of incarcerated persons and their wider communities, to housing policies whose adverse health effects have been robustly demonstrated, to inequitable tax laws that have been linked to increased infant mortality, to transportation policies that burden population health, to agricultural policies that subsidize sugar, and any other policy that has an evidence-based connection to adverse health effects. This HIA proposal is hardly too radical: it (merely) protects Americans from health harms the way that we already protect small businesses from economic harm.

Finally, in Chapters 6 and 7, I show that this same comparative sectoral approach can yield a viable proposal for how to incrementally build out not just a *negative* health liberty, but also an *affirmative* right to the material provision of health financing. An affirmative right to expensive healthcare has been precisely the type of state program considered far distant from the realm of political possibility in the United States. The claim to health aid that I propose is a claim to government "reinsurance" for backstopping catastrophic health risk. I argue that the state is already performing a reinsurance function whenever it absorbs catastrophic losses above a certain threshold in order to smooth out and shore up the underlying private risk market in other areas, and it ought to take on that function more explicitly in the health sector.

For all our vaunted aversion to entitlements, whenever we as a nation we have deemed a material interest to be vital—including housing, food crops, higher education, pensions, and banking—we have provided state guarantees, as I will show. These guarantees, however, have not necessarily backed the individual beneficiary, but rather the primary private insurer or financier who bridges beneficiary access to that good or service.

It turns out this demand for affirmative government reinsurance is commonplace in the context of other interests, though not yet so in health care. In domain after domain, the government stands behind insurers and other private entities to help absorb catastrophic costs whenever losses exceed what those institutions could be expected to bear. Yet the US government fails to reinsure the health plans of ordinary Americans, a step which would shield them from outlier health events.

In Chapter 6, I examine these types of commitments as they operate in non–health domains. Not only do they blanket our politico-legal landscape, but that they are in fact entrenched as virtual entitlements by the measure of David Super's yardstick. They have been endowed with the properties that we ascribe to rights-granting statutes, even if slightly outside the narrow viewfinder of our constitutional discourse. These reinsurance measures nearly always enjoy budgetary entitlement in the form of mandatory rather than discretionary funding, they confer positive entitlements to beneficiaries in the form of individually justiciable claims, and these non–health programs often qualify as "subjective," "responsive," and "functional" entitlements under Super's rubric insofar as the government has time and again vindicated the subjective expectations of reinsurance even in functionally like cases to which the positive law does not yet expressly extend.

Having laid out in Chapter 6 this argument for health reinsurance as desirable, if only so that health is valued on equal footing with competing interests, I continue in Chapter 7 to demonstrate the value and feasibility of a health reinsurance proposal in terms of how it could appreciably improve the US health system. I do so in part by showing how much we have already done along these lines through such statutory regimes as the ACA, Medicare, Medicaid, and the Employee Retirement Income Security Act (ERISA), and how beyond these programs, we could use reinsurance to begin to fill in the remaining gaps.

Dismantling Old Myths

But this health rights project, which I hope appears promising from the outline above, has been heretofore blocked. The barriers include the persistence of certain articles of faith that countless scholars have by now demonstrated that we ought to discard. In this book, I am writing against four main gaps and lacunae that afflict the conventional wisdom that a right to health is foreign to the US politico-legal system.

Dismantling the Documentary Premise

First, the stance rejecting American health rights has long overemphasized constitutions as a source of rights. But when right-to-health skeptics invoke the lack of express constitutional acknowledgment—the "documentary premise"— they reveal an ideological tilt.[10] After all, many have found implicit, atextual

---

[10] WILLIAM ESKRIDGE AND JOHN FEREJOHN, A REPUBLIC OF STATUTES: THE NEW AMERICAN CONSTITUTION 34, 65 (2010) (hereinafter A REPUBLIC OF STATUTES) introducing the notion of the documentary premise thus: "Unlike British constitutionalism, American Constitutionalism is closely connected to a single unified document whose canonical text is not in serious dispute. One implication of such a 'documentary premise' is that Constitutional claims must be linked to a written Constitution as amended." *Id.* at 34.

neo-*Lochner*ian protections for economic liberty throughout our constitutional jurisprudence.[11] I will argue that we have more resources within our legal corpus available for extrapolation, more ways to connect the dots than mere reinscription of the neoliberal image. I set out in this book to identify places in our body of law that suggest an implicit, unrecognized right to health. We already through our practices elevate and privilege a number of values without express acknowledgment, and I will show where we apply and where we deny this privileging to health as a value. If we know where to look to detect this rights-thinking, then we know what to support and extend.

But pushing back against the documentary premise requires recognition that entrenchment occurs in more ways than constitutional enshrinement alone. The scholarship in this vein has been robust. Bruce Ackerman has written of a mode of "higher lawmaking," that stands in for "our ability to write down our new constitutional commitments in the old-fashioned way."[12] He contends that whenever we "got serious about constitutional change [in recent times, we] pursued the paths marked out by the New Deal and civil rights revolutions . . . by passing a statute."[13] Some set of these important statutes are referred to by William Eskridge and John Ferejohn as "superstatutes."[14] Superstatutes, on their telling, entrench "small 'c' constitutional" norms. Once crystallized, these "institutional or normative principles have a broad effect on the law—including an effect beyond the four corners of the statute."[15] Hallmarks of these higher order laws include the extent of public deliberation in connection with these important statutory moments, the mobilization of institutions around such legislation, intertwining the fate of various interest groups with the fate of the statute, and an eventual acceptance of the norm by its original opponents.[16]

The Federal Reserve, for instance, with no official Constitutional mention, has become an anchor institution within our system of government. Central banks indeed depend for their functioning on an independence that allows them to make credible precommitments such that their stated intentions remain durable or "sticky" against later pressures and vicissitudes. Eskridge and Ferejohn

---

[11] *See, e.g.,* Elizabeth Sepper, *Free Exercise Lochnerism,* 115 COLUM. L. REV. 1453 (2015); *see also,* Abigail R. Moncrieff, *Safeguarding the Safeguards: The ACA Litigation and the Extension of Indirect Protection to Nonfundamental Liberties,* 64 FLORIDA L. REV. 639 (2012); Eugene Volokh, MEDICAL SELF-DEFENSE, PROHIBITED EXPERIMENTAL THERAPIES, AND PAYMENT FOR ORGANS, 120 HARV. L. REV. 1813 (2007).

Jeremy Kessler, *The Early Years of First Amendment Lochnerism,* 116 COLUM. L. REV. (2016); Jedediah Purdy, *Neoliberal Constitutionalism: Lochnerism for a New Economy,* 77 LAW & CONTEMP. PROBS. 195 (2014).

[12] BRUCE ACKERMAN, WE THE PEOPLE: THE CIVIL RIGHTS REVOLUTION 26–7 (2014)

[13] *Id.*

[14] *See* A REPUBLIC OF STATUTES at 11.

[15] William N. Eskridge, Jr. & John Ferejohn, *Super-Statutes,* 50 DUKE L.J. 1215, 1216 (2001).

[16] *See* A REPUBLIC OF STATUTES at 7.

themselves propose the US antitrust regime, the Social Security Act, and a handful of others as further examples of superstatutes.[17]

There is a lively literature around other examples and mechanisms of nonconstitutional entrenchment and the related concept of Congressional precommitment.[18] Beth Garrett and others have identified and explained a number of specific devices, like fast-track procedures or statutized rules of construction, by which legislatures try to alter the difficulty of select future decisions.[19] In addition to these procedural entrenchment strategies, Daryl Levinson and Benjamin Sachs further identify softer "functional" strategies that rely on normative or political pathways to insulate certain statutes from ordinary legislative change.[20]

Thus, a focus solely on the Constitution serves to distract attention from the real and consequential operation of the hidden machinery of prioritization that churns elsewhere in our system.

The notorious *Lochner* court elevated economic liberty as a political principle despite its absence from the positive text of the Constitution.[21] Even today a neo-*Lochner*ism pervades our law.[22] Why then impose documentary obstacles

---

[17] *Id.* For other literature on the candidacy of various superstatutes, *see* Kathryn E. Kovacs, *Superstatute Theory and Administrative Common Law*, 90 IND. L.J. 1207 (2015); Sam Simon, *How Statutes Create Rights: The Case of the National Labor Relations Act*, 15 U. PA. J. CONST. L. 1503 (2013); Lewis A. Grossman, *AIDS Activists, FDA Regulation, and the Amendment of America's Drug Constitution*, 42 AM. J.L. & MED. 687, 690–91 (2016); *see also* John D. Skrentny & Micah Gell-Redman, *Comprehensive Immigration Reform and the Dynamics of Statutory Entrenchment*, 120 YALE L.J. ONLINE 325, 332 (2011).

[18] Eric A. Posner & Adrian Vermeule, *Legislative Entrenchment: A Reappraisal*, 111 YALE L.J. 1665, 1671 (2002); John C. Roberts and Erwin Chemerinsky, *Entrenchment of Ordinary Legislation: A Reply to Professors Posner and Vermeule*, 91 CAL L REV 1773, 1775–76 (2003); Symposium, *"Paying the Alligator": Precommitment in Law, Bioethics, and Constitutions*, 81 TEX. L. REV. 1729 (2003) (with contributors including Robert H. Frank, John Ferejohn and Lawrence Sager, John Robertson, Daniel Brock, Samuel Issacharoff, Sanford Levinson, William Forbath, Steven Ratner, and others); PAUL STARR, ENTRENCHMENT (2020). Much of this work draws from seminal work by JON ELSTER, ULYSSES AND THE SIRENS: STUDIES IN RATIONALITY AND IRRATIONALITY (1990) (hereinafter SIRENS) and JON ELSTER, ULYSSES UNBOUND: STUDIES IN RATIONALITY, PRECOMMITMENT, AND CONSTRAINTS (2000) (hereinafter UNBOUND).

[19] *See, e.g.*, Elizabeth Garrett, *Framework Legislation and Federalism*, 83 NOTRE DAME L. REV. 1495, 1496 (2008). *See also*, Aaron Andrew-Bruhl, *Using Statutes to Set Legislative Rules: Entrenchment, Separation of Powers and the Rules of Proceedings Clause*, 19 J.L. & POL. 345 (2003). Andrew-Bruhl deems "statutized rules" to qualify as legislative entrenchment because they aim to change the relative burdens of certain subsequent Congressional acts from what they would have been otherwise. *Id.* at 372–73. *See also*, Michael J. Teter, *Recusal Legislating: Congress's Answer to Institutional Stalemate*, 48 HARV. J. ON LEGIS. 1, 8–12 (2011); Amandeep S. Grewal, *Legislative Entrenchment Rules in the Tax Law*, 62 ADMIN. L. REV. 1011(2010); John McGinnis & Michael Rappaport, *The Constitutionality of Legislative Supermajority Requirements: A Defense* 105 YALE L.J. 483, 504 (1996). Nicholas Quinn Rosenkranz, *Federal Rules of Statutory Interpretation*, 115 HARV. L. REV. 2085 (2002).

[20] Daryl Levinson & Benjamin I. Sachs, Political Entrenchment and Public Law 125 YALE L.J. 400, 454 (2015).

[21] Lochner v. New York, 198 U.S. 45 (1905).

[22] *See supra* n.11.

to deny such possibility for other values like human health? My effort answers a call that others have sounded; William Forbath, for instance, describes it thus:

> We're all familiar with the anti-redistributive, laissez-faire, or *Lochner* tradi-
> tion in American constitutional law and politics. . . . [*Lochner* revivalists] are
> wrong to claim that history can bind us to one particular account of our past
> constitutional commitments. In political economy, as elsewhere, our constitu-
> tional past is full of contending commitments and understandings; it offers less
> determinate and more choice-laden meanings for the present. . . . Movements
> for change need an account of past constitutional contests and commitments
> that add up to a vision of the nation that the Constitution promises to promote
> and redeem. . . . Lately, we progressives have not had any good constitutional
> narratives to counter the laissez-faire, *Lochner*-ian account of an America fun-
> damentally committed to rugged individualism, personal responsibility, and
> private property safe from state interferences and redistribution.[23]

If the political morality of economic rights serves to power the law, why not the political morality of health rights? The "false necessity" of the neoliberal back-ground norms has underwritten the denialism around health rights that I hope to contest.[24]

Debunking the Preference for Courts over Legislatures as Champions of Rights

This demand by the right-to-health skeptics for express constitutional acknowl-edgment exposes an additional problem, or lag, in the argument against an American right to health. A generation of scholars including Jeremy Waldron, Bruce Ackerman, Larry Sager, Larry Kramer, Mark Tushnet, Robin West, Philip Frickey, William Eskridge, and John Ferejohn have ushered in an era more cog-nizant of legislation and the polity as sources for entrenched rights.[25] This change makes room for my argument that health rights are incipient, and that much of

---

[23] William Forbath, *Social and Economic Rights in the American Grain: Reclaiming Constitutional Political Economy, in* THE CONSTITUTION IN 2020 56 (Jack Balkin and Reva Siegel, eds., 2009).

[24] ROBERTO MANGABEIRA UNGER, FALSE NECESSITY: ANTI-NECESSITARIAN SOCIAL THEORY IN THE SERVICE OF RADICAL DEMOCRACY 530 (1987).

[25] LAWRENCE SAGER, JUSTICE IN PLAINCLOTHES: A THEORY OF AMERICAN CONSTITUTIONAL PRACTICE (2004); LARRY KRAMER, THE PEOPLE THEMSELVES: POPULAR CONSTITUTIONALISM AND JUDICIAL REVIEW (2005); MARK TUSHNET, TAKING THE CONSTITUTION AWAY FROM THE COURTS (1999); Robin West, *Toward the Study of the Legislated Constitution*, 72 OHIO STATE L.J. 1343 (2011); Sam Moyn, The Court is Not Your Friend, Dissent (Winter 2020), https://www.dissentmagazine.org/article/the-court-is-not-your-friend; Jeremy Waldron, *The Core of the Case Against Judicial Review*, 115 YALE L. J. 1346 (2006).

their emergence has been and will be transacted outside of the Constitution and outside of the courts.

Many statutes, as Robin West puts it, can be

> understood to be central embodiments, not just peripheral glosses, of the constitutional mandate, enforced through political will rather than through judicial declaration, that both the federal government and the various states are "constituted" so as to promote public welfare . . . Those laws and others like them are the product of a political state that at least from time to time has taken very seriously not only to its obligations under the social compact to tend to the general welfare and promote domestic tranquility but its constitutional obligations to do so as well.[26]

We now enjoy a late flowering of work revealing how our nonjudicial institutions enact and fulfill important constitutional rights and duties.[27] My book dwells in this rich pocket of the scholarly landscape insofar as it treats the ACA, Medicare, Medicaid, and other health statutes as expressions of our constitutive norms, no less than if they were constitutionally motivated. While I examine many cases to plumb the content of our health law for rights hallmarks in Chapter 4, Chapter 3 also takes seriously the health governance decisions of our legislatures as a terrain for principled action and rights-based practice.

The solutions I focus on in Chapters 5 through 7 will also stress legislative next steps rather than constitutional change to be vindicated by courts. One reason is because we cannot wait any longer; our needs are pressing now, and they cannot be deferred beyond the horizon of constitutional change. Another reason is that socioeconomic rights, like the right to health, may have features that render them particularly suitable for legislative rather than judicial resolution. Such features include the complex polycentric nature of the disputes and their stakeholders.[28] Another characteristic is an inherent dynamism, given that our conception of healthcare and illness depends upon what morbidity and mortality is deemed "avoidable," a notion which changes with technology.[29] Finally,

---

[26] ROBIN WEST, NUSSBAUM AND LAW 200 (2015).

[27] *See, e.g.*, KAREN TANI, STATES OF DEPENDENCY: WELFARE, RIGHTS AND AMERICAN GOVERNANCE (2016). SOPHIA Z. LEE, THE WORKPLACE CONSTITUTION FROM THE NEW DEAL TO THE NEW RIGHT (2014).

[28] Lon Fuller, *The Forms and Limits of Adjudication*, 92 HARV. L. REV. 353 (1978).

[29] *See* NORMAN DANIELS, JUST HEALTH 145 (2008). NORM DANIELS AND JAMES SABIN, SETTING LIMITS FAIRLY: LEARNING TO SHARE RESOURCES FOR HEALTH 1–2 (2nd ed., 2008) ("The major force driving up health care costs . . . is the emergency of new technologies . . . Aging populations and increased expectations about what medicine can and should do for us mean there is ever- increasing demand for what technology makes possible"). INSTITUTE OF MEDICINE, ASSESSING MEDICAL TECHNOLOGIES 16 (1985). DANIEL CALLAHAN, TAMING THE BELOVED BEAST: HOW MEDICAL TECHNOLOGY COSTS ARE DESTROYING OUR HEALTH CARE SYSTEM (2009).

the right to health may also be susceptible to a certain amount of "moral under-determination" given the multiple policy options for satisfying the right, often involving broad coordination and detailed design.[30] I note each feature's relevance to health disputes briefly below.

Lon Fuller is credited with the notion that adjudication may be ill-suited for "polycentric" disputes, a term that he traces to Michael Polyani.[31] To illustrate a polycentric problem, Fuller gives the example of the task of:

[A]ssign[ing] players on a football team to their positions by a process of adjudication. I assume that we would agree that this is also an unwise application of adjudication. It is not merely a matter of eleven different men being possibly affected; each shift of any one player might have a different set of repercussions on the remaining players.[32]

Health disputes are frequently polycentric in part because the granting of health-care to an individual in a situation of competition for finite resources means that, to pick up on Fuller's words, the "shift" of health resources "of any one player might have a different set of repercussions on the remaining players." Katharine Young gives the following example: "In some cases, such as access to scarce vaccines . . . the [resolution of an individual claimant's] dispute directly diverts resources away from those on the government wait list."[33]

As for the technological and social dynamism characterizing health decisions, we start with the fact that our conception of health depends upon what we deem amenable to external intervention by way of treatment or prevention, a point I discuss more at the end of this chapter. Therefore our ability to recognize, conceptualize, and measure ill-health is related to our perception of "avoidable" morbidity or mortality. Certainly technological change affects the scope of what is avoidable, and one implication is that the governing institutions in health may require more expertise and more responsiveness than judge-made law is equipped to supply.[34]

Finally, recent commentators have pointed out that the multiplicity of policy options due to both the scope and pluralism of matters addressed under the banner of health may lead to moral under-determination: "Critical aspects of

---

[30] GREGOIRE WEBBER ET AL., LEGISLATED RIGHTS: SECURING HUMAN RIGHTS THROUGH LEGISLATION 22 (2018).

[31] Fuller, *supra* n.28 at 394 *citing* MICHAEL POLANYI, THE LOGIC OF LIBERTY (1951).

[32] Fuller, *id.* at 395.

[33] Katharine G. Young, *Rights and Queues: On Distributive Contests in the Modern State*, 55 COLUM. J. OF TRANSNAT'L L. 65, 103 (2016)

[34] DANIELS & SABIN, *supra* n.29 (explaining "The major force driving up health care costs. . . is the emergence of new technologies. . . . Aging populations and increased expectations about what medicine can and should do for us mean there is ever increasing demand for what technology makes possible").

human wellbeing can only be adequately protected and fostered in and through complex collective endeavors involving miscellaneous kind of conduct (including mutual restraint) by large numbers of persons. . . . Positive law is ideally suited to help communities set up and sustain salient, dynamic, and systemically coherent schemes of specific convergence. Law's central technique of legal validity makes it possible to mark specific courses of conduct in a widely salient way, in the face of both moral under-determination and moral controversy."[35] This type of broad, systemic coordination may best be achieved through detailed, publicly announced legislative and administrative statements of positive law.

Dismantling the False Binary of Negative Liberties and Affirmative Rights in Health

A third problem spot in the case against US health rights is the persistent and flawed divide between affirmative and negative rights. While it is true that health rights raise the question of the resources required to realize these rights, I will press in this book for more care in the use of this affirmative and negative rights distinction.[36]

An imperfect mapping of health rights onto the affirmative rights side of the divide, has enabled the highly dubious claim that because the United States enjoys a strong tradition of negative economic liberties, health rights fall outside our traditions.[37]

Much literature has already convincingly challenged the distinction between positive and negative rights. The difference is much exaggerated if not incoherent given that negative rights impose costs as well.[38] Meanwhile, what of our current conditions are not a function of some kind of state action? We can characterize any claim either as a demand to be free from state action of one particular

---

[35] WEBBER ET AL., *supra* n.30 at 22.

[36] *See, e.g.*, RICHARD A. EPSTEIN, MORTAL PERIL: OUR INALIENABLE RIGHT TO HEALTH CARE? 2 (1997) (declaring, "No one believes that the right to health care is so absolute that it sweeps aside all claims to food, clothing, or shelter. Yet by the same token, the scope of a more circumscribed duty turns out, at a philosophical level, to be well-nigh indefinable, no matter how many times we intone the words 'reasonable,' 'decent,' 'basic,' 'adequate,' or 'necessary'"). Epstein believes that health, or at least healthcare, could absorb every dollar because we have different preferences regarding healthcare, and cannot readily distinguish between useful and futile care. *Id.* at 59–79.

[37] *See, e.g.*, Frank Cross, *The Error of Positive Rights*, 48 UCLA L. REV. 857 (2001). *But see*, Susan Bandes, *The Negative Constitution: A Critique*, 88 MICH. L. REV. 2271 (1990). Among those who have pointed to the negative rights character of the US constitution as a reason why we lack a right to health in the United States. Abigail R. Moncrieff, *The Freedom of Health*, 159 U. PA. L. REV. 2209 (2011) at 2212–13, 2228–30; Benjamin Mason Meier & Dhrubajyoti Bhattacharya, *Health Care as a Human Right*, *in* DEBATES ON U.S. HEALTH CARE 32, 42 (Jennie Jacobs Kronenfeld et al. eds., 2012).

[38] *See, e.g.*, STEPHEN HOLMES & CASS R. SUNSTEIN, THE COST OF RIGHTS: WHY LIBERTY DEPENDS ON TAXES (1999) (discussing why both positive and negative rights require expenditure of resources by the State); Susan Bandes, *id.*

kind, or as a demand for state action or forbearance of another.[39] Our existing economic rights are not negative rights exactly: they are decisions to assure government backing for certain material holdings. State enactments backed by the state monopoly on force stands behind those decisions commonly regarded as negative liberties, as Robert Alexy clarifies: "[W]ithout the norms of contract law, there could be no *legal* act of formation of a contract; without the norms of company law, no formation of a company *in law*, without the law of marriage, no *legal* act of marriage, without procedural law no bringing of a *legal* action, and without electoral law, no *legal* act of voting."[40] These "freedoms" could not exist unless the state takes the affirmative step of supplying and enforcing the constitutive norms.[41]

This book employs and extends this line of work to debunk not only the false divide, but also the false assumption that if we insist upon the divide nonetheless, that health rights necessarily fall within the sphere of so-called affirmative rights. The HIAs I propose in Chapter 5, after all, fit the classical model of freedom from health-harming state action.

Pushing Back on Overclaiming about the Rights-Averse, Systemic Character of Health Measures

Sometimes the health rights opposition in the United States draws sustenance from a fourth influential view of human health and healthcare, namely that matters of health generally require a less individualistic and more systemic or collective approach that is focused on relationships of care, community, and interdependence. On this view, rights morality, as we will discuss in Chapter 2, exhibits structural features that tend toward individuation, and may be therefore less well-suited to achieving health justice. Many, including Karl Marx, scholars in the Critical Legal Studies tradition, and recently Jamal Greene, have faulted the individualistic, divisive character and effect of rights.[42] They point out that

---

[39] Robert L. Hale, *Coercion and Distribution in a Supposedly Non-Coercive State*, 38 POL. SCI. QUARTERLY 470 (1923).

[40] ROBERT ALEXY, A THEORY OF CONSTITUTIONAL RIGHTS 123 (Julian Rivers trans., 2002).

[41] *See also*, BERNARD HARCOURT, THE ILLUSION OF A FREE MARKET: PUNISHMENT AND THE MYTH OF NATURAL ORDER (2010) (explaining, "In all markets . . . the state is present. Naturally, it is present when it fixes the price of a commodity such as wheat or bread. But it is also present when it subsidizes the cultivation or production of wheat, when it grants a charter to the Chicago Board of Trade, when it permits an instrument like a futures contract, when it protects the property interests of wheat wholesalers").

[42] *See, e.g.*, Karl Marx, On the Jewish Question, *in* KARL MARX: EARLY WRITINGS 26 (T.B. Bottomore trans. & ed., 1963); Duncan Kennedy, *The Critique of Rights in Critical Legal Studies, in* LEFT LEGALISM/LEFT CRITIQUE 178 (Wendy Brown & Janet Halley eds., 2002); Paul D. Butler, *Poor People Lose: Gideon and the Critique of Rights*, 122 YALE L.J. 2176 (2013); Peter Gabel, *The Phenomenology of Rights-Consciousness and the Pact of the Withdrawn Selves*, 62 TEX. L. REV. 1563 (1984); Morton J. Horwitz, *Rights*, 23 HARV. C.R.-C.L. L. REV. 393 (1988); Mark Tushnet, *An Essay*

rights, whether by nature, or because of their historically contingent character in the United States, have tilted against recognition of the collective, mutually dependent nature of human life and flourishing, while suppressing attention to the multiple ways our choices are conditioned by and in turn condition the choices of others.[43]

Indeed in the context of health, we often speak of the urgent problems that require a collective approach. Pandemic response, often featuring community vaccination to achieve herd immunity, comes to mind. The benefits of community vaccination are difficult to break down into individual claims. While vaccines themselves may come in individual doses, the goal of disease control has more in common with "non-excludable, non-rivalrous public goods," as an economist would put it.[44] The recent debate over whether to undertake a COVID-19 vaccination campaign for younger children starkly illustrates this problem. Any individual child may face so little personal clinical risk from COVID-19 that the main justification for vaccinating them might not be the benefits that redound directly to the children themselves, but the benefits that are diffused through the population and enjoyed in large part by others. I quote the following defense of this approach over the more individualistic gaze that the US Food and Drug Administration (FDA) typically employs:

> When the FDA looks only at clinical risks and clinical benefits, like it did during the October 26 meeting [regarding vaccine approval for children age 5–11], it completely ignores all the benefits at the population level. They're pretending that children aged 5 to 11 do not live with other people. In short, they are very seriously underestimating the benefits of vaccines for this age group. As soon as you start accounting for prevention of onward transmission, the balance immediately tips toward vaccination.[45]

---

on Rights, 62 TEX. L. REV. 1363 (1984); Mark Tushnet, *The Critique of Rights*, 47 SMU L. REV. 23 (1993); Robin West, *A Tale of Two Rights*, 94 B.U. L. REV. 893 (2014); Robin L. West, *Tragic Rights: The Rights Critique in the Age of Obama*, 53 WM. & MARY L. REV. 713 (2011); Peter Westen, *The Rueful Rhetoric of "Rights,"* 33 UCLA L. REV. 977 (1986). While Horwitz maintains that the tendency of rights to emphasize individuals and their egoism over interconnectedness, Tushnet in *Critique of Rights* believes that this feature is only true in the particular historically contingent rights discourse we have developed. *See* Horwitz at 400 and Tushnet, Critique at 27. *See also*, JAMAL GREENE, HOW RIGHTS WENT WRONG: WHY OUR OBSESSION WITH RIGHTS IS TEARING AMERICA APART (2021).

[43] ROBIN WEST, REIMAGINING JUSTICE 82 (2003) (describing the neglect of harms and externalities caused by polluters, tobacco, and firearms).
[44] *Are Vaccines a Global Public Good?*, GLOBAL ACCESS TO VACCINES INITIATIVE (GAVI) (2020), https://www.gavi.org/vaccineswork/are-vaccines-global-public-good (May 29, 2022).
[45] Petra Zimmermann et al., *Should Children Be Vaccinated Against COVID-19?*, 107 ARCH. DIS. CHILD. e1–e8 (2022). Malia Jones, *The FDA Is Greatly Underestimating the Benefits of COVID Vaccines for Kids*, SLATE (November 2021), https://slate.com/technology/2021/11/covid-vaccines-kids-pfizer-fda-approval-clinical-benefits.html.

While infectious disease control might constitute the apex example of the collective nature of health inputs and outputs, the provision of healthcare is also rife with such situations. I have written elsewhere of how much of what we need governments to do in healthcare consists not in the providing easily parcel-able doses or procedures, or even the allotments of financing associated with those items. Instead what we urgently need from government is the "assurance of the *conditions* that enable the provision of financing, care, and services [which] literature refers to [as] the government's stewardship role, or its role in creating an 'enabling environment.'"[46] Investing in medical research and education to increase the baseline level of medical skill and science comprises part of this basic government function, as should the regulation of insurance companies and pharmaceutical prices.[47] In the past I have written with misgivings when other non–US health systems chose to focus on entitlements to medical savings accounts rather than "solving systemic and collective action problems, such as medical inflation, or the 'brain drain' of personnel from underserved rural areas."[48]

As you can see, I am sympathetic to this view that we must not focus so much on rights as to neglect health duties to the public-at-large. Rights cannot be the only norms that we bring to bear on the problem of health justice. But the situation in the United States right now is hardly one of an overly dominant rights-based frame for health to the exclusion of other normative tools. If anything, the quest for justice in health has been hobbled by the *occlusion* of health rights claims, the selective confiscation from health advocates of the one weapon arguably used most in the United States to secure greater prioritization and democratization. Moreover, the sample health rights proposals I elaborate in the latter half of this book will illustrate that if sensitively crafted, there are rights claims that can do both; they can serve as individual entitlements while also securing the systemic background conditions and enabling environment for the collective organization of health care and public health. For instance, health reinsurance might lend itself to rights claims while also constituting one of the basic government duties to assure public goods, not unlike the goods of stable currency, basic security, and national defense.

Others have, in the separate context of global health and international human rights, called for a similarly pluralistic approach, strategically promiscuous with respect to whichever tool best fits the task at hand. Again, I share their view

---

[46] *See* Sara C. Bennett and Michael K. Ranson, *Role of Central Governments in Furthering Social Goals through Microinsurance Units, in* SOCIAL REINSURANCE: A NEW APPROACH TO SUSTAINABLE COMMUNITY HEALTH FINANCING 255–57 (David Dror and Alexander Preker eds., 2002).

[47] Christina S. Ho, *Health Reinsurance as a Human Right, in* INSURANCE AND HUMAN RIGHTS 85 (Margarida Lima Rego and Birgit Kuschke eds., 2022).

[48] Christina S. Ho, *Health Rights at the Juncture of State and Market: The People's Republic of China, in* THE RIGHT TO HEALTH AT THE PUBLIC/PRIVATE DIVIDE: A GLOBAL COMPARATIVE STUDY 33 (Colleen Flood and Aeyal Gross eds., 2016).

"that human rights cannot constitute the whole of global health justice and that . . . other considerations—including the promotion of health-related global public goods—should also shape such policy."[49] I merely note the inarguable fact that we are in the United States right now far from any danger of rights-talk overspilling its potentially useful role in our health sector. In these last years, we have watched the cavalier abandonment of lives to COVID-19 denialism, gun-fire, border politics, climate disaster, police violence, deadly work conditions, gender and reproductive revanchism, rabid political tribalism, and more. Our feelings of mute outrage are telling. There is a giant discursive vacuum whenever we wish to articulate and insist upon the paramount importance of shielding people from death and suffering. To the White House COVID-19 strategists, to the Supreme Court, to the Border Patrol—somehow wherever we go to voice the basic tenet that the sacrifice of humans must be for reasons dear, not casual—we find ourselves grasping for an available language, casting about for a receptive frame. Rights would supply the grammar and vocabulary for that proposition, but somehow we have lost access to this mother tongue.

Working Definition of the Right to Health

Finally, before I begin the task of reclamation, I wish to clarify what I mean by "health" in the phrase "right to health." I particularly want to explain how I view the relationship between a right to "health" and a right to "healthcare." Following Norman Daniels, I will be using "health" as a shorthand for "health services" rather than health outcomes.[50] There are two aspects of this definition that I want to highlight at the outset. First, because the focus is on what we can do to serve health, rather than the end result of health itself, the implication is that "a right to health . . . is not violated when the socially controllable factors affecting health have been fairly distributed but health fails anyway."[51]

Second, there is something quite appealing about what Daniels means when he says "health-related services." Daniels says: "The reference to health should be construed as a handy way to characterize *functionally* the relevant, socially controllable actions."[52] He is therefore including not just medical services, but all the "various actions . . . that promote or maintain or restore . . . health" as well as forbearance "from actions that interfere with it."[53] What we typically consider

---

[49] John Tasioulas and Effy Vayena, *Just Global Health: Integrating Human Rights and Common Goods*, THE OXFORD HANDBOOK OF GLOBAL JUSTICE 139 (Thom Brooks, ed., 2020).
[50] *See* DANIELS, *supra* n.29 at 28.
[51] *Id.* at 145.
[52] *Id.* (emphasis in original).
[53] *Id.*

medical care fits under that heading, as do preventive services, or even changes in social conditions.

I find Daniels's definition a useful foundation because it emphasizes the continuities, rather than the differences, between "healthcare" and "public health" as I strive to do here as well. With this expansive domain of actions and forbearances to choose from, what can and should be claimed as an entitlement? This is our job as a legal and political community to determine, and it is this book's job to suggest how we have already begun to undertake Hercules's task and where next to train our efforts.

I do not presume to answer once and for all what belongs in the scope of the right to health that we should recognize in the United States. The content of this right, like our other rights, will necessarily be elaborated over time. However, this book will demonstrate that courts and legislatures have taken steps that show more movement toward a right to health than we have perceived and left us in a position to take more immediate action than we acknowledge. Mandatory HIAs and government reinsurance for health coverage are politically feasible yet meaningful ways to strengthen the right to health. Still, the significance of measures like these in establishing a right to health is often overlooked. I provide an alternate account by explaining how these steps can fit within but also enrich the broader popular conception of what we owe one another as part of our basic social compact. We find ourselves at a time of great yearning for renewed social and political grounding. Though the measures proposed here may seem modest, the implications could be transformative of our understanding of health and human flourishing as a material claim.

But before I do any of those things. I must first lay out my adopted account (or accounts) of rights so that we are working from common ground.

2

Methods

In this chapter I assemble a small toolkit for recognizing rights, something we can bring with us on the book's journey across our health decision domain.

At the same time, some account of the term "right" can also help explain why I choose to focus on rights at all, and thus offer a rejoinder to those who dismiss this strategy as less fruitful or worthwhile than other projects to advance human health interests. I believe that I can justify the choice in the face of the health problems we confront. My reasons lie in the nature of what we face in our polity when it comes to our health, and why we seem to be making little progress against such strong headwinds.

In the previous chapter, I identified our defining obstacle as the stark competition among interests, giving rise to tilted conflicts between the pursuit of those rival interests and the pursuit of health. Rights meet this problem head-on. Part of their genius as a tool lies in that they are purpose-built for situations when values inevitably conflict and a particular foundational value seems to be drawing short shrift.

The problem of resolving conflict between health and other values is connected with the prevailing US mode of public decision-making. For some time now we have been in the grip of a consensus, among the ruling conservatives and liberal centrists alike, that methods of collective ordering should default to cost-benefit analysis.[1]

Cost-benefit analysis (CBA) is typically understood as the decision method of weighing the aggregate costs of a regulatory decision against its aggregate benefits to assess and determine its desirability.[2] Its use has acquired default

---

With permission, Chapter 2 includes some minor material that was previously published in Christina S. Ho, *Are We Suffering from an Undiagnosed Health Right*, 42 AM. J. OF L. AND MED. 743 (2016), and in Christina S. Ho, *Health Impact Assessments: A Negative Procedural Health Right?* 50 SETON HALL L. REV. 643 (2020).

[1] *See, e.g.*, ELIZABETH POPP BERMAN, THINKING LIKE AN ECONOMIST: HOW EFFICIENCY REPLACED EQUALITY IN U.S. PUBLIC POLICY (2022).

[2] *See, e.g.*, Melissa Luttrell & Jorge Roman Romero, *Modernizing Regulatory Review Beyond Cost-Benefit Analysis*, L. & POLITICAL ECON. BLOG (October 11, 2021), https://lpeproject.org/blog/modernizing-regulatory-review-beyond-cost-benefit-analysis/ (defining "cost–benefit analysis" as "an applied economic technique that attempts to assess a government program or project by determining whether societal welfare has or will increase (in the aggregate more people are better off) because of the program or project").

status in US law, across state and federal landscapes alike.[3] A typical expression from a New York state judge captures the reigning attitude: "[C]ost-benefit analysis is the essence of reasonable regulation; if an agency adopted a particular rule without first considering whether its benefits justify its societal costs, it would be acting irrationally."[4]

This governing perspective, both boosted by and in turn burnishing the disciplinary primacy of economics, reinforces certain tendencies in legal decision-making as well, including the resort to balancing tests, and abstention from substantive value-judgments in favor of arms-length "counting" strategies instead.[5]

But the correctness or desirability of CBA is not so self-evident as this above quote might suggest. CBA reinforces a utilitarian view of the world in which values are aggregative and fungible, and thus capable of being traded off against one another.[6] In response, many have argued that the ascendance of CBA misvalues and ultimately displaces nonutilitarian values like rights, distribution, the integrity of human life, and dignity.[7] For instance, CBA privileges efficiency over distributive goals, as one commentator has succinctly described: "[A]ll transfer programs flunk standard CBA: one side loses what another gains, plus somebody pays for administrative costs."[8] Moreover, rights are given short shrift under CBA's utilitarian approach insofar as rights bind without much regard

[3] See Michigan v. EPA, 135 S. Ct. 2699, 2706–08 (2015) (requiring agency to weigh costs against benefits, unless Congress clearly states otherwise); see also Exec. Order No. 12,866, 58 Fed. Reg. 51, 735 (October 4, 1993) (which has been retained in substantially similar form through Reagan, Bush I, Clinton, Bush II, Obama, Trump, and Biden administrations); see generally Cass R. Sunstein, Cost-Benefit Default Principles, 99 MICH. L. REV. 1651 (2001).

[4] N.Y. Statewide Coal. Hispanic Chambers Com. v. N.Y.C. Dep't Health & Mental Hygiene, 16 N.E.3d 538, 546 (N.Y. 2014).

[5] T. Alexander Aleinikoff, Constitutional Law in the Age of Balancing, 96 YALE L.J. 943, 945 (1987); see also Duncan Kennedy, Proportionality and 'Deference' in Contemporary Constitutional Thought in TRANSFORMATION OF RECONSTITUTION OF EUROPE: THE CRITICAL LEGAL STUDIES PERSPECTIVE ON THE ROLE OF COURTS IN THE EUROPEAN UNION (Tamara Perišin & Siniša Rodin, eds.) (2018).

[6] See, e.g., SIDNEY SHAPIRO & ROBERT GLICKSMAN, RISK REGULATION AT RISK: RESTORING A PRAGMATIC APPROACH 54 (2002).

[7] See, e.g., BERMAN, supra n.1; Frank Ackerman & Liza Heinzerling, Pricing the Priceless: Cost-Benefit Analysis of Environmental Protection, 150 U. PA. L. REV. 1553 (2002) (discussing that it may not be possible to limit the effects of cost-benefit analysis to just those areas for which cost-benefit analysis is suitable because there are spillover or displacing effects, including that "cost benefit analysis turns public citizens into selfish consumers and interconnected communities into atomized individuals"); MICHAEL SANDEL, WHAT MONEY CAN'T BUY: THE MORAL LIMITS OF MARKETS (2012); Kristen Underhill, When Extrinsic Incentives Displace Intrinsic Motivation: Designing Legal Carrots and Sticks to Confront the Challenge of Motivational Crowding-Out, 33 YALE J. ON REG. 213 (2016).

[8] Adam Samaha, Death and Paperwork Reduction, 65 DUKE L. J. 279, 324 (2015) (citing Eric A. Posner, Transfer Regulations and Cost-effectiveness Analysis, 53 DUKE L. J. 1067, 1060–9 and 1076 (2003)). This pithy conclusion depends upon CBA being administered without regard to the fact that the relation between wealth and utility varies nonlinearly, such that the marginal decrease in a wealthy person's utility from the loss of a dollar might be lower than the marginal increase to a less well-off person from gaining a dollar.

to case-by-case consequences.[9] The nature of rights is such that an individual's rights cannot be sacrificed to the greater collective welfare as a matter of course.

Yet these prevailing views about how to handle value conflict have proven hard to dislodge. Observers note that our policymaking functions are now held to cost-benefit default requirements imposed both by courts,[10] and by an executive order that has proven durable regardless of the president's party affiliation.[11] Cass Sunstein has argued for an emerging "federal common law of regulatory policy" that presumes agency permission (and even duty) under its governing statutes to accommodate countervailing costs against benefits.[12]

One thing that CBA rightly assumes though is a world of plural concerns. Increasingly we live in a time of pluralism on overload, with a welter of interests, affiliations, values, demands, and priorities competing for scarce attention and re-sources. It is past time to assess how the dominant outlook associated with CBA and its brethren has fared along the dimension of our health. This book asks: What exactly is happening when our health interests runs up against other goals or purposes? How do we make those calls? Are we privileging health or is health at some unique disadvantage? What are our priorities and is there a tilt?

One question about this book could be posed as: Why rights and why now?[13] To this I would respond that rights are a familiar, indeed a primary tool for pushing pause. We urgently need such a tool given the conditions we face now, a situation where we bargain health away with little heed, where for all other social goals, we are paying in the currency of lives. As Justice Breyer observes, risk is all round us and we will always face trade-offs.[14] But rights are a way to stop and force the step of justification. They remain a way to trigger a reckoning each time to ask whether we are treading out of bounds, whether that step is worth it none-theless, or if we might better allocate those energies toward advancing health.[15]

---

[9] Even utilitarians can acknowledge rights as absolute and indefeasible in this sense. *See, e.g.,* John Stuart Mill, *Utilitarianism*, 1, 61–67, *in* UTILITARIANISM, ON LIBERTY, CONSIDERATIONS ON REPRESENTATIVE GOVERNMENT (H.B. Acton, ed., 1972) (distinguishing rights from expedience).

[10] *See* Michigan v. EPA, 135 S. Ct. 2699 (2015) (requiring agency to weigh costs against benefits, unless Congress clearly states otherwise); *see also,* Cass R. Sunstein, *Cost-Benefit Default Principles,* 99 MICH. L. REV. 1651 (2001).

[11] *See* Exec. Order No. 12,866, 58 Fed. Reg. 51,735 (October 4, 1993) (which has been retained in substantially similar form through Reagan, Bush I, Clinton, Bush II, and Obama administrations).

[12] Sunstein, *supra* n.3, at 1654–56.

[13] There are those who have argued that the multiplication of rights is precisely what ails rather than heals us in this moment. *See, e.g.,* JAMAL GREENE, HOW RIGHTS WENT WRONG: WHY OUR OBSESSION WITH RIGHTS IS TEARING AMERICA APART (2021).

[14] *See* Whitman v. American Trucking Association, 531 U.S. 457, 494 (2001) (Breyer, J., dissenting) ("But these words do not describe a world that is free of all risk-an impossible and undesirable objec-tive"). Breyer, speaking on proportionality, prefers transparency over the categorical approach. *See* STEPHEN BREYER, THE COURT AND THE WORLD: AMERICAN LAW AND THE NEW GLOBAL REALITIES 257 (2015).

[15] On the "culture of justification," *see* MOSHE COHEN-ELIYA & IDDO PORAT, PROPORTIONALITY AND CONSTITUTIONAL CULTURE 103–04 (2013) (citing Etienne Moreinik, *A Bridge to*

Rights are widely understood in the United States as a way to commit to the presumptive favoring and extra shielding of certain values in human flourishing.

What do they look like at work then—what is the machinery that enables rights to perform this function? The models of rights I have in mind are not exotic. I draw mainly from three legal and philosophical accounts of rights throughout the book. I explain them first here using the work of some of the primary exponents associated with each account. The first model is Ronald Dworkin's model of rights as trumps, the second is Robert Alexy's account of rights as proportionality, and the third is David Super's account of entrenched entitlements in the US politico-legal landscape.[16] These accounts are quite different; they certainly do not all operate in the same register, and while they pick out different emphases, they also share points of overlap. Yet each is recognizable within our legal system, and all provide important insights into how rights undertake the work of prioritization.

With these models in hand (both their signature traits and common elements) I can trace examples of distinctive rights-grammar throughout our existing health-related case law, as well as in our statutory enactments. I principally, though not exclusively, use Dworkin's model of lexical preclusion to detect rights grammar in the descriptive chapters, Chapters 3 and 4. Meanwhile, proportionality helps us spot the rights-form at work across the statutory and regulatory terrain of impact assessments that I discuss in Chapter 5. Finally, in Chapters 6 and 7, I employ Super's catalog of attributes associated with US legislative entitlements to pick out a species of affirmative right to material benefits that features across our policy landscape, namely state-sponsored reinsurance.[17]

My argument about the presence of rights-logic in the United States does not depend upon systemwide coherence or agreement over one conception of rights across all parts of the US legal corpus; indeed, it would be very strange to find that kind of agreement in a legal system embedded within a centrifugally plural society. It should come as little surprise that some judicial decisions take a decidedly more Dworkinian approach to rights, while I document a number of legislated rights that hew to a view of rights as proportionality.

Where?: Introducing the Interim Bill of Rights, 10 S. Afr. J. on Hum. Rts. 31 (1994)). *See also* Jamal Greene, *Supreme Court Foreword*, 132 Harv. L. Rev. 28, 35, 64 (2018).

[16] *See* Greene, *Supreme Court Foreword*, *supra* n.15, at 35, 64, for the overarching framework of rights theories as divided principally between Dworkinian and proportionality frames of reference. For David Super's schema for characterizing subconstitutional entitlements, *see* David A. Super, *The Political Economy of Entitlement*, 104 Colum. L. Rev. 633 (2004).

[17] *See* Super, *supra* n.16.

Ronald Dworkin

Dworkin argues that rights exist precisely in order to achieve a type of prioritization, which he calls "trumping" and which Jeremy Waldron compares to "lexical"
preclusion.[18]

Goals versus Principles

The key to understanding how Dworkin defines rights is knowing that he does
so by way of contrast with "utilitarian goals" which he also refers to as "policy"
values.[19] Policy goals can be pursued in a cumulative way, aggregated, maximized,
and indeed frictionlessly traded off against one another.[20] Thus "policy goals"
constitute a category of political norms that can be handled through CBA.

Rights instead are matters of principle, which for Dworkin are a type of
norm that "insists on distributional consistency from one case to the next."[21] He
explains what he means by comparing these principled rights norms with the
policy goals he has set up as their foil. Dworkin identifies "a political right [as] an
individuated political aim,"[22] emphasizing the necessity of individuated application of the norm to *each* rights-bearer in like cases. "Goals," on the other hand,
can be advanced whenever they prevail. Indeed if one person's welfare suffers
in any given transaction, another transaction can potentially offset that welfare
loss. But the impairment of a right in one case (say the deprivation of a right to
vote) is not rectified by giving someone two votes next time. Nor can we say that
the right has been fulfilled to an optimal degree and need not be satisfied in the
next case. Dworkin cites the right to contraception as an example: the protection of an individual's liberty to purchase contraception does not mean that the
next individual's liberty can be violated because "enough sexual liberty" has been

---

[18] Jeremy Waldron, *Rights in Conflict*, 99 ETHICS 503, 512–13 (1989). Lexical ordering is "an order
which requires us to satisfy the first principle in the ordering before we can move on to the second....
A serial ordering avoids, then, having to balance principles at all; those earlier in the ordering have
an absolute weight, so to speak, with respect to later ones." JOHN RAWLS, A THEORY OF JUSTICE 43
(1971). Waldron concedes that Dworkin's device of trumping falls somewhat short of *pure* lexical
ordering: "We surely think that some attention is due to considerations of ordinary utility, and while
it is reasonable to postpone that until the most striking of the requirements generated by rights
have been satisfied, it is not reasonable to postpone it forever while we satisfy duty after duty associated with rights." Waldron, *Rights in Conflict* at 513. Nevertheless, he extracts the following kernel
of cross-insight: "One possibility . . . is that lexical priority expresses the fact that a pair of moral
considerations are related *internally* to one another, rather than externally in the way that a purely
quantitative account of their respective importance would imply." *Id.* at 516 (emphasis in original).

[19] *See, e.g.*, RONALD DWORKIN, TAKING RIGHTS SERIOUSLY 91–92 (1978) (hereinafter "TRS").

[20] *See, e.g., id.*

[21] *Id.* at 88. See also *id.* at 90, where Dworkin states that "[p]rinciples are propositions that describe
rights; policies are propositions that describe goals."

[22] *See id.* at 91.

secured. No matter how much one serves the value that is a "right," the value is still undermined if it is not recognized in any single instance to which it applies.[23] This distributional consistency from one case to the next does not necessarily characterize goals as Dworkin points out: "It does not follow . . . that if the legislature awards a subsidy to one aircraft manufacturer one month it must award a subsidy to another manufacturer the next."[24] This principled aspect of rights explains why Dworkin's account accords with others on the distributed nature or "claimability" of rights, as I will return to shortly.

Resolving Conflict by Preclusion: Presumptive Privileging

But if rights must be honored in each case, how do we resolve conflict between rights and other values much less between rights and other rights? Does Dworkin's view imply that rights should always prevail at least over nonrights? Dworkin's contribution is to say of concrete rights that they already contain within them a view of the resolution of conflict between that principle and a competing right or value: "Concrete rights . . . are . . . precisely defined so as to express more definitely the weight they have against other political aims on particular occasions."[25] Herein lies the promise of rights: the fact that one value is already exalted in its particular form contains within itself the answer to the question of how to resolve conflict.

Waldron explains how this approach differs from simple "balancing" to resolve value conflict, while avoiding unadorned fiat:

> [W]hat looked like a brute confrontation between two rival interests, independently understood, turns out to be resolved by considering the internal relation that obtains between our understanding of the respective rights claims. The establishment of this sort of internal relation between moral considerations is an attractive way of justifying claims about lexical priority. Instead of announcing peremptorily that a certain interest just *has* absolute priority over some other interest ranked lower than it, we express our sense of a particular priority in our conception of the interest itself. In thinking about it, and singling it out for moral attention, we are already thinking about the type of consideration with which it is likely to conflict.[26]

---

[23] *See id.* at 88.

[24] *Id.* at 88.

[25] *Id.* at 93.

[26] Waldron, *supra* n.18, at 518. Waldron also says that this does not need to be a complete theory of social value: "However, this approach will not deal with all moral conflicts and there is no reason to want it to . . . What we were looking for was something to capture our sense that this is not always the whole story—our sense that sometimes, or in some conflicts, the issue is one of qualitative precedence rather than quantitative weight. I think the idea of internal connections helps to capture some

Thus, as Waldron emphasizes, the distinctive trumping property of rights is best understood not as a generalized trumping, but as trumping or preclusion of *particular justifications* identifiable because of the "internal" relationship they have with the reasons we value the right. This property distinguishes rights because it captures how rights arguments are arguments of "qualitative precedence rather than quantitative weight."[27]

Resolving Conflict by Preclusion: Requiring a Special Justification

Let us step back for a moment and understand the mechanism of rights in Dworkin's account, both its distinctive hallmarks but also its common ground with other understandings. His view certainly carries a whiff of absolutism, but it is only, as Jamal Greene says, a "presumptive absolutism."[28] Despite what the term might suggest, rights do not always "trump." There are special, or extraordinary justifications that Dworkin acknowledges can overcome the right.[29] As we will see for the adherents of proportionality, these countervailing justifications count as significant insofar as they are weighty. But what may be surprising is that Dworkin arguably allows for rights to be "outweighed" as well, at least in extreme cases. Two of the circumstances under which he says rights must yield include "when some competing right . . . would be abridged," and when "if the right were so defined, then the cost to society would not be simply incremental, but would be of a degree far beyond the cost paid to grant the original right, a degree great enough to justify whatever assault on dignity or equality might be involved."[30]

But the insight for which Dworkin's rights account is justly famous is that in judging the strength of any proposed rights-limiting justification, we must consider not only the weight, but also the nature of the justification for action detracting from the right. To understand a right as a trump means to recognize its importance over other considerations, and to use the right itself to answer the question of prioritization. For as Waldron says, "our conception of the interest's importance already tells us a lot about the sort of consideration to which it is appropriately opposed."[31]

---

of that. . . . We can establish qualitative priorities in some places, without thinking we have to establish qualitative priorities everywhere."

[27] *Id.* at 519.
[28] Greene, *Supreme Court Foreword, supra* n.15 at 35.
[29] *See* Waldron, *supra* n.18, at 516.
[30] *See* TRS, at 200.
[31] Waldron, *supra* n.18, at 517.

There is an inherent relationship between the right and the rejection of certain countervailing reasons, given that the purpose of ruling out those justifications is why the right exists to begin with.[32] Simply balancing everyone's interests is not sufficient to the task of resolving conflicts in society because some people's interests, such as the Nazis' preference for the oppression of Jewish people, must be precluded. A right (in this case the right to political independence) is the tool for barring consideration of those preferences.[33] Returning to Waldron again, he invokes John Stuart Mills's example: if we recognize a value as important enough to give it the status of a right, say free expression, for instance, then restricting speech because it upsets those who don't agree with the view expressed is presumptively ruled out as illegitimate. The "whole point" of speech rights is that the disutility of hearing something disagreeable should not count as a reason to curtail speech.[34] The "whole point" of having a right to political equality is precisely to preclude a Nazi sympathizer's invidious preference from counting validly against the Jewish individual's preference for her own civil and political equality. We prioritize one of those interests as a right, and in doing so, reject the other as a legitimate countervailing factor.

This constraint on the nature of permissible countervailing purposes characterizes those interests that we value as rights. And the law that governs human health is often characterized by this line of reasoning, as illustrated by the emerging norm that we should not deny health coverage to those with preexisting conditions. I would venture to guess that this norm has intuitive purchase because denying healthcare to someone precisely because they are in greater need of healthcare provokes an uncomfortable sense of contradiction with the purpose of valuing healthcare in the first place. I use this insight in Chapters 3 and 4 of the book as a litmus test to detect rights-thinking in our existing health-related case law, as well as our statutory enactments.

What types of considerations would be trumped in this way if the importance of health were recognized as though it were right? I submit that the types of considerations would be those that signal vulnerability, and indeed health need—the very conditions that concern us when we act to address people's health. Thus pointing to the neediness and medical vulnerability of those who would benefit cannot sensibly be considered as a reason to oppose or

---

[32] See id. at 516–17. "[R]ights are to prevail over utility precisely because the whole point of setting them up is to correct for the defects in the utilitarian arguments which are likely to oppose them." Id. at 516.

[33] See TRS, at 158 (explaining the right of political independence as expressly for preclusion of such preferences, given that it is by definition "the right that no one suffer disadvantage in the distribution of goods or opportunities on the ground that others think he should have less because of who he is or is not, or that others care less for him than they do for other people. The right of political independence would have the effect of insulating Jews from the preferences of Nazis").

[34] Waldron, supra n.18, at 517.

compromise any particular health response. The build out of our conception of health's importance is already happening in this way, as I will show by identifying the considerations that we deliberately subordinate to health. When we have mustered the political will to pass statutes prohibiting the denial of healthcare along certain categorical lines, these lines are often plausible proxies for health need. Even prior to the Affordable Care Act (ACA)'s rejection of health-status discrimination, US law already prohibited denial of health coverage on the basis of disability under the Americans with Disabilities Act (ADA), on the basis of age (if but feebly) in the Age Discrimination in Employment Act, based on genetic information under the Genetic Information Nondiscrimination Act, and on the grounds of diagnosis or condition in a grab-bag of other statutory provisions. We implicitly recognize the internal contradiction in allowing these considerations to factor in when they deny the whole reason we value health and accorded it political attention in the first place. This Dworkinian logic explains why we rule them out as potential countervailing factors.

Not only do we honor this intuition in statutes but in case law too, as I explore in Chapter 4. The set of "sensitive" considerations, whose use to limit health protection is condemned in these cases (age, diagnosis, disability, institutionalization, arbitrary physical characteristics, and sometimes even financial want or status as "the neediest among us") are plausibly explained insofar as they conflict "internally" with the reasons we value health in the first place. Across the cases I examine, this logic, sometimes correctly and sometimes mistakenly applied, underlies the judicial hostility toward exceptions drawn along these categorical lines.

Though Dworkin's account is especially useful in carrying out this book's descriptive project in Chapters 3 and 4, his observations are by no means irrelevant to the tasks undertaken in Chapters 5 through 7. Dworkin's rights as trumps account overlaps and supports some of the commonly observed features of rights that recur in the other accounts we examine, and which we utilize to both detect and craft rights-building programs of action. Dworkin offers one description of the method by which rights afford presumptive priority to their favored values: we might characterize this method as the requirement of a special, non-precluded justification in order to overcome the priority accorded by the right. In Dworkin's own words:

> We might, for simplicity, stipulate not to call any political aim a right unless it has a certain threshold weight against collective goals in general; unless, for example, it cannot be defeated by appeal to any of the ordinary routine goals of political administration, but only by a goal of special urgency.[35]

---

[35] Dworkin, *supra* n.19, at 92.

We might say that the "trumping" character or rights forces a "special" type of showing—a showing that cannot resort to certain precluded reasons—in order to justify compromising the right. While the types of special justification required are different, I will later show that the fact of requiring a special justification is common to both the Dworkininan and proportionality accounts of rights.

Distributed Character, or Claimability

Another commonality that emerges among the accounts is something I will loosely call the distributed nature or claimability of rights. I first introduced this point in the discussion above on Dworkin's characterization of rights as matters of principle.

In Dworkin's words, a person has a right

> if that person would be entitled to demand that protection from his government on his own title as an individual, without regard to whether a majority of his fellow citizens joined in the demand. It cannot be true, on this test, that anyone has a right to have all the laws of the nation enforced. He [may have] a right to have enforced laws against personal assault. . . . If the physically vulnerable members of the community—those who need police protection against personal violence—were only a small minority, it would still seem plausible to say that they were entitled to that protection. But the laws that provide a certain level of quiet in public places, or that authorize and finance a foreign war, cannot be thought to rest on individual rights. . . . There are laws—perhaps desirable laws—that provide these advantages to her, but the justification for these laws, if they can be justified at all, is the common desire of a large majority, not her personal right.[36]

The individuation distinctive to rights follows from Dworkin's imputation of integrity and consistency to rights as creatures of principle rather than policy.[37] In other words, Dworkin insists on this "distributed" quality because for him, the right redounds to some person in that particular instance as a matter of principled consistency, which must obtain in each like case.[38]

Although the individuation or distributed nature of rights for Dworkin flows from his distinctive account, I want to preview here that this insistence on individuation is also a point of commonality he shares with Alexy's

---

[36] *Id.* at 194.
[37] *See id.* at 82.
[38] *See id. See also,* text accompanying n.21–24.

account of rights under proportionality, and with David Super's account of statutory entitlements. Indeed it appears in the accounts of many other scholars, albeit grounded in their own outlooks on rights. Some operationalize the "individuated or "distributed" characteristic of rights in an even more demanding way, arguing that true rights must be able to be "claimed" by the rights-holder.[39] Joel Feinberg holds that the particular individuation to each rights-holder takes the form of "claimability," a property that distinguishes rights-based obligations from those based on duty or virtue.[40] This feature of rights and their individuation—the characteristic that they can be claimed by the individual or entity who holds them—is widely recognized. Various theories of rights may however dial up or dial down the stringency of this qualifying parameter.

D. N. MacCormick, for instance, describes that the line between rights which give rise to claimable duties and more general duties to the public-at-large as less a demarcation and more a choice of emphasis. He contrasts and connects the two categories thus:

When positive laws establish rights ... what they do is secure individuals ... in the enjoyment of some good or other. But not by way of a collective good collectively enjoyed, like clean air in a city, but rather an individual good individually enjoyed by each, like the protection of each occupier's particular environment as secured by the law of private nuisance. Such protection is characteristically achieved *by imposing duties on people at large*, for example, not to bring about certain kinds of adverse changes to the environment of land or premises occupied by someone else, *and further duties, which may be invoked at the instance of any aggrieved occupier*, to make good damage arising from adverse environmental change.[41]

He also suggests that the use of one frame or the other may adapt depending on what we wish to communicate:

[T]here may indeed be simple cases in which some general duty—e.g. a duty not to assault—is imposed upon everyone at large with a view to protecting

---

[39] *See, e.g.*, JOEL FEINBERG, *The Nature and Value of Rights, in* RIGHTS, JUSTICE, AND THE BOUNDS OF LIBERTY: ESSAYS IN SOCIAL PHILOSOPHY 143–55 (1980) (inventing the thought-experiment of "Nowheresville" expressly in order to highlight what is lost by protecting values using duties and virtues while failing to recognize the importance of individuals claiming on their own behalf. In other words, he argues that the distinctive advantage of the rights frame is that it focuses on the role of the claimant, the bearer of rights); *id.* at 155 (describing why "claiming," or the ability for each person to initiate the enforcement or recognition of that right, is an important feature of rights).

[40] *See id.*

[41] *See* Donald N. MacCormick, *Dworkin as a Pre-Benthamite*, 87 PHILOSOPHICAL REV. 585, 599 (1978) (emphasis added).

the physical security of each and every person in society, and where the "right not to be assaulted" is simply the correlative of the duty not to assault; no doubt in such simple cases the "terminology of rights" does not enable us to say very much more than can be said in the terminology of duty. But it may be well adapted even in this simple case to expressing a reason why people aggrieved by breaches of certain duties *should* be empowered to take various measures and actions at law to secure remedies therefore.[42]

How important is legal claimability to this account of rights? Indeed, Feinberg does not require that claimability necessarily entail the ability to invoke judicial redress in the form of a legal claim.[43] Dworkin acknowledges that moral rights may not garner full legal recognition, and admonishes that when one has a moral right against the government, there may be prudential and practical reasons why the organs of government may not furnish enforcement in court or otherwise.[44] Dworkin even contends that it may be wrong in certain contexts for moral right-holders themselves to press their claim.[45]

Nevertheless, rights do need to be distinguished from general duties to the public-at-large and we therefore in comparing various norms, will look to see if the duties they impose can be described in relation to some specific rights-holder, regardless of whether the rights-holder can always seek legal redress for violations of those duties.

And so we take from this discussion a couple of hallmarks of rights:

1) First we note the presumptive privileging achieved by rights such that their compromise requires special justification.
   a. For Dworkin, that special justification requirement takes the form of precluding certain kinds of ordinary countervailing justifications, a type of "internal" preclusion that constitutes the "trumping" quality of rights.
2) Second, we identify the necessarily distributed or "claimable" character of rights.

---

[42] DONALD. N. MacCORMICK, *Rights in Legislation, in* LAW, MORALITY, AND SOCIETY: ESSAYS IN HONOR OF H.L.A. HART 189, 203–04 (Peter Hacker & Joseph Raz, eds., 1979).

[43] *See* FEINBERG, supra n.39, at 154.

[44] *See* DWORKIN, *supra* n.19, at 184–97 ("some commentators . . . suppose that individual moral rights are fully protected by this [legal] system, but that is hardly so, nor could it be so").

[45] *See id.* at 196 (saying of the person's moral right in the face of unjust laws, "he must remember that reasonable men can differ about whether he has a right against the government. . . . He must take into account the various consequences his acts will have, whether they involve violence, and such other considerations as the context makes relevant").

Robert Alexy on Rights as Proportionality

While Dworkin's view of rights may tend toward absolutism, other accounts are more flexible. Fred Schauer characterizes values as rights if they can resist at least "low justification" or "small bore" countervailing reasons, with the implication that rights might still yield opposite certain "high justification" reasons.[46] Robert Alexy has extensively elaborated a theory of rights that holds, in contrast with Dworkin's, that rights are subject to a form of weighted balancing that we call "proportionality."[47]

One source of the contrast is Alexy's skepticism about both the possibility and desirability of ranking or ordering of norms to any significant degree of generality:

> In general we can say that an order of values or principles which determines con-
> stitutional adjudication in a way that is intersubjectively binding does not exist.
> But the impossibility of such a "hard" ordering says nothing about the technique
> of balancing interests. Soft orderings can be created in two ways: (1) through
> prima facie preferences in favour of particular values or principles or (2) through
> a network of concrete preference decisions. Soft orderings of constitutional
> values by way of prima facie preferences arise, for example when one establishes
> a burden of argumentation in favour of individual liberty, or equality, or certain
> collective interests. A soft ordering of a network of concrete preference decisions
> has been created by the case-law of the Federal Constitutional Court.[48]

For Alexy, there can be "no relation of absolute precedence" among principles by definition. We can only hope in each instance to "establish[] a conditional re-lation of precedence between the principles in light of the circumstances of the case."[49] He continues, "If an absolute relation of precedence is adopted between two values, in cases of conflict, they behave like rules."[50]

The Nature of Principles

This statement opens a window onto another difference between Dworkin and Alexy: principles for Alexy cannot be fulfilled with the kind of consistency and

---

[46] Frederick Schauer, *A Comment on the Structure of Rights*, 27 GA. L. REV. 415, 429–31 (1993).

[47] *See* ROBERT ALEXY, *Postscript, in* A THEORY OF CONSTITUTIONAL RIGHTS 388–425 (Julian Rivers, trans., 2002)

[48] ALEXY, *The Structure of Constitutional Rights Norms, in* A THEORY OF CONSTITUTIONAL RIGHTS 99–100.

[49] *Id.* at 50–54, 100.

[50] *Id.* at 100.

absoluteness that Dworkin envisions. The possibility of conflict among principles is in Alexy's world not rare but ubiquitous. Therefore principles are "*not definitive* but only *prima facie* requirements." In striking contrast to Dworkin, who believes that the resolution of right and counter-reason is already inherent in the conception of the right itself, Alexy declares, "How the relation between reason and counter-reason is to be stated is not decided by the principle itself. Principles lack the resources to determine their own extent in the light of competing principles and what is factually possible."[51] Principles can therefore only constitute *prima facie* reasons subject to an analysis of the justifications for their opposite.

But even as I point out these differences between the two accounts, I identify them against a backdrop of shared features. My contention is that a few structural features of rights are similar to both accounts, even if the stringency of the standards applied in the name of those features might vary with the theory of rights to which one subscribes.

Proportionality: Presumptive Privileging by Requiring Special Justification to Overcome a Right

Proportionality's proponents, as we previewed earlier, share the view that a special justification is needed to overcome a right. While the special justification that is required has qualitative particulars in Dworkin's telling, here, that justification must be one that can satisfy the "proportionality test."[52] Alison Young's explanation of rights under proportionality brings out this aspect of the theory:

> [R]ights . . . rule out some methods of balancing and [give] an element of
> additional weight to . . . rights in the balancing process . . . Proportionality is
> the best means of achieving this balancing because the test of proportionality
> is capable of assigning greater weight to . . . rights in the balancing exercise,
> and of restricting the range of justifications that can be used to restrict a . . .
> right.[53]

---

[51] *Id.* at 57.

[52] *See id.* at 100–101 ("[T]he justification model distinguishes between the mental process whichc leads to the determination of thes statement of preference and its justification. This distinction permits us to relate the requirement that the balancing be rational to the justification of the statement of preference and to say: a baolancing of principles is rational when the preferential statement to which it leads can be rationally justified." So the contrast with Dworkin is that these conditional preference statements have already been decided and need simply to be applied on their own authority").

[53] Alison L. Young, *Proportionality is Dead: Long Live Proportionality!, in* Proportionality and the Rule of Law: Rights, Justification, Reasoning 43, 47 (Grant Huscroft et al., eds., 2014).

The Proportionality Test Itself

The justification-forcing mechanism of rights is thus embedded in the proportionality test. To lay out the test itself, I start with the words of scholar-jurist Aharon Barak: "Proportionality . . . can be defined as the set of rules determining the necessary and sufficient conditions for a limitation of a constitutionally protected right by a law to be constitutionally permissible."[54] He proceeds to identify the four subcomponents of proportionality as follows:

> [A] limitation of a constitutionally protected right will be constitutionally permissible if:
>
> (i) it is designated for a proper purpose
> (ii) the measures undertaken to effectuate such a limitation are rationally connected to the fulfillment of that purpose
> (iii) the measures undertaken are necessary in that there are no alternative measures that may similarly achieve that same purpose with a lesser degree of limitation; and finally
> (iv) [there is] a proper relation (. . . or "balancing") between the importance of achieving the proper purpose and the social importance of preventing the limitation of the constitutional right.[55]

Little wonder that this schema feels familiar. As Jamal Greene notes:

> Some form of proportionality is practiced in courts throughout the world. . . . It is ubiquitous within the domestic constitutional courts of Europe, the European Court of Human Rights and the European Court of Justice. It is . . . the Canadian Supreme Court's default mode of analysts under the Canadian Charter of Rights and Freedoms. The last decade has seen a convergence on the use of proportionality in Latin American courts, including especially in the influential jurisdictions of Colombia, Brazil, and Mexico. It is the basic approach in the courts of South Korea, Taiwan, Hong Kong, and Malaysia. It is a standard tool of adjudication in South Africa and in Israel.[56]

The labels assigned to the steps of the test, as well as the decision about where to insert the breaks, may differ depending on the author and the jurisdiction. Yet the underlying analytical stages remain substantially similar. Alexy himself (having assumed implicitly the importance of the conflicting purpose or value

---

[54] AHARON BARAK, PROPORTIONALITY: CONSTITUTIONAL RIGHTS AND THEIR LIMITATIONS 3 (2012).
[55] Id.
[56] Greene, *Foreword: Rights as Trumps*, 132 HARV. L. REV. 28, 58–9 (2018).

that Barak identifies as his first step) goes on to specify components 2 through 4 as proportionality's three subprinciples, namely, "suitability [which in the United States is called mean-ends rationality], necessity (use of the least intrusive means), and proportionality in its narrow sense (that is the balancing requirement)."[57]

The Canadian case *R. v. Oakes* is often cited for its articulation of the test.[58] Canadian Supreme Court states:

> First, the objective to be served by the measures limiting a *Charter* right must be sufficiently important to warrant overriding a constitutionally protected right or freedom.... Second, the parting ... must show the means to be reasonable and demonstrably justified.... To begin the measures must be fair and not arbitrary, carefully designed to achieve the objective in question and rationally connected to that objective. In addition, the means should impair the right in question as little as possible. Lastly, there must be a proportionality between the effects of the limiting measure and the objective—the more severe the deleterious effects of a measure, the more important the objective must be.[59]

It is therefore no surprise that in the United States, when we engage in the presumption-privileged trade-off of a right, we often use strict scrutiny, a species of triggered proportionality test with preset weights.[60] Our constitutional rights doctrine in these instances often requires (1) a showing of sufficiency of purpose, (2) means-ends rationality such that the disputed measure furthers the important end, and (3) least-restrictive means.

I will tend to refer to these last two inquiries, otherwise known as Alexy's necessity and suitability components, under the umbrella term of "fit." The compromise of a rights-protected value is held to a sufficient purpose requirement and a fit requirement, presumably because the right is so important that the impingement, indeed the entire extent of impingement, must be justified by the sufficiently weighty countervailing purpose, without excess.[61] As we have discussed, many of these accounts of proportionality also add an explicit "balancing" prong at the end, but that prong often goes unmentioned in United States, perhaps

---

[57] ALEXY, *supra* n.48, at 66 (subdividing the "fit" prong into "suitability" and "necessity" inquiries).

[58] [1986] 1 S.C.R. 103 (Can.).

[59] *Id.* at 105–6.

[60] *See* Vicki Jackson, *Constitutional Rights in an Age of Proportionality*, 124 YALE L.J. 3094 (2015) (documenting how many tests for US constitutional rights qualify as proportionality tests, with some exceptions such as in First Amendment doctrine when examining speech inciting violence, and in Fourth Amendment law). For the distinctions among proportionality and other types of reasoning, *see* Duncan Kennedy, *Proportionality and Deference in Contemporary Constitutional Thought* (Harv. Pub. Law Working Paper No. 17-09, 2017), https://papers.ssrn.com/sol3/papers.cfm?abstract_id=2931220. *See also* Richard Fallon, *Strict Judicial Scrutiny*, 54 UCLA L. REV. 1267, 1316–1317 (2008).

[61] ALEXY, *supra* n.48 at 66.

because here the balancing is implicit in the notion that the privileged value can be overcome by the decision-makers in this context.[62]

To recap, it is not just in Dworkin's account that rights operate to defeat certain ordinary justifications. Any effective countervailing justification in Dworkin's world must be in some sense *extraordinary*. Meanwhile, the proportionality account also generates a presumptive priority for the rights-protected value by demanding a special justification, one that demonstrates sufficient purpose and fit, for any competing norm to prevail. Indeed, Alexy views the demand for justification as potentially even more central to his account than to Dworkin's in the following sense: in Dworkin's model, the outcome of a conflict between norms is predetermined by the ordering, or the authority of a "rule" that has been predecided. Alexy disparages this device, saying:

> By appealing to the concept of an order of values . . . talk about values destroys the transparency of judicial decision-taking and leads to an "arcanum" of constitutional interpretation. Decisions about competing principles and how to balance them are made on some other basis, masked with an "appearance of rationality" with the "real reasoning removed." "From a practical point of view," appeal to an order of values and the balancing of values is a formula for disguising judicial or interpretive decisionism.[63]

Alexy's case for proportionality is that, by contrast, whether a right stands or falls depends on reasoned justification that must be produced transparently each time.[64]

Proportionality: Individuation or Claimability

Proportionality also stresses the distributed, individuated nature of rights, even if short of legal claimability. Alexy rejects Hans Kelsen's definition that "the right in the specific sense of the word is the legal power to enforce an existing duty." He proposes instead, citing MacCormick, that it "might be better to see rights as reasons for the legal capacity to enforce them."[65] Thus while legal claimability is

---

[62] *See* Jackson, *supra* n.60 at 3118–19, 3140–41, 3141 n.222 (describing how in the United States we assimilate the balancing to the "less restrictive means" prong. The elision lies in how courts will demand a less restrictive means, but fail to say whether the alternate means would be "equally effective in carrying out the government's legitimately relevant interests, or instead that even if the [means] were less effective, [it] would be a sufficient alternative given the relatively greater importance of [the right intruded upon"). *Id.*

[63] *See* ALEXY, *supra* n.48, at 96.

[64] *See id.*

[65] ALEXY, *Constitutional Rights as Subjective Rights, in* A THEORY OF CONSTITUTIONAL RIGHTS 118 (citing MacCormick, supra n.42, at 204).

not necessary to a right in the most general sense for Alexy, he adds that a right combined with a "power" to enforce helps constitute a "complete right":

> These rights are combined with the *power* to challenge their infringement before the courts. When these three positions come together; a legal liberty, a right against the state to non-obstruction, and a *power* to challenge infringements before the courts, one has a completely constituted negative liberty right against the state.[66]

Alexy does view the right's ascription to individual right-holders as inhering in the notion of a right, What he emphasizes as distinctive about rights is their structure pin-pointing certain relations between (1) the duty-bearer, (2) the "object" of the right, and (3) the rights holder.[67] He thus formalizes a right as a three-point relation with the form "x has a right to G as against y."[68] A liberty right is specific case of this view, namely, a right with "a three-point relation whose third element is a *choice of actions* . . . x is free (or not free) from y, to do or not do z."[69]

Rights must as a formal matter feature both a right-holder (x) *and* an addressee of the right, (y), thereby distinguishing them from other norms, such as what we have called "duties-at-large," or what Alexy calls "reflex effects."[70] The example he cites to illustrate a "reflex effect" is a type of tariff:

> [Take] Ihering's example of a protectionist import duty. "The law which introduces a protectionist import duty in the interest of certain industries is to the *advantage* of workers in those industries, it *supports* them and *protects* them in their work, and yet it does not grant them any *rights*. All there is, is a *reflex effect*."[71]

The tariff here parallels MacCormick's aforementioned "clean air" law, or Dworkin's example of "laws that provide a certain level of quiet in public places." Each of these may benefit an individual, but do not arise from her entitlement.

---

[66] *Id.* at 149 ("These rights are combined with the *power* to challenge their infringement before the courts. When these three positions come together; a legal liberty, a right against the state to nonobstruction, and a *power* to challenge infringements before the courts, one has a completely constituted negative liberty right against the state").

[67] *See id.* at 117, citing Hans Kelsen, General Theory of Norms 324 (M. Hartney, trans., 1991).

[68] *Id.* at 120. Alexy cites by contrast "[t]he classic example of this situation is Ihering's example of a protectionist import duty. 'The law which introduces a protectionist import duty in the interest of certain industries is to the *advantage* of workers in those industries, it *supports* them and *protects* them in their work, and yet it does not grant them any *rights*. All there is, is a *reflex effect*." *Id.*

[69] *Id.* at 141.

[70] *Id.* Alexy considers liberties to conform to this three point relation also, "The broader concept of liberty, of which legal liberty is a particular expression, is thus [also] a three-point relation whose third element is a *choice of actions*. . . . X is free (or not free) from y, to do or not do z." *Id.*

[71] *Id.* at 120.

Alexy's account of rights thus shares with Dworkin's the following:

1) the requirement of, if not full claimability, at least some relational aspect that ties the duties generated by a right back to an individual rights-holder, and
2) that rights afford a presumptive prioritization requiring a special justification to overcome.
   a. And, that the required justification include some kind of fit component.

We will look for these two and a half—really three, partially nested—features in Chapter 5 as we try to identify rights-like policies like impact assessments that can be used to advance a right to health in the form of a classic negative liberty. In addition, our knowledge of the proportionality signature will come in handy as we sift through health sector case law for signs of rights-reasoning in Chapter 4. Though our most prominent use-case for Alexy's framework involves the task of identifying classic negative rights, I close this section by emphasizing that Alexy's framework is not restricted to what he calls "defensive" rights; his framework extends also to "positive" rights, which he terms, "entitlements."[72] "Every right to positive action on the part of the state is an entitlement," he says and he maintains that "entitlements, just like defensive rights, can have *prima facie*, or principled, character."[73]

With this schema in hand, I turn now from Alexy and toward a framework for denominating statutory "entitlements" in the US politico-legal landscape.

David Super

Because we in the US lack a strong tradition of constitutional guarantees to material claims, our subconstitutional "statutory entitlements" constitute the chief mechanism by which we frame state promises of affirmative material provision. Though not protected by the specific structural entrenchment that the US Constitution affords through its onerous Article V amendment requirements, statutory rights can acquire degrees of entrenchment in other ways.[74] Therefore, pinning down

---

[72] *See* ALEXY, *Rights to Positive State Action Entitlements in a Wide Sense, in* A THEORY OF CONSTITUTIONAL RIGHTS 294 ("Every right to a positive action on the part of the state is an entitlement"). He also says at 295 ("Rights to negative actions set limits to the purposes the state may pursue. But they say nothing about those purposes. Rights to positive action impose upon the state, to some extent, the purposes to be pursued"); 296 (Entitlements (in the wide sense) can be divided into three groups: (1) rights to protection, (2) rights to organization and procedure, and (3) entitlements in the narrow sense").

[73] *Id.* at 294, 297.

[74] U.S. CONST., art. V.

what an entrenched statutory entitlement consists of will assist us in Chapters 6 and 7, when we investigate the proposal for health reinsurance as an affirmative right to healthcare. To recognize examples of this category of affirmative state guarantee, we may be less in need of a philosophical theory of positive rights in general, requiring instead an account of the legal and political meaning of the term "entitlement" as used in the United States. For this purpose, David Super provides a comprehensive framework. Because the term is wielded strategically, often to disparage the dependence of recipients, Super sets out to clarify what "entitlement" could potentially refer to in recognizable usage as distinct from how it might appear in weaponized distortions. He considers six features that the label "entitlement" might be thought to imply and tests these characteristics against the actual programs to which this term commonly refers. Super does so even as he makes a normative case that some of these programs ought to come into closer conformity with a subset of these qualities to serve as even more effective entitlements. This exercise, while open-ended in its conclusions, will at least inform our judgment about which implications of the term "entitlement" hold up as descriptively accurate, or even necessary. The six features are, in his language, those of:

1) "unconditional entitlement," a characterization he deems misleading and unnecessary for a benefit to qualify as an entitlement,
2) "positive entitlement,"
3) "budgetary entitlement,"
4) "responsive entitlement,"
5) "functional entitlement," an aspirational property that is in the United States often honored in the breach, and
6) "subjective entitlement."

The first of these characteristics—entitlements as "unconditional"—need not concern us. Unsurprisingly, Super finds that there are virtually no material benefits that we provide to persons without *any* threshold qualification or definition of scope, despite the heated rhetoric of political opponents otherwise.

Similarly, he considers and largely rejects the descriptive necessity of the next-to-last trait listed above, namely that of "functional entitlement." To qualify as "functional," an entitlement must be sufficient to achieve a "particular mission or function" that would be "comprehensible to the layperson without a great deal of programmatic or economic knowledge."[75] In other words, the scope of a "functional" benefit should have some recognizable salience in the everyday world. Super illustrates by means of the Supplemental Nutrition Assistance (SNAP) or "food stamp" program. In lay understanding, SNAP is a program to "assure

---

[75] Super, *supra* n.16, at 657.

households of a minimally adequate diet."[76] Yet by 1985, the legal boundaries of the benefit were defined down to such an extent that "a minimally nutritious diet cost 26% to 54% more than food stamp allotments provided."[77]

A "functional entitlement" would make ready sense to the general public, and though this quality may be desirable, Super concedes that the entitlements that predominate in the United States tend to lack this functional character. Instead, any "understanding [of] the functional significance of an arbitrarily defined positive entitlement . . . hand is exceedingly difficult."[78] Many US benefit programs enacted under Congress's Spending Power foreground state flexibility by streaming money to states as primary actors and imposing only minimum conditions. Thus, over time, programs like SNAP and health or disability assistance have come to vary, containing obscure limits or technical cut-offs that would be hard for any layperson to fathom much less anticipate.[79] Although Super shows that our existing entitlements fall short of "functionality," he argues that we should aspire to this standard, both as a matter of political morality, but also for practical efficiency of administration.[80] Notably, we will see how this political morality of "functional" salience as opposed to arbitrary positive definition exerts a pull on US reinsurance programs in Chapter 6. In Chapter 4, we will also see the influence that "functional" understandings of benefits can exert as revealed by judicial tendencies to assure the coverage of "medically necessary" care, even when the strictly positive parameters of the scope of health coverage might purport to offer something short of beneficiary's medical needs.

Of the final four properties that "entitlements" could be understood to feature (numbers 2, 3, 4, and 6 in the list above) there are two—the quality of "positive entitlement" and that of "budgetary entitlement"—that Super considers widely characteristic and indeed necessary to the programs that we generally call entitlements. Another attribute, that of entitlements as "responsive," is also arguably necessary in his view. To Super, responsiveness in an entitlement means that "the number of eligible people seeking benefits and the amount for which they are eligible" determines the funding, not some extraneously introduced Congressional cap.[81] He admits, however, that this feature is occasionally

---

[76] Id. at 656.

[77] Id. at 656, 656 n.107 (citing Group Says Food Stamps Don't Assure Good Diet, L.A. TIMES, October 19, 1985, at 10).

[78] Id. at 657–58.

[79] See, e.g., How Benefits Cliffs and Financial Gaps Undermine the Safety Net for New Yorkers, FED'N PROTESTANT WELFARE AGENCIES (2021), https://www.fpwa.org/wp-content/uploads/2021/04/2104019_FPWA-benefitcliffs-rev2_FINAL_4.19.2021.pdf; Opportunities to Streamline Enrollment Across Public Benefit Programs, CTR. ON BUDGET & POL'Y PRIORITIES (November 2, 2017), https://www.cbpp.org/research/poverty-and-inequality/opportunities-to-streamline-enrollment-across-public-benefit.

[80] See Super, supra n.16, at 55–58.

[81] Id. at 654.

undercut in real life by the fierce political tug-of-war over entitlement programs that has stretched and rent their statutory configurations beyond coherence. Take the Social Services Block Grant as a stark example. Though it contains clear entitlement language, it then defines the entitlement to be *a capped aggregate amount per state even if recipient need should exceed expectation*: "Each State shall be entitled to payment under this subtitle . . . in an amount equal to its allotment for such fiscal year."[82] Such an "entitlement" is defined down to a rigid, unresponsive sum with so little functional salience as to be almost unworthy of its name. The final feature of entitlements that Super proposes, based on the "subjective" assurance a rights-holder would feel, is, he demurs, beyond his ability to assess. I take up this challenge where he leaves off. As we will see, this feature of "subjective entitlement" figures prominently in the context of the programs we demonstrate to be entitlements in Chapter 6.

I now turn to unpacking the meaning of each of these four candidate properties for entitlements to enable their use throughout the book.

Positive Entitlement

In keeping with the individuation or claimability of rights, Super takes the position that to distinguish a material benefit as an entitlement, one must start with the lawyer's understanding that "an entitlement is a legally enforceable right."[83] In Super's lexicon, this feature of a program renders it a "positive" entitlement.

Super explains that "a program's being a positive entitlement has . . . specific implications. First, an individual denied benefits can sue if they were turned away for reasons that an entitlement statute does not authorize."[84] In other words, to the extent that the statute spelled out the terms qualifying applicants for those legislatively prescribed benefits, a court can then require that those benefits be furnished in conformance with those statutory terms.[85] US law offers both statutory and constitutional avenues for claimants to vindicate their entitlements. These various legal pathways not only satisfy the "claimability" property that would allow us to classify these programs as rights; they also serve as mechanisms for demanding public justification, thereby rendering these entitlement programs rights-like according to the common features we identified in both Dworkinian and proportionality based accounts of rights above.

---

[82] 42 U.S.C. § 1397a(a)(1).

[83] Super, *supra* n.16, at 638.

[84] *Id.* at 649 (citing Rosado v. Wyman, 397 U.S. 397, 420 (1970) which in turn cites Goldberg v. Kelly, 397 U.S. 254, 261–2, 262 n.8 (1970) and Perry v. Sindermann, 408 U.S. 602–03 (1972)).

[85] *See id.*

I duly note in Chapter 6 whenever these claim-conferring *statutory* authorizations arise as we examine the different reinsurance models that a federal health backstopping program could emulate. Sometimes these legal claims are specifically authorized by that program's organic statute. But even without such authorization, well-specified legislation can trigger other general statutory causes of action, such as those available under the Administrative Procedure Act, 42 U.S.C. § 1983, or under, for instance, the Tucker Act, which authorizes "claim[s] against the United States founded either upon the Constitution, or any Act of Congress or any regulation of an executive department, or upon any express or implied contract with the United States, or for liquidated or unliquidated damages in cases not sounding in tort."[86]

Apart from assorted general statutory causes of action, Super spells out the constitutional pathway to suit as well. One crucial pathway opens insofar as "the rights an entitlement [granting statute] creates are sufficiently choate to constitute a property interest for purposes of the Due Process Clause."[87] In other words, a positive entitlement can back suits not only on statutory grounds, but also based on statutory characteristics that could trigger Constitutional grounds. Under Due Process doctrine familiar to us at least since *Goldberg v. Kelly* and the *Roth* and *Sindermann* line of cases, we have understood that if one's expectations of benefit "was grounded in the statute defining eligibility" or has legitimate backing in "rules or mutually explicit understandings," then that benefit will qualify as a constitutionally recognized property interest such that its deprivation triggers procedures for contestation that can be claimed through litigation.[88] In Chapter 6 we find numerous programs backed by statutory and constitutional causes of action among the reinsurance programs. Their availability bolsters this book's argument that state-sponsored reinsurance constitutes a type of affirmative material claim to benefits on which health rights could be modeled.

Budgetary Entitlement

The second necessary feature of a full entitlement in Super's view is that of "budgetary entitlement." As I have written elsewhere, "Entitlements generate budgetary consequences insofar as a beneficiary meeting the eligibility criteria outlined in law may sue to enforce the delivery of benefits specified in statute.

---

[86] 28 U.S.C. § 1491.

[87] Super, *supra* n.16, at 649 (citations omitted); *see also* Mathews v. Eldridge, 424 U.S. 319 (1976); Cleveland Bd. of Educ. v. Loudermill, 470 U.S. 532 (1985); *see generally* Charles Reich, *The New Property*, 73 YALE L. J. 733 (1964).

[88] Goldberg v. Kelly, 397 U.S. 254, 261–2, 262 n.8 (1970). Board of Regents of State Colleges v. Roth, 408 U.S. 564, 577 (1972) and Perry v. Sindermann, 408 U.S. 593, 601(1972).

Therefore, Congress cannot set contrary limits on the funding of such a program without changing the authorizing law."[89] This feature of "budgetary entitlement" is in one sense merely an implication triggered by the program's "positive entitlement" status, but the specifics of its operation bear further explanation.

A "budgetary entitlement" qualifies as such because it commands "mandatory," otherwise known as "direct" funding, rather than "discretionary" funding, in the US federal budget context. What makes an expenditure "mandatory or "direct" in nature is chiefly the fact that such expenditure is not conditioned on Congress's enactment of appropriations legislation. Matthew Lawrence and others have written to remind us that some entitlements are called "appropriated entitlements" and as a ministerial matter are included in annual appropriations bills.[90] But Tim Jost explains that whether an entitlement is considered appropriated or not has no bearing on whether the appropriations bill actually limits the payments made under those programs:

> [S]ome mandatory expenditures (such as Medicare) have permanent appropriations, others (including Medicaid) require annual appropriations, but in either case Congress must fund mandatory expenditures as needed to meet program obligations. . . . [Even when] entitlement programs require annual appropriations, actual outlays are determined by eligibility, benefit, and payment rules, which are established by the legislation that authorizes the programs.[91]

---

[89] Christina S. Ho, *Budgeting on Autopilot*, 50 TULSA L. REV. 695 (2015) ("The statutory language must, among other requirements, be sufficiently mandatory to admit of individual enforcement. And while 'shall' is one such indication of the mandatory nature of the provision, its effect can be undercut by language such as "subject to the availability of appropriations," or statements that under such law "there are authorized to be appropriated funds for"). *See also*, Timothy Westmoreland, *Standard Error*, 95 GEO. L.J. 1555, 1566 (2007).

[90] *See* Matthew Lawrence, *Disappropriation*, 120 COLUM. L. REV. 1 (2020); *see also* BILL HENIFF JR., CONG. RSCH. SERV., RS20129, ENTITLEMENTS AND APPROPRIATED ENTITLEMENTS IN THE FEDERAL BUDGET PROCESS (2012) (explaining, "Most entitlement spending bypasses the annual appropriations process altogether and is funded by permanent or multiyear appropriations in substantive law. Such spending becomes available automatically each year, without legislative action by Congress. Examples of such programs include Social Security, Medicare, and federal employee retirement. A portion of entitlement spending, such as Medicaid and certain veterans' programs, is funded in annual appropriations acts. Such entitlement spending, referred to as *appropriated entitlements*, comprises roughly 36–38 percent of funding provided in the annual appropriations acts") (emphasis in original).

[91] TIMOTHY S. JOST, DISENTITLEMENT?: THE THREATS FACING OUR PUBLIC HEALTH-CARE PROGRAMS AND A RIGHTS-BASED RESPONSE 47–48 (2003); *see also* HENIFF, supra n.90, at 2 ("[T]he funding is provided in the annual appropriations acts, the level of spending for appropriated entitlements is not controlled through the annual appropriations process. Instead, the level of spending for appropriated entitlements, like other entitlements, is based on the benefit and eligibility criteria established in law, and the amount provided in appropriations acts is based on meeting this projected level").

This authority for federal outlays, independent of appropriations legislation, is apparent from the definition of the term "entitlement authority" in 2 U.S.C. § 622(9)(A), especially the part emphasized in italics below:

> Entitlement authority is . . . *the authority to make payments (including loans and grants), the budget authority for which is not provided for in advance by appropriation Acts*, to any person or government if, under the provisions of the law containing that authority, the United States is obligated to make such payments to persons or governments who meet the requirements established by that law.

Plainly the distinction between authorizing and appropriations is a fundamental concept structuring Congress's work: "Authorizations establish, continue or modify programs or policies; appropriations fund authorized programs and policies."[92]

To further understand this distinction between authorization and appropriation, we need a picture of how Congress undertakes fiscal management and prioritization, starting with the budgeting process. Congress is engaged in the everyday process of passing laws, many of which authorize federal action of some kind. These authorized acts and programs typically require ongoing financial expenditure to effectuate. How much money will the universe of federal government activities consume each year? That amount must be "budgeted" annually, an action that takes the form of a budget resolution that is generally passed each spring by Congress following a proposal submitted by the president. The budget blueprint contains projections for mandatory spending as well as allotments for discretionary spending categories. Following that blueprint, certain funds must be "appropriated" accordingly in the course of the fiscal year.[93] The twelve appropriations subcommittees of Congress thus develop the appropriations bills that make the money available as budgeted. Legislation or appropriation that fails to conform to the budgeted discretionary spending allotments are subject to points of order, many of which require supermajorities to override.[94]

Neither appropriations nor annual budget limits, however, are enforceable against mandatory (direct) spending. While Congress has from time to time imposed a different type of direct spending discipline—namely "pay-as-you-go" points of order that require Congress to find spending or revenue offsets

---

[92] WALTER OLESZEK, CONGRESSIONAL PROCEDURES AND THE POLICY PROCESS 42 (7th ed. 2007).

[93] The Constitution commands, "No Money shall be drawn from the Treasury, but in Consequence of Appropriations made by Law." U.S. CONST., art. I, § 9, cl. 7.

[94] Congressional Budget Act § 302(f) (2)(A) and (B), as amended by the Budget Control Act of 2011, Pub. L. No. 112–25, 125 Stat. 240, at 25 (2011) (codified as amended at 2 U.S.C. § 633(f)(2)(A) and (B)) (imposing a Senate point of order on any legislation or appropriation that would cause the applicable allocation or suballocation from the budget resolution to be exceeded that can only be waived by three-fifths majority).

whenever new entitlement spending is authorized—that regime kicks in only for "legislated changes in entitlement programs and have no application when program expenditures increase due to increases in the number of persons eligible for the program or in the cost of benefits as determined by established payment rules."[95]

Certainly if new entitlement authorization legislation that changes eligibility, benefits, or payment rules is passed after the budget blueprint is adopted, and such legislation is projected to change spending, revenue, or debt thresholds, then the legislation would have to be reconciled with the budget. In anticipation of just such situations, the budget frequently contains instructions or reserve funds providing room for potential new authorizing legislation to emerge in the course of the legislative year.[96] Thus the process of authorizing legislation for entitlements usually works through this reconciliation pathway designed to assure that new laws match up with the budgeted parameters. Since reconciliation bills traverse this procedurally privileged pathway, Congress must use the so-called Byrd rule to impose supermajority points of order to fend off inclusions or amendments to such bills that could be deemed "extraneous legislation, not directed at changing outlays or revenues."[97] Otherwise, every member of Congress would try to hitch their legislative priorities onto the reconciliation train and ride to passage.

These somewhat arcane steps have grown up to satisfy the Constitutional command that "No Money shall be drawn from the Treasury, but in Consequence of Appropriations made by Law." How then can mandatory funding be spent "directly," according to the terms of the entitlement authorization statute, bypassing the limits that Congress would impose on available funds through the yearly appropriations bills? The reason is because the authorizing statutes for entitlements typically contain language that not only authorizes Congress to engage in the activities that incur expenses; they simultaneously include language to accomplish what appropriation would otherwise achieve in providing budget authority for outlays. They do so by means of verbal formulae like "there are hereby made available, in accordance with the provisions of this part, such sums as may be necessary to make loans to all eligible students," in the case of student loans, or "this constitutes budget authority in advance of appropriations acts," as in the case of Medicaid.[98] These mandatory funding instructions allowing

---

[95] Jost, *supra* n.91, at 48.

[96] *See* Richard Kogan & David Reich, *Introduction to Budget "Reconciliation*," Ctr. on Budget & Pol'y Priorities (May 6, 2022), https://www.cbpp.org/research/federal-budget/introduction-to-budget-reconciliation.

[97] Congressional Budget Act § 313; 2 U.S.C. § 644.

[98] *See* 20 U.S.C. § 1087a(a) (2012) ("There are hereby made available, in accordance with the provisions of this part, such sums as may be necessary to make loans to all eligible students."), cited in Lawrence, *supra* n.90, at 22; *see also* Medicaid language, 42 U.S.C. § 1396 ("[T]his constitutes budget authority in advance of appropriations acts."), cited in Timothy Westmoreland, *Standard Errors: How*

Treasury to spend without regard to the yearly appropriations, and that trait is what qualifies them as "budgetary entitlements," in Super's language. As the Supreme Court explained in *Maine Community Health Options v. U.S.*:

> Creating and satisfying a Government obligation . . . typically involves four steps: (1) Congress passes an organic statute (like the Affordable Care Act) that creates a program, agency, or function; (2) Congress passes an Act authorizing appropriations; (3) Congress enacts the appropriation, granting "budget authority" to incur obligations and make payments, and designating the funds to be drawn; and (4) the relevant Government entity begins incurring the obligation.[99]

A statute for a mandatory spending program accomplishes 2 and 3 at once without need for annual appropriations to effect step 3.

We have dwelled at some length on Congress's authorization and appropriation roles. The reason is because the upshot of these two tracks of Congressional action is that entitlements are subconstitutionally entrenched insofar as they comparatively exempt from the tribulations of this second track involving the yearly appropriations gauntlet. In sum, entitlements are relatively shielded from ongoing Congressional change or tampering when compared to ordinary legislation.

Responsive Entitlement

Recall from earlier that the budget mandating nature of entitlements flows in large part from the legal claimability of entitlements. Because the laws creating or authorizing these programs "establish[] sufficiently clear legal rights [such] that unsuccessful claimants could successfully sue for benefits,"[100] no predetermined funding level can guide or constrain the benefits disbursed. The relationship

---

Budget Rules Distort Lawmaking, 95 GEO. L.J. 1555, 1567 (2007). The Supreme Court even narrowly upheld the streaming of funds in excess of Congressional appropriations under the Contract Disputes Act, 41 U. S. C. §§ 601–613, when the underlying authorization statute used the words, "funds that the tribe . . . is entitled to receive," even if later language described the funds as "subject to the availability of appropriations." Salazar v. Ramah Navajo Chapter, 567 U.S. 182 (2012) (construing in part the quoted language at 25 U.S.C. §§ 5325(a)(3)(C) and (b)(5)).

[99] Maine Community Health Options v. United States, 590 U.S. ___, 10 (2020) (upholding HHS' position that risk corridor payments were an appropriated entitlement, even though Congress in 2014 passed a rider limiting the availability of appropriations for risk corridors payments). *Maine Community Health* also explains that "[b]udget authority is an agency's power provided by Federal law to incur financial obligations that will result in immediate or future outlays of government funds." *Id.* (citations omitted) (internal quotations omitted).

[100] Super, n.16, at 652 n.80.

would actually flow the other direction: the sum total would instead be determined by and must fluctuate to meet the detailed eligibility requirements and benefit payment specifications, even when the number of claimants exceeds what could have been predicted. As Super defines it, the responsiveness of an entitlement refers to when the program's capacity in terms of number of qualifying cases or recipients "rises and falls based on need without further legislative action."[101] For instance Medicaid enrollment grew by 16.1 million enrollees, or 22.7 percent during the pandemic period from February 2020 to February 2022.[102] This enrollment growth helps illustrate how entitlement programs expand and spending rises to match the need as more people lose income or meet disability-based eligibility requirements. The entitlement characteristic of "responsiveness" is in some sense entailed by the "positive" character of entitlements, and the associated "budgetary" entitlement status.

Even if Congress were to attempt to limit such mandatory spending by imposing appropriations caps, causes of action such as those under the Tucker Act prevent Congressional appropriations shortfalls from cutting off the government's obligations, as a recent Supreme Court decision illustrates.[103] The Court in *Maine Community Health Options v. U.S.* vindicated insurers' claims to risk corridor payments promised in the ACA, affirming that the "failure [of Congress] to appropriate funds to meet statutory obligations prevents the accounting officers of the Government from making disbursements, but such rights [remain] enforceable in the Court of Claims."[104] That such a channel of accountability exists testifies to why responsiveness as a property is worth mentioning separately and apart from budgetary entitlement. Congress has indeed attempted to buck the implications of its own acts in the past by setting appropriations or funding limitations short of the overall amount required to respond to the need as defined by the articulated program parameters. Congress's efforts have been repeatedly foiled as we see in *Maine v. Community Health Options v. U.S.*[105]

David Super identifies the mechanism by which courts bypass these congressional funding limits. Beyond the funds designated for a particular program, there exists a further reservoir of funding yet to meet these claims if they are

---

[101] *Id.*

[102] Bradley Corallo & Sophia Moreno, *Analysis of Recent National Trends in Medicaid and CHIP Enrollment*, KAISER FAM. FOUND. (June 6, 2022), https://www.kff.org/coronavirus-covid-19/issue-brief/analysis-of-recent-national-trends-in-medicaid-and-chip-enrollment/#:~:text=Data%20s how%20that%20Medicaid%2FCHIP,61.9%25%20(Figure%202).

[103] *See* Maine Community Health Options, 590 U.S.__ (2020).

[104] Greenlee Cty., Ariz. v. U.S., 487 F.3d 871, 877 (Fed. Cir. 2007) (citing N.Y. Airways, Inc. v. U.S., 369 F.2d 743, 748 (Ct. Cl. 1966)); *see also* U.S. GOV'T ACCOUNTABILITY OFF., A GLOSSARY OF TERMS USED IN THE FEDERAL BUDGET PROCESS: RELATED ACCOUNTING, ECONOMIC, AND TAX TERMS 57 (3d ed. 2013) ("Authorization for entitlements constitute a binding obligation on the part of the Federal Government, and eligible recipients have legal recourse if the obligation is not fulfilled").

[105] 590 U.S. ___. (2020).

brought in federal court under the Constitution or under cross-cutting statutes like the Tucker Act:

> A law creating a budgetary entitlement establishes sufficiently clear legal rights that unsuccessful claimants could successfully sue for benefits in the Court of Claims. For example, should eligible claimants be denied Medicaid assistance due them, they presumably could prevail under the requirement "that such assistance shall be furnished with reasonable promptness to all eligible individuals." 42 U.S.C. § 1396a(a)(8). If no funds appropriated for that program were available, those benefits would be paid from the *permanent unlimited appropriation for judgments against the United States*. 28 U.S.C. §§ 2414, 2517 (2000). Thus the law creating those enforceable rights to benefits is an exercise in "direct spending," i.e. no further action is required for the funds to be made available.[106]

The effect of such fiscal backing under this extra fund for claims, judgments and relief is therefore to ensure "a responsive entitlement," this third feature that Super considers arguably constitutive of entitlements. For a responsive entitlement, the determinative factors for whether a benefit is disbursed in a particular case depends on what Dworkin might call matters of "principle," those eligibility and treatment characteristics that render the situation a like case. This quality of responsiveness in accommodating a rise in eligible participants is what would allow the reinsurance measures described in Chapter 6, to serve much like Medicaid, as an automatic stabilizer to absorb whenever need surges during an economic recession, or in the event of some other unforeseen disaster.[107]

Super clearly favors a world where responsiveness would characterize all entitlements. However, because of fierce political contestation over entitlements, the reality is that sometimes caps have been imposed. The State Children's Health Insurance Program, passed in the chastened aftermath of the Clinton Health Reform campaign of the 1990s, could only win support in the contorted form of a "capped" entitlement to states for a certain amount of funding, like the Social Services Block Grant, shorn of any corresponding entitlement for individual beneficiaries.[108] Moreover, the funding language sunsets periodically, thus requiring affirmative Congressional action to assure continued authorization

---

[106] Super, *supra* n.16, at 652 n.80 (emphasis added); *see also* Lawrence, *supra* n.90, at 23 (citing 31 U.S.C. § 1304(a) and describing "[t]he Judgment Fund [as] a blanket, catch-all, permanent appropriation of "such sums" as might be necessary to honor federal court judgments, as well as certain compromise settlements negotiated by the Department of Justice in the context of Litigation").

[107] *See* Vivien Lee & Louise Sheiner, *What Are Automatic Stabilizers?*, BROOKINGS (2019), https://www.brookings.edu/blog/up-front/2019/07/02/what-are-automatic-stabilizers/.

[108] *See Key CHIP Design Features*, MEDICAID & CHIP PAYMENT & ACCESS COMM'N (accessed June 8, 2022), https://www.macpac.gov/subtopic/key-design-features/.

and appropriations.[109] This grudging design resulted in periodic state enroll-ment freezes whereby otherwise eligible children confronted waiting periods or even potential disenrollments until new funding tranches were approved.[110] The political instability of this position prompted passage of a provision in the ACA requiring states to catch CHIP-eligible children through the exchanges as a backup in the event of these funding shortfalls.[111]

Subjective Entitlement

Sixth and finally, Super notes that entitlements might be understood to (and in-deed deployed in order to) bring about a "subjective" sense of entitlement. A sub-jective entitlement is one that "induce[s] a subjective sense of security."[112] But a "sense of subjective entitlement," Super tells us, can "go well beyond any explicit promises."[113] Super finds that because the necessary conditions for a "subjec-tive entitlement" are "in the mind of the claimant," it is "impossible [for him] to generalize about whether this feature attaches descriptively to our entitlement programs." In Chapter 6, we will see how subjective expectations of reinsurance were repeatedly redeemed to an extent "well beyond any explicit promises."[114] These episodes show that government reinsurance can be regarded as a "sub-jective entitlement" in the United States, further strengthening the case that an extension of the reinsurance principle in healthcare might qualify as the kind of right we would call an entitlement.

Indeed, we find that all of Super's proposed properties of entitlements, short of unconditionality, are present to some extent in the "state-sponsored reinsurance"

---

[109] See Lawrence, *supra* n.90, at 37–9; *see also, e.g.*, HENIFF, supra n.90, at 1 ("Most entitlement spending, such as for Medicare, is not capped at a specific spending level, and typically increases (but may decrease) each year as the number of eligible beneficiaries and the authorized benefit payments increases (or decreases). However, some entitlement spending—particularly entitlement payments to states, such as the State Children's Health Insurance Program (commonly referred to as CHIP)—is capped at a specific level provided in the authorizing law").

[110] See *id.*; *see also* Tricia Brooks, Joan Alker, & Karina Wagnerman, *What Are the Consequences of Congressional Delay on CHIP?*, GEO. UNIV. HEALTH POL'Y INST. CTR. CHILD. & FAMS. 1, 10 n.3 (2017), https://ccf.georgetown.edu/2017/10/25/what-are-the-consequences-of-congressional-delay-on-chip/; Goodnough and Robert Pear, *The CHIP Program Is Beloved. Why Is Its Funding in Danger?*, N.Y. TIMES (December 5, 2017), https://www.nytimes.com/2017/12/05/health/childrens-health-insurance-program.html.

[111] See ACA § 2101(b)(1), 124 Stat. at 286–87; *see also* Key Provisions of Legislation Extending Federal Funding for the Children's Health Insurance Program, CTRS. MEDICARE & MEDICAID SERVS. 2–5 (2018), https://www.hhs.gov/guidance/document/key-provisions-legislation-extending-fede ral-funding-chip; Goodnough & Pear, *supra* n.109.

[112] Super, *supra* n.16, at 640 ("People believing they have rights feel and act differently than those believing their well-being is at the sufferance of others").

[113] *Id.*

[114] *Id.*

programs examined in Chapter 6. These features thereby render statutory rein-surance measures as entitlements that should be extended to health.

Soft Entrenchment

I anticipate some head-scratching over whether these subconstitutional rights truly count as "rights" in a way meaningful to my project. After all, if an ordi-nary legal right of action counts as what we seek under the slogan "the right to healthcare," then the aspiration deflates some and may not be worth all the fuss. I have at least two responses to this reaction. First is that my goal is to deflate the project insofar as its loftiness has been weaponized *against* the prospects of achieving any progress. Why would we reject the achievement of a clear, pre-sumptively privileged and broadly held right to sue for health and healthcare as a sign of meaningful progress? Our efforts thus far have been time and again stymied by business-led resistance and a conservative judicial movement to erect strong-form ERISA preemption of state remedial causes of action as recounted in Chapters 3 and 7, by expansive judicial holdings to preclude individual lawsuits under Medicare and erode the previously available rights to sue for Medicaid benefits under 42 U.S.C. § 1983 and the Supremacy Clause of the Constitution.[115] It is telling that we failed to achieve even such ordinary legal rights in healthcare and if anything pushback has grown only more formidable.

Second, as discussed in the previous chapter, exclusive focus on a judicialized, constitutionally documented right is misguided. Constitutions are not the only form of constitutive entrenchment. William Eskridge and John Ferejohn[116] have shown how some statutory schemes have become so embedded within our politico-legal landscape as to attain the status of superstatutes, resisting repeal. Richard Posner and Adrian Vermeule have championed legislatively imposed supermajority and other tools for Congress to constrain the decisions of future Congresses, calling to mind the budgetary privileging tools we saw at work just now.[117] And their proposal is just one intervention in a lively literature on the procedural methods that may be deployed to adjust the difficulty of repealing or amending certain types of legislation. Examples of these methods include man-datory prospective rules of statutory interpretation, the aforementioned points of order, differential imposition of the filibuster in the Senate, procedures for

[115] Bowen v. Michigan Acad. of Fam. Physicians, 476 U.S. 667 (1986), Armstrong v. Exceptional Child Center, Inc., 575 U.S. 320 (2015).
[116] WILLIAM ESKRIDGE AND JOHN FEREJOHN, A REPUBLIC OF STATUTES: THE NEW AMERICAN CONSTITUTION 34, 65 (2010).
[117] *See* Eric A. Posner & Adrian Vermeule, *Legislative Entrenchment: A Reappraisal*, 111 YALE L.J. 1665 (2002).

calendaring votes, and strategic committee jurisdiction.[118] Daryl Levinson and Benjamin Sachs meanwhile have teased out an additional range of entrenchment strategies that they call "functional" rather than "procedural" and which do not rely on explicit legal mechanisms, but utilize softer normative or political suasion instead. Some of their examples include politicians' explicit intentions to empower Social Security beneficiaries to stave off changes to the program, efforts to "burrow" certain decisions deeply and ineradicably into agency infrastructure, and moves to tie minimum capital requirements for banks to the Basel accords, and thereby entrenching these standards with "the greater political costs of violating international agreements."[119]

It is hard to deny that some forms of subconstitutional entrenchment exist, and the stickiness of norms can be measured on a gradient. As Paul Starr says, "Entrenchment . . . refers not only to a condition but to a process, and it is always a matter of degree . . . Entrenchment . . . can refer to any process whereby an institution, a technology, a group, or a cultural form—any kind of social formation—becomes resistant to pressures for change."[120] The multiple avenues for vindicating entitlements in court, the presumptive budgetary privilege that tilts resource allocation toward these programs, the durability and sacrosanct status of certain reinsurance institutions, like the Federal Reserve, the subjectively held implicit reliance and sense of entitlement that property holders harbor with respect to government backstops for flood and terrorism loss, all of which I detail in Chapters 6 and 7, reinforce the argument that these statutory guarantees exist at a kind of mezzanine level. This level enjoys insulated funding and stature at a tier above ordinary statutes, even if somewhere below Constitutional enshrinement.

Having examined these three main accounts of rights—Dworkin's, Alexy's, and Super's—and picked out an array of elements distinctive to the rights technology, we can turn to the task of seeking out the places in our health-related decision practices where these telltale elements cluster.

---

[118] *See, e.g.,* Larry Alexander & Saikrishna Prakash, *Mother May I? Imposing Mandatory Prospective Rules of Statutory Interpretation,* 20 CONST. COMMENT. 97 (2003); Nicholas Quinn Rosenkranz, *Federal Rules of Statutory Interpretation,* 115 HARV. L. REV. 2085 (2002); William N. Eskridge Jr., *Vertogates and American Public Law,* 31 J.L. ECON. & ORG. 756 (2012); Barry R. McNollgast, *Positive Canons: The Role of Legislative Bargains in Statutory Interpretation,* 80 GEO. L. J. 705, 707 (1992).

[119] Daryl Levinson & Benjamin I. Sachs, *Political Entrenchment and Public Law* 125 YALE L.J. 400, 454 (2015).

[120] PAUL STARR, UNDERSTANDING ENTRENCHMENT 2 (2019).

3

A Health Right By Any Other Name: Expression in Statute

In the previous chapter, we identified the features that are distinctive of the machinery of rights. Now we look to whether we can spot this machinery at work in health law and policy, our domain of inquiry.

We noted the Dworkinian logic of the ACA's hallmark declaration that health coverage should not be denied based on a person's health status or preexisting condition.[1] Denying someone health coverage because they are sick and therefore need costly healthcare displays exactly the kind of backward logic that Dworkin believes rights are designed to rule out—a logic where the reasons offered in favor of compromise internally contradict the purpose of valuing the right in the first place.

Of course, this norm, as we will see throughout this chapter, runs straight into the core practice of private health insurance, namely, "health-status underwriting" under which "insurers evaluate[] the health status, health history, and other risk factors of applicants to determine whether and under what terms to issue coverage."[2]

Here I review the development of the now-ascendant norm *against* health-status underwriting, a rather remarkable process that culminated in its codification in the Affordable Care Act (ACA).[3] But the ACA is far from the only

---

[1] Public Health Service Act (PHSA) § 2704, codified as 42 U.S.C. § 300gg-3 and PHSA §2705, codified as 42 U.S.C. § 300gg-4.
With permission from the original publisher, Chapter 3 adapts minor material contained in the following previously published work: Christina S. Ho, *Are We Suffering from an Undiagnosed Health Right*, 42 AM. J. OF L. AND MED. 743 (2016).
[2] Gary Claxton et al., *Pre-existing Conditions and Medical Underwriting in the Individual Insurance Market Prior to the ACA*, KFF (2016) (alteration in original), https://www.kff.org/health-reform/issue-brief/pre-existing-conditions-and-medical-underwriting-in-the-individual-insurance-market-prior-to-the-aca/ (accessed December 11, 2021).
[3] 42 U.S.C. § 300gg-91(b)(19). Health-status underwriting is actually specified in the Public Health Service Act: "The term 'underwriting purposes' means . . .

    (A) rules for, or determination of, eligibility (including enrollment and continued eligibility) for benefits under the plan or coverage;
    (B) the computation of premium or contribution amounts under the plan or coverage;
    (C) the application of any pre-existing condition exclusion under the plan or coverage; and
    (D) other activities related to the creation, renewal, or replacement of a contract of health insurance or health benefits."

expression of resistance to using an individual's poor health as reason to cut back on their healthcare. Our battle-scarred health law and policy landscape is littered with other statutes that operate on related rationales.

One might have expected to find a natural reservoir among the laws that "require" certain types of healthcare to be included in the benefit basket, whether in the form of benefit mandates, or Medicare, Medicaid, and ACA benefit packages. These are certainly relevant, and others have looked at and continue to examine these norms. In this chapter, I will turn over a different rock. Rather than seeking those laws that require provision, I will focus on those laws that selectively *prohibit* certain "sensitive" factors from triggering denial. In some sense these laws are the photo negative of where one might expect to find the right to health. Instead of looking for the categories that entail the requirement of health provision, we will look for the categories along which denial is prohibited. Indeed, Dworkin teaches us to look here for the functions of a right—at the factors and justifications that are precluded from valid consideration to support *denial* of that right.

Many of these statutes cluster around a suggestive list of factors that we have in piecemeal fashion ruled out from consideration in determining eligibility for healthcare. For instance, the Americans with Disabilities Act of 2000, itself preceded by the Rehabilitation Act of 1978, precludes *disability* as grounds for denying health coverage. Medicaid and other statutes have in sporadic ways likewise fleshed out the intuition that access to healthcare in the form of health coverage ought not to be limited based on the factor of a person's *diagnosis or health condition*. The Age Discrimination in Employment Act and the Age Discrimination Act ostensibly prevent the consideration of *age* in employer-sponsored and federally funded health coverage, though various bouts of political contestation have eviscerated their effect in that regard. And the Genetic Information Nondiscrimination Act of 2008 prohibits the collection and use of *genetic information* in decisions about health coverage.

It turns out these prohibited categories (age, disability, diagnosis or health condition, and genetics) can plausibly be explained as stand-ins for health need.[4] Their preclusion from health access decisions thereby conforms to the pattern we might expect to find if we were looking for evidence that health interests trump select countervailing considerations in our polity. The problem that motivates these statutes is indeed the common view that it is precisely when one is old, disabled, genetically predisposed, or afflicted by a particular health condition that

---

[4] *See generally* Jessica L. Roberts, *The Genetic Information Nondiscrimination Act as an Antidiscrimination Law*, 86 NOTRE DAME L. REV. 597 (2013); John Jacobi, *The Ends of Health Insurance*, 30 U.C. DAVIS L. REV. 311, 335–37 (1997); Govind Persad, *Evaluating the Legality of Age-Based Criteria in Health Care: From Nondiscrimination and Discretion to Distributive Justice*, 60 BOS. COLL. L. REV. 889 (2019).

one needs health coverage the most. Allowing these features to constitute valid reasons to deny access to healthcare would undercut the purpose of prioritizing healthcare in the first place.

I do not mean to suggest that any of these factors is fully coincident with health need—the relationships between these factors and health are complicated—but just to suggest that they are widely understood as proxies.[5]

Affordable Care Act (ACA)

Let us start by outlining the express health-status nondiscrimination norm embodied in the ACA and briefly how we got here. Much of the ACA aims to realize this vision of barring illness or health need itself from counting against the provision of healthcare. This achievement is no small matter given the force of such health-need-related factors as the ordinary grounds of health insurer cost-control. I start with the core provisions addressed toward these purposes, namely §§ 2701–2712 of Public Health Service Act (PHSA).[6] These measures generally apply to any "group health plan and . . . health insurance issuer offering group or individual health insurance coverage." "Group health plan" is stipulated to include the "employee welfare benefit plans" that may be self-funded rather than fully insured, a specification whose significance I turn to in the next subsection.[7] This scope of application thus assures broad effect for these standards across all types of private health coverage, including individual plans, small employer plans, and even, for a subset of these norms, the large employer plans.[8]

---

[5] *See* Elizabeth Weeks & Jessica L. Roberts, Healthism: Health-Status Discrimination and the Law 55–56 (1st ed. 2018); *see* Persad, *supra* n.4.

[6] 42 U.S.C. § 300gg et seq.; The Patient Protection and Affordable Care Act of 2010 (ACA) Pub. L. 111–148 § 1201 (2010).

[7] 42 U.S.C. § 300gg-91(a)(1); Interim Final Rules 75 Fed. Reg. 34,538, 34,539 (June 17, 2010) cited in Timothy S. Jost, *Loopholes in the Affordable Care Act: Regulatory Gaps and Border Crossing Techniques and How to Address Them*, 5 St. Louis Univ. J. of Health L. & Pol'y 27, 52–3 (2011) (elaborating on the application of title 27 of the PHSA to employer plans as such title interacts with ERISA or the tax code, citing: "The Affordable Care Act also adds section 715(a)(2) of ERISA, which provides that, to the extent that any provision of part 7 of ERISA conflicts with part A of title XXVII of the PHS Act with respect to group health plans or group health insurance coverage, the PHS Act provisions apply. Similarly, the Affordable Care Act adds section 9815(a)(2) of the Code, which provides that, to the extent that any provision of subchapter B of chapter 100 of the Code conflicts with part A of title XXVII of the PHS Act with respect to group health plans or group health insurance coverage, the PHS Act provisions apply").

[8] Jost, *supra* n.7, at 28–29 ("Large group plans are, for example, not subject to the essential benefits package requirement, the risk adjustment program").

Adverse Selection and the Basic Anatomy of the US Private Insurance Market

Let me pause for a moment to specify some of the components and distinctions that characterize the private insurance market in the United States.

Individual Market

Those who seek health insurance independently of their employers are shopping in the "individual market." Transactions in this market are beset by an information imperfection that insurers call "adverse selection." To pool the cost and probability of high-loss insurable events in any given policy year, insurers could theoretically, in an oversimplified model, charge everyone in the pool based on what the predicted yearly costs would be when averaged across all members. However, potential customers usually know more about their health status than insurers do. Therefore those who anticipate high medical costs are the most likely to purchase health insurance, or purchase more of it, calculating it to be financially worthwhile. Meanwhile, those who are healthier than average generally suspect they are unlikely to use enough healthcare for potential insurance payouts to make up for the average premium costs they must incur to buy insurance. Those in this self-identified "healthier" segment are therefore more tempted to forgo insurance. Thus the insurers' enrolled membership will tend to skew sicker and the "average" cost of those who actually purchase insurance will tend to be higher than the average premium if calculated across the population as a whole. As John Cogan puts it, "If this scenario plays out on a larger scale—too many sick people buy insurance and too many healthy people forgo it—the insurer's claims costs will be higher than expected. The premium collected will not cover claims costs and the insurer will lose money."[9] As more insurers lose money and exit the market, premiums will spiral higher, exacerbating the skewed disincentives to buy coverage and possibly triggering an insurance "death spiral."[10]

Group Market

However, the employer-sponsored health system that grew up in the United States dampened the effects of these insurance market flaws, at least while it prevailed. Due in part to wage controls during World War II that forced employers to use

---

[9] John A. Cogan Jr., *Does Small Group Health Insurance Deliver Group Benefits? An Argument in Favor of Allowing the Small Group Market to Die*, 93 WASH. L. REV. 1121, 1130 (2018).

[10] Peter Siegelman, *Adverse Selection in Insurance Markets: An Exaggerated Threat*, 113 YALE L. J. 1223, 1224 (2004) (explaining an insurance death spiral as when "good risks begin to exit, the average quality of those insureds remaining falls and prices rise in a vicious circle, [and eventually] no one is covered").

fringe benefits to compete for labor, and due in part to the tax exclusion for compensation paid in the form of health coverage, an employer-based system of private health coverage took hold in the United States.[11] Even today, about half of Americans receive their health coverage through their employers.[12] Employer groups were less afflicted by adverse selection "[s]ince employees came to the group for a reason other than to buy insurance (i.e., to get a job)."[13] Their job choices tended not to reflect individuals' propensity to be sick enough to need healthcare.

Because group insurance is sold not to individuals but to employer-based groups, the group market is less wracked by adverse selection on the whole. Unfortunately, the group market is bifurcated. Larger employers, typically defined as firms with more than fifty employees (sometimes defined as over a hundred employees), comprise the "large group market."[14] The situation confronting the large group market as compared to the small group market is quite different as Tim Jost has summarized:

> Historically, the large group market has functioned pretty well. Large groups have bargaining power with insurers and present insurers with a reasonably uniform risk profile . . . The worst abuses in the large group market—pre-existing condition exclusions and health status underwriting within the group—were addressed by HIPAA [in 1996]. . . . The small group and individual markets, on the other hand, have been more dysfunctional and have been the traditional targets of state regulation. They have suffered the most from health status underwriting, pre-existing condition exclusions, and arbitrary and unreasonable insurer practices, such as rescissions or unconscionably low annual limits.[15]

---

[11] JILL QUADAGNO, ONE NATION, UNINSURED: WHY THE U.S. HAS NO NATIONAL HEALTH INSURANCE 49–51 (2006); *Timeline: History of Health Reform in the U.S.*, KAISER FAMILY FOUNDATION (2011), https://www.kff.org/wp-content/uploads/2011/03/5-02-13-history-of-health-reform.pdf.

[12] *Health Insurance Coverage of the Total Population*, KAISER FAM. FOUND. (2019), https://www.kff.org/other/state-indicator/total-population/?currentTimeframe=0&sortModel=%7B%22collId%22:%22Location%22,%22sort%22:%22asc%22%7D

[13] Cogan, *supra* n.9, at 1133 (alteration in original).

[14] Cogan, *supra* n.9, at 1123, n. 2 ("The ACA amended these definitions to enlarge the small employer group market to include employers with up to 100 employees as of January 1, 2016") (citations omitted). Congress later amended the ACA to retain the original definitions of large and small group employers. Protecting Affordable Coverage for Employees Act, Pub. L. 114–60, § 2(a)(1)-(2), 129 Stat. 543 (2015) (codified in scattered sections of 42 U.S.C.). Four states-California, Colorado, New York, and Vermont—currently extend their small group market to cover employers with up to 100 employees according to Sabrina Corlette et al., *Repeal of Small-Business Provision of the ACA Creates Natural Experiment in States*, COMMONWEALTH FUND (March 22, 2016), https://www.commonwealthfund.org/blog/2016/repeal-small-business-provision-aca-creates-natural-experiment-states.

[15] Jost, *supra* n.7, at 29–30.

Self-Insured versus Fully Insured and the Effects on Small Employers

Increasingly however, employers, especially smaller-employers, have ceased to offer health benefits to their workers, and even those who do continue tend to opt out of buying health insurance on the "fully insured" market. Instead, some offer so-called self-funded or self-insured employer plans, where the employer ostensibly elects to pay directly for their employees' health benefits out of their own funds. Self-insured plans thus assume direct financial responsibility for absorbing unpredictably large claims rather than buying so-called fully insured group health insurance off-the-shelf to perform that cushioning for them.[16] This approach has been attractive ever since the emergence of an ERISA doctrine which, by saving state insurance law but preempting the application of that law to self-funded plans, made self-funding a means of escaping costly state consumer protections. We will discuss this development in greater depth in Chapters 6 and 7. Self-funding may be particularly attractive to more cost-conscious employers or those anticipating a *healthier* overall pool of workers whose costly tail risk is therefore comparatively minimal for the employer. This inclination tends to segment the group market so that healthier groups self-fund and thereby *adversely select out* of buying fully insured plans for their employees. The resulting market for fully insured plans thus faces on average, a higher-risk customer base, in addition to a more stringent set of regulatory requirements and therefore higher premiums overall.

These overlapping dynamics differentially burden smaller employers. To insurers selling in the group market, small groups already pose greater volatility because "[t]he larger the pool of insureds, the more accurately future claims can be predicted. For smaller groups, claims experience is much less predictive," again placing upward pressure on the premiums that insurers charge small groups in the fully insured group market.[17] Meanwhile, large firms are well-incentivized and better able to select out of the higher-cost fully insured group market and to sustain the risks of self-insurance. This comparative advantage holds true at the most basic level because large firms have a larger employee base over which to spread those risks, and thereby gain the financial advantages, and the regulatory advantages that we describe later. The statistics accord with these tendencies: the universe of self-funded plans skews toward large firms: according to a 2020 report, "21% of covered workers in small firms and 82% in large firms, are enrolled

---

[16] *See* Gary Claxton et al., *Employer Health Benefits 2020 Annual Survey*, KAISER FAM. FOUND. 167, 170 (October 8, 2020), https://files.kff.org/attachment/Report-Employer-Health-Benefits-2020-Annual-Survey.pdf (defining self-funded plans on page 170; showing that a great majority of these self-funded plans actually purchase additional stop-loss to help them cushion the costs, via Figure 10.9 on page 167).

[17] Cogan, *supra* n.9, at 1137.

in plans that are self-funded."[18] This market splitting effect further works against stability in the small group market.

Higher costs and stricter regulation in the fully insured market then prompt some small employers to drop health benefits altogether. Other small groups, seeking lower costs, turn to insurers who compete to offer lower rates to groups with "healthier" characteristics while spurning less attractive groups, namely, insurers who underwrite on the basis of health status. This kind of employer-driven adverse selection and insurer-driven medical underwriting generates even more administrative cost and inflationary pressure on premiums. Medical underwriting strips healthy employer groups from the rest of the group market, further hindering risk pooling and courting an insurance death spiral.

It is little surprise that in recent years, "[o]nly 29% of small employers . . . offer[ed] health insurance to their employees, down from 51% in the mid-1990's."[19] The private health coverage pie at the time the ACA passed thus consisted of "large employers, which currently insure 133 million enrollees,"[20] "[s]maller employers, which currently insure 43 million enrollees,"[21] and 17 million enrollees in the individual market.[22]

The Dworkin-Inflected Insurance Protections in the ACA

The ACA therefore trained its firepower mostly at the individual and small group markets where the problems were most dire, a marked contrast from the earlier Clinton-era health reform's more wide-ranging approach as we will see. For instance, the ACA amended the Public Health Service Act (PHSA) § 2702 to enact a "Guaranteed Issue" provision expressly for the fully insured part of the market, in part to address the availability of insurance in the small group and individual markets. Under § 2702, "each health insurance issuer that offers health insurance coverage in the individual or group market in a State must accept every employer and individual in the State that applies for such coverage . . . without regard to the claims experience of those individuals, employers and their employees (and their dependents) or any health status-related factor."[23] PHSA § 2703 extends this protection to the *renewal* of insurance as well. The statute plainly precludes

---

[18] *2020 Employer Health Benefits Survey—Section 10: Plan Funding*, KAISER FAM. FOUND. (October 8, 2020), https://www.kff.org/report-section/ehbs-2020-section-10-plan-funding/.

[19] Cogan, *supra* n.9, at 1123 (alteration in original).

[20] Jost, *supra* n.7, at 39 (citing Interim Final Rules, 75 Fed. Reg. 34,538, 34,550 (June 17, 2010) (codified at 45 C.F.R. pt. 147)) (97 million in private plans and 36 million in governmental plans).

[21] Jost, *supra* n.7, at 34, 39, 550 (alteration in original).

[22] *Id.* at 40.

[23] 42 U.S.C. § 300gg-1.

health-status–related factors from counting as acceptable reasons to deny enrollment in health coverage. It might appear at first glance that employees of
self-insured plans, more likely to be those working for large-employers, are not
addressed by these provisions. However, they were already protected under an
ACA precursor statute, the Health Insurance Portability and Accountability Act
of 1997 (HIPAA), which barred group health plans from turning away specific
individual members of the group for health-status reasons, as we will discuss
later.[24]

The enshrinement of guaranteed issue into federal law did mark a major
change in the general approach to employer sponsored health insurance that
prevailed from mid-century through the 1980s. Starting in the 1950s, the commercial insurers used so-called experience-rated discounts to lure the healthier
employer groups—those whose employees exhibited less experience of medical
use—away from the flat-rate provider-run Blue Cross-Blue Shield-style plans
that had arisen during the Depression.[25] Commercial insurers also took the otherwise pooled rates, and imposed group-specific upward premium adjustments
on small employers who were considered riskier and less desirable. Under pressure of adverse selection and these "destructive medical underwriting techniques,"
the group market had begun to fray by the 1980s and early 1990s.[26] Mila Kofman
and Karen Pollitz summarized the corresponding regulatory situation: by and
large "states [had] allowed commercial insurers not to sell to groups with medical
needs. In many states, however, Blue Cross Blue Shield plans offered coverage on a
guaranteed-issue basis. In the 1980s, the market became more fragmented . . . and
commercial carriers became more selective in who they would cover."[27] In this
destabilizing situation, federal regulation was even less availing. The only major
federal law governing employer-based coverage, ERISA, was fundamentally deregulatory because it preempted state laws, as we have mentioned and will return
to repeatedly.[28] The conditions were ripe for some type of intervention, but that

[24] Jost, *supra* n.7, at 29, n. 22; *see also* ERISA § 702(a)(1), 29 U.S.C. § 1182(a)(1) (a group health
plan "may not establish rules for eligibility (including continued eligibility) of any individual to enroll
under the terms of the plan based on any of the following health status-related factors"). But under
(a)(2) other than limitations on preexisting conditions, this nondiscrimination language "shall not
be construed to require a group health plan . . . .to provide particular benefits . . . .or to prevent such a
plan or coverage from establishing limitations or restrictions on the amount, level, extent, or nature
of the benefits or coverage for similarly situated individuals enrolled in the plan or coverage" (citing
29 U.S.C. § 1182).

[25] Cogan, *supra* n.9, at 145–6.

[26] *Id.* at 1148 citing Mark A. Hall, *The Political Economics of Health Insurance Market Reform*,
HEALTH AFF. Summer 1992, at 111.

[27] *See also, id.* at 146–48; Jost, *supra* n.7, at 148; Mila Kofman & Karen Pollitz, *Health Insurance
Regulation by States and the Federal Government: A Review of Current Approaches and Proposals for
Change*, GEORGETOWN UNIV. HEALTH POL'Y INST. 2 (2006), https://www-tc.pbs.org/now/politics/
Healthinsurancereportfinalkofmanpollitz.pdf.

[28] *See generally* Claxton et al., *supra* n.16.

intervention took a circuitous path until the nondiscrimination provisions of the ACA, like guaranteed issue, were finally passed in 2010.

Thus, the PHSA § 2702 guaranteed issue provision was what John McDonough, one of the engineers for both for the Massachusetts health reform and the federal ACA, called the "cornerstone requirement" for both addressing these problems and building a system where persons with health needs can access health coverage.[29] For guaranteed issue to work, though, it needed supplementation, so the ACA included other provisions as well. Guaranteed issue only forbade health plans from denying coverage outright; it did not prevent the plans from hiking premiums, reducing benefits, or adding other costs based on health status. An issuer might comply in name by issuing a health plan, meanwhile riddling the plan terms with special carveouts for anticipated high-cost healthcare needs. For instance, a regime of guaranteed issue alone would not prevent an issuer from delaying or excluding coverage for those very conditions that we would seek coverage to treat, namely those that could be considered "preexisting."[30] It also would not restrict a plan from imposing annual or lifetime caps on the reimbursement they furnish for particular disfavored diagnoses, or limiting the particular treatments or providers needed for expensive conditions.[31] This constellation of interlocking techniques was addressed by a corresponding set of protections included in the ACA.

The ACA, for instance, contained PHSA § 2701, a modified "community rating" provision to outlaw discriminatory pricing.[32] Under a limited list of exceptions, insurers may only vary premiums by age, though with constraints on how widely. In setting premiums, the ACA also provides exceptions under which insurers can consider tobacco use, geographical region, and to some extent, participation in wellness programs.

It is true that ACA's community rating proposals did not apply to large group plans, but those were again already subject to HIPAA rules that banned *intragroup* premium discrimination, meaning that high-risk individual enrollees in a large-group plan, whether self-insured or fully insured, could not be treated differently from other enrollees in either premiums or required contributions.[33] HIPAA, which contained its own guaranteed issue provision

---

[29] JOHN E. MCDONOUGH, INSIDE NATIONAL HEALTH REFORM 120 (2011).

[30] *How Private Insurance Works: A Primer*, KAISER FAM. FOUND. 7 (2008) (hereinafter How Private Insurance Works), http://www.kff.org/insurance/upload/7766.pdf (accessed November 30, 2008) (defining preexisting conditions as one diagnosed in a specified period prior to when the enrollee sought health coverage).

[31] John Jacobi, *supra* n.4, at 317 (1997) ("health insurers and health plans have singled out individuals with expensive medical conditions by imposing extremely low limits on coverage for their expensive conditions").

[32] Public Health Service Act (PHSA) § 2701, 42 U.S.C. § 201.

[33] Jost, *supra* n.7, at 29, n. 22; ACA § 1201 amending PHSA § 2701, 42 U.S.C. § 201 (defining its scope "[w]ith respect to the premium rate charged by a health insurance issuer for health insurance coverage offered in the individual or small group market"). *See* ERISA § 702(b).

for the group market, had also prohibited *intergroup* health-status discrimination in issuance and renewal, banning small group market insurers from refusing to sell insurance to an employer due to claims experience, medical risk, or other health-status–related factors.[34] On the other hand, HIPAA expressly permitted the practice of intergroup differentiation in *premiums* between employers.[35] Thus any given large employer could potentially face higher rates because of the medical profile of its employees. This remains true even today because the ACA community rating provisions do not regulate the pricing offered in the large group market. But on the whole, large groups have been less afflicted by medical underwriting in part because of the logic we described earlier whereby the larger the group, the more likely it is that medical experience of the group is likely to average out and blunt the impact of anomalous high cost enrollees.[36] Thus ACA community rating still struck a major blow against health-status–based discrimination in the pricing of health plans.

The legislation also contained numerous other provisions designed to combat health-status discrimination. The ACA prohibited preexisting conditions exclusions in PHSA § 2704 and annual or lifetime caps on benefits in PHSA § 2711. PHSA § 2707 standardized the individual and small-group benefits package to the parameters set by the Essential Health Benefits Package with certain cost-sharing limitations as well.[37] The ACA also contained "network" adequacy requirements at least for individual and small group plans sold on the ACA exchanges to help address the potential exclusion of certain providers.[38] It included guaranteed renewal in PHSA § 2703 and a restriction on rescissions of coverage in PHSA § 2712.[39] These provisions assure that insurance, once issued without regard to health status, could not be canceled or not renewed just when an enrollee got sick and needed insurance the most.

These are just some of the major provisions that embody and further specify the Dworkian norm in the ACA regime. This Dworkinian impulse is often

---

[34] HIPAA § 102, creating PHSA § 2711 codified as 42 U.S.C. § 300gg-11, amended by the ACA § 1201 ("each health insurance issuer that offers health insurance coverage in the small group market in a State must accept every small employer . . . in the State that applies for such coverage; and must accept for enrollment under such coverage every eligible individual . . . who applies for enrollment during the period . . . ." This requirement allowed certain exceptions for minimum participation rules, poor fit with the service area of the network, or for issuers' financial capacity limits, if those limits are applied uniformly to all employers).

[35] PHSA § 2702(b)(2), 42 U.S.C. § 201 ("Nothing in paragraph (1) shall be construed to restrict the amount that an employer may be charged for coverage under a group health plan").

[36] Cogan, *supra* n.9, 1126; *see generally* Claxton et al., *supra* n.2.

[37] PHSA § 2707, added by ACA § 1201 (codified at 42 U.S.C. § 300gg-6); ACA § 1302(b)(1)(A)-(J) (codified at 42 U.S.C. § 18022). For cost sharing limitations, *see* ACA § 1302(c)(2)(A)(i), (ii) (to be codified at 42 U.S.C. § 18022).

[38] ACA § 1311(c), 42 U.S.C. § 18011.

[39] PHSA § 2712, 42 U.S.C. §300gg-12.

misunderstood. It is somewhat misleading to describe these ACA provisions as aimed at nondiscrimination rather than substantive entitlement, since these principles forbidding the consideration of health status are not typically seen in contexts outside of the provision of health insurance. This observation is one we will return to unpack later in this chapter, especially when discussing the history and application of the so-called genetic nondiscrimination norm.

Contrast with Pre-ACA Contestation of Norms: Defamiliarization of the Health-Status Nondiscrimination Norm

The triumph of this norm in the past decades can perhaps best be appreciated not by demonstrating its unchallenged acceptance, but instead by demonstrating the sway exerted by the countervailing arguments that it has arguably vanquished since. For a considerable interval during the history of our health system, this norm was locked in political battle with another tenet governing health coverage, one that goes by the name "actuarial fairness."

Deborah Stone famously spelled out this notion of actuarial fairness in her article "The Struggle for the Soul of Health Insurance."[40] She contrasted it with an alternate principle of "social solidarity," as Stone terms it, or "Dworkinian preclusion," as I suggest we frame it.[41] Actuarial "fairness" she defines as the view that the pooling of equal premiums (and common expectation of payout should the insurable event materialize) is only "fair" when all members of the pool have the same risk. Tellingly, it is a quote from insurance lawyers arguing for insurers' prerogatives to consider HIV status that Stone cites to illustrate how the actuarial fairness principle has been articulated: "[A]n insurer has the 'responsibility to treat all its policyholders fairly by establishing premiums at a level consistent with the risk represented by each individual policyholder.' "[42] This objective of knowing as much as possible about a person's risk in order to match their premium to their risk-level, is, as Stone says, the "keystone" to the project of commercial insurance, which requires insurers to "price correctly" in a competitive market.[43] But this type of risk classification has social consequences. As Stone

---

[40] Deborah A. Stone, *The Struggle for the Soul of Health Insurance*, 18 J. OF HEALTH POL., POL'Y AND L. 287 (1993).

[41] *Id.* at 290–92 ("Social insurance operates by the logic of solidarity. Its purpose is to guarantee that certain agreed-upon individual needs will be paid for by a community or group . . . having decided in advance that some need is deserving of social aid, a society undertakes to guarantee that the need is met for all its members." She concludes that "the ideal of the solidarity principle is that we should strive to distribute medical care according to medical need and to limit the influence of ability to pay, past consumption of medical care, or expected future consumption").

[42] *Id.* at 293 (alteration in original) (quoting Karen A. Clifford and Russell A. Iuculano, *AIDS and Insurance: The Rationale for AIDS-Related Testing*, 100 HARV. L. REV. 1806 (1987)).

[43] *Id.* at 294–95.

observes, "It is a method of organizing mutual aid by fragmenting communities into ever-smaller, more homogeneous groups."[44] As a result, "[i]nsurance underwriting, far from being a dry statistical exercise, is a political exercise in drawing the boundaries of community membership."[45]

Insurers believe their central purpose is risk prediction for loss management and that medical need is in fact the main predictor of medical expense and high claims. Thus, in the health sector, "[a]ctuarial underwriting or discrimination based on an individual's health status is a business feature of the voluntary private insurance market."[46] Kenneth Abraham walks through how this form of risk segmentation, unless banned from the marketplace, will be deemed necessary for business survival by health insurers:

> When there is . . . competition among insurers for premium dollars, the value of risk classification to insurers becomes [clear]. The more refined (and accurate) an insurer's risk classifications, the more capable an insurer is of skimming good risks away from insurers whose classifications are less refined. If other insurers do not respond, either by refining their own classifications or raising prices and catering mainly to high risks, then their book of risks will contain a higher mixture of poor risks who are still being charged premiums calculated for average risks. Additional poor risks will gravitate toward these insurers whose classifications have not isolated and charged poor risks higher premiums. The resulting adverse selection will further disadvantage these insurers' competitive positions. This prospect tends to explain the proliferation of risk classifications in insurance markets. . . . [U]p to the point where the cost of refining classifications is not worth the competitive benefit derived, all insurers will classify at roughly the same level of refinement.[47]

To tell the story of how the Dworkinian preclusion of health-status factors in health coverage has *become the dominant view*, one must call upon the readers' intuitive recognition of its "normalcy" in the present while conveying how the norm was strange, even impossible to imagine, in the past. The Abraham passage helps us to understand how embedded the competing view was, because risk classification was in fact the bread-and-butter of insurance practice.[48] It

---

[44] *Id.* at 290.

[45] *Id.* at 299 (alteration in original).

[46] Sara Rosenbaum, *Insurance Discrimination on the Basis of Health Status: An Overview of Discrimination Practices, Federal Law and Federal Reform Options* 1, THE O'NEILL INST. FOR NAT'L AND GLOB. HEALTH L. AT GEORGETOWN UNIV. (2009).

[47] KENNETH S. ABRAHAM, DISTRIBUTING RISK 67–68 (1986) (alteration in original).

[48] EMMETT J. VAUGHAN & THERESE M. VAUGHAN, FUNDAMENTALS OF RISK AND INSURANCE 133 (11th ed. 2014) (calling underwriting an "essential element in the operation of any insurance program").

is a measure of the extent to which the preclusion of health-status factors has become entrenched that to see it as impossibly utopian is now somewhat difficult: we have to defamiliarize ourselves by looking at alternate contexts.

Stone, as we noted earlier, flagged one such era in the late 1980s to the early 1990s when AIDS panic and anti-gay animus were at a peak. *McCann v. H & H Music* is a case dating from this time when the earlier pre-Dworkinian norm prevailed. McCann was an employee who was diagnosed with AIDS and filed claims for care related to his medical needs. Shortly afterward his employer took two steps. It capped the lifetime cost of AIDS care that would be reimbursed to just $5,000, while leaving coverage for all other illnesses subject to a higher cap of $1 million. The employer also changed the employer plan from fully insured to self-funded status to escape Texas state regulations, which at that time limited insurers' ability to carve HIV care out of their policies.[49] The question was whether ERISA prevented the employer's discrimination on the basis of McGann's medical needs. The court found "nothing in the record to suggest that defendants' motivation was other than as they asserted, namely to avoid the expense of paying for AIDS treatment . . . , no more for McGann than for any other present or future plan beneficiary who might suffer from AIDS."[50] Note the opinion's underlying assumption that a person living with AIDS would be on equal footing with any other employee-beneficiary insofar as all would face lower AIDS treatment limits. The countervailing factor of health status strikes the 5th Circuit as central, rather than suspect. This passage on the health plan's motivation reveals the judges' easy acceptance that economic savings suffice as a rational reason for compromising on health provision, acknowledging that "the record supported *the employer's motive as saving money*."[51] And from this perspective, consideration of health status was natural and necessary for saving money.

As Jacobi explains later in the article, this link between health status and economic savings gains force from the famously skewed distribution of health expenditures across the population, where "one percent of the population accounts for twenty-five percent of expenditures; four or five percent of the population accounts for fifty percent of expenditures."[52] For any health plan in a competitive market to survive, they will face enormous pressure to select against or increase premiums for those highest-risk, sickest patients. After all, "[a]voiding even a small number of high-cost individuals can substantially

---

[49] Jacobi, *supra* n.4, at 349 (citing Eric C. Sohlgren, *Group Health Benefits Discrimination Against AIDS Victims: Falling Through the Gaps of Federal Law - ERISA, the Rehabilitation Act, and the Americans with Disabilities Act*, 24 LOYOLA L.A. L. REV. 1247, 1248 (stating that Texas law prohibits limitation of HIV coverage in group insurance plans)).

[50] McGann v. H & H Music Co., 946 F.2d 401, 404 (5th Cir. 1991).

[51] Jacobi, *supra* n.4, at 350 (emphasis added).

[52] Jacobi, *supra* n.4, at 394 (citing Anne K. Gauthier et al., *Risk Selection in the Health Care Market: A Workshop Overview*, 32 INQUIRY 14, 14–15 (1995)).

reduce an insurer's losses."[53] Any other business strategy for controlling costs would be rendered inconsequential by enrollment of merely a few of the sickest patients in the distribution. Indeed, saving money to achieve economic viability would seem the paradigm of *ordinary legitimate business justification* for the insurers' actions. Yet something about this instance struck observers then and now as difficult to swallow, even though seeking to reduce claims and classify similar risks to pool together seem like textbook legitimate ends for insurance companies to pursue.[54] "The very same risk-assessing and cost-minimizing strategies that disadvantage the sick are the practices that make private health insurance profitable."[55]

In this light, it is remarkable that the preclusion of costly health need as a countervailing factor in allocating health coverage came to be a pillar of the Affordable Care Act. It has become so deeply ingrained in public sentiment that its metonym, "protecting those with preexisting conditions," is a potent political rallying cry. Even those calling for repeal-and-replace of the ACA dared not admit if they were crosswise to "protecting preexisting conditions," as Trump put it in his mangled and disingenuous vows.[56] "I think it's gotten to the point where every politician has to say they're for protecting people with pre-existing conditions," said Larry Levitt, the executive vice president for health policy at the Kaiser Family Foundation."[57]

A change this significant could not have transpired with the passage of the ACA alone. How had this norm developed? It did so in through fits and starts and scattered developments that dot the healthcare lawscape.

States Reforms Round 1: The HIV Wars

Background state insurance laws in the latter decades of the twentieth century were generally weak on the matter of private health-status underwriting. They addressed risk discrimination typically only in the form of Unfair Trade Practice Acts (UTPAs) limiting "unfair discrimination." What was prohibited as "unfair" was generally vague and undefined. For instance, the model Unfair Trade Practice Act drafted by the National Association of Insurance Commissioners

---

[53] Kofman & Pollitz, *supra* n.25, at 2.

[54] Jacobi, *supra* n.4, at 322–23; *see* Jessica L. Roberts, *Healthism: A Critique of the Antidiscrimination Approach to Health Insurance and Health-Care Reform*, 2012 UNIV. OF ILL. L. REV. 1159 (2012).

[55] Roberts, *supra* n.54, at 1170.

[56] Margo Sanger-Katz, *Trump Says He Will "Always" Protect Those With Pre-Existing Conditions. He Hasn't*, N.Y. TIMES (September 24, 2020), https://www.nytimes.com/2020/09/24/upshot/pre-existing-conditions.html.

[57] *Id.; see also*, Sabrina Corlette, *Where's the Plan? Trump Executive Order Fails to Include any Policy to Protect Health Care if the ACA is Struck Down*, CHIRBLOG (September 28, 2020), http://chirblog.org/wheres-the-plan-trump-eo/.

in 2001 specified that the prohibition was directed at "unfair discrimination between individuals of the same class and of essentially the same hazard."[58] This language suggests that refusing to cover or rating up the sick would qualify as perfectly fair, since a sick individual necessarily presents a different hazard for health insurers than a relatively healthy individual.[59]

With the advent of HIV/AIDS in the 1980s, as *McGann* illustrates, some states like Texas passed laws that restricted insurers from using information about HIV status in their underwriting decisions.[60] Though these measures concerned only those insurance terms that targeted HIV, one health condition among many, rather than addressing discrimination across all costly conditions, this episode still registers as an instance where "social concerns regarding specific, actuarially significant characteristics overcame the principle of accurate risk segmentation."[61] Advocates saw HIV status as a discrete indicator of health need that came to serve as a focal case for "societal responsibility to all people . . . with serious illness or risk of illness."[62] But this early test skirmish came to naught. These state prohibitions against consideration of HIV status were either repealed or struck by courts.[63]

States did, however, return to the broader issue of "all people . . . with serious illness or risk of illness," and they did so in response to the same social forces that fueled the Clinton health reform, as we will see.

Popular discontent over healthcare surged at the turn of the 1990s. Americans polled as concerned about "job lock," fearing in part that because any employer could exclude their preexisting conditions from employer-sponsored health plans, any given worker in the United States might no longer have health coverage if they changed jobs.[64] Jacob Hacker describes this concern as part of the

---

[58] MODEL UNFAIR TRADE PRACTICES ACT (Nat'l Ass'n of Ins. Comm'rs 2001) § 4(G)(2) (quoted in Mary Crossley, *Discrimination Against the Unhealthy*, 54 UNIV. OF KAN. L. REV. 73, 109–110 (2005)).

[59] *See* Mary Crossley, *Discrimination Against the Unhealthy*, 54 UNIV. OF KAN. L. REV. 73, 109 (2005) ("To put it more bluntly: does the law prohibit health insurers from discriminating against the unhealthy? Admittedly posing this question often provokes an incredulous response: isn't that exactly what health insurers do all the time? Indeed, when an insurer classifies an individual or small group on the basis of risk, medical information about the prospective insured is typically central to the classification process. One might wonder whether any valid predictive basis for risk classification exists if an insurer cannot classify risks of future medical expenses based on an applicant's past or existing health conditions").

[60] ROBERT H. JERRY II, UNDERSTANDING INSURANCE LAW 145–47 (3d ed. 2002) (cited in Crossley, *supra* n.58 at 110 (2005)); Karen A. Clifford and Russell A. Iuculano, *The Need of HIV Testing*, 100 HARV. L. REV. 1806, 1815–16 (1987).

[61] Jacobi, *supra* n.4, at 324.

[62] Deborah A. Stone, *The Rhetoric of Insurance Law: The Debate over AIDS Testing*, 15 L. & SOC. INQUIRY 385, 404 (1990).

[63] Jacobi, *supra* n.4, at 325.

[64] *See* Brigitte C. Madrian, *Employment-Based Health Insurance and Job Mobility: Is There Evidence of Job-Lock?*, 109 THE QUARTERLY J. OF ECON 27 (1994); *see also* Jonathan Gruber, *Health Insurance and the Labor Market*, NAT'L BUREAU OF ECON. RSCH. WORKING PAPERS (1998), https://www.nber.org/system/files/working_papers/w6762/w6762.pdf.

dawning realization that "the efforts of employers to control costs and of insurers to screen out high-risk individuals were 'undoing some of the middle-class insulation from health care costs.'"[65] As several veterans of the Clinton health reform effort put it: "The middle class perceived itself as having three goals: (1) making sure they do not lose insurance coverage when they change or lose their job (2) making sure they are not charged more if someone in their family gets sick; and (3) reducing the insurance premiums and out-of-pocket costs they and their employers had to pay."[66] So often the purpose of health reform is phrased as "the problem of the uninsured." But the creep of associated worries into the middle class took a particular Dworkinian form. It also created the political opening to take on national health reform once again after decades of neglect.

Federal Reforms Round 1: The Clinton Health Security Act

The Clinton Health Security Act contained numerous provisions that would have precluded sickness from factoring into people's health access. It featured an employer mandate and directives so that nearly all low and high-risk groups in a region would participate in one common pool in the form of a purchasing alliance. These regional purchasing alliances can be understood as beefed-up ACA exchanges that actually negotiated and purchased on behalf of consumers, in addition to offering menus of different health plans for enrolling consumers to choose from. By pooling risk, the regional health alliances would thus help smooth and equalize cost and access among not only individual purchasers, who faced vicious medical underwriting, but also among employers who had otherwise been separating into sick and healthy market segments. One major difference between these alliances and the Obamacare exchanges lay in the extent to which employers had to funnel their employer-sponsored coverage through these alliances. Only very large firms with more than five thousand employees could opt out and constitute their own independent purchasing alliance, and only on condition of accepting financial assessments and growth constraints. Smaller employers, by merging buying clout with the rest of the employers in the alliance, thus gained "access to community rates negotiated by a large, monopsonistic purchasing cooperative" and better volume discounts from providers.[67]

---

[65] JACOB HACKER, THE ROAD TO NOWHERE: THE GENESIS OF PRESIDENT CLINTON'S PLAN FOR HEALTH SECURITY 16 (Ira Katznelson et al., eds., 1997) (citing Paul Starr, *The Middle Class and National Health Reform*, THE AM. PROSPECT (December 5, 2000), https://prospect.org/health/middle-class-national-health-reform/).

[66] David Cutler & Jonathan Gruber, *Health Policy in the Clinton Era: Once Bitten, Twice Shy*, NBER (September 2001), https://www.nber.org/papers/w8455.

[67] Hacker, *supra* n.65, at 59 and 114.

Employers would have to pay 80 percent of premiums, but with guarantees that they would never owe more than a certain proportion of payroll.[68] Individuals would make set contributions as well, though with subsidies for those lower on the income scale, and the opportunity to "buy up" to more expensive plans if they wished.[69]

Given the community rating requirements, the plans' charges could not differ based on health status, and benefits would be largely standardized across plans, thereby prohibiting disadvantageous exclusions or limits on the particular benefits that sicker patients tend to need most. The purchasing alliances would also try to curb other more creative types of risk selection by risk adjusting premiums paid to various plans. These adjustments would have helped correct for any advantage plans might have gained if their overall enrolled population looked healthier than average, or correct in the other direction if the population looked sicker than average.

Many of the provisions in the Clinton health plan look quite familiar to us from our earlier description of the ACA. In addition to complying with community rating requirements and standardized benefit packages, health plans had to honor prohibitions on health-status underwriting, bans on preexisting condition exclusions, fair marketing standards, and requirements to include essential community providers in their networks.

To assure that there was money to pay for these features and that the budget-enforcing Congressional Budget Office (CBO) would score sufficient savings, the Clinton Health Security Act also imposed caps on overall growth in premiums and other payments. To the bill's opponents, these caps smacked of state command-and-control and forced rationing over time.[70] Meanwhile, employers feared the burden of mandates and the cost of required contributions.[71] And the lack of a reference point for these behemoth purchasing alliances made for difficult public relations.[72] The effort collapsed in spectacular fashion.

Though health reform may have failed, the underlying political forces to which it was responding persisted. As David Cutler and Jonathan Gruber observed, "The fear of being dropped from coverage, losing coverage when changing jobs,

---

[68] Health Security Act of 1993, H.R. 3600, 103rd Cong. §§ 6121–6123 (1993). *See also*, Paul Starr, *What Happened to Health Care Reform?* THE AM. PROSPECT (November 19, 2001), https://prospect.org/health/happened-health-care-reform/.

[69] Health Security Act of 1993, H.R. 3600, 103rd Cong. §§ 6101–6115 (1993).

[70] Hacker, *supra* n.65, at 134–35 (describing the following examples of complaints lodged at the time, "Paul Ellwood informed Magaziner that the Jackson Hole Group would only support the President's proposal if it eschewed binding budget constraints . . . The Chamber of Commerce wrote Magaziner . . . stating its 'grave concern over what seems to be a movement toward a government financed and controlled system' ").

[71] Starr, *supra* n.68.

[72] Hacker, *supra* n.65, at 143 ("Only 22 percent of respondents claimed to know what a 'consumer purchasing cooperative' or 'health alliance' was").

or having insurance premiums increase when someone became sick did not go away with the demise of the Health Security Act."[73]

State Reforms Round 2: The 1990s Insurance Market Reforms

States could not but respond even amid the decline and fall of the federal reform efforts. Unfortunately, their reach was preempted in the self-insured segment of the large and small group markets. States tried nevertheless to do what they could within their ambit to address the most precarious, least stable parts of the fully insured market, namely those issuers selling to "small groups," and to those "individual" customers buying without affiliation to any employer-based group. Observers noted: "While most states made significant changes to the regulation of their small group markets, a more modest number took the additional step of also changing their individual insurance laws."[74] It was in this context that a subset of states in the 1990s passed laws imposing guaranteed issue and community rating.[75]

In 2004, the Robert Wood Johnson Foundation gathered information on the individual market laws that states had enacted in the 1990s. In that review, they found that from 1990 to 1998, 14 states had enacted guaranteed issue laws, 42 had enacted guaranteed renewal, 29 had limited preexisting condition exclusions, 8 forced some kind of rating bands, and 10 imposed some measure of community rating to restrict the extent to which individuals with higher risk of health expenses could be charged higher rates.[76] Some of the guaranteed issue and renewal laws only required carriers to make at least one policy available to all applicants, rather than all its products.[77] However, some of the states that undertook the most aggressive reforms despite their limited tools and limited reach over self-insured health plans, ended up de-stabilizing their markets: "In Kentucky and Washington, states that initially imposed guaranteed

---

[73] Cutler & Gruber, *supra* n.66.

[74] Claudia Williams & Beth Fuchs, *Expanding the Individual Health Insurance Market: Lessons from the State Reforms of the 1990's*, The Robert Wood Johnson Found. 23 (2004), file:///C:/Users/David/Downloads/rwjf18005_1.pdf.

[75] Kofman & Pollitz, supra n.25, at 2 (describing how commercial carriers, other than Blue Cross Blue Shield, could refuse to sell to groups with unattractive medical needs but that "[b]y the mid-1990's, 36 states had" some form of guaranteed issue law "requiring all insurers to offer at least two health insurance policies to small businesses regardless of the medical conditions of the employees or their dependents." *Citing State Legislative Health Care and Insurance Issues: 2005 Survey of Plans*, BCBS 57 (December 2005)).

[76] Williams & Fuchs, *supra* n.74, at 7.

[77] *Id.* at 10.

issue, community rating, and very tight limits on the use of pre-existing condition exclusions, only one or two insurers remained in the market."[78]

States took similar measures in the small group market. By the mid-1990s,
thirty-six states had guaranteed issue requirements (and 46 had guaranteed renewal), requiring "all insurers to offer at least two health insurance policies to
small businesses regardless of the medical conditions of the employees or their
dependents."[79] Mila Kofman and Karen Pollitz document 37 states with some
kind of restriction on "how much [small group] insurers can vary premiums
for each policyholder based on the health and claims of the policyholder."[80] But
these regulations still permitted a significant range of health-status discrimination. The National Association of Insurance Commissioners' (NAIC's) model
rating law from that time, which was followed by many states, allowed premium
variation of up to 200 percent based on health status, and also permitted adjustment based on other factors including age as long as actuarially justified.[81] By
2004, 12 states had gone further and enacted some kind of community rating in
the small group market.[82] The Texas HIV law from our *McGann* discussion was
an early condition-specific example.

Insurers could also discriminate against the relatively sicker segments of the
market and shield themselves from cost exposure by manipulating the particular
contour of benefits offered. In other words, they could carve out of coverage for
the care that expensive patients would need. States tried to curb these practices
through so-called mandated benefit laws. For instance, forty-six states required
health plans "to cover or offer to cover benefits for diabetes supplies and education."[83] These states recognized that "[o]ne way to spread the cost of a medical
condition or treatment among a broad population, making it less expensive for
the group of people who need such coverage, is through a benefit mandate."[84]

In sum, these state laws were all geared toward limiting the extent to which
insurers could discriminate against the sick. Many had mixed success—in the
states with tighter community rating, premiums tended to increase in reaction,
and the states that undertook the most comprehensive reforms tended to see
overall coverage in the states *decline*.[85] Because ERISA preempted state laws as
applied to employer self-insured plans, states lacked full jurisdiction over all the
segments of private insurance, thus spurring an exodus of the lower-risk small
groups to the unregulated self-insured part of the market whenever the states

[78] *Id.*
[79] Kofman & Pollitz, *supra* n.25, at 2.
[80] *Id.* at 3
[81] *Id.*
[82] *Id.*
[83] *Id.* at 4.
[84] *Id.*
[85] *Id.* at 11, 12.

tried to flex their regulatory muscle. This dynamic raised premiums for everyone else who remained in the fully insured portion of the market. Many states were legally or politically thwarted in their ability to enact requirements like the individual or employer mandates, which might have blunted similar opt-out selection in response to their piecemeal underwriting and rating reforms.[86] Without the full suite of tools at their disposal, states were partially undermined in their regulatory efforts, as could have been predicted by the basic economic theory regarding insurance markets.

It is no surprise that states had to continue to tinker with these laws, many of which they repealed or amended over time.[87] This spate of legislation nevertheless represented a recognition that use of one's health status to determine price and access to health insurance was becoming unacceptable.[88]

Federal Reforms Round 2: HIPAA

Out of the wreckage of the Clinton campaign for health reform, the Health Insurance Portability and Accountability Act (HIPAA) sought to salvage some residual indication of our commitment to healthcare. In 1997, the Federal government followed the lead of many of the states who were passing piecemeal insurance market reforms in the 1990s. The federal legislation was called HIPAA, also known as "Kassebaum-Kennedy."[89]

To illuminate what HIPAA meant at the time, Paul Starr's contemporaneous account is useful:

> President Clinton's signing of the Health Insurance Portability and Accountability Act was a bittersweet occasion for those of us gathered on the South Lawn yesterday who had worked on the original Health Security Act in 1993 and 1994. "Better than nothing" was the sentiment heard frequently among the former health reform staffers. The bill limits preexisting condition exclusions and for the first time makes the regulation of private health insurance a federal responsibility. . . . and while it prohibits insurance companies from refusing to renew coverage, it sets no limits on what they can charge. The true achievement of the bill was underlined by Merrit Kimball of the Alliance for Health Reform, who spoke eloquently of how personal the problem of

---

[86] *See, e.g.*, Retail Indus. Leaders Ass'n v. Fielder, 475 F.3d 180 (4th Cir. 2007).

[87] Leigh Wachenheim & Hans Leida, *The Impact of Guaranteed Issue and Community Rating Reforms on States' Individual Insurance Markets*, MILLIMAN (2012), http://www.statecoverage.org/files/Updated-Milliman-Report_GI_and_Comm_Rating_March_2012.pdf; Williams & Fuchs, *supra* n.74.

[88] Williams & Fuchs, *supra* n.74.

[89] Cutler & Gruber, *supra* n.66, at 21.

preexisting conditions had become for her when she was recently diagnosed with breast cancer.[90]

It is evident from this passage that despite the relative insignificance of what could be achieved or expected from this legislation, the core impulse that it expressed was an impulse to preclude health status from standing in the way of eligibility for health coverage. And the stagecraft around this bill trumpeted broad spectrum embrace of that principle. The Kassebaum-Kennedy name foregrounded bipartisan support. Soon-to-be House Republican leader Dennis Hastert joined the signing ceremony.[91] Republicans like Senator Judd Gregg echoed the then-prevalent message that "basic flaws in the regulation of health care caused American families" to be "subject to unfair discrimination in their access to health insurance if they have a medical condition that has required treatment before they joined that health plan."[92]

What in fact did HIPAA do? One part of HIPAA addressed the group market. It prohibited employment-based health plans, both self-insured and fully insured, from rejecting, refusing to renew, or differentiating premiums for health coverage based on a person's health status.[93] It also prevented those plans from excluding care for preexisting conditions, as long as the individual had maintained creditable coverage without major lapses.[94]

That group health insurance issuers could not consider "health status-related factors" in their decisions about whether to offer coverage, was a significant statement. But its effect was modest. While individuals within the employer group (intragroup) could not be discriminated against in premium pricing, a health

---

[90] Paul Starr, *The Signing of the Kennedy-Kassebaum Bill*, EPN (August 22, 1996), https://www.princeton.edu/~starr/articles/signing.html.

[91] *Id.*

[92] 142 CONG. REC. S9513 (daily ed. August 2, 1996).

[93] HIPAA § 101(a) adding ERISA § 702(a)(1) codified at 29 USC § 1182(a)(1) ("A group health plan, and a health insurance issuer offering health insurance coverage in connection with a group health plan, may not establish rules for eligibility (including continued eligibility) of any individual to enroll under the terms of the plan based on any of the following health-status related factors"). For language prohibiting variation in premiums, see ERISA § 702(a)(2) codified at 29 USC §1182(a)(2) ("A group health plan, and a health insurance issuer offering health insurance coverage in connection with a group health plan, may not require any individual (as a condition of enrollment or continued enrollment under the plan) to pay a premium or contribution for a similarly situated individual enrolled in the plan on the basis of any health-status related factor in relation to the individual or to an individual enrolled under the plan as a dependent of the individual").

[94] 29 U.S.C. § 1181(a)(2006) (stating that insurers may only impose a preexisting condition exclusion when "(1) such exclusion relates to a condition (whether physical or mental), regardless of the cause of the condition, for which medical advice, diagnosis, care, or treatment was recommended or received within the [six month] period ending on the enrollment date; (2) such exclusion extends for a period of not more than [twelve] months (or [eighteen] months in the case of a late enrollee) after the enrollment date; and (3) the period of any such preexisting condition exclusion is reduced by the aggregate of the periods of creditable coverage"). "Creditable Coverage" was defined in 26 U.S.C. § 9801(c)(1) (2006); 29 U.S.C. § 1181(c)(1) (2006); 42 U.S.C. § 300gg(c)(1) (2006).

insurer could still decide to charge the *entire group* a higher intergroup premium rate based on the adverse health of the members within the group.[95] Thus price discrimination among different groups based on health status remained unregulated by federal law until the ACA, even though some states continued to limit or at least narrow the differences on the fully insured side of the market through rating reforms, as we saw above.[96] Furthermore HIPAA expressly left group health plans with an avenue for health-status underwriting in the form of how they shaped their benefits to reduce their exposure to high claims costs. Though crude preexisting condition exclusions were limited, the law disavowed benefit mandates. It maintained that its nondiscrimination language "shall not be construed . . . to require a group health plan, or group health insurance coverage, to provide particular benefits other than those provided under the terms of such plan or coverage, or . . . to prevent such a plan or coverage from establishing limitations or restrictions on the amount, level, extent or nature of the benefits or coverage for similarly situated individuals enrolled in the plan or coverage."[97] In other words, the plan could still potentially refuse to cover HIV/AIDS drugs or diabetes supplies and not technically run afoul of HIPAA.

What about HIPAA's effects outside the confines of the relatively stable group market? If an individual was moving from employer-sponsored coverage to buying on their own in the individual market, HIPAA again required insurers to offer coverage.[98] But this protection was peppered with so many qualifications as to be nigh meaningless. The requirement only applied to those applicants coming from group coverage without significant lapses in their insured status,[99] and only as a last resort if the individual had no other options.[100] If a state offered a high-risk pool, for instance, that policy would constitute an available option exempting the individual insurer from the guaranteed issue requirements, even though the high-risk pools were often prohibitively expensive, or had inadequate

---

[95] HIPAA § 101(a) adding ERISA § 702(b)(2) codified at 29 USC § 1182(b)(2) ("Nothing . . . shall be construed to restrict the amount that an employer may be charged for coverage under a group health plan").

[96] Cutler and Gruber, *supra* n.66, at 41.

[97] HIPAA § 401(a) adding 26 U.S.C. § 9802(a)(2)(b).

[98] HIPAA § 111(a) adding PHSA § 2741(a) codified as 42 U.S.C. §300gg-41 ("[E]ach health insurance issuer that offers health insurance coverage . . . in the individual market in a State may not, with respect to any eligible individual . . . desiring to enroll in individual health insurance coverage, decline to offer such coverage to, or deny enrollment of, such individual, or impose any preexisting condition exclusion").

[99] HIPAA § 111(a) adding PHSA § 2741(b) codified as 42 USC § 300gg-41(b) (defining "eligible individual" as someone "whose most recent prior creditable coverage was under a group health plan, governmental plan or church plan (or health insurance coverage offered in connection with any such plan)").

[100] *See*, HIPAA § 111(a) adding PHSA § 2741(b) codified as 42 USC § 300gg-41(b) (also defining "eligible individual" as someone not eligible for other coverage including Medicaid or Medicare, and had exhausted their COBRA coverage where eligible).

benefits featuring annual caps on coverage as low as $75,000 per year.[101] Even when applicable, the law imposed no limits on premiums, so the promise of access to coverage did not translate into access to *affordable* coverage.[102]

As Mary Crossley has said, HIPAA protected "the health insurance 'haves' from loss of coverage while doing little to help the health insurance 'have nots' access coverage."[103] Yet it marked out a striking normative position, writing into federal law a textual preclusion against considering health-status–related factors, defined to encompass:

(A) Health status;
(B) Medical condition (including both physical and mental illnesses)
(C) Claims experience;
(D) Receipt of health care;
(E) Medical history;
(F) Genetic information;
(G) Evidence of insurability (including conditions arising out of domestic violence;
(H) Disability)."[104]

Because HIPAA followed states' lead in responding to the temper of the times, it basically adopted into federal law, with grave flaws and loopholes, a subset of the reforms that had been taken up already across the states. Therefore, it was no surprise that "essentially all analyses of the effect of HIPAA on health insurance markets suggest that the HIPAA legislation by itself had virtually no effect on rates of insurance coverage, premiums paid, or job mobility."[105] HIPAA at least extended some of these protections to the self-insured plans that states had been unable to reach, but beyond that, its significance was largely symbolic.[106] The fact that lawmakers were insistent upon achieving its passage despite its scant effects should signal that this expressive statement must have been important indeed. Given that this exact health-status preclusion language is now part of the

[101] Jean Hall, *High-Risk Pools for People with Preexisting Conditions: A Refresher Course*, THE COMMONWEALTH FUND (2017), https://www.commonwealthfund.org/blog/2017/high-risk-pools-people-preexisting-conditions-refresher-course (accessed December 30, 2021). For the HIPAA language providing such state flexibility *see*, HIPAA § 111(a) adding PHSA § 2744(c) codified as 42 USC § 300gg-44(c).

[102] *See*, HIPAA § 111(a) adding PHSA § 2741(f)(1) codified as 42 USC § 300gg-41(f)(1) ("Nothing in this section shall be construed to restrict the amount of the premium rates that an issuer may charge an individual for health insurance coverage provided in the individual market under applicable State law").

[103] Crossley, *supra* n.59, at 117.

[104] 29 U.S.C. § 1182(a)(1) (2000).

[105] Cutler & Gruber, *supra* n.66, at 42.

[106] *Id.*

above-mentioned constellation of risk-pooling regulations built out by the ACA, we can in hindsight view this statutory inscription as an important normative declaration despite its notorious impotence at the time.

But even as this frontal battle for the Dworkinian norm ran its course, many side skirmishes took place as well. Starting as early as the late 1960s and 1970s, Congress picked up on public discomfort with the use of certain factors to deny health coverage. These factors, such as age, disability, diagnosis, and genetic information, all point toward the kind of health-status–related factors that the ACA ultimately banned wholesale from use in health coverage eligibility and pricing decisions.

Age

As the existence of Medicare and the ACA's age-rating exception to community rating both demonstrate, age is one of the risk factors most salient to health expense. Federal regulation of private health insurance prior to the ACA also translated this recognition into halting efforts to *restrict* the consideration of age, a phenomenon which loses some of its puzzling character if we understand it as a nascent expression of the Dworkinian approach to the encroachment of other considerations upon health access. As early as the late 1960s, the Age Discrimination in Employment Act of 1967 (ADEA) limited the use of age in employer-sponsored health plans, and the Age Discrimination Act of 1975 (the Age Act) restricted age discrimination by any recipient of federal financial assistance, thus capturing a large swathe of health institutions.[107] The effect of these statutes on age as a factor in health coverage was neutered both in the statutes' conceptions as well as over time. But it is worth noting their existence.

The ADEA was signed by Lyndon B. Johnson in 1967 just two years after the historic passage of Medicare and Medicaid, but the act was not addressed solely to problems of access to health coverage. Instead, President Johnson invoked what he called "arbitrary age discrimination" in the workforce, illustrated by the finding that "half of all private job openings were barred to applicants over 55, and a quarter to those over 45."[108] The ADEA was therefore enacted to prohibit "discriminat[ion] against any individual with respect to the compensation, terms, conditions, or privileges of employment because of such individual's

---

[107] Medicare and Medicaid have been found by courts to qualify as federal financial assistance programs. *See* United States v. Baylor Univ. Med. Ctr., 736 F.2d 1039, 1042 (5th Cir. 1984); United States v. Univ. Hosp., 575 F. Supp. 607, 612 (E.D.N.Y. 1983) *aff'd on other grounds*, 729 F.2d 144 (2d Cir. 1984).

[108] 29 U.S.C. § 621–34. Aid for the Aged, Message from the President of the United States, Jan, 23, 1967, *printed at* 113 Cong. Rec. 1089–90 (January 23, 1967) (for President Johnson's remarks).

age," and access to health benefits was chief among those terms conditions and privileges.[109] Because of the concerns that motivated its passage, the statute restricted its focus to discrimination on the basis of "old age" by protecting only those applicants and employees over the age of forty.[110] However, age parameters can prove harmful and irrational when imposed on other age groups as well, as the exclusion of certain children from transplants has shown. This problem awaited the development of other regimes to address, as we will discuss in the next chapter.[111]

The ADEA's promise itself was never realized because of all the exemptions written into the statute. The broad prohibition may sound sweeping, but the nondiscrimination text turned out to be less important than the exceptions to the prohibition because the exceptions capture so much of normal employer practice. The act designated a list of "lawful practices" that were safely harbored from the scope of the law in § 623(f). These exempted practices included conditioning employment upon age as a "bona fide occupational qualification[] reasonably necessary to the normal operation of the particular business." The law also exempted practices that would produce broadly disparate impacts for older employees as long as "differentiation is based on reasonable factors other than age." This exception immunized employer use of a whole host of factors that are correlated with age but might meet minimal rationality. The ADEA also protected any "bona fide seniority system," and most importantly for our purposes "any bona fide employee benefit plan . . . which is not a subterfuge to evade the purposes of this [Act]."[112] This so-called (f)(2) exemption of bona fide employee benefits thus addresses age discrimination in employer-sponsored health benefits and has undergone significant contestation and change over time. The US Department of Labor had interpreted the "not a subterfuge" requirement narrowly, thereby granting employers correspondingly wide permission for age distinctions in their fringe benefits.[113] The agency interpretation allowed employers to make "age-based reductions in employee benefit plans . . . where such reductions are justified by significant cost considerations . . . . [Thus] benefit levels for older workers may be reduced to the extent necessary to achieve approximate equivalency in cost for older and younger workers."[114]

From one standpoint, this interpretation seems outrageous. The ADEA is hard to understand as motivated by anything other than a concern that older

---

[109] 29 U.S.C. § 623(a)(1) (alteration to original).

[110] 29 U.S.C. § 631(a).

[111] Persad, *supra* n.4, n.922 (citing Complaint for a Temporary Restraining Order and Preliminary and Permanent Injunctive Relief in Murnagham v. Dep't of Health and Human Servs., No 13-CV-03083 (E.D. Pa. June 5, 2013).

[112] 29 U.S.C. § 623(f)(2) (1985); Jacobi, *supra* n.4.

[113] 29 C.F.R. § 1625.10 (1989).

[114] 29 C.F.R. § 1625.10(a)(1).

employees would receive worse treatment in the terms and benefits of employment, and reducing the health benefits of older workers because their health coverage would cost more would seem to fall squarely within that scope of concern. However, the courts, Congress, agency, and many commentators adhered to some version of the this early interpretation by the Department of Labor, called the "equal benefit or equal cost" test, which "acknowledge[ed] the higher cost of providing health coverage or other insurance for older employees" and allowed the employer to satisfy the test without providing equal benefits. Employers need only provide benefits that satisfy the equal cost standard of comparison between older and younger workers.[115] This test allows certain ordinary economic justifications to serve as legitimate countervailing reasons to cut back on healthcare, thus permitting "age-related cost justification[s] or 'a substantial business purpose' for any age-based reduction in benefits."[116]

While this interpretation was temporarily rejected by the Supreme Court in 1989 in favor of an intent-based standard that became associated with other statutory regimes containing the "not a subterfuge language,"[117] Congress then overrode that decision one year later to restore the cost-equivalency standard.[118]

Congress's Older Workers Benefit Protection Act of 1990 replaced the "not a subterfuge" language with new language expressly exempting from the ADEA any benefit plan where "for each benefit or benefit package, the actual amount of payment made or cost incurred on behalf of an older worker is no less than that made or incurred on behalf of a younger worker."[119] After this language, employers could once again provide lesser benefits to older workers, in essence violating the "equal benefits" test, as long as the older workers' benefits cost the employer as much as the younger workers' benefits, thereby meeting the "equal cost" prong.[120] The courts ultimately affirmed this approach under the new language.[121] The possibility of expensive health needs is exactly what health coverage exists to protect against, and the correlation of those needs with old age

---

[115] Crossley, *supra* n.59, at 96.

[116] Pub. Emp. Ret. Sys. of Ohio v. Betts, 492 U.S. 158 (1989) (rejecting an interpretation where a sixty-one-year-old could not get disability retirement benefits due to age, and thereby abandoning the equal cost standard only to have it reinstated by Congress).

[117] *Id.*

[118] Older Workers Benefit Protection Act, Pub. L. No. 101–433, 104 Stat. 978 (1990). Signed on October 16, 1990.

[119] 29 U.S.C. § 623(f)(2)(B)(i).

[120] Older Workers Benefit Protection Act, Pub. L. No. 101–433, 104 Stat. 978 (1990). (Instructing that the ADEA should be understood as "prohibit[ing] discrimination against older workers in all employee benefits except when age-based reductions in employee benefit plans are justified by significant cost considerations."; *see also* Auerbach v. Bd. Of Educ., 136 F. 3d 104 (2d Cir. 1998).

[121] Crossley, *supra* n.59, at 96–97, n. 115 (*citing* Auerbach v. Bd. of Educ., 136 F.3d 104, 110 (2d Cir. 1998)) ("Realizing that the costs of providing certain employee benefits increases with age, Congress decided that employers need not provide 'exactly the same benefits' to older employees as they do for younger ones, when to do so would result in excessive benefit costs that would discourage employers from hiring older workers in the first place").

is exactly why age is objectionable when used as an excuse to cut back on an employee's benefits. The ADEA on its face seemed designed to thwart employer tendencies to dump older workers because of their expense, but the subsequent wrangling over the bona fide employee benefit plan exception favored the "actuarial fairness" alternative to the Dworkinian norm.

The Age Discrimination Act of 1975 also appears at first glance to be a broad, and potentially an even more transformative tool, given its coverage over all recipients of federal financial assistance and its application to all ages, including younger persons. The basic prohibition seems expansive, but only if one overlooks the introductory proviso: "[E]xcept as provided by § 6103(b) and § 6103(c) of this title, no person in the United States shall, on the basis of age, be excluded from participation in, be denied the benefits of, or be subjected to discrimination."[122] However, like the ADEA, the Age Act's prohibitory language was almost entirely undercut by the exceptions in §§ 6103(b) and (c). One of the leading scholars in this area has declared the statute "so unfocused in conception and so compromised by a series of broad caveats that it is questionable whether it could be of anything more than minimal practical utility to those who might seek to invoke its protection."[123] Eglit goes on to explain the statute's history, revealing an ill-informed and hasty legislature. Congress had enacted a broad prohibition with little understanding of the underlying problems it was trying to solve, and almost no research on the extensive scope of ordinary business practice that might be disrupted by the prohibition: "After all, the use of age distinctions in our society is common; age lines regularly are used for the allocation of social and economic resources, and for the imposition of rights and responsibilities."[124] Thus Congress, fearing the consequences of its own actions, in the very same breath attempted to ward off these undesired results by building in caveats to allow the relatively smooth continuation of the practices that so much of our social ordering had come to rely upon.

The four primary exceptions allow age-based discrimination if:

- such action reasonably takes into account age as a factor necessary to the normal operation or the achievement of any statutory objective of such program or activity,
- the differentiation made by such action is based upon reasonable factors other than age, or

---

[122] 42 U.S.C. § 6102 (alteration in original).

[123] Howard Eglit, *Health Care Allocation for the Elderly: Age Discrimination by Another Name?*, 26 HOUS. L. REV. 813, 873 (1989).

[124] *Id.* at 873–75. *See also* Peter Schuck, *The Graying of Civil Rights Law: The Age Discrimination Act of 1975*, 89 YALE L. J. 27, 82 (1979) ("These exceptions and exclusions appeared to be designed to afford a broad scope for precisely the kinds of allocative criteria—age classifications—that the nondiscrimination provision flatly condemned").

- [if the discrimination is part of] any program or activity established under authority of any law which (A) provides any benefits or assistance to persons based upon the age of such persons; or (B) establishes criteria for participation in age-related terms or describes intended beneficiaries or target groups in such terms.[125]

In light of these exceptions, the prohibitory language is of little use. Any ordinary statutory objective, normal operation, or discrimination by way of providing benefits, not burdens would render the age-discrimination lawful.

These two legislative attempts to address age as a factor in the denial of health coverage thus amount to little. Perhaps their failure is not the narrative feature that proves surprising, though. Instead, one is left wondering how, in the face of an overwhelming business lobby and the prevailing deference to employers, did it come to be that age was recognized at all as a salient category to prohibit from consideration? Why did Congress pass these statutes that look outwardly like important civil rights, only to turn right around and permit all the ordinary justifications that would otherwise have been precluded? What powered that surface impulse and recognition? Were these laws like HIPAA, a symbolic strike against the use of age, inserted into the code with the hope that this norm could be built upon later? The sensitivity of this category is of longstanding ostensible concern in our legal corpus, and has persisted in the legal imagination, even in case law as we will see in the next chapter, culminating finally in the restriction of age as a factor in health coverage with the passage of the ACA.

Disability

We have shown similarly deep resistance to disability as an obstacle to health coverage. The Rehabilitation Act has since 1973 prohibited recipients of federal funds from discriminating against qualified individuals on the basis of disability, but key segments, including the private sector, escaped its reach.[126] When the Americans with Disabilities Act (ADA) was passed in 1990, it had the benefit of the Rehabilitation Act as a statutory foundation from which to build.[127] One of the key drafters of the ADA said, "Indeed, one of the best 'selling points' of

---

[125] 42 U.S.C. § 6102.

[126] Rehabilitation Act of 1973, Pub. L. No. 93–112, 87 Stat. 355 (codified as amended at 29 U.S.C. § 701 (1998)) ("This section, Section 504, provided that: "no otherwise qualified handicapped individual in the United States . . . shall, solely by reason of his handicap, be excluded from the participation in, be denied the benefits of, or be subjected to discrimination under any program or activity receiving federal financial assistance").

[127] The Americans with Disabilities Act of 1990 (ADA), 42 U.S.C. §§ 12101–12213 et seq.

the ADA was that Congress would simply be extending to the private sector the requirements of an existing law, Section 504 of the Rehabilitation Act."[128]

Despite this strategically modest characterization, many believed that the ADA would prove a transformative event. Some, including Paul Stevens Miller of the EEOC at the time, hailed the ADA as announcing a "new paradigm" of civil rights, because "the traditional civil rights model of treating people 'exactly the same' does not apply to disability discrimination."[129]

This extension of the principles from the Rehabilitation Act to the ADA, not unlike the transmutation of HIPAA into the ACA, captures something essential to the viewpoint pressed in this book. In the world as observed here, path-breaking norms are rarely disjoint from what came before. Accounts that present our law as either fully made or fully found can be distorting. In this and each of the following chapters, I will instead highlight the ways that the norms we seek to cultivate have been present all along. I will show how the principled extension of these norms to similar situations can proceed along a legislative timeline, to no less effect than through the more familiar channels of judicial precedent.

The scope of the norm as prescribed by the ADA was expansive indeed. It prohibited discrimination on the basis of disability whether by private employers, state and local governments, or entities regarded as public accommodations. A wide range of the motley US institutions that furnish health coverage are thus swept within its ambit. Title I addressed employers who provide employer-sponsored coverage, whether through the purchase of group insurance or by self-funding of their employees' claims costs. Title II of the ADA covered state and local government services, such as Medicaid programs. And Title III, which expressly lists "insurance offices" among the covered public accommodations, extended the ADA to private insurance in the individual market outside of the employment context as well.[130]

This frame still left open questions as to how this norm would translate into meaningful health access. What would it mean for someone HIV-positive like McGann, whose employer modified its health plan to newly cap the overall amount of HIV/AIDS treatment covered?[131] Would the ADA carve out as nondisabled a person whose condition could be managed through medication, when the availability of that medication depends on the fringe benefits

[128] Chai R. Feldblum, *Definition of Disability under Federal Anti-Discrimination Law: What Happened? Why? And What Can We Do about It?*, 21 BERKELEY J. EMP. & LAB. L. 91, 92 (2000). *See also* Chai R. Feldblum, *Antidiscrimination Requirements of the ADA*, *in* IMPLEMENTING THE AMERICANS WITH DISABILITIES ACT: RIGHTS AND RESPONSIBILITIES OF ALL AMERICANS 37 (Lawrence O. Gostin & Henry A. Beyer, eds., 1993) (affirming that the substantive requirements of the ADA came from Section 504 of the Rehabilitation Act of 1973).

[129] Paul S. Miller, *Disability Civil Rights and a New Paradigm for the Twenty-First Century*, 1 UNIV. PA. J. OF LAB. AND EMP. L. 511, 514 (1997).

[130] 42 U.S.C. § 12181(7)(F).

[131] McGann v. H & H Music Co., 946 F.2d 401 (1991).

associated with their contingent employment?[132] Certainly disability rights advocates lobbied hard for the ADA to preclude these types of consequences based on diagnoses or health conditions that need treatment.[133] They secured a statement in the committee reports to suggest how the ADA's nondiscrimination norm should apply in the context of expensive health benefits, translating it into a bar against some forms of medical underwriting: "[E]mployers may not deny health insurance coverage . . . to an individual based on the person's diagnosis or disability."[134] Meanwhile, many had harbored hopes that the ADA could inaugurate an era with new tools to limit the extent to which those considered "sick" are subject to health-status discrimination. For instance, John Jacobi, in an influential article from the 1990s, took the measure of the times and concluded that the requirement that disabilities be treated the same as other more popular conditions for coverage purposes would not end in leveling down coverage for stigmatized expensive conditions like HIV that arguably qualify as "disabilities." In his view, the market and political pressure to cover other more "popular" expensive conditions like heart disease would help ensure that care for the "unpopular" discrete conditions would be leveled up, rather than insurers choosing to eliminate coverage for all actuarially expensive conditions altogether.[135] Prohibiting private plans from differentiating benefits on the basis of health condition—a potentially disability-based distinction—would have approached realization of the Dworkinian norm that someone's status as needing care for a health condition is an illegitimate factor to consider in limiting health coverage.

But certain textual artifacts and judicial trends became obstacles to the goal of prying open greater healthcare access. First, disability was not exactly coincident with health status. Not every health condition rises to the level of a disability, thereby limiting the ADA's ability to incarnate the norm prohibiting health conditions, much less health status more generally, from being used to deny health coverage.

The definition of disability in the ADA encompasses three prongs:

---

[132] Sutton v. United Air Lines, Inc., 527 U.S. 471 (1999) (determining whether employee had a disability that substantially limits major life activities must also take into account the effects of mitigating measures like medications or devices); Matczak v. Frankford Candy & Chocolate Co., 136 F.3d 933, 937–38 (3d Cir. 1997); see also Baert v. Euclid Beverage, Ltd., 149 F.3d 626, 629–30 (7th Cir. 1998); Arnold v. United Parcel Serv., Inc., 136 F.3d 854, 859–66 (1st Cir. 1998); Ellis v. Mohenis Serv's., Inc., No. CIV. A. 96–6307, 1998 WL 564478 (E.D. Pa. August 24, 1998).

[133] Stone, supra n.40, at 310 (citing Mark A. Rothstein, Genetic Discrimination in Employment and the Americans with Disabilities Act, 29 Hous. L. Rev. 23–84 (1992) ("The disability rights community lobbied hard for protection against medical underwriting in the 1991 Americans with Disabilities Act and probably failed").

[134] The Americans with Disabilities Act of 1989, S. Rep. No. 101-116 at 29 (1989).

[135] Jacobi, supra n.4, at 363–66.

(1) physical or mental impairment that substantially limits one or more major life activities,

(2) record of such an impairment, or

(3) [being] regarded as having such an impairment.[136]

But the notion of what constitutes an impairment or a major life activity carried shades of the longstanding social construction of disability as an inability to function in society, particularly an inability to *work*. Chai Feldblum narrates the development of our conceptions of disability from the time of the nineteenth-century almshouses through World War I, a time during which the prevailing exclusionary "approach to people with disabilities meant that people with a range of medical conditions, who were able to function in society despite their medical conditions, were not considered 'disabled.' They might well have been considered 'sick' or 'ill,' of course, but they were not considered disabled. The sine qua non of disability was inability to function in society."[137] This discourse fed into a line of case law early in the years following the ADA's passage that construed the definition of disability narrowly, excluding those whose illnesses were responsive to healthcare such that they could still work. This line of cases erected a barrier to relief.[138] Feldblum cites an indicative passage from a judge at the time, ultimately denying that someone who suffered a heart attack counted as a person with a disability:

> The question is whether it produced a permanent disability that he can't perform his work. It's obvious he's a salesman, and he's still selling. . . . In order for the Plaintiff to recover in this case, the Plaintiff must make a showing that he has some type of permanent impairment . . . There's been no showing of that in this case. The only evidence is that he had a blocked artery that was opened by a balloon angioplasty. . . . People recover from heart attacks and go on with life's functions . . . I have decided it as a matter of law . . . the Plaintiff failed to prove that he had a permanent disability resulting from his heart attack.[139]

Even though the definition of disability did not require the degree of "permanent" dysfunction or untreatability that this passage seems to suggest, and instead contemplates the inclusion of even those with only a record of impairment in the past, this judicial passage raises the threshold showing needed to qualify for ADA protection. Indeed, this strain of case law became so problematic that it

---

[136] 42 U.S.C. § 12102 (2000).

[137] Feldblum, *supra* n.128, at 95.

[138] *Id. See*, Steven S. Locke, *The Incredible Shrinking Protected Class: Redefining the Scope of Disability Under the Americans with Disabilities Act*, 68 Univ. Colo. L. Rev. 107, 109 (1997).

[139] Katz v. City Metal Co., 87 F.3d 26, 26–27 (1st Cir. 1996).

finally prompted Congressional action in the form of a legislative override in the ADA Amendments Act of 2008, intended to restore the broad remedial thrust of the ADA.[140]

Meanwhile, § 501(c) of the ADA threw up an additional obstacle to the reformers' hopes drawing from the actuarial fairness tradition introduced above. Section 501(c) contained a safe harbor for underwriting and risk classification practices by insurers, managed care organizations, and bona fide health benefit plans whether fully insured or self-funded. The only caveat in the safe-harbor provision was that these practices could not be a "subterfuge" for disability-based discrimination.[141] The language instructed that the ADA "shall not be construed to prohibit or restrict" an insurer or anyone connected with providing bona fide employer-sponsored health plans from "underwriting risks, classifying risks or administering such risks."[142] In Mark Rothstein's words, this text and "[t]he legislative history of § 501(c) indicates that arbitrary, invidious discrimination in health insurance against individuals with disabilities is unlawful but that actuarially-based discrimination is permissible."[143]

The subterfuge language, borrowed from the contested ADEA context discussed earlier, tinged this safe harbor language with suggestions of the "actuarial" fidelity standard from the ADEA as it existed at that time.[144] As we have seen, this "actuarial fidelity" conception of the "not a subterfuge" requirement certainly allowed room for the health-status discrimination and "actuarial fairness" that Deborah Stone deplored. Would this test of actuarial fidelity thereby stifle the health-status precluding potential of the ADA's prohibition of disability-based discrimination? The whole problem is that people who have health conditions, like people who are older, will likely cost more to a health plan. So allowing their treatment under the health plan to reflect their actuarial costs means that the insurer could take into account their high-cost health needs and restrict the coverage of their particular health needs downward accordingly.

Courts were moving alarmingly in this direction, undercutting whatever promise the ADA might have heralded in preventing insurer health-status discrimination.

Judges issued rulings like that of *Doe v. Mutual of Omaha*, which erected a judge-made threshold test distinguishing between "access" and "content" discrimination. *Doe* upheld an insurance policy that imposed a lifetime cap of

---

[140] Pub. L. 110–325 (September 25, 2008).

[141] 42 U.S.C. § 12201.

[142] 42 U.S.C. § 12201(c).

[143] Mark Rothstein, *Genetic Discrimination in Employment and the Americans with Disabilities Act*, 29 Hous. L. Rev. 23, 81–82 (1992) (citing House Educ. and Lab. Comm., H.R. Rep. No. 485, 101st Cong., 2d Sess., pt. 2, at 137 (1990) (stating that refusals limitations, and rate differentials are allowed if based on sound actuarial principles).

[144] Jacobi, *supra* n.4 at 356–58.

$25,000 on AIDS coverage for any beneficiary, when all other care faced a looser lifetime cap of $1 million. In doing so, *Doe* came to stand for the proposition that insurers were not restricted by the ADA with regard to the "content" of benefits offered. Under *Doe*, the ADA could be seen as only regulating insurers to the extent that they provided differential "access" to persons with disabilities, no matter how gravely benefits disfavored the treatments that high-need patients might require. As Judge Richard Posner declared, relying on "common sense" rather than a solid textual anchor, "the common sense of the statute is that the content of the goods or services offered by a place of public accommodation is not regulated. A camera store may not refuse to sell cameras to a disabled person, but it is not required to stock cameras specially designed for such persons."[145] By analogy an insurance policy does not discriminate against people with people living with HIV when it offers a product that carves out any coverage of HIV/AIDS, so long as it allows both customers with HIV and customers without HIV to purchase a policy featuring this condition-specific carve-out. This view was previewed in *McGann*, and has been echoed by the opponents of the ACA as well. I have noted the legacy of this reasoning elsewhere in the following terms: "Posner's position is that people with AIDS and those without are treated equally insofar as both may buy a policy that imposes special restrictions on people with AIDS. Similarly, men and women are equally offered health insurance without contraception or pregnancy-related benefits," an argument that Congressional Republican Rep. John Shimkus made recently when trying to repeal-and-replace the ACA.[146]

Had these interpretations of the ADA fully prevailed, the project of precluding health status as an underwriting factor would have been extinguished from yet another statutory regime. But other nonjudicial actors were dealt their interpretive turns and thereby helped ADA doctrine retain its Dworkinian cast. For instance, the Equal Employment Opportunity Commission (EEOC), which enforces Title I of the ADA as it applies to employers, issued an interim guidance in 1993 articulating how it would enforce the ADA to govern disability-based distinctions in employer-sponsored health plans. This guidance was dubbed "interim," though by its own terms, the guidance document "remains in effect until rescinded or superseded."[147] Thus it governs EEOC enforcement today. The

---

[145] 179 F.3d 557, 559 (2000).

[146] *See* Christina S. Ho, *Commentary on Doe v. Mutual of Omaha*, FEMINIST JUDGMENTS: HEALTH LAW REWRITTEN 206, 235–6 (2022); *see also* Rothstein, *supra* n.143, at 80 (lamenting that under this view, "[e]mployers are free to discriminate against certain disabilities; they are not free to discriminate against certain individuals with disabilities. For example, an employer's health insurance plan can exclude or restrict coverage for kidney dialysis, but an otherwise qualified individual with adult polycystic kidney disease (APKD) who is receiving dialysis treatment cannot be denied health insurance coverage altogether, so long as insurance is made available to other employees. The individual receiving dialysis is still entitled to health insurance coverage for a broken leg, influenza, pneumonia, or other conditions made available to employees without disabilities" (alteration in original).

[147] *Interim Enforcement Guidance on the Application of the ADA to Disability-Based Distinctions in Employer-Provided Health Insurance*, U.S. EQUAL EMPLOYMENT OPPORTUNITY COMMISSION

guidance contemplates a limit to the practice of health-status discrimination by employer-sponsored health plans under Title I of the ADA.[148]

I walk through the interpretive steps of the Guidance here. The ADA on its face prohibits persons from being discriminated against on the basis of disability, and Title I extends this prohibition to the employment context.[149] But the question at hand is to what extent this prohibition restricts employer plans from offering differential health coverage along the lines of a health-status–related factor. This question remains somewhat open for the two main reasons that we flagged above. The first is the aforementioned gap between the definition of "disability" and concept of "health condition" such that a difference in coverage between two conditions does not necessarily constitute "disability-based discrimination." The second reason is the ADA § 501(c), which offers a safe harbor for bona fide underwriting practices that are "not a subterfuge."

The EEOC guidance articulates the following test for when the agency will consider a distinction in coverage differentiating among conditions to constitute disability-based discrimination: a prima facie case of discrimination is made out if the coverage restriction or carve-out treats a "discrete group of related or similar conditions" differently. In subsection III(B), the guidance illustrates by way of contrast: "Blanket pre-existing condition clauses that exclude from the coverage of a health insurance plan the treatment of conditions that pre-date an individual's eligibility for benefits under that plan also are not distinctions based on disability, and do not violate the ADA." Presumably the category of preexisting conditions cover such a "multitude of dissimilar conditions" that the differential treatment of preexisting conditions cannot be said to be based on a "discrete group of related or similar conditions" amounting to a classification by disability. The guidance goes on to identify another permissible condition-based distinction: "[S]ome health insurance plans provide fewer benefits for 'eye care' than for other physical conditions. Such broad distinctions, which apply to the treatment of a multitude of dissimilar conditions and which constrain individuals both with and without disabilities, are not distinctions based on disability."[150]

But the guidance contrasts such restrictions across a broad category of dissimilar conditions with the following benefit boundary, which it deems discriminatory: "A term or provision is 'disability-based' if it singles out a particular disability (e.g., deafness, AIDS, schizophrenia), a discrete group of

---

NOTICE No. 915.002 (June 8, 1993), https://www.eeoc.gov/laws/guidance/interim-enforcement-guidance-application-ada-disability-based-distinctions-employer ("This Notice will remain in effect until rescinded or superseded").

[148] *Id.*
[149] 42 U.S.C. § 12182.
[150] *Interim Enforcement, supra* n.147.

disabilities (e.g., cancers, muscular dystrophies, kidney diseases), or disability in general (e.g., noncoverage of all conditions that substantially limit a major life activity)."[151]

The guidance thus specifically rejects the results of *Doe*, at least as those results apply to employer-sponsored health coverage. The agency instead describes a differential carveout of HIV/AIDS from the general annual limits as discrimination singling out a discrete disability, and therefore a possible violation of the ADA.

The guidance also identifies another example of forbidden disability-based distinction: the example of a "health insurance plan that excludes from coverage treatment for any pre-existing blood disorders for a period of 18 months, but does not exclude the treatment of any other pre-existing conditions. [Such a narrow] pre-existing condition clause only excludes treatment for a discrete group of related disabilities, e.g., hemophilia, leukemia, and is thus a disability-based distinction."[152]

In the EEOC's hands, the ADA manages to cabin health-status–based distinctions to some degree, as long as those distinctions group together interrelated conditions for unfavorable treatment. Nevertheless, there it leaves open the question of when conditions are so dissimilar as not to mark out a disability-based distinction.[153] What is so dissimilar about the conditions that require eye care when blood disorders by contrast constitute a discrete and interrelated category, even though such disorders span conditions from leukemia and high blood cholesterol to sepsis and hemophilia?

The EEOC guidance was somewhat less successful at salvaging a Dworkinian preclusion of health considerations from the second obstacle we flagged, namely the § 501(c) safe harbor for bona fide underwriting practices. The EEOC hewed to the "actuarial fairness" standard that was imported from the ADEA along with the "not a subterfuge" proviso, allowing limitation of benefits for certain health conditions as long as actuarially justified. According to the guidance, "'[s]ubterfuge' refers to disability-based disparate treatment that is not justified by the risks or costs associated with the disability."[154] Thus the health benefits offered could be constricted for one type of illness or condition if equal benefits for that condition would otherwise result in much greater cost. This result is in keeping with the "equal benefit or equal cost" standard inherited from the language's ADEA lineage.

While this approach may appear to do little more than permit ordinary factors, like cost, to weigh validly against medical need in the proffering of benefits, the

[151] *Id.*
[152] *Id.*
[153] *Id.*
[154] *Id.*

EEOC guidance contains at least some suggestion of rights-like preclusion and prioritization nonetheless. In the following passage, the guidance assigns the burden of proof to the employer to "prove that the challenged disability-based distinction is not being used as a subterfuge," and "bear this burden of proving entitlement to the protection of section 501(c)."[155] This feature can be understood as operating to require the employer to provide *special justification for actions that injure the prioritized value*, consistent with the form of rights under proportionality. And indeed the types of justification that the guidance sets forth as potentially satisfying such requirement are the distinctive showings that proportionality requires. For instance, the guidance recognizably articulates what proportionality proponents call "necessity" as one of the showings, a requirement that is otherwise known as "tailoring" or "least-restrictive means" in the US parlance. In subsections C(2)(c) and (d), the guidance advises that to take advantage of the safe harbor, the employer could show that the unfavorable treatment for a particular health condition is:

> necessary (i.e., that there is no nondisability-based health insurance plan change that could be made) to ensure that the challenged health insurance plan satisfies the commonly accepted or legally required standards for the fiscal soundness of such an insurance plan . . . [or] that there is no nondisability-based change that could be made) to prevent the occurrence of an unacceptable change either in the coverage of the health insurance plan, or in the premiums charged.[156]

Apparently, even before the Clinton health reform wars, before HIPAA, and long before the Affordable Care Act, the ADA marked a battlefield over which advocates struggled to gain ground for the Dworkinian preclusion that signals a rights-like prioritization of health. Though the campaigns proceeded along multiple fronts in courts, agencies, and legislatures, narrow footholds were ultimately secured for this incipient rights norm.

Diagnosis/Health Condition

The normative discomfort with denying coverage based on a person's condition or diagnosis crops up in statutes aside from the ADA as well.

The State Children's Health Insurance Program (CHIP), like HIPAA, was passed in the late 1990s to salvage some health improvements from the wreckage

---

[155] *Id.*
[156] *Id.*

of Clinton health reform.[157] CHIP expanded health coverage to more children, going beyond Medicaid to extend eligibility to children in higher-income households.[158] The CHIP authorizing language granted considerable leeway to states in drawing eligibility lines to fit state need conditions, and it permitted eligibility to vary based on geographic location, age, income, and access to other overage. Yet the language barred disability status from restricting eligibility. It also specifically admonished that "standards may not discriminate on the basis of diagnosis."[159]

The US Medicaid program has also developed a presumption against denying coverage based on diagnosis or condition. Medicaid is a health coverage safety net program that arose with strong links to welfare and social security assistance categories. Congress codified Medicaid in its modern form in 1965, alongside the passage of Medicare, a story we refer to in Chapter 4 and recount more in detail in Chapter 7.[160] Unlike the federally administered Medicare program, which provides near-universal health coverage for Americans and their spouses aged sixty-five and older, Medicaid is jointly overseen by federal and state governments, and generally only furnishes health coverage to select populations in need of a safety net. These populations have canonically included low-income parents and children, low-income elderly and disabled persons, with low-income pregnant women added later.[161] States are not required to establish Medicaid programs, but if they do so, the federal government will provide them with matching funds for such expenditures as long as the state programs conform to certain federal standards.[162] These standards include coverage of the *mandatory* eligibility categories and of certain *mandatory* benefits, as well as compliance with some cross-cutting general standards that I will discuss in more depth shortly.[163] However states can choose to cover additional optional eligibility categories or optional benefits above and beyond these mandatory floors. The mandatory eligibility categories for Medicaid, namely the above-listed

---

[157] Balanced Budget Act of 1997, Pub. L. No. 105-33, § 4901, 111 Stat. 251, 558 (codified as amended at 42 U.S.C. § 1397 *et seq* (2012)).

[158] *See, e.g.,* Matthew Lawrence, *Disappropriation*, 120 COLUM. L. REV. 1, 37 (2020).

[159] 42 U.S.C. § 1397bb(b)(1).

[160] *See* discussion in Chapters 2 and 7.

[161] ROBERT STEVENS & ROSEMARY STEVENS, WELFARE MEDICINE IN AMERICA: A CASE STUDY OF MEDICAID 6 (2003).

[162] 42 U.S.C. §1396b; SSA § 1903. *See generally* ANDY SCHNEIDER ET AL., THE MEDICAID RESOURCE BOOK 4 (2003), https://www.kff.org/medicaid/report/the-medicaid-resource-book/.

[163] *See generally* discussion in Chapter 7. For mandatory populations, *see* Social Security Act § 1902(a)(10)(A)(i), 42 U.S.C. § 1396a(a)(10)(A)(i). For mandatory benefits, *see,* 42 U.S.C. § 1396a(a) (10) ("A State plan for medical assistance must . . . provide"); 42 U.S.C. § 1396d(a)(1)–(5), (17), (21), (28). *See also,* Harper Jean Tobin & Rochelle Bobroff, *The Continuing Viability of Medicaid Rights After the Deficit Reduction Act of 2005*, 118 YALE L.J. POCKET PART 147 (2009), http://yalelawjournal.org/the-yalelaw-journal-pocket-part/legislation/the-continuing-viability-of-medicaid-rights-after-the-deficit-reduction-act-of-2005/.

categories historically associated with eligibility for social assistance programs, are often referred to as the "categorically" needy groups who had to meet both the characteristics for their eligibility category but also certain poverty thresholds to qualify.[164] The optional populations that states could choose to make eligible for Medicaid include the so-called medically needy, whose incomes were too high to qualify for Medicaid, but had such burdensome medical bills that they were deemed to have "spent down" to Medicaid levels.[165]

Medicaid thus features an approach whereby federal guidelines set a baseline for what a state program must cover to qualify as a Medicaid program.[166] While failure to reach the minimum standards will cause the state to lose matching funds, states have considerable freedom in the other direction to layer more generous eligibility or benefits atop the federally required floor. The provision of this optional assistance garners federal matching funds if it falls within the parameters of general Medicaid requirements.[167]

One of the crosscutting Medicaid standards mandated by statute has come to be understood as a restriction on the use of diagnosis as a factor in the denial of benefits. We will turn to the case law that elaborates this interpretation in greater depth in Chapter 4, but here we lay out some of the statutory and regulatory underpinnings of this doctrinal preclusion.

The Medicaid statute requires that "[a] State plan for medical assistance ... include reasonable standards ... for determining eligibility for and the extent of medical assistance under the plan which ... are consistent with the objectives of this [Act]."[168] This language is fairly general, requiring mere "reasonable standards ... consistent with the objectives of this [Act.]" This requirement has been construed by both courts and HHS alike to incorporate the "almost-universal contractual standard for [health insurance] coverage" of "medical necessity," itself a fairly general formulation that has taken on a richly specified meaning by virtue of long customary usage, as we will see in the next chapter.[169]

While neither the statutory language, nor the medical necessity standard that it is deemed to incorporate speaks explicitly to a ban on diagnosis-based distinctions, HHS has issued a regulation that interprets "reasonable standards ... consistent with the objectives of this Act" language to mean:

---

[164] Stevens and Stevens, *supra* n.161 at 29–65.

[165] *Id. See also,* Fullington v. Shea. 320 F. Supp. 500 (D.Colo. 1970).

[166] Nicole Huberfeld, *Bizarre Love Triangle: The Spending Clause, Section 1983, and Medicaid Entitlements,* 42 U.C. DAVIS L. REV. 413, 418–24 (2008).

[167] Christina S. Ho, *Exceptions Meet Absolutism: Outlawing Government Underreach in Health,* 93 DENV. L. REV. 109, 157–160 (2015).

[168] 42 U.S.C. § 1396a(a)(17).

[169] Maxwell G. Bloche, *The Emergent Logic of Health Law,* 82 S. CAL. L. REV. 389, 413 (2009). For judicial endorsement on interpretations of (a)(17) to incorporate the "medical necessity" standard, *see* Beal v. Doe, 432 U.S. 438, 444–45 n.9 (1977).

[Benefits] must be sufficient in amount, duration and scope to reasonably achieve their purpose. With respect to the required services for the categorically needy . . . and the medically needy . . . *the State may not arbitrarily deny or reduce the amount, duration or scope of [such] service[s] to an otherwise eligible beneficiary solely because of the diagnosis, type of illness or condition.* The agency may place appropriate limits on a service based on such criteria as medical necessity or on utilization control. . . .[170] (emphasis added)

This translation of the rather capacious statutory requirement of "reasonableness" into a ban on denials or reductions "solely because of diagnosis, type of illness or condition" is startling. How did this preclusion of health condition factors arise within the realm of positive Medicaid law? This view seems hardly compelled by the statute terms. Here is where a health rights hypothesis might furnish an answer. With an implicit right to health propelling this turn, we could explain how this otherwise vaguely worded statute has come to harbor an underlying view of both the purposes of healthcare as well as a view of which countervailing justifications will trump those purposes once states have decided to provide that care.

One of the crucial cases cementing this view of the "reasonableness" standard was *White v. Beal.*[171] In the 1970s, the Pennsylvania Department of Public Welfare offered eyeglasses, an optional benefit, as part of its Medicaid program.[172] But state law restricted the extent of coverage: if the need for eyeglasses stemmed from an eye disease, like strabismus, Medicaid would cover the treatment, but if the need stemmed from refraction error, such as near-sightedness, the program would not.[173] A federal court in *White v. Beal* struck this benefit design as contrary to the Medicaid statute. This result was puzzling. The state is not required to provide eyeglasses at all, so how can it be required to extend them to both those with eye disease and those with refractive error alike, and on such slight statutory basis as the command that benefits be reasonable given Medicaid's objectives? The Third Circuit explained its decision thus:

[T]he restriction on furnishing eyeglasses results neither in furnishing them to those who are most visually handicapped (and thus most in need) nor to those whose impairment would most likely be improved . . . We find nothing in the federal statute that permits discrimination based upon etiology rather

---

[170] Formerly 45 C.F.R. § 249.10(a)(5)(i), now 42 C.F.R. § 440.230 (b) and (c).

[171] 555 F.2d 1146 (1977) [White II].

[172] White II at 1148. Eyeglasses, however, would not be optional for children who enjoy mandatory Early Periodic Screening Diagnostic and Treatment (EPSDT) benefits under 42 U.S.C. §1396a(a)(43) (A).

[173] White II at 1148 & n.1.

than need for the service. By permitting the state plans to provide only part of the cost, the statute must be construed to envision an evenhanded sharing of benefits and burdens among those having the same needs. We conclude that when a state decides to distribute a services as part of its participation in [Medicaid], its service must be distributed in a manner which bears a rational relationship to the underlying federal purpose of providing the service to those in greatest need of it.[174]

If the notion of "reasonableness" imports certain minimum norms regarding a state's determination of the extent to which it wishes to lend "extra" assistance to its Medicaid population, that is indeed remarkable. It appears we are so averse to denying healthcare along lines associated with medical need that this notion of prohibiting the conditioning of benefits by diagnosis turns up unbidden.

Pivoting to a different statutory context, the Pregnancy Discrimination Act of 1978, Congress again appears to balk when reduced health access turns on medically significant conditions, in this case the particular health condition of pregnancy.[175] The Pregnancy Discrimination Act amended the civil rights laws to define discrimination based on "pregnancy, childbirth, or related medical conditions" as a form of prohibited sex discrimination in the employment context. The Supreme Court has in turn applied this statute to prohibit pregnancy-based discrimination in employer sponsored health coverage,[176] declaring, "the 1978 Act makes clear that it is discriminatory to treat pregnancy-related conditions less favorably than other medical conditions."[177]

One district court even applied the Pregnancy Discrimination Act to forbid the differential exclusion of prescription contraception as a preventative response to potential pregnancy.[178] However, the Eight Circuit declined to follow, reciting from the same script that Representative Shimkus invoked against the ACA: that men and women alike had equal access to health insurance without contraception benefits.[179] The Eight Circuit opined accordingly that PDA "does not require coverage of contraception because contraception is not a gender-specific term . . . but rather applies to both men and women."[180] Courts also stopped short of applying the PDA's restriction on pregnancy-specific benefit carve-outs to employers' exclusion of infertility treatments.[181]

---

[174] White II at 1151.
[175] Pub. L. No. 95-555 (1978), 92 Stat. 2076 *codified* as 42 U.S.C. 2000e-(k).
[176] Newport News Shipbuilding & Dry Dock Co. v. EEOC, 462 U.S. 669 (1983).
[177] *Id.* at 684.
[178] Erickson v. Bartell Drug Co 141 F. Supp. 2d 1266 (W.D. Wash. 2001).
[179] In re Union Pac. R.R. Emp. Pracs. Litig., 479 F.3d 936 (8th Cir. 2007).
[180] *Id.* at 942 (8th Cir. 2007) The EEOC expressly rejected that view in its 2015 Enforcement Guidance: Pregnancy Discrimination and Related Issues.
[181] *See* Saks v. Franklin Covey Co., 316 F.3d 337 (2d Cir. 2003); Krauel v. Iowa Methodist Med. Ctr. 95 F.3d 674 (8th Cir. 1996).

The Pregnancy Discrimination Act, though weakened by some of these spotty case outcomes, nevertheless purports to prevent a certain type of diagnosis or condition—namely pregnancy—from serving as grounds for reduced health access.

Another set of laws that zoom in on a specific condition, rendering it invalid as a basis for reduced coverage, is mental health parity. Such statutes arose in the states around the time of the 1980s and 1990s state benefit mandates discussed earlier this chapter. Parity laws respond to the problem that "[t]he result of the empirical association between mental health use and total cost is that competitive health plans will seek to discourage enrollment of high-cost enrollees by not offering an attractive MH/SA [mental health/substance abuse] benefit."[182] In other words, contra *McGann* and its embrace of actuarial fairness, the mental health parity measures reject the reason of cost-savings from denying care for a specific condition as sufficient to justify the benefit disparity for that condition. Just as Congress followed the states' lead in enacting HIPAA, it also took a cue from them in passing a federal Mental Health Parity Act (MHPA) in 1996. MHPA only barred plans from imposing lower lifetime or annual caps on treatments for mental health conditions as compared to the caps for "medical and surgical" benefits. MHPA also only regulated group health plans, that is, those in the employer market whether self-insured or fully insured. However, in 2008, federal mental health parity protections were enlarged by Congress in the Mental Health Parity and Addiction Equality Act (MHPAEA).[183] MHPAEA barred other types of benefit restrictions as well—both quantitative and nonquantitative limitations—to assure that the parameters were no less favorable for MH/SA than for other conditions. Unfortunately the law allowed numerous exemptions, including exceptions for small employers, for large employers who opt out, and for those employers for whom such provisions would increase costs by more than 1 percent. Nevertheless, the mental health parity laws can also be understood as legislative efforts to counter discrimination based on a particular condition associated with high cost and unmet need. As we will see next chapter, the definition of the scope of care that belongs in our conception of healthcare remains a subject of contest among courts, agencies, and legislature. Behavioral health, like sexual and reproductive health, may well represent one contested front in these

---

[182] Richard G. Frank et al., *Solutions for Adverse Selection in Behavioral Health Care*, 18 HEALTH CARE FIN. REV. 109 (1997).

[183] MHPA of 1996, Pub. L. No. 104-204 (1996) (prohibiting separate lifetime and annual limits for mental health coverage offered in the group market). *See*, The Mental Health Parity and Addiction Equity Act of 2008 (MHPAEA) Pub L. No. 110-343 (2008). The ACA effectively extended these standards to the individual market through the Essential Health Benefits requirement, PHSA § 2707, added by ACA § 1201 (codified at 42 U.S.C. § 300gg-6); ACA § 1302(b)(1)(A)-(J) (codified at 42 U.S.C. § 18022).

battles over the scope of what should be prioritized against the countervailing protests of medical expense associated with treating those afflicted.

Genetic Information and Rebutting the Counterargument of Formal Equality

Finally, genetic information emerged as a health-status–related factor whose use was trumped or precluded by the passage of state and then federal health protections. Throughout the 1990s, states engaged in the bottom-up development of the norm of "genetic nondiscrimination."[184] These state laws were foremost concerned with barring the use of genetic information in determining access to health coverage specifically. Some of the state laws, however, restricted its use in life insurance, disability insurance, and employment as well.[185]

Once again following the states' lead, Congress passed a federal counterpart in the form of the Genetic Information Nondiscrimination Act of 2000 (GINA).[186] GINA outlawed the use of genetic information in the health insurance and employment contexts. Specifically, it prohibited health plans from denying or pricing coverage on the basis of genetic information. It also banned the use of such information in imposing preexisting condition exclusions. Health plans cannot require genetic testing nor collect genetic information prior to enrollment and employers are barred from acquiring genetic information or making employment-related decisions based on such information. Some of the touchstone stories that gave rise to the passage of GINA featured everyday employees whose workplaces, upon receiving information about their genetic predispositions for breast and ovarian cancer, or Huntington's Disease, fired them precisely in order to exclude them from employer-sponsored health benefits.[187]

Neither age nor disability aligned perfectly with health status. HIV/AIDS, pregnancy, and behavioral health were plucked out as emblems of health need. Similarly, the concerns over genetic discrimination were perhaps symbolic of rather than coterminous with our concerns over health-status discrimination. Yet genetic information was always identified as a category of concern and listed

---

[184] Deborah Hellman, *What Makes Genetic Discrimination Exceptional?* 29 AM. J. L. & MED. 77, 78 (2003) ("[T]he question that dominates current literature is whether genetic discrimination is meaningfully different from discrimination on the basis of general health status") (alteration in original); *see* Jacobi, *supra* n.4, at 318 ("describes a growing consensus among state legislatures that statistically valid genetic indicators of future illness may not be used to deny or set prices for health coverage").

[185] *Id.* at 77.

[186] 42 U.S.C. § 2000ff et seq, Pub. L. No. 110-233, 122 Stat. 881.

[187] Faces of Genetic Discrimination: How Genetic Discrimination Affects Real People, National Partnership for Women and Families (July 2004), http://go.nationalpartnership.org/site/DocServer/FacesofGeneticDiscrimination.pdf.

among the health-status–related factors that were defined in HIPAA and later incorporated into the ACA's prohibition on health-status–based discrimination. Moreover, as Jacobi recognizes, banning consideration of genetic information would "ban[] insurers from considering much information relevant to calculating the expected risk of loss for applicants. After all, the percentage of risk that can be attributed to testable genetic factors . . . is currently unknown . . . but it is certainly substantial."[188] Thus GINA, like the other statutory schemes we have examined, could be understood as an imperfect strike against the use of the risk of health need itself to deny health coverage.

All of these points add to the plausibility that our telltale Dworkinian rights impulse—the preclusion of countervailing considerations like health need by virtue of our choice to value healthcare—lay behind the passage of GINA. The fact that GINA in its initial form focused solely on health insurance and employment terminations that were designed to exclude an individual from health coverage suggests less of a generalized antidiscrimination concern with respect to genetic information, and instead a more particular objection to the use of the genetic information as a factor in denying access to healthcare.[189] The form that the federal law eventually assumed extended the prohibitions to employers on the rationale that employers are major sources of health insurance.[190]

There is a potential counterargument challenging my characterization of this entire suite of prohibited considerations as trumped Dworkinian considerations. This counterargument chalks these health-status nondiscrimination statutes up to a concern with formal equality, rather than substantive Dworkinian rights. This view has some appeal. The fact that we term many of these nondiscrimination statutes rather than rights statutes must have meaning, otherwise what are we to make of the substantive rights implications of our entire body of antidiscrimination law? Why not understand these statutes as silent on the question of what people are owed substantively, and view them instead as merely signifying that whatever the actors subject to these laws decide to provide, these laws simply require that they provide it equally, without regard to health status?

This account, though, is wide of the mark. A venerable line of scholarship exists explaining as a general matter how the application of an equality norm is merely incidental to an underlying substantive rights conception.[191] Thus, any

---

[188] Jacobi, *supra* n.4, at 335.

[189] Sonia Suter et al., *The Persistent Lack of Knowledge and Misunderstanding of the Genetic Information Nondiscrimination Act (GINA) More Than a Decade After Passage*, 23 GENETICS MED. 2324 (2021).

[190] *See* Anya Prince & Daniel Schwarcz, *Proxy Discrimination in the Age of Artificial Intelligence and Big Data*, 105 IOWA L. REV. 1257, 1263–64 (2020).

[191] *See* Peter Westen, *The Empty Idea of Equality*, 95 HARV. L. REV. 537 (1982); Christopher Peters, *Equality Revisited*, 110 HARV. L. REV. 1210 (1997); Paul Gowder, *Equal Law in an Unequal World*, 99 IOWA L. REV. 1021, 1032 (2013); ROBIN WEST, REIMAGINING JUSTICE 121–4 (2003) (describing

argument resting on formal equality is actually smuggling in a substantive rights claim. Equality, under this view, refers to just our own moral conventions about what features matter when justifying particular treatment. In other words, the categories that we think suspect, or morally irrelevant, we deem to be so only with an eye to their use as standards of likeness *for the purposes of some treatment accorded*. We cannot consider their relevance without also assuming something about the purpose or treatment against which their relevance would be measured.

I describe a modified version of the example Peter Westen gives to illustrate this point. He says that the statement that all persons should be treated equally usually implies some conception of "a substantive right of persons to be treated with human respect."[192] Otherwise it is difficult to know whether certain borderline candidates—human embryos, persons in irreversible comas, or legal persons such as corporations—qualify for like treatment. Westen says:

> In trying to make the decision, one gets nowhere by intoning that all persons are equal, because the very question is whether the three [borderline] candidates are indeed "persons" within the meaning of the rule. Nor does it do any good to say that likes should be treated alike, because the very question is whether the three candidates are indeed alike for purposes of human respect. Rather, one must first identify the trait that entitles anyone to be treated with respect and then ascertain empirically whether the trait appears in one or more of the three candidates.

If the substantive right that one has in mind when speaking of equality is not "human respect" but political speech or voting rights, then one might reasonably exclude all three candidate "persons," the fetus, the comatose patient, and the corporation. If the substantive treatment one has in mind is healthcare, one would exclude corporations but favor the comatose person. If the entitlement in question was legal immunity, one would be more likely to reject distinctions based on status as a corporate legal person rather than natural person. Our answers as to which traits we consider impermissible discrimination might differ as the traits relevant to one's entitlement to a substantive right will differ.

---

critical legal studies scholars' observations along these lines); Kent Greenawalt, *"Prescriptive Equality": Two Steps Forward*, 110 HARV. L. REV. 1265 (1997). *Cf.*, Kenneth W. Simons, *The Logic of Egalitarian Norms*, 80 B.U. L. REV. 693, 723–29 (2000) (distinguishing formal equality, which he calls, "lexical equality," which he concedes may be problematic as a norm, from other types of egalitarian, or comparative norms); Kenneth Simons, *Equality as a Comparative Right*, 65 B.U. L. REV. 387, 390, 394 (1985).

[192] Westen, *supra* n.191, at 549–50.

GINA's history illustrates why it is hard to imagine that formal equality is the norm actually doing the hidden work in the statutes we have discussed. Neither GINA, nor mental health parity, nor HIPAA were drafted as cross-cutting nondiscrimination statutes, and their terms suggest a clear viewpoint on the antecedent question of "equality in virtue of what?" It is after all striking that housing, credit, and criminal enforcement are settings where we still allow the use of genetic information. Only health coverage and employment were the domains where this nondiscrimination norm emerged.[193] Thus GINA clearly expresses a view about the traits that are relevant (and those that are irrelevant) to a person's substantive claim to health access. The ACA's norm against excluding people with preexisting conditions similarly does not apply outside the health context.

I will continue to argue in the next chapter that the laws excluding these health-status–related lines of justification from weighing against medical need amount to the delineation of a right—a declaration about which traits entitle a person to some domain of treatment.

Consider a right in the abstract form, where S is the set of conditions (traits, eligibility standards) that qualify someone to right, R. Thus, the state may invoke failure to meet S when denying R. A substantive rights claim takes the form: an individual meets S and therefore has a right to R. The laws we have examined all share the same form, identifying a trait that may *not* serve as one of the conditions in S that can qualify or disqualify a person from R. Congress's selection of instances wherein to permit or strike the use of such reasons implicitly demarcates not only S by process of elimination (traits *cannot* include age, diagnosis, or genetics), but also R (ACA plans and employer-sponsored benefits, but not housing or credit).

In this chapter, I have tried to show that it is through manifold pathways, charted by our legislatures and agencies no less than our courts, that an American health right has burrowed its way deep into our legal corpus. Dworkin teaches that the elevation of a right operates by precluding certain countervailing justifications. Having applied this insight in our inquiry, we find, in true Dworkinian fashion, that the principle of a right to health both fits and explains much of the legal material pertaining to health coverage.

That we are looking at statutory rather than constitutional language does not render this embedded principle any less constitutive of our rights, and here I quote Ed Rubin in a passage that rings true:

---

[193] *Id.* at 548; *see,* Mark A. Rothstein & Laura Rothstein, *How Genetics Might Affect Real Property Rights,* 44 J.L. Med. & Ethics 216 (2016) (describing that only select states, California prominently, have statutes that protect against genetic discrimination in housing and lending).

[P]eople understand, at some politically visceral level, a feature of constitutional law that has been underemphasized in the scholarly literature; namely, that statutes as well as judicial decisions interpret the Constitution. Not every statute is relevant to our understanding of the Constitution, of course, but many significant ones are and the PPACA is a prime example. The Act's passage suggests that the U.S. Constitution guarantees so-called positive rights, such as rights to . . . basic health care. The mere fact of its enactment secures the place of these rights on our political agenda and encourages the Supreme Court to declare them part of the Constitution.[194]

---

[194] Edward Rubin, *The Affordable Care Act, the Constitutional Meaning of Statutes, and the Emerging Doctrine of Positive Constitutional Rights*, 53 WILLIAM & MARY L. REV. 1639 (2012) (alteration in original).

4

A Health Right By Any Other Name: Expression in Case Law

In this chapter, I turn to case law to show that courts have already laid considerable groundwork in the United States for the delineation of a health right; we have simply yet to acknowledge these examples as rights-building. I began in the last chapter by locating signs of the Dworkinian rights grammar of internal preclusion in our statutes—but where might we find it in case law? Recalling our earlier discussion of the problems that health rights are distinctively positioned to solve, I looked at cases where health came prominently into conflict or competition with other values or interests. Are there patterns to how we handle such cases?

A curious phenomenon seemed to recur: health protections were jeopardized by their underreach, that is, their failure to do enough to protect health. When a health measure accommodated some competing consideration, where the law carved out an exception to acknowledge conflicting interests, those concessions would often expose the health policy to invalidation. Repeatedly, in high-stakes cases, judges framed their decisions, *while striking the measure*, as somehow valuing or honoring the sanctity of health and protecting it from unjustified compromise. This sanctimonious posturing has imperiled our most hard-won health policy victories.

Take, for instance, the fate of FDA's 1995 tobacco rule. The US FDA has longstanding authority to regulate drugs and devices, granted under a statute that defines those terms broadly to include "any . . . article (other than food) *intended* to affect the structure or function of the [human] body."[1] For decades, science and the public understood that nicotine affected the body's functions by stimulating the nervous system, suppressing appetite, and triggering cravings, resulting in addiction. However, manufacturers maintained that they marketed the products without "intending" those effects, no matter how consumers elected to use them. Big Tobacco contended that they were merely offering cigarettes for people's lifestyle, recreation, or other nonspecific, nonphysiological purposes.

With permission, Chapter 4 adapts but substantially changes and augments material that was originally published in Christina S. Ho, *Are We Suffering from an Undiagnosed Health Right*, 42 AM. J. OF L. AND MED. 743 (2016), and from Christina S. Ho, *Exceptions Meet Absolutism: Outlawing Governmental Underreach in Health Law*, 93 DENVER. L. REV. 109 (2015).

[1] FDCA §201(g) and (h) (emphasis added).

In the 1990s, groundbreaking litigation against the tobacco companies brought to light internal documents showing that they had deliberately altered and selected cigarette design features that would optimize cigarettes' ability to "exert psychoactive, or mood-altering, effects on the brain, cause and sustain addiction, tranquilize and stimulate." The intent of industry was finally unmistakable.

Thus in 1995, the FDA issued a rule claiming authority over cigarettes as devices (articles that do not depend on being metabolized) intended to deliver nicotine (a drug operating by chemical action). The FDA characterized smoking, because of its origins in the physiological and behavioral change of minors, as a pediatric disease and thus prohibited the marketing, sale, and distribution of cigarettes to anyone under eighteen. The FDA elected not extend the ban to *adults* because other factors weighed more heavily in that population. The agency cited potential health harms from widespread withdrawal, adult smokers' autonomy with respect to hedonistic utility, and their greater capacity at the outset to consent to the effects, even including addictive effects, of tobacco.[2]

The tobacco industry promptly sued, and in *FDA v. Brown & Williamson*, the Supreme Court struck the tobacco rule as contrary to Congress's statutory authorization, faulting, in part, the rule's failure to protect *adults* from cigarettes. Justice O'Connor's majority opinion declares: "[T]he FDA quite exhaustively documented that 'tobacco products are unsafe' . . . These findings logically imply that if tobacco products were 'devices' under the FDCA, the FDA would be required to remove them from the market."[3] Relying in part on the strength of this reading, O'Connor decides that Congress barred the agency's compromise strategy: adults should never have been left out of the rule's protective ambit.

Consider also the landmark ACA case, *NFIB v. Sebelius*.[4] While Chief Justice John Roberts upheld the ACA's individual mandate, he also assembled a large majority to strike the expansion of Medicaid to a new mandatory population of childless adults, those with incomes up to 133 percent of poverty.[5] Under Medicaid, the federal government offers to match qualifying state health spending, but those matching funds come with conditions for state programs, such as coverage of certain mandatory benefits for certain mandatory populations. These populations include low-income children and parents, pregnant women, and the contemporary analogs to the customary welfare categories of the "aged, blind, and totally and permanently disabled." The Roberts plurality

---

[2] *See* Regulations Restricting the Sale and Distribution of Cigarettes and Smokeless Tobacco to Protect Children and Adolescents, 61 Fe. Reg. 44396, 44113 (August 128, 1996) (codified in scattered parts of 21 C.F.R.).

[3] 529 U.S. 120, 135 (2000).

[4] 567 U.S. 519 (2012).

[5] Chief Justice Roberts's Medicaid views, outlined in Part IV of the *Sebelius* opinion, were joined by Justices Breyer and Kagan, while Justices Scalia, Kennedy, Thomas and Alito dissented, rendering a 7–2 decision.

opinion establishes that Congress, by adding a new mandatory expansion population, overstepped its Spending Power. But curiously, Roberts pinpoints
Congress's misstep not so much in the ambitious scope of its coverage expansion, but in having left nonexpansion states out of being able to claim even "old
Medicaid" matching funds, thus threatening to *reduce* coverage. Robert explains
the ACA's flaw thus: "What Congress is not free to do is to penalize States that
choose not to participate in that new program by taking away their existing
Medicaid funding."[6] Justice Roberts's plurality opinion later leans into this
rhetoric of solicitude for those whose funding might be threatened by the conditional funding design of the ACA's Medicaid expansion. He laments that the
"old Medicaid" recipients who would be endangered by the threat of funds withdrawal actually rank as "the neediest among us."[7]

As we consider the somewhat surprising level of courthouse resistance to various types of exceptions, conditions, or limits written into our health laws, the
question poses itself: Why, under current law, would judges reject some lines of
compromise, or the accommodation of some countervailing factors, as especially sensitive? Isn't this sensitivity particularly strange since these displays of
special judicial concern for health have paradoxically undermined some of our
most hard-won health achievements? Are there unstated fit norms at work, and
can we divine them?

We now know that carving out those over eighteen from tobacco protection
draws extra friction, as does withholding funds from the "neediest among us."

The following are just a few more of the types of exceptions that courts deemed
unacceptable. None were dictated by the statutory preclusions we examined last
chapter.

In *Tummino v. Torti*, a judge struck FDA's decision to make Plan B emergency contraceptives available over the counter (OTC), *except to women under
eighteen*.[8] In the final judicial analysis, this age-exception feature rendered the
FDA's decision "arbitrary and capricious" as compared to blunter, less-contoured
measures. After all, other emergency contraceptives, like ella, are prescription-
only, thus *entirely* restricted from OTC availability to women of *all* ages.[9] These
blunt bans on OTC access still prevail. Even the levonorgestrel birth control
pill (the "mini-pill") remains available only by prescription, though it consists

---

[6] 62 out of 153.

[7] 59 out of 193.

[8] Tummino v. Torti (*Tummino I*), 603 F. Supp. 2d at 519 (E.D.N.Y. 2009); Tummino v. Hamburg
(*Tummino II*), 936 F. Supp. 2d 162 (E.D.N.Y. 2013); Tummino v. Hamburg (*Tummino III*), No. 12-
CV-763, 2013 WL 2631163 (E.D.N.Y. June 12, 2013).

[9] *See* Olga Khazan, *Birth Control Without a Prescription*, ATLANTIC (September 19, 2014), http://
www.theatlantic.com/health/archive/2014/09/toward-a-prescription-free-birth-control-pill/380
464/ (citing the vice chair of the American College of Obstetricians and Gynecologists Committee
on Gynecologic Practice Bulletins saying that the mini-pill should be the first to be offered over the
counter because of its safety profile).

of exactly the same chemical entity as Plan B and differs only insofar as it is marketed for nonemergency contraception.[10] The judge seems to envision the FDA's range of action for postintercourse levonorgestrel as restricted to fully OTC or fully prescription, with no ability to offer OTC access with an age-based exception.

Meanwhile, the health protection at issue in *Lorillard v. Reilly* was a Massachusetts' regulation banning in-store tobacco advertising near schools, *unless placed above the 5-foot sight line.*[11] Part of what doomed the measure was its performance under the third prong of the *Central Hudson* test, how well the regulation advanced the substantial countervailing interest that is weighed against speech.[12] In this case the countervailing interest was children's health protection, and thus the Court struck the regulation in part *because of its failure to protect the health of children taller than five feet.*

In *Hays v. Sebelius*,[13] the circuit court struck the Secretary of Health and Human Services' policy of covering certain outpatient drugs and medical items under Part B, *but only reimbursing up to the price of a drug's least costly alternative.* Beneficiaries would thereby sustain greater burden if their treatment plan involved the more costly version of the drug. HHS clearly wished to incentivize switches in treatment. Otherwise the patient would either have to pay more or go without. Trimming down the generosity of reimbursement for covered items in this way was, in the D.C. Circuit's view, contrary to the Medicare statute; the appeals court interpreted that text as allowing HHS a measure of judgment on which items and services were reasonable and necessary, but not judgment on the allowable rate for those items and services. By the court's lights, "the Secretary may make only a binary coverage decision, namely to reimburse at the full statutory rate or not at all."[14]

We even detect this striking for under-inclusion phenomenon in *Florida ex rel. Bondi v. DHHS*, one of the appellate cases that culminated in *NFIB v. Sebelius*.[15] Indeed the 11th Circuit in *Florida v. DHHS* was the only one of the circuit-level precursors to *NFIB* to invalidate the individual mandate on its merits. Notably, the majority did so because the mandate to maintain minimum essential coverage featured *exemptions and lenience in enforcement*, thereby marring the fit of the mandate enough to fail the means-ends test required under the Necessary

---

[10] *See also*, Scout Richters, *The Moral Interception of Oral Contraception*, 22 J. OF L. & POL'Y 393, 408 (2013) (identifying levonorgestrel as the substance in progestin-only mini-pills).

[11] *See* Lorillard, 533 U.S. 525, 566 (2001).

[12] *See* Central Hudson Gas & Elec. Corp. v. Pub. Serv. Comm'n, 447 U.S. 557, 566 (1980).

[13] Hays v. Sebelius, 589 F.3d 1279 (D.C. Cir. 2009).

[14] 589 F.3d at 1281 (D.C. Ct. 2009).

[15] Florida ex rel Bondi v. DHHS, 648 F.3d 1235, 1307-11 (11th Cir. 2011) (finding that the individual mandate fails the "essential to a larger regulatory scheme" standard for qualifying as an exercise of the Necessary and Proper clause of Article I), *overruled by* NFIB v. Sebelius, 567 U.S. 519, 132 S. Ct. 2566 (2012).

and Proper Clause of Article I. Without a viable Article I Power to authorize Congress's enactment of the mandate, in the 11th Circuit's view, the mandate was unconstitutional. The panel in its majority opinion therefore scolds Congress for its broad, untailored exclusion of certain uninsureds from the protective ambit of the mandate:

> The government's assertion that the individual mandate is "essential" to Congress's broader economic regulation is further undermined by components of the Act itself. In [*Gonzalez v. Raich,*] Congress devised a "closed regulatory system," designed to eliminate all interstate marijuana traffic. Here, by contrast, Congress itself carved out eight broad exemptions and exceptions to the individual mandate (and its penalty) that impair its scope and functionality . . . Congress has hamstrung its own efforts to ensure compliance with the mandate by opting for toothless enforcement mechanisms. Eschewing the IRS's traditional enforcement tools, the Act waives all criminal penalties for noncompliance and prevents the IRS from using liens or levies to collect the penalty. Thus, to the extent the uninsureds' ability to delay insurance purchases would leave a "gaping hole" in Congress's efforts to reform the insurance market, Congress has seen fit to bore the hole itself.[16] (citations omitted)

In each of these cases certain carveouts from health protection were contested and cited as the reason for invalidating the entire health measure. Why should judges invalidate rules that have been narrowed to fit varied and conflicting considerations, especially when none of these situations ran expressly afoul of the statutory preclusions we examined last chapter? Are judges carrying the project of Dworkinian preclusion further on their own? What pressures combine with the denormalization of health rights to force judges into maneuvers that limit lawmakers to a seemingly all-or-nothing range of action with no ability to trim a measure to accommodate different factors? Such sanctimony has all too often left beneficiaries with nothing, as the case of *White v. Beal* from the last chapter illustrated.[17] As a result of the court ruling requiring Pennsylvania to provide an optional benefit, namely eyeglasses, to all relevant diagnoses, rather than limiting the benefit to only certain eye conditions, Pennsylvania ultimately found eyeglasses to be unaffordable and withdrew coverage altogether.[18]

Though the case data is unquestionably "noisy," the carveouts that draw scrutiny still tend to cluster. Certain disfavored factors recur—indeed, ones that bear

---

[16] Florida ex rel Bondi v. DHHS, 648 F.3d 1235, 1310–12 (11th Cir. 2011).
[17] White v. Beal (*White II*), 555 F.2d 1146 (3d Cir. 1977).
[18] *See* White v. Beal (*White III*), 447 F. Supp. 788, 798 (E.D. Pa. 1978).

a familial resemblance to the factors statutorily designated as "suspect" in the last chapter. Cases frequently condemn exclusions based on the following categories:

- Diagnosis
- Age
- Institutionalization
- Economic want
- Arbitrary physical attributes

Once again, these considerations are all plausibly explained as exclusions that conflict "internally" with the reasons we value health provision in the first place. Or, to requote Waldron: "Once again, our conception of the interest's importance already tells us a lot about the sort of consideration to which it is appropriately opposed."[19]

Under a Dworkinian account of how a health right exerts precedence, we would predict that limits based on these and similar factors would be subject to "trumping," or "lexical preclusion." Indeed, a scan of cases suggests that when exceptions are based on factors that could arguably proxy for health need, the statute, regulation, or provision at issue becomes legally vulnerable and notably vulnerable for *underprotecting* health.

Diagnosis

Let us revisit *White v. Beal (White II)*, which we discussed in the previous chapter. *White II* introduced us to the notion that state Medicaid programs, though they may choose not to provide optional services, are not "unbridled" in their discretion over the *extent* to which they provide such services.[20] But, as flagged earlier, the choice to make diagnoses or health conditions the point at which insurer discretion ceases is essentially judge-driven. The Medicaid statute, after all, requires only "reasonable standards . . . for determining eligibility for and the extent of medical assistance . . . consistent with the objectives of th[e Act]."[21] And for

---

[19] Jeremy Waldron, *Rights in Conflict*, 99 ETHICS 503, 517 (1989).

[20] *See* White II, 555 F.2d at TK. White III, 447 F. Supp. at 798.

[21] 42 U.S.C. § 1396a(a)(17). For managed care, 42 U.S.C. §1396b(i)(26) requires necessary, reasonable limits. *See also* 42 U.S.C. § 1396a(a)(19). Note that advocates sometimes warn against sourcing these standards for reasonableness in amount, duration, and scope to particular statutory provisions rather than to more diffuse federal common law. *See* Stan Dorn et al., *Maximizing Coverage for Medicaid Clients ("Bridges over Troubled Waters")*, 20 CLEARINGHOUSE REV. 411, 412 n.11 (1986) (regarding case law that "relied on 42 U.S.C. §[] . . . 1396a(10)(C)(, and 45 C.F.R. § 249.10(a)(5)(i), now 42 C.F.R. § 440.230(d)").

private employer-sponsored coverage, ERISA certainly contains no more stringent requirement of reasonability.

White II turns out not to be an anomalous data point in the case law. It keeps company with a number of similar cases, such as *Weaver v. Reagan*.[22] In *Weaver*, the judge struck Missouri's coverage of AZT because it extended to only some HIV-related indications and not others. AZT is an antiretroviral used to treat certain viral infections, but the State Medicaid program offered it only to select HIV-positive persons, such as those diagnosed with pneumocystis carinii pneumonia (PCP). PCP is only one type of opportunistic infection to which HIV-positive patients are vulnerable. Yet Missouri refused AZT for other characteristic HIV side-infections, such as oropharyngeal/esophageal candidiasis, even though physicians commonly prescribed AZT under those circumstances as well. Indeed, AZT represented the only approved treatment for HIV infection at the time. In other words, distinguishing among HIV-positive individuals who had one opportunistic diagnosis rather than another violated the reasonableness standards of the Medicaid statute, just as the *White v. Beal* eyeglasses carveout did.

Some of the other cases in this family do not cite the cross-cutting Medicaid statutory requirement of "reasonableness" for support, but the cross-cutting "comparability" requirement instead, showcasing the judge-led, rather than statutorily mandated quality of this doctrinal preclusion. *Davis v. Shah* represents such a case.[23] When New York confronted budget crises in 2011, the state limited its optional benefits covering orthopedic footwear and compression socks (classified as prosthetics) to only the most common diagnoses. The special footwear was approved for a short list of qualifying conditions, including "to correct accommodate or prevent a physical deformity or range of motion malfunction [in children] . . . as a component of a comprehensive diabetic treatment plan . . . or to form an integral part of an orthotic brace."[24] Compression socks were limited to "coverage during pregnancy and for venous stasis ulcers."[25] While the court rejected plaintiffs' other claims—including contentions that the limitations ran afoul of the ADA and the Rehabilitation Act—and found no violation of the reasonableness standard from *White II*, the court did ultimately invalidate New York's benefit cutback under Medicaid's "comparability" condition.

The Medicaid statute actually features two different "comparability" provisions. One merely prohibits states from providing optional beneficiaries with more benefits than mandatory beneficiaries.[26] This distinction was not at

---

[22] 886 F.2d 194 (8th Cir. 1989).

[23] 621 F.3d 231 (2d Cir. 2016).

[24] *Id*. at 257 (citing New York 18 NY.C.R.R. § 505.5(a)(4)).

[25] *Id*. at n.2 (citing New York 18 N.Y.C.R.R. § 505.5(a)(4)).

[26] *See* 42 U.S.C. 1396a(a)(10)(B)(ii).

issue here. The other provision, which did concern the Second Circuit, demands that "the medical assistance made available to any [categorically needy] individual . . . shall not be less in amount, duration, or scope than the medical assistance made available to any other such individual."[27] At least within the class of "categorically needy" beneficiaries, this provision "prohibits states from discriminating . . . by 'provid[ing] benefits to some . . . individuals but not to others.'"[28] The statement that the medical assistance provided to one categorically needy plaintiff "shall not be less . . . than the medical assistance made available to any other such individual" hinges, of course, on who constitutes "any other such individual." The state cannot violate the comparability provision if the realm of comparators is sufficiently narrowed. Thus, New York State tried to argue that it could define the benefit as only for the treatment of certain conditions. Under New York's reading, the term "such individual" to whom the state had to provide comparable treatment could never even include a person with a different condition. The Second Circuit rejected this extreme positivism.

The comparability provision thus resembles the hollow pronouncements of purely formal equality that, as discussed in the last chapter, depend on a prior conception of the legal treatment for which the relevant claimants are being evaluated. In other words, the court must have an idea of the nature of the legal entitlement to draw from when deciding what qualities would be relevant to evaluating an individual claim of equal entitlement to that treatment. What quality would make "such individuals" alike? In *Davis*, the idea is one familiar from the many statutes and cases we have now examined—the idea that *medical need* is the relevant quality that entitles one to coverage of medical treatment. Medicaid is thus precluded from denying coverage on the basis of a medical diagnosis when that diagnosis is a valid indicator of medical need:

> [A]llowing a state to deny medical benefits to some categorically needy individuals that it provides to others with the exact same medical needs simply by defining such services . . . as aimed at treating only some medical conditions would risk swallowing the comparability provision whole . . . that provision prohibits discrimination among individuals *with the same medical needs stemming from different medical conditions.* . . . To the extent that such a provision might be read simply as precluding discrimination among individuals with the very same medical conditions, indeed it would simply govern the equitable administration of a state plan not the formal terms of that plan.[29]

---

[27]   42 U.S.C. 1396a(a)(10)(B)(i).

[28]   Davis v. Shah, 821 F.3d 231 (2d Cir. 2016) (quoting Rodriguez v. City of New York, 197 F.3d 611, 615 (1999) (finding the benefit design and implementation for personal care service hours did not discriminate on the basis of disability)).

[29]   Davis v. Shah, 821 F.3d at 258 (emphasis added).

Medicaid is not the only source of statutory language that has been hijacked in the service of this norm against denying healthcare on the grounds of diagnostic conditions. For private employer plans, no less than public, the Americans with Disabilities Act limits the distinctions based on *disability*. And, as we discussed last chapter, the EEOC has, in the context of employer-based health coverage, also interpreted the ADA to impose limits on the distinctions that can be drawn between coverage for one *diagnosis* and coverage for another. The EEOC's Interim Enforcement Guidance offers this formulation: a term or provision differentiating among diagnoses can be potentially discriminatory "if it singles out a particular disability (e.g., deafness, AIDS, schizophrenia) [or] a discrete group of disabilities (e.g., cancers, muscular dystrophies, kidney diseases)." Meanwhile, it maintains that "some health insurance plans provide fewer benefits for 'eye care' than for other physical conditions [and that] such broad distinctions, which apply to the treatment of a multitude of dissimilar conditions" remain permissible.[30] Why kidney diseases constitute a more "discrete group of disabilities" than conditions requiring eye care is unexplained, but the clear implication is that at least some condition-based exclusions fall under the ADA's ban.

Our broad acceptance of this normative kernel now—namely, the wide-spread discomfort with health coverage denials on the basis of diagnosis—in some ways impedes my account of how such a judicial pattern constitutes a noteworthy normative commitment to health rights. To understand why the recurrence of this theme is significant, even startling, we have to, as we did last chapter, defamiliarize a now prevailing view.

The reason this condemnation of diagnosis-based distinctions can be thought strange is because there are many circumstances when it is rational to treat distinct diagnoses differently for therapeutic and coverage purposes. For instance, starting in the late 1980s, high-dose chemotherapy with autologous bone marrow transplant (HDCT/ABMT) was widely prescribed for breast cancer, though the regime had previously been used successfully for only certain blood cancers.[31] Women with breast cancer, along with their doctors, mounted lawsuit upon lawsuit challenging insurance restrictions on their access to this treatment, winning stunning victories in the bulk of these cases.[32] However, randomized clinical

---

[30] *Interim Enforcement Guidance on the Application of the ADA to Disability-Based Distinctions in Employer-Provided Health Insurance*, U.S. EQUAL EMPLOYMENT OPPORTUNITY COMMISSION NOTICE NO. 915.002 (June 8, 1993), https://www.eeoc.gov/laws/guidance/interim-enforcement-guidance-application-ada-disability-based-distinctions-employer.

[31] *See* RICHARD RETTIG ET AL., FALSE HOPE: BONE MARROW TRANSPLANTATION FOR BREAST CANCER (2007).

[32] Peter D. Jacobson and Stefanie A. Doebler, *"We Were All Sold A Bill of Goods": Litigating the Science of Breast Cancer Treatment*, 52 WAYNE L. REV. 43 (2006); Mark Hall et al., *Judicial Protection of Managed Care Consumers: An Empirical Study of Insurance Coverage Disputes*, 26 SETON HALL L. REV. 1055 (1996).

trials later failed to show any therapeutic benefit for extending HDCT/ABMT to breast cancer. Thirty thousand women had already by that time suffered under the application of this punishing regimen.[33] A restriction of this treatment solely to proven diagnoses could well have been justified, though courts too often sided with the sympathetic patient-claimants in these cases. Only later did the case law ultimately settle out to permit private insurers to deny bone marrow transplants to patients with some cancers but not others.[34]

Of course, diagnosis-based distinctions can be abused for invidious reasons. Recall from last chapter the notorious ADA case *Doe v. Mutual of Omaha*, where benefits for HIV/AIDS care were capped at an annual limit lower than the limit for benefits under any other diagnosis. This differential ceiling applied even though the insurer could have achieved the same savings with a lower but more evenhanded cap.[35] Seventh Circuit Judge Richard Posner permitted the differential cap, relying upon another notorious case, *Lenox v. Healthwise of Kentucky Ltd.*, where an insurance term that covered some organ transplants, but not heart transplants was nevertheless lawful under the ADA.[36] This case law has helped the occasional insurer prevail even in one notable instance when the plan denied coverage for liver transplants unless transplant candidates "have six months of sobriety and [are] in treatment for substance abuse," a rather heavy-handed distinction to make in the rescue value of two human lives.[37] What this backdrop conveys is that not only do background medical justifications often exist for differential treatment of diagnoses, but that even beyond medical rationality lies a bedrock norm of individual choice and prerogative for market participants. Each of these reasons inclines us away from the preclusion of diagnosis as a factor available for the limitation of health financing. And yet we regularly encounter instances where the diagnostic nondiscrimination norm prevails.

Case outcomes fail to break reliably for insurers, and diagnosis-based denials seem ever to court searching judicial scrutiny. Insurance plans have been blocked when they furnish "liver transplants only for biliary atresia and certain

---

[33] *See* E. Haavi Morreim, *from the Clinics to the Courts: The Role Evidence Should Play in Litigating Medical Care*, 26 J. HEALTH POL., POL'Y & L. 409, 411–13 (2001).

[34] *See, e.g.*, Hilliard v. Bellsouth Medical Assistance Plan, 918 F. Supp. 1016 (S.D. Miss. 1995) (holding that such denials were consistent with the ADA); Clark v. Kmart, 1992 WL 106935 (C.A.3 (PA)) (holding that private insurers can exclude HDCT/ABMT for breast cancer); Bechtold v. Physicians Health Plan of Northern Indiana, 19 F.3d 322 (7th Cir. 1994) (defining 'experimental treatment plan' by reference to the Medicare Coverage Issues manual, saying that HDCT for breast cancer could be excluded ... and "that a participant's right to 'full and fair review' does not include the right to challenge the underlying medical judgment of a clear contractual exclusion"). *But see* Pirozzi v. BCBS 741 F.Supp. 586 (E.D.Va. 1990) (holding that there cannot be a denial of HDCT/ABMT because there was never explicit incorporation of the internal "technology evaluation criteria").

[35] *See* 179 F.3d 557 (7th Cir. 1999).

[36] *See* 149 F.3d 453 (6th Cir. 1998).

[37] Neal v. Christopher & Banks Comprehensive Major Med. Plan, 651 F. Supp. 2d 890 (E.D. Wis. 2009).

congenital metabolic disorders" but not for cirrhosis, as was the case in *Hyde v. Humana*.[38] The insurance plan in that case had a rider articulating its transplant policy, and in that rider, it reserved the authority to determine coverage of transplants based on its written criteria and procedures. The court held this language was not enough to alert the enrollee—who brought contract and bad faith claims under state law—that Humana's transplant coverage criteria could cleave along these condition-specific lines. This kind of judge-crafted notice-based ruling, which does not rest on any statutory ADA or Rehabilitation Act text, both presumes and enforces a shared expectation of what would be covered based on our common understanding. It is exactly the kind of ruling that through common law accretion could begin to form a conception of what we have a right to expect in our health coverage.

Likewise, ERISA has been roped in to police private plans that draw objectionable diagnosis-based distinctions. In *Heasley v. Belden & Blake Corp.*, a plan denied liver transplants based on a dividing line between metastatic and nonmetastatic cancers.[39] Plaintiff had a neuroendocrine tumor, called a gastrinoma, which can affect the liver. The Plan had ruled out the plaintiff's liver transplant request based on the standard policy term excluding experimental treatment. In doing so, the Plan relied on its own decision rule that adults with metastatic malignancies do not qualify for liver transplants because of the chance of cancer regrowth.[40] But the Third Circuit took a deep dive into the medical rationality of this distinction, ultimately arguing that, based on the literature, neuroendocrine tumors differ from other metastatic cancers in their slow rate of growth. Thus the broad exclusion of metastatic cancer patients as requesting experimental transplants did not make sense in this individual case. The insurer tried to cut the diagnostic category yet finer, contending that even if neuroendocrine tumors differed from other metastatic cancers, nevertheless within the category of neuroendocrine tumors, gastrinoma transplant experience was still relatively sparse. The Appeals Court however insisted upon the inclusion of gastrinomas under the coverage terms based on its own analysis of the similarity of the medical properties of gastrinomas to other neuroendocrine tumors (slow growth, tendency not to spread beyond liver and not to recur in liver after transplant). The Plan's diagnostic distinctions triggered a degree of judicial scrutiny that seems to far exceed mere rationality review. The Plan's policy had even featured language granting insurer discretion on the question of whether a procedure was medically necessary, language that in the ERISA context normally

---

[38] Hyde v. Humana, 598 So. 2d 876 (Al. 1992).
[39] *See* 2 F.3d 1249 (3d Cir. 1993).
[40] *See id.*

assures deferential judicial review for nonarbitrariness.[41] Yet this Circuit ruled that absent an additional specification of discretion *particular to the experimental procedure exclusion*, the courts could undertake their own inquiry *de novo*, and a demanding one it proved.[42]

Time and again, courts have shown misgivings about diagnosis-based denials of health coverage, even when no clear statutory text raises this concern.

Age

Age-related cut-offs are also lightning rods for judicial reappraisal, despite the frequent inapplicability and conceded impotence of the age discrimination statutes we reviewed last chapter. Just as tobacco marketing protections focused solely on children drew particular scrutiny, so did denials of over-the-counter Plan B access for women under eighteen in the cases flagged earlier.

Age distinctions by private plans draw fire as well. In *DiDomenico v. Employers Co-op Industry Trust*,[43] the ERISA-governed plan, as in *Beasley*, expressly excluded transplants that were "considered experimental," but stipulated that "[t]ransplants of a kidney, cornea or a liver (for a child under age 12) are not considered experimental." The insurer later claimed this policy was consistent with the "Merck Manual" and Medicare guidelines, though these technical bodies were not expressly referenced in the plan as the source of the age cut-off. Because plaintiff was an *adult* with biliary cirrhosis of the liver, the plan denied his transplant. The District Court found the above exclusionary provision, with its under-twelve safe-harbor, to be "ambiguous." Therefore, under the doctrine of *contra proferentum* which instructs courts to favor the insured when the terms are unclear, the District Court construed the provisions to permit coverage of adult liver transplants. It then ruled that the plan's exclusion of adult liver transplants from the definition of medical necessity was arbitrary and capricious, lacking sufficient reasonable basis and thus failing the *Firestone* arbitrary

---

[41] *See* Firestone Tire & Rubber Co. v. Bruch, 489 U.S. 101, 109 S.Ct. 948 (1989) (stating when the "arbitrary and capricious" standard should be used by the courts in judging whether the contract terms of an ERISA plan were violated and remediable under ERISA § 502(a)). The Court held that the arbitrary and capricious standard, hereinafter "the A&C standard," obtains whenever "the benefit plan gives the administrator or fiduciary discretionary authority to determine eligibility for benefits or to construe the terms of the plan"). *Id.* at 113–14.

[42] Heasley v. Belden & Blake Corp., 2 F.3d 1249 (3d Cir. 1993). Because *Firestone* introduced the A&C standard as an exception to the default de novo review standard for ERISA-governed plan terms, nearly all employers post-*Firestone* made sure to draft into their contracts a provision to grant their administrators and fiduciaries discretionary authority to determine eligibility and construe the terms of the plan. *Heasley*, however, limited the scope of such provisions such that applicability to the experimental procedure exclusion of the policy would have required greater clarity.

[43] 676 F. Supp. 903 (N.D. In. 1987).

and capricious standard for judicial review of employer plan decisions. The judge confronted these questions in the context of deciding plaintiff's motion for preliminary injunction, a doctrinal setting which overlays its own traditional factors for the courts to weigh. In addition to the likelihood of irreparable harm to the movant, the court must consider the public interest factor and in doing so, the District Court declared, "it suffices to state that the interest in the sanctity and quality of life is paramount."[44] Thus the posture under which these private insurance claims cases arise can lend itself to this kind of rights-talk, where the "trumping" weight of a paramount value can enter the analysis especially in the third prong. This is a point we will revisit below.[45]

Medicaid case law is rife with courts scrutinizing, and not infrequently striking down, age-based limits.[46] *Radaszewski v. Maram* concerned a beneficiary who required round-the-clock medical care as a result of a pediatric brain tumor and stroke.[47] Eric Radaszewski had been under private-duty nursing care in his parents' home for sixteen hours a day. His parents, having received specialized training, supplied the remaining hours of care. Private-duty nursing, an optional Medicaid benefit, is, as the court describes, "nursing service provided to a person who requires more individualized and continuous care than would routinely be provided by a visiting nurse or by the nursing staff of a hospital or skilled nursing facility."[48] Illinois supplied the sixteen hours of this care to Eric under a Medicaid waiver for "medically fragile children." Upon reaching twenty-one, Eric aged out of the program and lost state private duty nursing for all but five hours a day under the new cap that he faced in Illinois' separate private-duty nursing benefit for adults. Illinois' age-based differentiation, though permissible under the limited statutes on age discrimination, was nevertheless struck by the appeals court as disability-based discrimination, and thereby inconsistent with the ADA and the Rehabilitation Act.

Medicaid has characteristically made aid available to whose medical needs are severe enough to need institutional care.[49] But the de-institutionalization

---

[44] *Id.* at 908.

[45] *See* Mark Hall and Gerard Anderson, *Health Insurers' Assessment of Medical Necessity*, 140 U. PENN. L. REV. 1637, 1655 (1992).

[46] *See, e.g.*, Conley v. Dep't of Health, 2012 WL 4450154 at *15 (Utah Ct. App. September 27, 2012) (finding that "SACDs cannot reasonably be prosthetics and communication equipment for those individuals under age twenty-one and pregnant women, but only be speech pathology services for non-pregnant individuals age twenty-one and older"); *see also id.* at *12 (citing opinions refusing to recognize age-based coverage distinctions).

[47] Radaszewski ex rel Radaszewski v. Maram, 383 F.3d 599 (7th Cir. 2004).

[48] *Id.* at 601 (citing 42 C.F.R. § 440.80, categorized as optional under Social Security Act § 1905(a) (8), 42 U.S.C. § 1396a(a)(8)).

[49] Robert Stevens and Rosemary Stevens, WELFARE MEDICINE IN AMERICA: A CASE STUDY OF MEDICAID, 29–30 (rev. ed. 2003) Kerr-Mills included help not just for those receiving OAA cash benefits, but those medically indigent whose incomes did not qualify, but nevertheless had such high medical costs that their income was insufficient in that light. Kerr-Mills, though mostly lax in terms of federal standards "required each plan to include both institutional and noninstitutional care as

movement sought to extend noninstitutional, or home and community-based options, to this Medicaid population as well. Thus, starting in the late 1970s, Illinois secured waivers from certain Medicaid requirements to gain the flexibility to provide care for some beneficiaries in home and community-based settings instead.[50] Under these waivers, Illinois extended a suite of in-home or other medical and support services—including private duty nursing—to qualified beneficiaries who would otherwise have received Medicaid funding for institutional care. These waivers therefore enabled some Medicaid beneficiaries to live in more integrated settings, hopefully costing Medicaid less money. One of Illinois' home- and community-based service (HCBS) waivers was called the Medically Fragile and Technology Dependent Children program (MFTDC), which covered those eligible up to the age of twenty-one. Illinois also operated a Home Services Program (HSP) that was *not* restricted to children. This divided program structure set up the age-based benefit boundary that Eric Radaszewski confronted in his case.

When Eric aged out of MFTDC, he sought continued in-home private nursing through the HSP program. But as previously noted, HSP would only provide him with a maximum of five hours of similar service while taking "the position that if funding at [that] rate was insufficient to provide for Eric's care at home, then he would have to move to an institutional setting in order to receive care."[51] Eric's parents countered that while a certain degree of medical supervision would be available at an institution, Eric's needs required more constant individualized attention.

The courts decided that with these factual questions at issue, Eric's complaint of an ADA violation based on Illinois' age cut-off was sufficient to at least

---

a condition of federal sharing." *Id.* at 30; *see also id.* at 33–34 (stating that Kerr-Mills MAA funding was designed with some characteristics, like no upper limits, that led to a focus on institutional care: "Massachusetts, for example, began its Kerr-Mills program in October 1960 by transferring 14,000 persons—recipients needing and receiving long-term nursing home care—from other public assistance programs; these persons represented 89 percent of the initial recipients under MAA"); Social Security Act § 1902(a)(10)(ii)(IV), 42 U.S.C. § 1396a(a)(10)(ii)(IV) sometimes known as the "Long Amendment," overrode the earlier Social Security Act ban on vendor payments or other assistance to "[p]ersons who would be eligible for assistance if they were not in a medical facility, including those over 65 who are in mental or tuberculosis institutions." Prior to Medicaid, these specific institutions would not have been eligible for vendor payments because of those bars on vendor payments to such institutions that were traditionally thought of as the responsibility of states to maintain. *Id.* at 62.

[50] *See* 42 U.S.C. § 1396n(c)(1). Illinois' early "Community Care Program," focused on the aged but later extended to other populations, was one of the first in the nation. Brian B. Melamed, *An Examination of Issues Related to How Home and Community-Based Services Programs Operate Within Fixed Budgets and to the Administrative Linkages Between Eligibility Determination, Needs Assessment and Care Planning Functions*, U.S. DEP'T HEALTH & HUMAN SERVICES (December 1994), https://aspe.hhs.gov/reports/examination-issues-related-how-hcbs-programs-operate-within-fixed-budgets-administrative-linkages-0.

[51] Radaszewski, 383 F.3d at 604.

survive summary judgment. Title II of the ADA, which pertains to state and local governments, requires that "no qualified individual with a disability shall by reason of such disability, be excluded from participation in or be denied the benefits of the services, programs, or activities of a public entity, or be subjected to discrimination by such entity."[52] The District Court had originally rejected Eric's argument that this language prohibited the age distinction, protesting that "neither the Rehabilitation Act nor the ADA 'require[s] that the State create and fund a program that does not already exist' in order to enable a disabled person to be cared for in the most integrated community setting possible; rather what the statutes require is even-handed treatment."[53]

But when treatment should count as even-handed is the precise question at issue, and one that is underdetermined by the statutory text. When does treatment qualify as a "special" new benefit, and when does it consist simply of providing the healthcare called for under the circumstances such that denying it violates the standard coverage term of "medical necessity" construed as the requirement to meet needs evenhandedly? After all, a decision that requires leveling up to some other comparator to meet the requirement of "nondiscrimination" with respect to medical need can smuggle in claims to material provision, or what Super might consider a "functional" entitlement. Such determinations are made by courts and require a substantive conception of the contours of "adequate" healthcare and what it looks like to meet "medical needs." Indeed, the *Radaszewski* District Court at first recognized and resisted this implication of Eric's argument, complaining, "The [State] is not required to provide the handicapped more coverage than the non-handicapped individual to assure 'adequate health care.'"[54] Yet the Seventh Circuit decision, in reversing the District Court, proceeded to require exactly that, arguing that the provision of reduced nursing care, on the view that patients with greater needs should otherwise default to institutionalization to obtain such care, would amount to a prohibited exclusion of an individual with a disability from participation in society. They essentially declared that such conditioning of this increment of care upon institutionalization could not be considered healthcare remotely adequate for a person as a member of society.

Consistent with the then-recent landmark Supreme Court decision, *Olmstead v. L.C. ex rel Zimring*, which we will examine shortly, the Seventh Circuit in *Radaszewksi* interpreted the ADA's nonexclusion command to entail a so-called integration mandate. This mandate has been articulated by the Department of Justice regulations as a requirement for public entities to "administer services,

---

[52] 42 U.S.C. § 12132 (emphasis added).

[53] Radaszewski, 383 F. 3d at 607 (quoting Radaszewski v. Garner, 2002 WL 31045384 (N.D. Ill. September 10, 2002) at *3).

[54] *Id.*

programs and activities in the most integrated setting appropriate to the needs of qualified individuals with disabilities."[55] Making sufficient nursing care available only through institutional settings ran counter to this mandate.

Of course, *Olmstead* did not contemplate nor require bottomless resources: "[T]he State always has the opportunity to show that adapting existing institution-based services to a community-based setting would impose unreasonable burdens or fundamentally alter the nature of its programs and services, and for that reason, it should not be required to accommodate the plaintiff."[56] This standard resembles a proportionality test of the type that we discussed in Chapter 2. Such a test typifies the analysis that would be conducted in a right-to-health jurisdiction to determine whether a particular claim to healthcare could be limited. Under proportionality, the state does not have an absolute, indefeasible duty with regard to all possible sticks in the healthcare rights bundle; to defeat plaintiff's claim to any particular stick, the state could show weighty countervailing burdens. Mere recitation of cost burden would not suffice to overcome the rights-claim. And indeed, *Radaszewski* did not set the bar so low; it required a showing of such financial strain that the requirement would "fundamentally alter the nature . . . of programs and services."

In Eric Radaszewski's case, the appeals court determined that he was not laying claims to a new or fundamentally altered service: "The fact that the State already provides for some private-duty nursing tends to belie the notion that providing such care to Eric . . . would require the State to alter the substance of its Medicaid programs by creating an entirely 'new' service."[57] Here the court verges on the curious all-or-nothing, maneuver we observed earlier in situations where the courts felt plainly helpless to mandate provision. Is the Circuit Court suggesting that had the State not provided private duty nursing to children, its defense that extended nursing required "fundamental alteration" would have found more purchase? And that if it was to offer some benefits along these lines, it could not exclude adults? This case adds to the accumulated signals that some deeper pattern underlies these cases where courts reject line-drawing in health benefits.

Much of the rest of the Seventh Circuit *Radaszewski* opinion walks through the application not just of this test for the "fundamental alteration" defense, but also of the overarching test from *Olmstead* gauging whether the integration mandate is satisfied. This test consists of three prongs. First:

---

[55]   28 C.F.R. § 35.130(d).
[56]   Radaszewski, 383 F. 3d at 611 (citing 28 C.F.R. 35.130(b)(7) (implementing _____)).
[57]   *Id.* at 612.

[t]he State is obliged to provide community-based treatment for individuals with disabilities, so long as the State's treatment professionals find that such treatment is appropriate, [second] the affected individuals do not oppose community-based treatment, and [third] placement in the community *can be reasonably accommodated, taking into account the State's resources and the needs of others with similar disabilities.*[58]

This test, particularly the third prong italicized above, once again serves as a vehicle for rights-as-proportionality reasoning. In *Radaszewski*, the court's analysis under this prong weighs two competing considerations. On one hand, the plaintiff contends that "it would cost the State no more and possibly less to care for Eric at home than it would to care for him in an institution." Against this factor, the State argues that "moving one resident of a state-funded institution into the community does not necessarily mean that the State immediately could close or reduce the size of that institution," given that

[the State] may not always be able to fully realize the cost savings of placing an individual in a community setting rather than an institution. . . . A court must therefore take care to consider the cost of a plaintiff's care not in isolation but in the context of the care it must provide to all individuals with disabilities comparable to those of the plaintiff.[59]

This analysis again echoes typical right-to-health jurisprudence, involving fact-based determinations about the likelihood of polycentric cost impacts. For instance, the South African Constitutional Court, in applying a constitutionally guaranteed right to health, performs a similar analysis in the landmark case, *Minister of Health v. Treatment Action Campaign* (hereinafter *TAC*). In *TAC*, the South African Ministry of Health tried to defend its decision to offer nevirapine (a drug that prevents the transmission of HIV/AIDS during childbirth) only at certain pilot sites. The Ministry defended its limited program based partly on the budgetary burdens associated with providing a package of nevirapine support services, such as formula feeding and counseling, considered adjunct to administering the drug.[60]

Just as the *Radaszewski* court considers the likelihood that private nursing in the home will reduce spending on more expensive institutional care,[61] the

---

[58] *Id.* at 609 (emphasis added) (citing Olmstead v. L.C. ex rel Zimring, 527 U.S. 581, 607, 119 S. Ct. 2176, 2190 (1999)).

[59] Radaszewski, 383 F.3d at 614 (citing Olmstead, 527 U.S. at 604, 119 S.Ct. at 2189).

[60] Minister of Health v. Treatment Action Campaign 2002 (5) SA 721 (CC) at para. 71 (S. Afr.).

[61] Radaszewski, 383 F.3d at 614 ("If the State would have to pay a private facility to care for Eric, for example, and the cost of that placement equaled or exceeded the cost of caring for him at home, then it would be difficult to see how requiring the State to pay for at-home care would amount to an unreasonable, fundamental alteration of its programs and services").

TAC court had to consider the possibility of offsetting cost-savings for providing infant formula as part of the nevirapine support services package: "The
point is made here that the cost of providing breastmilk substitutes must also
be compared with or offset by the savings in preventing newborn babies being
infected with HIV and consequently needing care."[62] The court reasoned that
"the use of nevirapine would result in significant savings in later years because it
would reduce the number of HIV-positive children who would otherwise have
to be treated in the public health system for all the complications caused by the
condition."[63]

Ultimately in *Radaszewski*, the US appeals court concludes that there are legitimate factual issues that require a weighing of the likelihood of additional savings accruing to the offer of sufficient nursing in patients' homes rather than in
institutional settings alone. These issues suffice for Eric Radaszewski's claims to
survive the State's motion for judgment on the pleadings.

Radaszewski was indeed a signal case, one whose outcome reflects a judge-
led aversion to the implications of an age-limit to Eric's nursing care. The use of
Olmstead to achieve this result is hardly commanded by the Medicaid statute,
but a feat of judicial ingenuity. But it did not represent an isolated occurrence.
Radaszewski was followed a few years later by *Grooms v. Maran*, where the district court allowed the plaintiff-beneficiary's claims that his aging out of certain services under the Illinois Medicaid waiver also violated the ADA and the
Rehabilitation Act.[64] The judge rejected the state's motion for summary judgment and granted the plaintiff-beneficiary preliminary relief, signaling openness
to the claim that Illinois must reasonably accommodate a request for continued
home care when someone aged out.[65] The Washington State Supreme Court
ruled similarly in *Samantha A. v. Departments of Social and Health Services*,
striking a state formula that automatically reduced in-home personal care services if the beneficiary was a minor. In the state supreme court's eyes, this broad
age-based presumption regarding existing in-home help violated the Medicaid
comparability requirements discussed above.[66]

[62] Minister of Health v. Treatment Action Campaign 2002 (5) SA 721 (CC) at para. 91 (S. Afr.)
(hereinafter TAC). *See also id.* at para. 116 ("the use of nevirapine would result in significant savings
in later years because it would reduce the number of HIV-positive children who would otherwise
have to be treated in the public health system for all the complications caused by the condition").
[63] TAC (5) SA 721 at para. 116.
[64] 563 F.Supp.2d 840 (N.D. Ill 2008).
[65] *See id.* at 843.
[66] *See* Samantha A., 171 Wash.2d 623 (Wash. 2011).

Institutionalization

The *Radaszewski* age cut-off case is worth discussing at length because it prepares our discussion of institutionalization as a line of demarcation along which services are provided or denied. Not only were these Medicaid age cases about denials of healthcare to certain beneficiaries because of their age—they were also about the permissibility of institutionalization as the consequence of those cut-offs. Death and adverse health are ever at stake when the patient is denied care. Here, institutionalization was also in play as it represented the only other pathway to life-prolonging care that remained open to these Medicaid enrollees. A number of related cases therefore do not involve age but still feature a benefit boundary that requires patients to forsake living in the community-at-large in order to receive care. Such cases regularly rouse judicial sensitivity.

Olmstead, as noted earlier, was the seminal case. It was brought by two women with mental disabilities who were confined to an inpatient psychiatric hospital, even though their treating professionals judged their conditions capable of management in community-based programs. Georgia demurred in part because home- and community-based care for such patients was not required and indeed needed a waiver of Medicaid regulations at the time.[67] Had the state offered no home and community-based care enabling benefits, it is possible that in a similar suit by plaintiffs demanding such care, the state might have been able to avail itself of the "fundamental alteration defense" to the integration mandate. In other words, the law seemed to offer an all-or-nothing range of action, much like that in *White v. Beal* and the other cases noted above.[68] But Georgia actions occupied an awkward range of partial provision. The state had made available some possibility for nonconfined care management. The Court ruled that therefore the benefit could not be offered in a discriminatory manner consistent with the ADA. As the Supreme Court pointedly characterized it:

> Dissimilar treatment correspondingly exists in this key respect: in order to receive needed medical services, persons with . . . disabilities must because of those disabilities, relinquish participation in community life they could enjoy given reasonable accommodations, while persons without [such] disabilities can receive the medical services they need without similar sacrifice.[69]

---

[67] *See Intermediate Care Facilities for Individuals with Intellectual Disability*, CTRS. FOR MEDICARE & MEDICAID SERVS., https://www.medicaid.gov/medicaid/long-term-services-supports/institutional-long-term-care/intermediate-care-facilities-individuals-intellectual-disability/index.html (accessed December 16, 2022).

[68] *See, e.g.*, White III, 447 F. Supp. at 798.

[69] Olmstead, 527 U.S. at 600–01, 119 S. Ct. at 2187.

This type of treatment disparity between those who submit to institutional care and those who do not—a disparity that persons who are not severely disabled need not confront—was also illustrated in a 2003 case from the Tenth Circuit, *Fisher v. Oklahoma Health Care Authority*.[70] In *Fisher*, the court struck Oklahoma's newly imposed cap of five prescription drugs per month for those beneficiaries under the Medicaid Home and Community Based Services (HCBS) waiver program. Medicaid recipients in nursing facilities faced no such restriction. As with eyeglasses, prescription drugs remain officially an optional benefit under Medicaid, despite the fact that all states have chosen to offer them. Oklahoma Health Care Authority (OHCA) had been providing "all the prescriptions that are medically necessary" to persons institutionalized in nursing homes.[71] In the mid-1990s Oklahoma had also obtained a federal waiver for its Advantage Program, designed to extend home- and community-based medical and support services (HCBS) to beneficiaries whom they would otherwise have covered had they been in nursing homes.[72] Initially, the pharmaceutical coverage of these new beneficiaries was also uncapped.

The background statute neither required Oklahoma to cover prescription drugs, nor required the state to cover this category of HCBS beneficiaries at all. So why was the state barred from offering a select range of these optional services for the specified beneficiaries?

Oklahoma's HCBS prescription cap, which went into effect October 2002, "was based on a budgetary shortfall; defendants anticipated that capping the number of prescriptions available would save the state $3.2 million."[73] The Tenth Circuit held that this situation plausibly violated the ADA prohibitions against disability discrimination, in particular the integration mandate announced in *Olmstead* that charges governed entities with "administer[ing] services programs, and activities in the most integrated setting appropriate to the needs of qualified individuals with disabilities."[74] *Fisher v. Oklahoma* was among the spate of cases in *Olmstead*'s wake that demonstrated how substantive benefits might be claimed, or benefit cutbacks successfully challenged, by virtue of this principle that ostensibly required mere formal equality. The case was settled following this decision with Oklahoma's HCBS waiver participants ultimately permitted prescriptions beyond the mere five as long as they obtained prior authorization.[75]

[70] 335 F. 3d 1175 (10th Cir. 2003).

[71] *Id.* at 1178 (citing Okla. Admin. Code. § 317:35-3-2(15)(B)).

[72] Robert Mollica et al., *Home and Community Based Services in Oklahoma: A Systems Review*, NAT'L ACAD. FOR STATE HEALTH POL'Y (September 2005), http://muskie.usm.maine.edu/Publicati ons/2005/HCBS-OK-Systems-Review.pdf.

[73] Fisher, 335 F. 3d at 1178–79.

[74] 28 C.F.R. § 35.130(d).

[75] Jennifer Mathis, *Where Are We Five Years After Olmstead?*, 38 CLEARINGHOUSE REV. J. POVERTY L. & POL'Y 561, 574 (January–February 2005).

This result was especially striking in light of background cases like *Curtis v. Taylor* and *Alexander v. Choate*, upholding across-the-board benefit cut-offs.[76]

In *Curtis v. Taylor*, neither constitutional equal protection principles nor the Medicaid statute barred Florida's Medicaid program from capping physician visits to three per month. In *Alexander v. Choate*, the Supreme Court upheld Tennessee Medicaid's fourteen-day limitation on annual in-patient hospital care as consistent with the nondiscrimination provisions of the Rehabilitation Act, which, as we know, prohibited disability-based discrimination by recipients of federal funds long before the ADA came into force.[77] The Tennessee Medicaid recipients pointed out in *Alexander v. Choate* that people with disabilities would suffer disproportionately from this hard cap on inpatient days: "27.4% of all handicapped users of hospital services who received Medicaid required more than 14 days of care, while only 7.8% of nonhandicapped users required more than 14 days of inpatient care."[78] Nevertheless, the US Supreme Court ruled that this disparate impact did not violate § 504 of the Rehabilitation Act nor its implementing regulations. Instead, the Court upheld Tennessee's policy design despite the possibility that budgetary goals could have been fulfilled by more tailored limits on covered days, such as caps on days per spell of illness, without limiting the number of illness spells overall. The Court thus determined that "Tennessee is free, as a matter of the Medicaid Act, to choose to define the benefit it will be providing as 14 days of inpatient coverage."[79] This, the Court said, would comport with Medicaid's grant of discretion to the states to "set the contours of the amount, scope, and duration limitations on coverage, as long as care and services are provided in 'the best interests of the recipients.'"[80] As to the Rehabilitation Act claim, the Court rejoined: "The state has made the same benefit—14 days of coverage—equally accessible to both handicapped and nonhandicapped persons.... [T]he State is not obligated to modify its Medicaid program by abandoning reliance on annual durational limitations on inpatient coverage."[81]

This chapter poses the question: In light of precedents like *Alexander*, why are age, diagnosis, institutionalization or other kinds of limitations not equally within the state's discretion? Why doesn't this judicial latitude extend to states that contour benefits by limiting them to five prescriptions a month unless the beneficiary resides inpatient?

---

[76] 625 F.2d 645 (5th Cir. 1980); 469 U.S. 287 (1985).
[77] Alexander, 469 U.S. 287, 302–03 (1985).
[78] *Id.* at 290.
[79] *Id.* at 303 (citing 42 U.S.C. § 1396a(a)(19)).
[80] *Id.* (citing 42 U.S.C. § 1396a(a)(19)).
[81] *Id.* at 309.

These strangely vulnerable benefit boundaries seem to wither under the judicial gaze not only in the context of state Medicaid packages, but when used in private plans as well. In *K.F. ex rel Fry v. Regence Blueshield*, the employer-sponsored plan provided that "[a]s an alternative to hospitalization or other inpatient care, the Benefits of this Contract . . . will be provided for . . . home health care."[82] But it also contained other sections listing exclusions, one of which expressly denied payment for hourly nursing services.[83] This provision effectively restricted the beneficiary to institutional care in order to obtain the range of health services. The District Court refused to uphold this express carve-out, employing *contra proferentum* and the "reasonable expectations doctrine" to construe ERISA plan benefits language in such a way as to ensure that the reasonable expectations of the insured were met.[84]

Earlier we noted how courts policed the contours of state optional benefits, resisting benefit designs that were too meager, even while conceding the states' discretion to eliminate the benefits altogether. The body of ERISA benefits denial law as a whole dramatizes this same all-or-nothing pattern: when courts reject a cut-back in benefits, they are ironically disciplining the employer's limitation of benefits that they need not have offered in the first place under the voluntary system of employer-sponsored coverage. In *Fry*, the employer did not have to offer health benefits at all to its employees, much less health benefits that include home care.[85]

However, when an employer benefit plan purports to offer home care, then, according to *Fry*, it cannot be read on the one hand to promise home care as an alternative to inpatient nursing facility, while then significantly limiting nursing services in the home setting. Such a distinction based on "institutionalization status" would defy the "reasonable expectations" of what coverage for home care should constitute.

---

[82] 2008 U.S. Dist. WL 4330901 at *12 (W.D. Wash. September 19, 2008) (sic).

[83] *See id.* at 4.

[84] McHenry v. Pacificsource Health Plans, 679 F. Supp. 2d 1226, 1247 (D. Or. 2010) (explaining *Fry* thus: "In Fry, an ERISA-governed medical benefits plan provided home health care for medically necessary inpatient care. The plaintiff sought payment for hourly nursing services to provide that care, However, the plan expressly excluded payment for hourly nursing services. The court concluded that interpreting the plan to exclude in-home nursing would render its promise of substituted services illusory in most circumstances because one of the primary reasons for inpatient care is round-the-clock nursing services. More importantly, the court found that the exclusion for hourly nursing services did not clearly apply to the substituted service provision").

[85] *See Benefits Health Plans Must Cover under Washington State Law*, OFF. INS. COMM'R, https://www.insurance.wa.gov/benefits-health-plans-must-cover-under-washington-state-law (accessed December 16, 2022) (noting that home care is not among the mandated health benefits for individual or group health insurance in Washington State, but even if it were, under ERISA law, the employer has the option to self-insure rather than buy an insurance produce from a separate carrier and escape the mandated benefits); *see also* Metropolitan Life v. Massachusetts, 471 U.S. 724 (1985).

Each of these cases show courts reining in the use of a patient's institutionalization status as a parameter for benefit denial. This pattern comports with our prediction that the sensitive factors that courts are liable to reject will tend to be proxies for health need, or in some way central to the notion of what healthcare is for and why it matters. Indeed, this same parameter of institutionalization is identified in the ACA regulations as one of the canonical health-status–based factors along which discrimination is prohibited in the individual and small group markets. The relevant section in the Code of Federal Regulations reads:

(1) *Nonconfinement provisions*—(i) *General rule.* Under the rules of paragraphs (b) and (c) of this section, a plan or issuer may not establish a rule for eligibility (as described in paragraph (b)(1)(ii) of this section) or set any individual's premium or contribution rate based on whether an individual is confined to a hospital or other health care institution.[86]

As we noted in the previous chapter, the ACA has since catalyzed the formalization and codification into statute of some strands of this proto-rights thinking that had previously circulated in the courts.

Economic Want

We even see cases where courts, extending this logic, balk when insurers clip benefits along lines differentiating patients who lack financial resources.

These cases surprise our expectations in a number of ways. First, it is widely known that the US healthcare system exhibits a comparatively strong market-orientation; the individualized process of "weighing health against [one's] wallet" serves as an unfortunate primary sorting mechanism to determine who receives healthcare and who is denied.[87] Beyond this generalized conventional ideology, we find that our legal doctrine parrots a related view. Our case law contains numerous references to the background principle that US laws do not interfere with the plenary discretion of insurers to define benefits at will, even if those laws purport to hold insurers to the coverage that they ultimately choose to promise under these conditions of discretion. Typical is the language found in the Medicaid case, *Dodson v. Parham*:

---

[86] 29 C.F.R. § 2590.702(e).

[87] *See* Roosa Tikkanen & Robin Osborn, *Does the United States Ration Health Care?* COMMONWEALTH FUND (2019), https://www.commonwealthfund.org/blog/2019/does-united-states-ration-health-care (describing "weighing health against your wallet").

There is no requirement that a state fund every medically necessary procedure or item falling within a service it covers under its plan. To begin with, medical necessity and coverage are distinct concepts; a patient's medical necessity does not determine whether a particular item or services is covered . . . Title XIX afford states great latitude in determining the scope and extent of coverage of medical services.[88]

This statement, from a case involving a restrictive prescription drug formulary, seems to announce at-will discretion for Medicaid programs to shape their coverage footprints at the outset. They could choose to insure merely those items within a defined scope of coverage. Within that scope, each benefit authorization would be held to the medical necessity test, but some threshold benefit decisions would be instead a determination of whether the benefit category fell within the scope of coverage at all. Under this model, not every coverage delimitation is subject to the test of whether that benefit exclusion itself tracks the logic of medically necessity. However, this quote from *Dodson*, with its clear demarcation of scope of benefits as a zone of insurer discretion (apart from the test of medical necessity), is belied by the actual outcome of even that case itself.[89] We will return to discussion of *Dodson* later.

The background expectation that the health plan has discretion in defining the benefits it will cover as a step separate from the consideration of medical necessity extends even more readily to the private health plan context. In a landmark ERISA case, *Reid v. BCBSM Inc.*, the judge reaffirms that the threshold question of the scope of benefits is set by bargained-for employer health plan terms: "ERISA permits a plan participant, such as Reid, to sue 'to recover benefits due to [her] under the terms of [her] plan.'" The judge proceeds to distinguish as follows: "However, Reid's claim is not that [the benefit she seeks] *is* covered by her plan, her claim is that it *should* be. So she is not seeking to recover benefits due under the terms of the plan, she is seeking to change the terms of the plan, which ERISA does not permit."[90] In *Pegram v. Herdrich*, a unanimous Supreme Court recognizes that this distinction between the two facets of the coverage question can be a fine one to draw:

A great many . . . coverage questions are not simple yes-or-no questions, like whether appendicitis is a covered condition (when there is no dispute that a

---

[88]   Dodson v. Parham, 427 F.Supp. 97, 108 (N.D. Ga. 1977).

[89]   *See also* DeSario v. Thomas, 139 F.3d 80, 88 (1998) ("The district court's approach elides a threshold question. No matter how medically necessary a thing may be to a particular person (gloves are medically necessary to persons exposed to frost; a dwelling is medically necessary to an agoraphobe) or even to the population as a whole, the state need not (and in fact cannot) provide it unless it falls within a covered medical service").

[90]   984 F. Supp.2d 949, 955 (2013).

patient has appendicitis), or whether acupuncture is a covered procedure for pain relief (when the claim of pain is unchallenged). The more common coverage question is a when-and-how question.[91]

A number of ADA cases are notoriously sharp in distinguishing the "content" of the coverage product, reserved for the insurer's discretion, from the notion of "access" to the product, which the courts concede is subject to ADA nondiscrimination norms. This distinction is the one we saw operating in *Doe v. Mutual of Omaha*, where Seventh Circuit Judge Richard Posner reasoned: "A camera store may not refuse to sell cameras to a disabled person, but it is not required to stock cameras specially designed for such persons,"[92] just as "a store is not required to alter its inventory in order to stock goods such as Braille books that are especially designed for disabled people."[93] This notion of the insurers' discretion over what they offer as a market participant appears deeply rooted in the notion of private health coverage as a contract with all the preconceptions of voluntariness and discretion that attend our understanding of which contract terms a party offers and assumes.[94]

What is strange is that *despite* this background, we find unexplained pockets of resistance to the insurer's prerogative to define benefits in ways that shift the cost-burden onto patients. In reading these cases, one feels an almost palpable pressure on the courts, constantly threatening to collapse these matters of purported benefit design back into pure judgments of medical necessity, which beneficiaries, when supported by the authority of medical professionals, can more easily contest. If a service lacks medical necessity, the courts are demonstrably more comfortable finding against patient-beneficiaries and upholding insurance benefit denials; any other line-drawing begins to ratchet up judicial strain. This chapter tests the hypothesis that some exclusions seem to particularly rankle courts, and proposes that those exclusions tend to be the ones that not only fail to track the distinction between medically necessary and unnecessary care, but seem perversely to proxy for *greater* healthcare need. Economic want could conceivably fall in that category.

Medicaid, given the economic vulnerability of its population, underscores this dynamic whenever a benefit design imposes limitations on those with more costly needs. See, for instance, *Bontrager v. Indiana Family and Social Services Administration.*[95] Indiana Medicaid had limited its optional dental benefit to

---

[91] 520 U.S. 211 (2000).

[92] 159 F.3d 557, 560 (7th Cir. 1999).

[93] *Id.* at 559.

[94] *See generally*, Brian Bix, *Theories of Contract Law and Enforcing Promissory Morality: Comments on Charles Fried*, 44 SUFFOLK U. L. REV. 719 (2012).

[95] 697 F.3d 604 (7th Cir. 2012).

an annual maximum of $1,000. The Seventh Circuit nevertheless enjoined the cap because it was not "sufficient in amount, duration, and scope to reasonably achieve its purpose." The court rejected the State's argument that "the $1,000 cap does not prevent coverage of any medically necessary dental procedures," responding:

> [T]he cap prevents the State from providing coverage for all medically necessary services, and partial payment for such services does not constitute "some coverage," as the State would have us believe. To illustrate, a medically necessary procedure that costs $1,200 is not "covered" since the State's cap prevents full reimbursement to the provider. Although the State agrees to pay $1000, an indigent individual will likely be unable to pay the remaining $200 and will have to go without the procedure. The State's monetary contribution has no effect (i.e., the State ends up paying nothing) and the Medicaid recipient is left without recourse.[96]

The fact that this case asserting improper Medicaid benefits denial presented as a motion for preliminary injunction, adds a layer of doctrine that, as we saw earlier, favors the granting of entitlements to the patient seeking care. As Mark Hall and Gerard Anderson explain, the preliminary injunction context "requires the courts to balance the equities between the parties in a manner that inevitably favors avoiding the possible loss of life over the insurers' monetary loss."[97] This is because after considering the first prong of the preliminary injunction test, likelihood of success on the merits, courts must then weigh the likelihood of irreparable harm to the patient, and balance those harms with the harm that the preliminary injunction would inflict on the defendant-health plan, and finally whether the injunction would be in the public interest. This framework for handling the countervailing justifications as against the health interests once again calls to mind a weighted proportionality analysis.

In *Bontrager*, we accordingly find the court performing an analysis that also would not look out of place in a right-to-health jurisdiction. In *Bontrager*, the Seventh Circuit declared:

> The State's potential budgetary concerns are entitled to our consideration but do not outweigh the potential harm to Bontrager and other indigent individuals, especially when the State's position is likely in violation of state and federal

---

[96] *Id.* at 609.

[97] Mark Hall and Gerard Anderson, *Health Insurers' Assessment of Medical Necessity*, 140 U. PENN. L. REV. 1637, 1655 (1992) (citing Dozsa v. Crum & Forster Ins. Co., 716 F. Supp. 131, 140 (D. N.J. 1989) as standing for the proposition that "[w]eighing the various equities presents no difficulties. . . . Failure to provide treatment will probably result in death in a matter of months").

law. . . . The same reasoning applies to our consideration of the public interest. The Medicaid statute was designed to pay for the healthcare costs of "the most needy in the country."[98]

The court then cites *Dominguez v. Schwarzenegger* for the proposition: "We have repeatedly recognized that individuals' interests in sufficient access to health care trump the State's interest in balancing its budget."[99] The *Bontrager* opinion proceeds to suggest that the state could have considered less restrictive alternatives, apart from a crude dollar-based limit on services, to achieve its countervailing budgetary purposes:

> Moreover, there are other avenues by which the State can limit its exposure to significant Medicaid costs. . . . [for instance] "[a] state may also limit required Medicaid services based on its judgment of degree of medical necessity so long as such limitations do not discriminate on the basis of the kind of medical condition" . . . [and] the state may limit coverage "by narrowing the definition of medical necessity."[100]

This analysis—demanding sufficient weight for a countervailing financial interest to overcome the presumption in favor of protecting health, and then analyzing whether such methods of financial prudence were sufficiently tailored and least restrictive to health—is tantamount to a proportionality test. The judge in *Bontrager* imposes these rights-like constraints on State benefit design in the face of Indiana's threat that if it could not cap the benefit it might choose to "end coverage of all dental services under its Medicaid plan."[101] The judge retorts, "[T]he state's likely violation of state and federal law cannot be ignored in order to preserve the status quo."[102] One wonders if the awkward all-or-nothing posture of these cases is a symptom of the discursive constraint imposed by the weaponized marginalization of a right to health.

Formulary-style fee schedules for Medicaid prescription drugs, though less crude, also feature exclusions that inevitably throw up moments of conflict with enrollees' medical needs under financial straits. These, too, have had to bow to judicial pressure to accommodate medical necessity. In the aforementioned *Dodson* case, where the judge purported to espouse clear separation of the definition of the scope of benefits covered from the determination of medical necessity, we observed that the result belied the judge's stated principle. The judge

---

[98] Bontrager, 697 F.3d at 611–12.
[99] *Id.* at 612 (citing 596 F.3d 1087, 1098 (9th Cir. 2010)).
[100] *Id.* (citations omitted).
[101] *Id.*
[102] *Id.*

proclaimed in dicta that restrictive formularies were, in theory, permitted. Yet the actual case outcome enjoined the state drug formulary because Georgia did not have emergency exceptions or a "medically sound and effective prior approval system which would make non-[formulary] pharmaceuticals available to those who truly need them."[103] As for Georgia's protest that even without this emergency process, Medicaid recipients could simply pay first and then seek reimbursement later, the judge responded, "[W]e would be blinking reality to conclude that Medicaid recipients in the State of Georgia, who are by definition the 'categorically needy,' would have the financial capability to have diverse prescriptions filled in the interim."[104] Thus the provision of some emergency authorization in cases of medical necessity was judicially required.

Even in *Desario v. Thomas*, where the Second Circuit *accepted* formulary-style fee lists for durable medical equipment (DME) despite certain exclusions, court approval appeared to depend on Connecticut having furnished some opportunity for individual plaintiffs to appeal the reasonableness of any item's exclusion from the formulary.[105] The appeals court reasoned, "Given the availability of this hearing, any imperfection in the fee schedule can be cured through hearing-by-hearing consideration of the legality of excluding individual items of DME. Thus the use of the fee schedule to deny coverage does not violate Title XIX."[106] We will return to *DeSario* later as a counterexample to health-right-grounded internal preclusion and what that signifies for our hypothesized right to health.

Newton-Nations v. Betlach is yet another case that showcases judicial reluctance when it comes to beneficiary cost-sharing measures.[107] In the early 2000s, Arizona sought and received waivers from the George W. Bush administration lifting the statutory prohibition on imposing beneficiary copayments. Arizona sought to collect these copayments on optional and other ordinarily ineligible expansion groups, in particular childless adults under the poverty line. The state pointed out that these populations, covered by the grace of the state, would otherwise qualify for nothing whatsoever under Medicaid. Even limited by the condition that they shoulder a copayment in order to receive care, these groups were at least receiving some services compared to a baseline of zero. The Bush administration HHS agreed, granting Arizona its waiver. But the Ninth Circuit invalidated the copayment permission, even as to these nonmandatory "expansion" populations that might not otherwise have been eligible for Medicaid.

---

[103] Dodson, 427 F. Supp. at 108.

[104] *Id.* at

[105] DeSario, 139 F.3d at 97 n.13 ("For the purposes of this opinion, we assume that Connecticut will continue its practice of affording Medicaid recipients an opportunity to demonstrate at a fair hearing that the absence of the requested item of DME from the fee schedule renders the schedule unreasonable and inadequate with respect to the needs of the Medicaid population of the state").

[106] *Id.*

[107] 660 F.3d 370 (9th Cir. 2011).

As courts do when evaluating a potential rights infringement, the *Newton-Nations* court demanded that the Secretary produce a special justification for limiting coverage along this axis of increased beneficiary cost-burden. What doctrine underlay the courts interjection of this rights-based lens? The Secretary's waiver decision, subject to ordinary administrative law, must meet the Administrative Procedure Act (APA) standard that agency action not stray so far as to be "arbitrary and capricious." Over time, the application of the arbitrary and capricious standard to the government's § 1115 waiver approvals under the Social Security Act has assumed the form of a three-prong test, articulated in *Beno v. Shalala*.[108] First, the administrative record must support that the proposal has value as a demonstration, experimental or pilot project. Second, the project must be "likely to assist in promoting the objectives of the Act."[109] And third, the Secretary must show that "'the extent and period' for which she approves the proposal is necessary."[110] The prongs of this test map closely onto the type of proportionality reasoning that countries with health rights perform in enforcing those rights. The first prong asks if there is a sufficient value in the countervailing interest in scientific knowledge generation such that it might justify compromising the interest in enrollees' health. The second prong emphasizes that the interest of health is the primary value prioritized by virtue of the Medicaid statute, that is, the value or purpose that the court will generally expect state action to serve. And the third prong looks like a fit, or tailoring element—asking that the waiver of the protection last no more than necessary with respect to "the extent and period" of the waiver. Failure to produce this multi-part justification will render the Secretary's decision arbitrary and capricious.

In *Newton-Nations*, the Secretary's justification failed. The Ninth Circuit declared, "There is no evidence that the Secretary made 'some judgment that the project has a research or a demonstration value.' "[111] "The Secretary's second obligation under *Beno* is to 'consider the impact of the state's project on the' persons the Medicaid Act 'was enacted to protect,' "[112] and by the court's lights, the Secretary failed. The defect lay in the Secretary's absence of sufficient "consideration of the impact Arizona's demonstration project would have on the economically vulnerable."[113] When Arizona tried again to impose higher copayments on childless adults in poverty, this time under the Obama administration's grant of waiver authority, the Ninth Circuit acted yet again to strike down the

---

[108] 30 F.3d 1057, 1069 (9th Cir. 1994) (holding that § 1315 waiver to cut benefits statewide to recipients of AFDC was A&C because the Secretary, within the administrative record, must have "examine[d] each of th[ree] issues").

[109] *Id.*

[110] Newton-Nations, 660 F.3d at 380 (citing Beno, 30 F.3d at 1071).

[111] *Id.* at 381 (citing Beno, 30 F.3d at 1069).

[112] *Id.* (citing Beno, 30 F.3d at 1070).

[113] *Id.*

waiver for failure to meet the prongs of the *Beno* test.[114] The appeals court found that the Secretary's approval could not be shown likely to assist in promoting the objectives of the Act. The judge faulted the Secretary's silence in the face of accumulated evidence that increased copays do not produce savings and that deterring preventative primary care and essential medications leads instead to greater incidence of emergency room care and hospitalization for serious medical conditions.[115]

Earlier, we flagged the *NFIB* Medicaid holding as another decision that partakes of this seeming logic, namely, one where a healthcare provision that excludes the financially or otherwise needy from healthcare particularly offends the courts. Roberts proclaimed the new Medicaid expansion unconstitutional because it carved nonexpansion states out from the entitlement to "old" Medicaid funding as well. What was so sacrosanct about "old" Medicaid funding? Hesitant to pin the outcome solely on the size of conditional federal funding at stake, Roberts goes on to emphasize that taking away the money for "old" Medicaid leaves the "neediest among us" without funding. He seems to draw on some arguably extralegal norm—one suggesting that the health of any state's neediest should not be held hostage as an example to convince other states to participate.

Of course, the contradiction in the idea of health coverage structured to deny healthcare to those who are economically strained is at its most heightened in the context of Medicaid. Yet the imposition of higher cost-sharing also draws judicial heat in the Medicare context. *Hays v. Sebelius*, described at the outset of this chapter, serves as case in point. Medicare's "least cost alternative" (LCA) policy caps Medicare Part B reimbursement for a drug at the cost of any drug deemed to be a therapeutic alternative. Any surplus cost of the expensive drug above the LCA ceiling would fall upon the patient as an additional financial burden. The expectation was that this additional cost burden would incline patients and their providers to use the cheaper alternative instead.[116] Whatever the policy merits of this incentive structure, the measure was struck on statutory grounds, starkly dramatizing the all-or-nothing bind that courts have imposed in case after case. The drug could be covered or not in the court's view. Where this court drew the line was when Medicare chose instead to reimburse less. Rather than denying the drug outright, Medicare sought to influence patient choice by shifting the cost burden onto patients, and in this, it exceeded its authority.

Beyond Medicaid and Medicare, we have even caught hints of this judicial temper in the evaluation of private health plans against the scant regime of discipline we impose there. As implausible as it may seem, judicial tolerance for

---

[114] *See* Wood v. Betlach, 922 F.Supp. 2d 836 (2013).

[115] *See id.* at 850.

[116] *See The "Least Costly Alternative" Approach for Payment of Medicare Part B Drugs*, PEW CHARITABLE TRS. (2016), http://pew.org/1UfucUl (accessed August 23, 2021).

private insurer discretion over the extent of the cost-sharing they impose may also have its limits. Conventional wisdom might question why the terms and contours of private employer coverage would be anything but a matter for employer discretion. Certainly, employers can be held to their promises, but they are private employers, so they need not promise anything at all, or so the thinking goes. And yet in the case *In Re Epipen*, plan participants sued over the excessive cost-sharing they were charged for this important drug to prevent anaphylactic shock. The participants argued that based on the plan administrators' (pharmaceutical benefit managers in this case) negotiated price structures that inflated the list price for EpiPens, plaintiffs' coinsurance and deductible payments rose as a result. The excessive list prices had to be paid in full by those patients who had not reached their deductible. Moreover, the pricing structure increased patients' coinsurance burden, since those payments are typically set as a percentage of the list price, which plaintiffs argued was inflated. A federal district court permitted the case to go forward, finding that plan participants plausibly stated a claim under ERISA for breach of fiduciary duty.[117]

Arbitrary Physical Characteristics

Courts also flinch from measures that deny health protection based on arbitrary physical traits. In *Lorillard* as mentioned before, the Supreme Court struck the no-lower-than-5-foot restriction on indoor advertising *in part because of its failure to protect the health of taller children*.[118] This under-protection of health doomed the rule's chances under the *Central Hudson* test, which is ironically not a health rights doctrine, but a test for the protection of speech rights.[119] The doctrinal pathway to the Court's rejection of height-based exclusions runs through the tailoring prong of this First Amendment test. The Court conceded that Massachusetts' interest in protecting children's health from tobacco was "substantial, and even compelling," but the under-inclusiveness of the five-foot rule "provides only ineffective or remote support for the government's purpose."[120] Therefore, the tobacco advertising restriction isn't justified; it doesn't draw enough justificatory force as a health protection to qualify as a permissible limitation of speech. Health provisions are thus scrutinized for their adequacy. Under *Central Hudson* prong three, they must directly and materially advance the asserted governmental interest. And this reasoning has curious implications. Would expanding health protection to taller children have satisfied the Court,

---

[117] 341 F.Supp.3d 1015 (D.Minn. 2018).

[118] Lorillard Tobacco Co. v. Reilly, 533 U.S. 525 (2001).

[119] Central Hudson Gas & Elec. Corp. v. Pub. Serv. Comm'n, 447 U.S. 557 (1980).

[120] Lorillard, 533 U.S. 525, 564 and 566 (2001).

and what are we to make of a First Amendment doctrine that might have required *greater* restriction of speech, and correspondingly *greater* protection of children's health?

In the end, this decision may reveal less about how we value speech, and more about our conception of health. What we learn is that the height parameter strikes the Court as an irrational way to mark off the protection of health. As I have said of this case before:

> Differentiation by height or sightlines may not perfectly align with the needs Massachusetts was trying to address through health protection, but is it particularly sensitive . . . To be sure, this intervention does not cast judicial competence at elaborating health rights in the best light. However, granting the Court the benefit of the doubt, it may have bridled at the irrationality of using natural physical endowments as a disqualification from health protection, since health provision is meant precisely to minister to people in whatever physical circumstances they may confront. The Court, in short, ascribes trumping qualities to health values such that brute luck physical attributes must be precluded as reasons for denying health protection.[121]

Take also the case of *Reed v. Walmart Stores, Inc.*[122] In *Reed*, the employer plan denied autologous stem cell transplant for a breast cancer patient because less than ten of her lymph nodes were affected. The court condemned this distinction as arbitrary and capricious, given evidence in the record that "[p]laintiff's six node disease[] 'was biologically exactly the same as the patient that [the Defendants] would cover under the plan.'"[123]

The employer protested that in denying Reed the procedure, it was consistent in following its own decision rule that Stage II patients with the involvement of ten or more lymph nodes would be included among the "[p]atients who are at high risk of relapse who could benefit from this therapeutic approach."[124] Because Reed did not meet this criterion, her procedure would be considered experimental by Walmart.

The District Court took a deep dive into the record and found the treatment at issue would not help those with ten or more positive lymph nodes either, because "the treatment, *across the board*, has not been proven to be more effective than standard adjuvant therapy." The judge's medical reasoning was sound in this case as we learned from our earlier discussion of the medically justified, though

---

[121] Christina S. Ho, *Are We Suffering From an Undiagnosed Health Right*, 42 AM. J. OF L. & MED. 743, 769 (2016).
[122] 197 F.Supp. 2d 883 (E.D. Mich. 2002).
[123] *Id.* at 891.
[124] *Id.* at 886.

legally ineffective insurance restriction on HDCT/ABMT for breast cancer starting from the late 1980s. The judge continues,

> Since the treatment, *across the board*, has not proven its efficacy, it would appear that the Plan would offer it to no one, regardless of the number of nodes affected. Yet the Plan chooses to cover only women with Stage II breast cancer with 10 or more lymph nodes affected.[125]

The District Court plainly recoils from deciding based on the arbitrary physical distinction of the number of nodes affected: "[I]t was medically irrational to distinguish between ten node disease and six node disease with aggressive pathology."[126] This passage reeks of the all-or-nothing attitude we have now grown accustomed to in so many health cases.

The judge therefore declared Walmart's denial "arbitrary and capricious," violating the minimum rationality to which employer plans are held. The judge also ruled that the terms "experimental" and "investigational" were ambiguous, and therefore triggered *contra proferentum* to favor the insured in construction of the terms of the health plan.[127]

In *Baker v. Physicians Health Plan of Northern Indiana Group Health Plan*, a court also questioned the rationality of a coverage denial that hinged on a physical characteristic, namely consistency of breast tissue.[128] Under the patient's plan terms, breast reduction surgery could either count as cosmetic, and therefore excluded, or as medical in nature and thereby covered. The plan employed a set of guidelines to sort surgeries into the categories of "cosmetic" or "medically necessary" based on the relationship between weight of the tissue removed and body surface area. These guidelines drew from a study which found that lower ratios of removed tissue relative to body surface correlated with women's nonmedical motivations for the procedure. The *Baker* court rejected this crude associational approach, objecting that "the paper says nothing about the actual health benefits of mammoplasty or how much tissue must be removed to reduce symptoms."[129]

In *Baker*, the plaintiff would have had to reach a numerical threshold of 750 grams of tissue removed from each breast to qualify as receiving medically necessary surgery. Her surgeon's notes had in the preapproval process estimated that 800 grams would be removed, thus qualifying the plaintiff for coverage of the mammoplasty. However, in the course of the surgery, the actual weight of the tissue removed was just short of 600 grams per breast, and the plan refused

---

[125] *Id.* at 890.
[126] *Id.* at 893.
[127] *See id.* at 888.
[128] 2007 WL 1965278 (N.D. Ind. 2007).
[129] *Id.* at 4.

to pay.[130] Her physician explained that the difference in actual versus predicted tissue mass is because "[t]issue deep within the breast is quite variable in its consistency as well as its weight." He also emphasized the medical purpose of the intervention, noting that "the patient's symptoms have been greatly helped, which was the whole medical indication for this procedure."[131]

The *Baker* judge ruled that because the dispositive factor under these guidelines (the weight of breast tissue excised) was so far removed from whether the procedure improved women's health and quality of life outcomes, the plan's criterion was therefore "downright unreasonable."[132] The plan's definition of cosmetic procedures, the judge reasoned, did not depend upon the patient's motivation. Instead, the plan defined a cosmetic procedure as one "that improves physical appearance but does not correct or materially improve a physical function."[133] The judge decided in *Baker* that the surgery did improve a physical function and that denying coverage of such a procedure was arbitrary and capricious and therefore a violation of ERISA.

Discussion

For those who have stuck with this *tour d'horizon* of US health law jurisprudence, it should be clear that the phenomenon is not a one-off. The sheer mass of cases exhibiting the various hallmarks of rights reasoning that we identified in Chapter 2 is remarkable.

To be sure, this jurisprudence does not advertise itself as "rights protection." It is instead *proceeding under the guise of other doctrines*. Sometimes the underprotective health law is struck as arbitrary and capricious, which is as we have seen, a subconstitutional standard scrutinizing fit. The judicial application of this "arbitrary and capricious" standard under some recurring circumstances, like the review of § 1115 waivers in Medicaid, can sediment into articulated tests whose coincidence with the signature proportionality-style tests of rights protection we have noted in this chapter.

In other cases, exceptions were ruled to be violations of medical necessity, a standard coverage term in health statutes and contracts, thus rendering the exclusions contrary to medical need, and thereby subject to internal preclusion. Dworkinian rights grammar has, in this sense, burrowed into our methods of statutory and contractual interpretation.

---

[130] *See id.* at 4–5.
[131] *Id.* at 6.
[132] *Id.* at 8.
[133] *Id.* at 11.

Certain canons in the construction of contract terms facilitate this rights-like analysis. As we found repeatedly above, whenever courts find ambiguity, the background maneuver of *contra proferentum* allowed them to apply a presumption in favor of granting the insured's health coverage demand.[134]

Moreover, under longstanding ERISA jurisprudence,[135] courts typically reviewed an employer's administration of its contractual plan terms under the "arbitrary and capricious" standard, thus creating new opportunities for courts to import their own fit norms by declaring that the parameter by which the plan clipped its scope of coverage to be "arbitrary," or a breach of "fiduciary duty." Cases where courts strike down a plan denial as inconsistent with the insurer's promise to provide necessary care (or to provide care sufficient for persons to live as "integrated" members of the community) inevitably reflect what judges think necessary, normal, and adequate healthcare looks like.[136]

As we noted earlier, these cases seeking private or public coverage of healthcare also frequently arise in the preliminary injunction context, and the balancing test governing preliminary injunctions also lends itself to analysis closely resembling that of rights-based proportionality tests.

Rights-like reasoning can also appear as questions of constitutional fit, but under the auspices of far less rights-oriented constitutional norms, such as various tests for the enumerated powers under Article I, or the First Amendment balancing test of *Central Hudson*.

Counterexamples

Once we hypothesize that rights-thinking is at work, we can, with this account, explain not only when the internal preclusion logic appears but also when it does not.

There are many instances when courts deem ordinary countervailing reasons good enough to justify an exclusion or carve-out from health protection. There are countless cases where courts conspicuously decline to question the form that carveout takes. The pattern we have discerned thus far exerts its influence as an arguably "extralegal," unacknowledged norm, so it should not surprise us when it is not consistently followed. What does surprise is that such a hidden norm determines outcomes to the extent that it does, something we have tried to

---

[134] *See* Mark A. Hall & Gerard F. Anderson *Health Insurers' Assessment of Medical Necessity*, 140 U. PA. L. REV. 1637, 1684 (1992).

[135] *See* Firestone, 489 U.S. 101.

[136] *See, e.g.*, Wit v. United Behavioral Health, 2019 WL 1033730 at *13; Arnold v. Blue Shield of California, 2012 WL 5904735 (N.D. Cal. 2012); Egert v. Connecticut General Life Ins., 900 F.2d 1302 (7th Cir. 1990); Baker v. Physicians Health Plan of Northern Indiana Group Health Plan, 2007 WL 1965278 (N.D. Ind. 2007); Evans v. W.E.A. Ins. Trust, 361 N.W.2d 630 (Wis. 1985).

demonstrate by showing the veritable raft of cases where it operates. Moreover, we would expect this snip of rights DNA to be absent from judicial reasoning sometimes just by virtue of the background noise of case outcomes overall. But I would like to suggest here that sometimes the absence of this rights-logic reveals something about the cultural conception of health that judges harbor.

Courts, for instance, shy away from imposing this level of scrutiny in cases relating to sexual and reproductive health. This reticence over time hints that the implicit judicial conception of the scope of necessary healthcare may not extend to certain kinds of sexual, gender-affirming and reproductive healthcare. Such an explanation can also account for the judicial failure to police exclusions in certain cases involving durable medical equipment.[137]

Abortion Funding Cases

Dobbs v. Jackson Women's Health Organization has upended the constitutional status of abortion such that legislatures may now regulate, limit or even prohibit this medical procedure altogether.[138] But even when abortion decisions were considered part of the constitutionally protected right to privacy under *Roe v. Wade* and its progeny, claims to funding and coverage of the procedure were viewed as having no greater purchase than the funding and coverage of other medical services, and indeed came to be treated somewhat worse.[139]

While a pre–Hyde Amendment line of case law had permitted state Medicaid programs to exclude what were called "non-therapeutic" abortions, namely, ones that were not "medically necessary," certain states went further and excluded a number of "therapeutic" abortions from their Medicaid programs as well.[140] In those restrictive states, even a medically necessary abortion could be denied coverage unless the mother's life, severe health complications, or, sometimes, rape or incest, were at issue. In *Preterm, Inc. v. Dukakis,* the First Circuit had originally struck this type of coverage restriction, following the pattern of the cases we have documented throughout this chapter until this point. The First Circuit held that it was inconsistent with Medicaid's statutory "reasonableness" requirement for a state to prohibit medically necessary abortions except the subset of medically necessary abortions required to save the woman's life.[141]

---

[137] *See* DeSario, 139 F.3d. 80 (1998).

[138] 597 U.S. ___ (2022).

[139] Roe v. Wade, Wade, 410 U.S. 113 (1973); Planned Parenthood of Southeastern Pa. v. Casey, 505 U.S. 833 (1992).

[140] *See, e.g.,* Beal v. Doe. 432 U.S. 438, 440–41 (1977); Maher v. Roe, 4 32 U.S. 464, 481 (1977).

[141] *See* Preterm, Inc. v. Dukakis, 591 F.2d 121, 126–27 (1st Cir. 1979).

However, Congress had by then begun to modify the underlying Medicaid funding conditions themselves, ultimately undercutting this holding. The Hyde Amendment was adopted as a yearly appropriations rider starting in 1976 and it *prohibited* states from using federal Medicaid matching funds to provide abortions, whether therapeutic or otherwise. The only exceptions to this federal Medicaid ban were again those cases involving rape, incest, severe health effects, and life-endangerment for the mother.[142] States could, however, use their own funds to provide some level of abortion-coverage beyond Hyde levels, and the vast majority have.[143] In *Harris v. McRae*, the Supreme Court broke from the direction charted in *Preterm v. Dukakis* and proceeded instead to uphold the Hyde Amendment, affirming that states had no legal obligation to provide even medically necessary abortions above the Hyde-defined minimum.[144] The judicial authorization to deny abortion as a medical service to those in need clearly flouts the rationality of internal preclusion, thus contrasting with the judicial treatment of other healthcare services that we have observed. Yet the exclusion of abortion excited little if any scrutiny for fit. The Court breezily declared the Hyde measure to be "rationally related to the legitimate governmental objective of protecting potential life."[145]

The Supreme Court's tolerance for abortion carve-outs extends to non-Medicaid subsidies as well. Missouri state funded certain public hospitals to provide medical care, including pregnancy-related services. However, the state banned public employees and public facilities from performing or assisting in abortions, preserving only a narrow exception for cases of life-endangerment. Advocates challenged this law with an all-or-nothing type of argument now familiar to us. In the grip of the conventional wisdom that we lack a right to health, they concede that Missouri did not have to use its discretionary state funds for public hospitals at all. But as long as the state did, they argued that it should not be allowed to condition those funds in such a way as to burden Due Process rights like those protected at that time under *Roe v. Wade*.[146] Nevertheless, the Court declined to treat the abortion carve-out as sensitive, despite the then-constitutionally recognized status of abortion. It allowed ordinary political preferences to weigh against the medical needs of women with unwanted

---

[142] Hyde Amendment, Pub. L. No. 94–439, § 209, 90 Stat. 1418, 1434 (1976). Initially, the Hyde Amendment included exceptions if the mother faced endangerment of life, severe endangerment of health, or in cases of rape or incest. *Id.* In the 1980s, the Congress pared these exceptions back to instances where the life of the mother was endangered. Supplemental Appropriations and Rescission Act of 1981, Pub. L. No. 97-12 § 402, 95 Stat. 14, 95-96 (1981).

[143] *See Whose Choice? How the Hyde Amendment Harms Poor Women*, CTR. FOR REPROD. RTS. (September 13, 2010), http://www.reproductiverights.org/sites/crr.civicactions.net/files/docume nts/Hyde_Report_FINAL_nospreads.pdf?_ga = 1.126399437.1959154140.1477102676.

[144] *See* 448 U.S. 297, 326 (1980).

[145] *Id.* at 325.

[146] *See id.* (citing Roe, 410 U.S. 113 (1973)).

pregnancies, saying, "[T]he Constitution does not forbid a State or city, pursuant to democratic processes from expressing a preference for normal childbirth as St. Louis has done."[147] Weighing countervailing considerations in the ordinary political trade-off process is enough, and nowhere did the Court display any impulse to preclude ordinary trade-offs from consideration.

By contrast, prescription drugs, private duty nursing, and even eyeglasses and dentistry were presumptively valued against financial considerations. But medical response to pregnancy is not granted that presumption. Indeed, these women's claims can be traded off and overcome by nearly any countervailing preference; ordinary political choice in favor of childbirth is sufficient. Clearly courts in this domain ceased to invoke the "trumping" function of rights to preclude countervailing considerations. By implication, coverage of abortion does not warrant treatment as a right in the Court's eyes.

Gender-Affirming Surgery Cases

When Medicaid excludes gender-affirming surgery, we have seen the courts similarly decline to preclude the countervailing arguments that are weighed against medical need.

In *Smith v. Rasmussen*, the Iowa Medicaid program covered medically necessary care but specifically *carved out gender-affirming surgery*. The appeals court upheld the states' discretion to exclude this care, denying the medical necessity of these procedures. In rejecting the plaintiffs' health need for these treatments, the court perceived no internal contradiction between excluding transition surgery and valuing health.[148] Iowa's line-drawing was thus permissible, rather than suspect, and in the Eighth Circuit's view, did not exclude medically necessary care on the basis of "diagnosis, type of illness, or condition." In rendering this decision, the appeals court notably cast aside a prior case, *Pinneke v. Preisser*, and the precedential force it carried.

In *Pinneke*,[149] the Eighth Circuit had earlier found, relying on *White II*, that Medicaid's reasonableness requirement forbade Iowa's exclusion of sex-reassignment surgery if such a procedure represented the only therapy for the condition of gender dysphoria.[150] "We find that a state plan absolutely excluding the only available treatment known at this stage of the art for a particular condition must be considered an arbitrary denial of benefits based solely

---

[147] Webster v. Reproductive Health Services, 492 U.S. 490 (1989).
[148] *See* Smith v. Rasmussen, 249 F.3d 755 (8th Cir. 2001).
[149] 623 F.2d 546 (8th Cir. 1980).
[150] *See id.* at 548 n.2.

on the 'diagnosis, type of illness, or condition.'"[151] Just as had transpired with abortion procedures, though, this application of the *White II* Medicaid reasonableness doctrine to gender-affirming surgery was abruptly suspended. By the time *Smith* came along, the Eight Circuit surmised that there were other treatment alternatives, and thus Iowa enjoyed the leeway to choose among treatment options. To explain its changed stance, the Eighth Circuit pointed to the fact that Iowa had in the meantime commissioned a review from an outside medical peer review organization which discovered post-*Pinneke* research and divergent medical views questioning the efficacy of the surgery and suggesting that other therapies such as "hormone treatment, psychotherapy, and situational treatment may be more appropriate, and at times more effective."[152]

Contrast that framing with the *Pinneke* opinion, announcing that "[t]he decision whether or not certain treatment or a particular type of surgery is 'medically necessary' rests with the individual's physician and not with clerical personnel or government officials."[153] The *Pinneke* judge deferred to the judgment of the physician on what was needed in an individual case with its particular circumstances. By the time of *Smith v. Rasmussen*, however, Iowa had conducted a survey of states and found that the vast majority of state Medicaid programs did not provide coverage for gender-affirmation surgery, and therefore reinstated its exclusion.[154] The *Smith* decision upheld Iowa's reinstated exclusion, concluding that as long as *some* treatment for gender dysphoria is covered, the carveout did not draw lines on the basis of diagnosis. Because the treatment was not thereby judged medically necessary, the benefit exclusion did not conflict with, or serve as a proxy for, health need. Dworkinian preclusion was not activated.

The contrast between this case and the handling of carve-outs for other types of treatment prompts the question: Are judges really treating gender-affirming surgery as a part of healthcare, with the kind of regard and scrutiny that has been accorded elsewhere on that score? As demonstrated by Congress's intervention through the Hyde amendment, courts may not have the final say. The conversation to settle on a conception of healthcare, the need for which is treated as peremptory against countervailing considerations, is necessarily a dialogue among different actors. Agencies and legislatures may, and indeed do, countermand the conception proffered by the courts. For instance, Medicare, although it has declined to issue a National Coverage Determination mandating coverage, has as of May 13, 2014 lifted its national coverage rule mandating exclusion.[155]

---

[151] *Id.* at 549.

[152] Smith, 249 F.3d at 760.

[153] Pinneke, 623 F.2d at 550.

[154] *See* Smith, 249 F.3d at 761 n.5.

[155] *See* Memorandum from Ctrs. for Medicare and Medicaid Servs., Final Decision on Gender Reassignment Surgery for Medicare Beneficiaries with Gender Dysphoria (August 30, 2016),

Since then, states have weighed in. The Washington state legislature, for example, enacted S.B. 5313, which requires its Medicaid program and state-regulated health insurance plans to cover medically necessary gender-affirming healthcare as of 2022.[156] At the other end of the political spectrum, Alabama and Arkansas have criminalized certain gender-affirming care, only to face lawsuits to block implementation.[157]

Durable Medical Equipment Cases

Some types of durable medical equipment (DME) also seem to overstep the courts' implicit conception of medical care, causing judges to conspicuously abstain from questioning the lines of partial exclusion when those items are involved. As we saw in *DeSario*, Connecticut had limited the DME that it would reimburse to those items listed on its fee schedule, specifically excluding categories such as air conditioners, room size humidifiers, and air purifiers.[158] The court tolerated these categorical exclusions, despite the precedent set by *Dodson v. Parham*. In *Dodson*, as we recall, the court enjoined Georgia's formulary-style drug list that left out categories of medically necessary drugs. The *Dodson* judge ruled that Georgia's discretion to slice the scope of its benefits stopped short of what it had done here. The state should have left an individualized escape hatch, some "medically sound and effective prior approval system which would make non-[formulary] pharmaceuticals available to those who truly need them."[159] *Dodson* exemplifies the resistance to benefit cut-offs that fail to accommodate medical need, and the judicial tendency to meld consideration of medical necessity into the judgment of whether the state decides to cover that scope within its benefit basket at all.

Compare that attitude to the court's decision in *DeSario* rejecting the District Court's injunction of Connecticut's DME formulary exclusions:

https://www.cms.gov/medicare-coverage-database/view/ncacal-decision-memo.aspx?proposed= N&NCAId=282.

[156] *See* S.B. 5313, 67th Leg., Regular Sess. (Wash. 2021), https://www.billtrack50.com/billdetail/ 1276290/17935.

[157] H.B. 1507 93rd Gen. Assembly, Regular Sess. (Ark. 2021), https://www.arkleg.state.ar.us/Bills/ Detail?id=HB1570&ddBienniumSession=2021%2F2021R.. *See* Alabama ban on gender-affirming care for transgender youth takes effect, NBC NEWS (May 9, 2022), https://www.nbcnews.com/nbc- out/out-politics-and-policy/alabama-ban-gender-affirming-care-transgender-youth-takes-effect- rcna27913 (accessed June 13, 2022).

[158] DeSario, 139 F.3d at 83.

[159] Dodson, 427 F. Supp. at 108.

We give ready deference to the Secretary's assessment. [The State's] definition of DME establishes a rational distinction between equipment that is primarily medical in nature and devices principally employed for non-medical purposes that might incidentally benefit someone with a particular condition.[160]

The judge then describes a parade of horribles that would otherwise demand inclusion as well, including "clear glass cookware and table dishes," "electric heaters," "all natural bedding," "vacuum cleaner[s] designed for allergic and chemically sensitive people," "organic food," and "bottled water in glass bottles."[161]

Connecticut had tellingly never even argued against plaintiffs' medical need for the DME items they requested. "Instead," as the court explains, "the [State] has taken the position that the requested equipment [is] excluded from coverage under her definition of DME because the items are useful to individuals in the absence of illness or injury."[162]

Why did courts treat the prescription drug formulary differently from the DME formulary? Why is the state's leeway to define the scope of benefits, regardless of medical necessity, accepted for the latter but not the former? Why does the court scrutinize drug formularies for rationality, but accept the rationality of DME lists? What drives the court's distinction is a skepticism about whether the DME items are within the domain of healthcare.

In *DeSario*, the appeals court accepts as "rational" the state's "distinction between equipment that is primarily medical in nature, and devices that can be employed for nonmedical purposes that might incidentally benefit someone with a particular condition."[163]

This definition of the outer boundary of what constitutes healthcare that we might presumptively prioritize in cases of medical need was advanced by a Second Circuit judge in *DeSario*. But the dialogue continued across other branches of government. In response to this case, HHS, a federal agency issued what has come to be known as "the *DeSario* Letter," announcing in 1998 that states had permission to "develop a list of pre-approved items . . . as an administrative convenience," but only on the condition that they supply a "reasonable and meaningful procedure for requesting items that do not appear on a State's pre-approved list." Reasonability would be judged according to the procedure's "consisten[cy] with the objectives of the Medicaid statute."[164] Once again, pure

---

[160] DeSario, 139 F.3d at 89.
[161] Id.
[162] DeSario v. Thomas, 963 F. Supp. 120, 133 (D. Conn. 1997).
[163] DeSario, 139 F.3d at 80.
[164] Letter from Sally K. Richardson, Dir., Dept. Health & Human Servs., to Dir. Ctr. for Medicaid & State Operations (September 4, 1998), https://www.medicaid.gov/Federal-Policy-Guidance/downloads/SMD090498.pdf.

discretion over which benefit categories to offer, without regard to medical need, was forbidden.

That articulation has itself come under pressure. Sixteen years later, in *Detgen*, the Fifth Circuit permitted Texas to exclude ceiling lifts categorically regardless of this letter guidance. The court tried to navigate the tension between its position and the HHS guidance using the following analysis:

> Deference to the [*DeSario* Letter] is not an issue, because the state has not violated its requirements: the letter says only that if a state has a pre-approved list, there must be some way to prove need for items not on it. This letter says nothing about the possibility of a state's deciding that some items shall be on a "never approved list," that is some items may be categorically excluded. It would be perfectly consistent with federal law and this letter to adopt a list of pre-approved devices for convenience and a list of categorical exclusions if based on reasonable grounds, such as the availability of more cost-effective alternatives, and to permit a beneficiary to demonstrate need for an item on neither list.[165]

Texas Medical Home Health Services thus denied coverage for chair lifts because its list of durable medical equipment excluded "[s]tructural changes to homes, domiciles, or other living arrangements . . . Patient lifts requiring attachment to walls, ceilings, or floors . . . are not a benefit of Home Health Services."[166] Texas did provide coverage for what the court characterized as "more cost-effective alternatives," thereby rendering the exclusion "reasonable" under to the Fifth Circuit's rubric above. Such alternatives included "transfer boards, freestanding track . . . lifts, transfer chair systems for use with the bath or commode, and manually or electronically operated floor lifts."[167]

The Fifth Circuit also declined to question the distinctions it might have found sensitive in other contexts. For instance, the plaintiffs protested that "the state provides ceiling lifts to those younger than twenty-one" as part of the child-focused EPSDT benefits required in the Medicaid statute. But the opinion brushes aside this argument. It does so by pointing to the unusual statutory language describing the special Early Periodic Screening, Diagnostic and Treatment (EPSDT) benefits that Medicaid guarantees specifically to children with a textual provision mandating that states provide medically necessary services arising in this category "whether or not such services are covered under the state plan."[168] The Fifth Circuit reasoned that the existence of this language

---

[165] Detgen v. Janek, 752 F.3d 627, 632–33 (5th Cir. 2014).
[166] Detgen v. Janek, 945 F. Supp 746, 756, 757 (N.D. Tex. 2013) (citing Sections 2.2.14.26 and 2.2.24 of the Texas Medicaid Provider Procedures Manual).
[167] Detgen, 752 F.3d at 632.
[168] *Id.* (citing 42 U.S.C. § 1396d(r)(5)).

would be superfluous unless the background law contemplated the possibility of distinctions made by age and by coverage status of services. If adults were not limited by the state plan's delineation of benefit boundaries, there would be no need for the statute to insist on special access for children under the EPSDT protections to services not covered.[169]

Thus, *Detgen* held that ceiling lifts could be provided as a categorical matter by Texas Medicaid to children only, but denied to those over twenty-one, even if medically necessary.

These examples show that in the context of durable medical equipment, courts may decline to administer the same scrutiny they bring to other categories of benefits. The language in these opinions also suggests that a conception of whether the claimed items are healthcare or some other category of product, be it home improvement or consumer appliance, drives the courts' selective scrutiny. While the courts' behavior in this regard is not terribly consistent, this explanation might account for some of the most prominent outlier cases, including *Detgen v. Janek, Smith v. Rasmussen*, and *Harris v. McRae*.[170]

Courts are defining which traits and circumstances qualify a person for health protection and doing so by process of elimination. Judges are, in the course of their work, inevitably declaring which properties one should *not* use to disqualify a patient from treatment: namely, diagnosis, age, institutionalization, arbitrary physical characteristics, even, on occasion, lack of financial resources.

Yet as the counterexamples show, courts are simultaneously selecting the health measures to subject to this scrutiny. Courts decide where they will and where they won't add this extra measure of friction even when these sensitive lines crop up. This court behavior is tantamount to picking and choosing the treatments that they view as within the scope of the right.

Judges are inescapably picking and choosing the items and services that they subject to heightened scrutiny over line-drawing, meanwhile leaving others to ordinary political trade-off or market discretion. How is this sorting any different from deciding which sticks belong in rights bundle?

Judges' selection of triggering fact patterns to scrutinize for the justifiability of limiting factors implicitly demarcates not only the permissible and impermissible boundaries of eligibility (e.g., prohibiting limits based on age, diagnosis, height), but also the domain of the entitlement subject to such justification requirements (e.g., eyeglasses but not gender-affirming treatments, tobacco control but not abortions).

---

[169] *Id.* at 633.
[170] *See, e.g.*, Koenning v. Suehs, 2012 WL 4127956 (S.D. Tex. September 18, 2012); Davis, 821 F.3d 231.

Judge-Made Conceptions of Health Rights

It should be plain to us by now that judges cannot avoid engaging in a common law elaboration of their substantive visions of the right to health. Through every decision they render, they are in effect selecting the attributes that *cannot* disqualify a person from the treatment, as well as which treatments they will subject to such close, justification-demanding review. Recall in the last chapter our model of "a right in the abstract form, where S is the set of circumstances (traits, eligibility standards) that qualify someone to right, R." The specification of a right thus involves asking "What is in the set of traits S that qualify you for the right, R?" If judges are defining S by process of elimination, that is, identifying traits that cannot be included in S, and if they are at the same time defining R by declaring the treatments for which medical need is the qualifying trait, then judges are limning a health right.

One of the payoffs of this lens, which shows where judges are engaging in rights-building, is that it also reveals where we must focus our advocacy. We have uncovered a map locating the treatments whose coverage denials are not scrutinized by judges for their reasonableness, despite insurers' use of parameters that conflict internally with the need for healthcare in the first place. Those pockets show us where we must cultivate an inclusive conception of health, incorporating such items as the structural aspects of a dwelling including lifts and air purification. Housing infrastructure is a powerful determinant of health, a truth at which the judges in *DeSario* and *Detgen* seem to scoff. Reproductive and sexual healthcare could not be more intimately connected with human flourishing, but have been invidiously carved out. The battle on these fronts should be joined with every tool at our disposal, and my call here is not to overlook the right to health as a weapon at hand. With that, we turn from the descriptive to the prescriptive chapters of this project.

5

Health Impact Assessments as a
Negative Right to Health

The greatest health challenges today are complex and have many linked contributing factors, some of which operate far upstream, outside what we conventionally regard as health policy. It is by now widely recognized that policies beyond the traditional health sector affect our health outcomes no less than policies within our so-called health system.[1] An oft-cited early report from the Centers for Disease Control credited medical care with only 10–15 percent of the reductions in mortality achieved during the twentieth century.[2] Our knowledge base has now grown to recognize how "social determinants of health" may have at least as much effect on health outcomes.[3]

The Need to Consider Health Even in Deciding
Non–Health Policies

Thanks to environmental law, many of us recognize that hazardous chemical exposures in our air, water, food, and workplaces burden human health. But we are increasingly learning more about the importance of our social and economic conditions as well.

Despite what the judges in the *Detgen* and *DeSario* cases from Chapter 4 insisted, housing and our built environment are examples of upstream policy-driven factors that affect population health in complex socially mediated ways.[4] For instance, lopsided mortgage interest subsidies to the affluent divert resources from quality affordable housing options, which we know in turn subjects people

With permission, chapter 5 contains material that was originally published in Christina S. Ho, *Health Impact Assessments: A Negative Procedural Health Right?* 50 SETON HALL L. REV. 643 (2020).

[1] *See, e.g.*, Centers for Disease Control and Prevention (CDC), *Ten Great Public Health Achievements—United States 1900–1999*, 48 MMWR MORB MORTAL WKLY REP. 241 (April 1999).

[2] *Id.*

[3] *See, e.g.*, Jessica Mantel, *Tackling the Social Determinants of Health: A Central Role for Providers*, 33 GA. ST. U. L. REV. 217 (2017).

[4] Lauren Taylor, *Housing and Health: An Overview of the Literature*, HEALTH AFFS., Health Policy Brief, June 7, 2018, doi: 10.1377/hpb20180313.396577. For discussion of *Detgen* and *Desario* cases, *see* Chapter 4, text accompanying notes 104 and 157–69.

to hazardous exposures such as lead or mold. Indeed, our policy paradigms, such as those that beget urban sprawl, have been associated with numerous other health effects. One study found that for every 1 percent increase in county compactness (a sprawl index), "traffic fatality rates fell by 1.49 percent and pedestrian fatality rates fell by 1.47 percent.[5] These effects are a function of government action.[6] For example, federal housing financing has long favored low-density single-family homes.[7] Government-financed roads literally paved the way for the automobile.[8] Development assumed its particular character because of single-use zoning laws as well as ordinances stipulating setbacks and parking.[9] The effects on human well-being, through physical, mental, and social pathways, have been manifold.[10] Meanwhile, housing instability among renters gravely harms health, especially the health of children in the household.[11] Yet the US Department of Housing and Urban Development under the Trump administration pursued new work requirements to encumber what housing assistance we do make available.[12]

The governance of work itself has permitted scheduling and other arrangements to offload ever more contingency onto workers, exacerbating toxic stress and fatigue.[13] And each sector we examine reveals the source of additional health burdens. Our transportation policies often create new accident

[5] Reid Ewing and Shima Hamidi, *Compactness v. Sprawl: A Review of Recent Evidence from the United States*, 30 J. OF PLANNING LIT. 413 (2015), Paula Braveman, *Housing and Health*, Robert Wood Johnson Foundation Issue Brief No. 7, EXPLORING THE SOCIAL DETERMINANTS OF HEALTH (2011).

[6] KENNETH T. JACKSON, CRABGRASS FRONTIER: THE SUBURBANIZATION OF THE UNITED STATES 229–30 (1985).

[7] See *id*. See also, Emily Badger, *How the Federal Government Dramatically Skews the U.S. Real Estate Market*, CITYLAB, January 8, 2013 (documenting that even recently "FHA, for instance, funneled just one-tenth of its $1.2 trillion in loan guarantees over the past five years toward multi-family housing"). See also, Heather Hughes, *Securitization and Suburbia*, 90 OR. L. REV. 359 (2011) (tracing how laws governing commercial finance facilitate sprawl).

[8] See Jackson, *supra* n.6.

[9] *Id*.

[10] Andrew L. Dannenberg et al., *The Impact of Community Design and Land-Use Choices on Public Health: A Scientific Research Agenda*, 93 AM. J. PUB. HEALTH. 1500, 1500–1508 (2003).

[11] Megan Sandel et al., *Unstable Housing and Caregiver and Child Health in Renter Families*, 141 PEDIATRICS 2017 (2018), doi: 10.1542/peds.2017-2199.

[12] Kriston Capps, CITYLAB, HUD May Push New Work Requirements for Public Housing Residents (February 2, 2018), https://www.citylab.com/equity/2018/02/hud-floats-work-requireme nts-for-public-housing-residents/552173/.

[13] See, e.g., HUMAN IMPACT PARTNERS, SCHEDULING AWAY OUR HEALTH (July 2016), http://www. humanimpact.org/wp-content/uploads/Scheduling-Away-Our-Health_rev3.pdf. Such transformation of the workforce has been facilitated by government designation of these workers as outside certain categories of protection. See, e.g., KARLA WALTER AND KATE BAHN, CENTER FOR AMERICAN PROGRESS, RAISING PAY AND PROVIDING BENEFITS FOR WORKERS IN A DISRUPTIVE ECONOMY (October 13, 2017), https://www.americanprogress.org/issues/economy/reports/2017/10/13/440 483/raising-pay-providing-benefits-workers-disruptive-economy/. See also JEFFREY PFEFFER, DYING FOR PAYCHECK (2018).

and other risks, as the rise of the railroad[14] and the automobile have made clear.[15]

Our agricultural and economic development subsidies may be transferring risk from agricultural and fast-food enterprises to individuals. When we subsidize corn rather than fruits and vegetables, even as cheap high-fructose corn syrup has fostered excessive consumption of added sugars, do we consider the potential health effects?[16] Meanwhile, the Small Business Administration has poured funding into fast food franchises in low-income neighborhoods in the name of urban revitalization,[17] even as land, zoning, and other regulations deterred supermarkets from locating there.[18]

Socioeconomic conditions, including relative social position, are powerful determinants of health.[19] Even when poverty and deprivation are not themselves pressing health threats, the health effects of socioeconomic status (SES) factors do not disappear. The level of inequality in a society itself can impose health burdens on the community.[20] Comparing equally wealthy countries, health outcomes are superior in egalitarian societies compared to ones with steeper

[14] MARK ALDRICH, DEATH RODE THE RAILS: AMERICAN RAILROAD ACCIDENTS AND SAFETY 1828–1965 (2006). For discussion of how tort law responded to this externalization of costs by railroads onto others, see MORTON HORWITZ, THE TRANSFORMATION OF AMERICAN LAW 1780–1860 97–101 (1977) (observing that "most of the cases involving injuries to persons or property after 1840 were brought about by the activity of canals or railroads").

[15] See, e.g., JERRY L. MASHAW & DAVID L. HARFST, THE STRUGGLE FOR AUTO SAFETY (1991). See, e.g., Sandro Galea, Making the Acceptable Unacceptable, Dean's Note (June 4, 2015), https://www.bu.edu/sph/2015/06/14/making-the-acceptable-unacceptable/ (observing that "Despite a dramatic increase in number of vehicle miles traveled, we reduced, in just one generation, the risk of motor vehicle fatality five-fold [through] road safety, advocacy for safer driving, and legal disincentives for unsafe driving"). For a recent example of our subsidization of transportation technologies, including self-driving automobiles presumably with inadequate regard for health risk, see Jerry Hirsh, Elon Musk's growing empire is fueled by $4.9 billion in government subsidies, L.A. TIMES (May 30, 2015), http://www.latimes.com/business/la-fi-hy-musk-subsidies-20150531-story.html.

[16] See, e.g., Scott Fields, The Fat of the Land: Do Agricultural Subsidies Foster Poor Health? 112 ENVIRONMENTAL HEALTH PERSPECTIVES A820 (2004). See also, David Wallinga, Agricultural Policy and Childhood Obesity: A Food Systems and Public Health Commentary, 29 HEALTH AFF. 405 (2010).

[17] Karina Christiansen, Franchising Inequality, 36 HEALTH AFF. 1141 (June 2017), https://doi.org/10.1377/hlthaff.2017.0575.

[18] Alan Ehrenhalt, The Grocery Gap, GOVERNING (April 2006), http://www.governing.com/topics/mgmt/Grocery-Gap.html.

[19] MICHAEL MARMOT, STATUS SYNDROME: HOW SOCIAL STANDINGS AFFECT OUR HEALTH AND LONGEVITY (2004); R. G. WILKINSON, UNHEALTHY SOCIETIES: THE AFFLICTIONS OF INEQUALITY (1996), R. G. WILKINSON, MIND THE GAP: HIERARCHIES, HEALTH AND HUMAN EVOLUTION (2000). Angus Deaton, Health Inequality and Economic Development, Working Paper, Princeton University Research Program in Development Studies and Center for Health and Wellbeing, 2001). See also, Joshua Holland, High Inequality Results in More US Deaths Than Tobacco, Car Crashes and Guns Combined, MOYERS & COMPANY (April 19, 2014), http://billmoyers.com/2014/04/19/high-inequality-results-in-more-us-deaths-than-tobacco-car-crashes-and-guns-combined/#.VY1GJPrs9dk.twitter

[20] For a succinct account, see, NORMAN DANIELS, JUST HEALTH 83–7 (2008); NORMAN DANIELS et al., IS INEQUALITY BAD FOR OUR HEALTH (2001).

economic gradients.[21] Yet our tax policies are ever more unequal with predictable health impacts.[22] For instance, every ten percent reduction in the Earned Income Tax Credit increases infant mortality by 23.2 per 100,000 births.[23]

Education is arguably the socioeconomic status factor most profoundly correlated with health outcomes. Globally, educational status, especially of that of the mother, as well as literacy,[24] particularly male-female disparity in adult literacy, are among the strongest predictors of life-expectancy.[25] Meanwhile, our system leaves far too many behind as the fashioning of choice or charter policies and diversion of funding to private schools reinforce disparity in educational opportunity.[26]

Incarceration policies harm prisoner health in lasting ways while also affecting the children of incarcerated parents. Even the health of other members of the community suffers from what has been memorably dubbed "toxic exposure" to mass incarceration.[27]

As yet uncertain-health threats lurk in other non–health sector policies: for instance special immunities granted to social media platforms subsidize them at the expense of young people who face more mental health risks, particularly if

---

[21] RICHARD WILKINSON, MIND THE GAP: HIERARCHIES, HEALTH AND HUMAN EVOLUTION (2000). *See also* Kate Pickett and Richard Wilkinson, *Income Inequality and Health: A Causal Review*, 128 SOC. SCI. AND MED. 316 (2015). *See also* Marmot, *supra* n.19; Nancy Adler et al., *Reaching for a Healthier Life: Facts on Socioeconomic Status and Health in the U.S*, The John D. & Catherine T. MacArthur Foundation Research Network on Socioeconomic Status and Health (2008), http://www.macses.ucsf.edu/downloads/reaching_for_a_healthier_life.pdf.

[22] Tax Cuts and Jobs Act of 2017, Pub. L. 115–97, 131 Stat. 2054 (2017).

[23] Peter A. Muenig et al., *Cost Effectiveness of the Earned Income Tax Credit as a Health Policy Investment* 51 AM. J. PREVENTIVE MED. 874, 874–881 (2016). *See also*, William H. Dow et al., *A Way Out from Rock Bottom: Economic Policies Can Reduce Deaths of Despair* (July 7, 2019), https://voxeu.org/article/economic-policies-can-reduce-deaths-despair.

[24] Emmanuela Gakidou et al., *Increased Educational Attainment and Its Effect on Child Mortality in 175 Countries Between 1970 and 2009: A Systematic Analysis*, 376 THE LANCET 959 (2010).

[25] *See* DANIELS, *supra* n.20 at 85 (2008).

[26] D. Goldman & J. P. Smith, *The Increasing Value of Education to Health*, 72 SOC SCI MED 1728, 1728–37(2011); Stuart J. Olshansky et al., *Differences in Life Expectancy Due to Race and Educational Differences Are Widening, And Many May Not Catch Up*, 31 HEALTH AFF. 1803 (2012). *See also*, Bruce D. Baker, *Exploring the Consequences of Charter School Expansion in U.S. Cities*, ECONOMIC POLICY INSTITUTE (November 30, 2016), http://www.epi.org/publication/exploring-the-consequences-of-charter-school-expansion-in-u-s-cities/#_ref14.

[27] ERNEST DRUCKER, A PLAGUE OF PRISONS: AN EPIDEMIOLOGY OF MASS INCARCERATION IN AMERICA (2013) (describing in Chapter 8 the effects of the "toxic exposure" to mass incarceration on individuals and their communities). Christopher Wildeman, *Imprisonment and (Inequality in) Population Health*, 41 SOC. SCI. RES. 74 (2012) (showing that parental incarceration substantially increases infant mortality risk). Mark L. Hatzenbuehler et al., *The Collateral Damage of Mass Incarceration: Risk of Psychiatric Morbidity Among Nonincarcerated Residents of High-Incarceration Neighborhoods*, 105 AM. J. PUB. HEALTH 138 (2015). *See also*, Ingrid Binswanger et al., *Epidemiology of Infectious Disease–Related Death After Release from Prison, Washington State, United States, and Queensland, Australia: A Cohort Study*, 131 PUB HEALTH REP. 574 (2016), https://www.ncbi.nlm.nih.gov/pmc/articles/PMC4937119/. Prison Policy Initiative, *New Data: State Prisons Are Increasingly Deadly Places*, https://www.prisonpolicy.org/blog/2021/06/08/prison_mortality/ (accessed June 11, 2021).

they are vulnerable because of gender, sexual identity, or other characteristics.[28] Whole literatures exist to examine the relationship between global trade and human development.[29]

A structured regime of health impact assessments (HIAs) would provide a way to frame some of these arguments in the language of a procedural right, one that is not altogether unfamiliar to us. We already in some contexts provide that whenever non–health laws are deliberated, people are entitled to demand an accounting of the associated health burden and a justification of the attendant suffering.[30] We have yet to extend this approach to its logical conclusion.

When trade agreements and economic legislation affect health, as they have by fostering the global spread of tobacco, why are the trade proponents exempt from proving that there is no less health-restrictive alternative?[31] After all, nations that impose sanitary and phytosanitary policies must justify them as the least trade-restrictive.[32] Health should be accommodated when laws grant government monopolies that raise the price of drugs, and indeed there are scattered but underutilized provisions for public health-based exceptions from government-granted exclusivities for inventions and plant varieties.[33] In theory, a frank embrace of health rights could equip us to trim back federal grants of liability relief to gun manufacturers to narrowly tailor the impingement on health-health interests.[34]

The institutionalization of what is often called a "Health in All Policies" approach is desirable for reasons that have been set forth powerfully and thoroughly by others. My case for HIAs is different; I argue that we should do so to correct the tilt against health that arises because we have already enacted

---

[28] 47 U.S.C. § 230 (providing liability relief to internet platforms); David D. Luxton et al., *Social Media and Suicide: A Public Health Perspective*,102 Am. J. Pub. Health S195, S195–S200 (2012); Rae Ellen Bichell, *Suicide Rates Climb in U.S., Especially Among Adolescent Girls*, National Public Radio (April 22, 2016), http://www.npr.org/sections/health-shots/2016/04/22/474888854/suicide-rates-climb-in-u-s-especially-among-adolescent-girls.

[29] *See, e.g.*, Amartya Sen, Development as Freedom (1999).

[30] *See infra* text accompanying n.63 to n.68.

[31] *See, e.g.*, Benn McGrady, Trade and Public Health: The WTO, Tobacco, Alcohol, and Diet (2011).

[32] *See* Benn McGrady & Christina S. Ho, *Identifying Gaps in International Food Safety Regulations*, 66 Food & Drug L.J. 183, 190 (2011).

[33] 7 U.S.C. § 2404 (2012); 28 U.S.C. § 1498(a); 35 U.S.C. § 203. *See also*, World Intellectual Property Organization, Exclusions from Patentability and Exceptions and Limitations to Patentees' Rights (2015). *See also* 42 U.S.C. § 7608 (allowing compulsory licenses for devices for reducing air pollution).

[34] 15 U.S.C. §§ 7901–7903. Charles E. Koop & George Lundberg, *Violence in America: A Public Health Emergency Time to Bite the Bullet Back*, 267 JAMA 3075 (1992). *See also* Robin West, Re-Imagining Justice: Progressive Interpretations of Formal Equality, Rights, and the Rule of Law (2003) (describing a case where a Texas district court judge held that a man's constitutional right to bear arms trumps the public safety policy protected by a federal law forbidding domestic violence offenders from owning firearms.) *citing* U.S. v. Emerson, 46 F. Supp. 2d 598 (N.D. Tex. 1999), *rev'd* and *remanded* 270 F.3d 203, 261–63 (5th Cir. 2001) (reversed on the basis that though the federal law protecting public safety did not protect a right, it was sufficiently narrowly drawn to coexist with the right to firearms).

analogous requirements that cultivate rights around competing non–health values. Indeed, without HIAs, our current regime of regulatory analysis privileges those values over health using rights-grammar in a way that has long gone unobserved and unexplained. These *other* regulatory impact assessments (RIAs) elevate economic freedom for small business, freedom from paperwork, economic protection for states and localities, religious liberty, and more.[35] To institutionalize HIAs would not represent an unprecedented normative leap, but a mere recalibration of the playing field.

These other purposes compete with and burden health and we need some means of checking them. There are human costs to the unfettered pursuit of human welfare and development narrowly construed as consumption, production, and trade.[36] HIAs supply a way of making these arguments so that government action advancing neoliberal interests at the expense of human health can be tailored, mitigated, or even blocked.

HIAs and Their Significance

Use of HIA to call for an accounting of such government policies would not necessarily take the form of a right to affirmative provision, but a claim of freedom from these health-harming measures. The claim contrasts with the approach of some libertarian scholars who conceptualize the negative right to health as a freedom from government restriction of *choice* in medical treatment.[37] Their narrower medical autonomy right would disfavor mandatory vaccination and possibly invalidate FDA premarket drug approval requirements.[38] This is a blinkered and not necessarily health-promoting view of the government's role in health, as Jennifer Prah Ruger and others have deplored.[39] But a negative right to health properly conceived in the form of an HIA regime would meaningfully address some of the major health challenges we confront today.

HIA has been defined as "a combination of procedures, methods, and tools by which a policy, program, or project may be judged as to its potential effects on

---

[35] For the argument that religious liberty is a new guise for economic libertarianism, *see*, Elizabeth Sepper, *Free Exercise Lochnerism*, 115 COLUM. L. REV. 1453 (2015).

[36] *See, e.g.*, Joseph Stiglitz et al., FOR GOOD MEASURE: ADVANCING RESEARCH ON WELL-BEING METRICS BEYOND GDP, (2018), https://doi.org/10.1787/9789264307278-en.

[37] Abigail R. Moncrieff, *The Freedom of Health*, 159 U. PA. L. REV. 2209 (2011). Abigail R. Moncrieff, *Safeguarding the Safeguards: The ACA Litigation and the Extension of Indirect Protection to Nonfundamental Liberties*, 64 FLA. L. REV. 639 (2012) (hereinafter Moncrieff, *Safeguarding*); Eugene Volokh, *Medical Self-Defense, Prohibited Experimental Therapies, and Payment for Organs*, 120 HARV. L. REV. 1813 (2007).

[38] *Id.*

[39] Jennifer Prah Ruger, *Responding to Eugene Volokh, Medical Self-Defense, Prohibited Experimental Therapies, and Payment for Organs*, 120 HARV. L. REV. 1813 (2007).

the health of a population, and the distribution of those effects within the population."[40] In short, the HIAs I propose would subject federal government action to a routine accounting of its impact on health and the distribution of health.[41]

HIAs conventionally involves six stages: screening, scoping, assessment, recommendations, reporting, and finally, monitoring and evaluation.[42] Sometimes called the Liverpool approach, the sequence of steps has been specified in the literature as follows:

> [A]pplying a screening procedure to select policies or projects for assessment; defining the scope of the health impact assessment in terms of depth, duration, spatial and temporal boundaries, methods, outputs, and the like; policy analysis; profiling the areas and communities likely to be affected by the policy; collecting qualitative and quantitative data on potential impacts from stakeholders and key informants, using a predefined model of determining health impact; evaluating the importance, scale, and likelihood (and, if possible, cost) of potential impacts; searching for the evidence to validate data; undertaking option appraisal (i.e., developing and choosing from alternative options) and developing recommendations for action; and monitoring and evaluating results following implementation.[43]

HIA differs from some related tools.[44] Risk assessments, for instance, are focused on discrete chemical exposure scenarios rather than the comprehensive consideration of a wider array of upstream health determinants.[45] Cost-benefit analysis (CBA) includes less qualitative information than HIA, and HIA emphasizes a deliberative process, rather than an analytical approach, especially in the screening, scoping, assessment, and recommendation steps.[46]

---

[40] Andrew L. Dannenberg et al., *Use of Health Impact Assessment in the U.S.: 27 Case Studies, 1999–2007*, 34 AM J PREV MED 3 241–256, 241 (2008). *See also* National Research Council, IMPROVING HEALTH IN THE UNITED STATES: THE ROLE OF HEALTH IMPACT ASSESSMENT 5 (2011) (hereinafter "For the Public's Health") (defining HIA much as the Gothenburg paper, *infra* n.57, does, to mean "[a] systematic process that uses an array of data sources and analytic methods and considers input from stakeholders to determine the potential effects of a proposed policy, plan, program, or project on the health of a population and the distribution of those effects within the population. HIA provides recommendations on monitoring and managing those effects").

[41] In this chapter, I explore the policy of a federal HIA requirement, although, HIA requirements at state, transnational and other levels are also important steps forward.

[42] *See* For the Public's Health at 7.

[43] Eileen O'Keefe & Alex Scott-Samuel, *Human Rights and Wrongs: Could Health Impact Assessment Help?* 30 J.L. MED. & ETHICS 734, 735 (2002).

[44] *See e.g.*, Center for Disease Control and Prevention, *Different Types of Health Assessment*, Healthy Places (last updated October 21, 2016), https://www.cdc.gov/healthyplaces/types_health_assessments.htm; World Health Organization, *Other Impact Assessments*, Health Impact Assessment (HIA), http://www.who.int/hia/tools/other_IA/en/ (accessed January 15, 2018).

[45] James Hodge et al., *Integration of Health and Health Impact Assessments Via Environmental Policy Acts*, The Network for Public Health Law (December 22, 2016), https://www.networkforphl.org/_asset/ltcwv8/PEW-HIA-NEPA-Stage-1---Report-FINAL.pdf.

[46] For the Public's Health, *supra* n.42, at 127–128.

Link Between Health Impact Assessment and Equity

Equity itself is often said to be integral to the project of population health.[47] For instance the effect of socioeconomic status (SES) factors on health is steeper for those who are worse off. Therefore "transfers of resources from the best-off to the worst-off SES groups would improve aggregate health and would have little negative effect, if any, on the best-off groups."[48] The implication is that improving population health, and certainly doing so within a resource horizon, necessitates equity. Also, built into the conventional methods of health impact assessment are a number of equity-promoting features, First, the identification of affected groups and communities is integral to the methodology, as we see in the six stages described above.[49] HIAs by nature screen for differential impact, thereby detecting disparities both in baseline health, but also in the health outcomes attributable to a given policy. Furthermore, the analytical steps described above specifically call for the participation of stakeholders.[50] Some observers have also argued that when non–health policies impose health burdens, those burdens tend to fall unequally, "disproportionately affect[ing] the already disadvantaged."[51] Given this persistent pattern, efforts focused on health impacts will tend to promote equity, rather than remain neutral to distribution.[52]

Moreover, as I mentioned earlier, there is accumulating evidence that inequality is a major determinant driving poor health outcomes. Therefore any measure that screens for detriment to health will tend to flag for scrutiny those policies that exacerbate inequality.[53]

However, as is the case with all rights, the equity-promoting valence of HIAs can be disrupted or reversed.[54] The National Research Council is careful to note

---

[47] For one view of how population health inherently contemplates health equity, see David Kindig & Greg Stoddart, What Is Population Health?, 93 AJPH 380 (2003).

[48] NORMAN DANIELS, JUST HEALTH 85 (2008).

[49] Stakeholder Participation Working Group of the 2010 HIA in the Americas Workshop, Guidance and Best Practices for Stakeholder Participation in Health Impact Assessment (March, 2012), http://www.pewtrusts.org/~/media/assets/2012/03/01/guidance_best_practices_stakeholder_pa rticipation_hia.pdf.

[50] See supra text accompanying n.43.

[51] See O'Keefe supra n.43 at 735.

[52] Id. See also, R. Quigley et al., Health Impact Assessment International Best Practice Principles. Special Publication Series Number 5, International Association for Impact Assessment: Fargo USA. (2006) (on file with author) (outlining a set of values underlying HIAs); but see, For the Public's Health, supra n.40, at 94.

[53] See supra text accompanying n.19–21. Richard Wilkinson & Kate Pickett, The Science Is In: Greater Equality Makes Societies Healthier and Richer, EVONOMICS (January 26, 2017), http:// evonomics.com/wilkinson-pickett-income-inequality-fix-economy/.

[54] See, e.g., Duncan Kennedy, The Critique of Rights in Critical Legal Studies, in LEFT LEGALISM/ LEFT CRITIQUE 178 (Wendy Brown & Janet Halley eds., 2002); Paul D. Butler, Poor People Lose: Gideon and the Critique of Rights, 122 YALE L.J. 2176 (2013); Peter Gabel, The Phenomenology of Rights-Consciousness and the Pact of the Withdrawn Selves, 62 TEX. L. REV. 1563 (1984); Morton J. Horwitz, Rights, 23 HARV. C.R.-C.L. L. REV. 393 (1988); Mark Tushnet, An Essay on Rights, 62 TEX. L. REV. 1363 (1984); Mark Tushnet, The Critique of Rights, 47 SMU L. REV. 23 (1993); Robin West, A

that the pro-equity character of HIAs is a contingent and possibly temporary feature: "HIA could conceivably contribute to health inequities if more socio-economically or politically advantaged communities develop greater capacity to demand HIA or if health issues that are highlighted in HIA are focused on the health needs of the advantaged."[55]

History and Precedent

HIAs are what I have called a "shovel-ready" proposal insofar as they are familiar and increasingly widely employed both domestically and internationally. Some have sourced the HIA tool's origins in the World Health Organization (WHO) Ottawa Charter on Health Promotion of 1986, which called for the "systematic assessment of the health impact of a rapidly changing environment—particularly in areas of technology, work, energy production, and urbanization."[56] WHO followed with a Gothenburg Consensus document on HIAs in 1999.[57] In 2006, HIAs were recommended as a standard for screening large World Bank projects and are now adopted by the Bank's private sector counterpart, the International Finance Corporation.[58] Their use has proliferated globally. British Columbia and Quebec require HIAs for all government legislation.[59] HIAs are included in the Thai constitution. The London mayor's office construed HIAs as part of the office's statutory remit for a number of years.[60] Finland, Australia, New Zealand, Wales, and the European Community have to varying extents adopted HIA practices.[61]

Tale of Two Rights, 94 B.U. L. REV. 893 (2014); Robin L. West, *Tragic Rights: The Rights Critique in the Age of Obama*, 53 WM. & MARY L. REV. 713 (2011); Peter Westen, *The Rueful Rhetoric of "Rights,"* 33 UCLA L. REV. 977 (1986). *See also*, Octavio Luiz Motta Ferraz, *The Right to Health in the Courts of Brazil: Worsening Health Inequities?*, 11 HEALTH & HUM. RTS. 33 (2009). *See also* Solomon R. Benatar, *Human Rights in the Biotechnology Era*, 2 BMC INT'L HEALTH AND HUM. RTS. 3 (2002). *See also* discussion in JONATHAN WOLFF, THE HUMAN RIGHT TO HEALTH 36–38 (2012).

[55] For the Public's Health, *supra* n.40 at 127–128.

[56] Rajiv Bhatia, Health Impact Assessment: A Guide for Practice, Human Impact Partners (2011), http://www.pewtrusts.org/~/media/assets/2011/01/01/bhatia_2011_hia_guide_for_practice.pdf.

[57] GOTHENBURG CONSENSUS PAPER: HEALTH IMPACT ASSESSMENT MAIN CONCEPTS AND SUGGESTED APPROACH. EUROPEAN CENTRE FOR HEALTH POLICY AND WHO REGIONAL OFFICE FOR EUROPE (1999), https://docs.google.com/viewer?url=http%3A%2F%2Fwww.who.dk%2Fdocum ent%2FPAE%2FGothenburgpaper.pdf.

[58] Ben Harris-Roxas et al., *Differing Forms, Differing Purposes: A Typology of Health Impact Assessment*, 31 ENV. IMPACT ASSESSMENT REV. 396 (2010).

[59] For the Public's Health, *supra* n.40, at 131–135.

[60] J. Mindell et al., *Health Impact Assessment as an Agent of Policy Change: Improving the Health Impacts of the Mayor of London's Draft Transport Strategy*, 58 J. EPIDEMIOLOGY & COMMUN. HEALTH 3, 169–174 (2004), http://jech.bmj.com/content/58/3/169.

[61] For the Public's Health, *supra* n.40, at 127–128; Laura Gottlieb & Paula Braveman, *Health Impact Assessment: A Tool for Promoting Health in All Policies*, Robert Wood Johnson Foundation, Issue Brief No. 11 at 6 (2011,) https://www.rwjf.org/content/dam/farm/reports/issue_briefs/2011/rwjf70449.

This practice is already in increasing, if sporadic, use in US states and localities as well.[62] In one study, 22 of 36 sampled jurisdictions in the United States have made some legal provision for HIAs when environmental and energy policies are considered, while 7 out of the 36 jurisdictions do so for agriculture or transportation policies.[63] HIAs are sometimes included as part of the environmental impact assessment required by the National Environmental Policy Act (NEPA), which I discuss in greater depth later. NEPA regulations include health among the "direct, indirect, and cumulative effects" of the proposed action and alternatives that must be considered in environmental impact reporting.[64] While EPA can take health into account by using alternative tools, it has deliberately chosen the HIA methodology within its environmental assessments as part of its Sustainable and Healthy Communities Research Program. EPA concluded in its April 2014 briefing paper that employment of the HIA methodology "helped raise awareness and bring health into decisions outside traditional health-related fields."[65] During Barack Obama's second term, Susan Bromm declared an EPA preference for HIAs over narrower risk assessments in the environmental impact reporting process because they capture the range of direct, indirect, and cumulative effects.[66] However, for reasons including institutional insularity and gaps in the research connecting policies to their ultimate health effects, this HIA mechanism remains underutilized, and health effects are not always identified in the environmental impact assessment process.[67] Furthermore, NEPA-based health assessments cannot account for the health effects of many policies like tax measures that operate through economically or socially mediated pathways.[68]

---

[62] Andrew L. Dannenberg et al., *Use of Health Impact Assessment in the U.S.:27 Case Studies, 1999–2007*, 34 Am. J. Prev. Med. 3 241–256, 241 (2008). *See also*, Jonathon Heller et al., *Promoting Equity through the Practice of Health Impact Assessment*, PolicyLink (2013), https://kresge.org/sites/default/files/Promoting-equity-through-health-impact-assessment-2013.pdf.

[63] Alicia Corbett et al., *Legal Review Concerning the Use of Health Impact Assessments in Non-Health Sectors*, IssueLab (April 4, 2012), http://www.issuelab.org/resource/legal_review_concerning_the_use_of_health_impact_assessments_in_non_health_sectors; *see also* Doug Farquhar, *An Analysis of State Health Impact Assessment Legislation*, National Conference of State Legislatures (2014), http://www.ncsl.org/Portals/1/Documents/environ/HealthImpactAssessments314_for_NCSL.pdf.

[64] 40 C.F.R. §1502.16 and § 1508.14.

[65] U.S. Environmental Protection Agency, Office of Research and Development, Science in Action: Innovative Research for a Sustainable Future 2 (Revised April 2014) (on file with the author). *See also* Jessica Wentz, *Incorporating Public Health Assessments into Climate Change Action, in* Climate Change, Public Health, and the Law (Michael Burger & Justin Gundlach, eds.) (2018).

[66] Memorandum from Susan E. Bromm & Michael Slimak on Promoting the Use of Health Impact Assessment to Address Human Health in Reviews Conducted Pursuant to the National Environmental Policy Act and Section 309 of the Clean Air Act to the Regional NEPA Directors (November 10, 2015), https://www.epa.gov/sites/production/files/2016-03/documents/hia_memo_from_bromm.pdf.

[67] *See* Hodge, *supra* n.26.

[68] Psychosocial Pathways and Health Outcomes: Informing Action on Health Inequalities, Public Health England and University College of London Institute of Health Equity (September 2017), https://www.gov.uk/government/publications/psychosocial-pathways-and-hea

Rights in Regulatory and Legislative Impact Assessment Statutes

To contend that health impact assessments are a form of a right to health, I use the prevailing model of rights as proportionality from Chapter 2. From the model of rights as proportionality that Robert Alexy elaborated, we distilled three nested operative features of rights.[69] These three elements, if present, signal that a value is being treated as a right, particularly against the background of flat cost-benefit analysis (CBA), which predominates in the policy realm.[70] We can be alerted to rights-reasoning at work whenever we see an interest whose trade-off requires (1) a special justification invoking sufficiently important purpose, (2) a special showing of fit as part of that justification, and (3) conferral of some claim upon an individual rights-holder, albeit not always a judicial claim.

These elements are familiar to us from the type of scrutiny attached to such fundamental rights as those protected under US substantive due process doctrine and the First Amendment.[71] Vicki Jackson has pointed out other areas of US constitutional law, like Takings doctrine, where a similar type of proportionality test is used.[72] Richard Fallon explains the rise of this type of scrutiny as stemming from the court's need to privilege certain rights over other constitutional values in the decades after the *Lochner* era, when courts were trying to both (a) correct for a lopsided solicitude for economic libertarian concerns (as I claim exists now in RIA domain) and (b) render meaningful the protection of some rights even amid an overall acceptance of policy trade-offs (which the current vogue for CBA represents as well).[73] However, few proceed to note that RIA requirements are also rife with this three-part logic of heightened justification.

---

lth-outcomes. *See also*, David Blane et al., *Social-biological transitions: how does the social become biological?*, 4 LONGITUD. LIFE COURSE STUD. 136–146 (2013).

[69] *See* Vicki Jackson, *Constitutional Rights in an Age of Proportionality*, 124 YALE L.J. 3094 (2015) (discussing other methods in the US constitutional tradition, like categorical rules). *See also* AHARON BARAK, ALTERNATIVES TO PROPORTIONALITY 493–527 (2012) (discussing methods like categorization or absolute rights, particularly as applied to a right's "core").

[70] *See* Michigan v. EPA, 135 S. Ct. 2699 (2015) (requiring agency to weigh costs against benefits, unless Congress clearly states otherwise). *See also*, Cass R. Sunstein, *Cost-Benefit Default Principles*, 99 MICH. L. REV. 1651 (2001); Exec. Order No. 12,866, 58 Fed. Reg. 51,735 (October 4, 1993) (which has been retained in substantially similar form through Reagan, Bush I, Clinton, Bush II, and Obama administrations); Portman-Heitkamp Regulatory Accountability Act, S. 951, 115th Cong. §3(b)(5) (2017), https://www.congress.gov/bill/115th-congress/senate-bill/951/text. *See also*, Regulatory Accountability Act, H.R. 5, 115th Cong. (2017) (requiring all agencies, including independent agencies, to consider a "reasonable number of [regulatory] alternatives" and select the "most cost-effective" rule, unless "the additional benefits of the more costly rule justify the additional costs of that rule." This requirement is sometimes called the "super mandate").

[71] *See* Richard Fallon, *Strict Judicial Scrutiny*, 54 UCLA L. REV. 1267, 1316–1317 (2008).

[72] *See* Jackson, *supra* n.69 at 3104–3105.

[73] *See* Fallon, *supra* n.71. For examples of the ascendance of cost-benefit analysis *see supra* n.70.

The scholarly attention paid to regulatory impact analysis has focused mostly on CBA and its critiques, chief among which is the methodology's insensitivity to nonfungible, nonutilitarian values.[74] But it turns out that CBA is not the only kind of regulatory analysis that must routinely be conducted. We have accrued a list of special burdens that trigger their own procedural requirements and even substantive judicial review. These RIA measures include the Paperwork Reduction Act (PRA), the Regulatory Flexibility Act (RFA) as amended by the Small Business Enforcement Regulatory Flexibility Act (SBERFA), the Unfunded Mandates Reform Act (UMRA), and the National Environmental Policy Act (NEPA).

Apart from these widely recognized RIAs,[75] my inventory includes a number of less-canonical provisions that are similar in structure. The Endangered Species Act permits burdens to biodiversity only under strict conditions including showings of fit and purpose. Some executive orders (EOs) even resemble these rights-like RIAs, despite the lack of judicial enforcement available for EOs.[76] For instance, the Reagan-era EO 12630 (1988) required special assessment of regulatory burdens on private property even when the scrutinized regulations did not rise to the level of regulatory takings.

The Religious Freedom Restoration Act (RFRA), passed in 1993, is analogous because independently of the Constitution, it singles out certain burdens as triggering heightened justification involving showings of fit and purpose for valid regulatory or legislative action. The chief ostensible difference between RFRA and the classic RIA is that such showings can be enforced by the mechanism of judicial review under RFRA. However, we shall see that under the Regulatory Flexibility Act, NEPA, Title II of UMRA, and the Endangered Species Act, judicial review is available as well.[77]

In each of these examples, we have elected to impose a heightened justification requirement that has the structure of a right, exhibiting three key elements (1) requiring sufficiency of countervailing purpose, (2) demanding careful fit, and (3) conferring some degree of claim to enforcement. Claimability in this

---

[74] See, e.g., Frank Ackerman & Liza Heinzerling, Pricing the Priceless: Cost-Benefit Analysis of Environmental Protection, 150 U. PA. L. REV. 1553 (2002) (discussing how it may not be possible to limit the effects of cost-benefit analysis to just those areas for which cost-benefit analysis is suitable because there are spillover or displacing effects, including that "cost benefit analysis turns public citizens into selfish consumers and interconnected communities into atomized individuals"). See also, MICHAEL SANDEL, WHAT MONEY CAN'T BUY: THE MORAL LIMITS OF MARKETS (2012); Kristen Underhill, When Extrinsic Incentives Displace Intrinsic Motivation: Designing Legal Carrots and Sticks to Confront the Challenge of Motivational Crowding-Out, 33 YALE J. ON REG. 213 (2016).

[75] MAEVE P. CAREY, CONGRESSIONAL RESEARCH SERVICE, CROSS-CUTTING REGULATORY ANALYSIS REQUIREMENTS 4, December 9, 2014 (including these four in the discussion).

[76] PETER STRAUSS ET AL., GELLHORN AND BYSE'S ADMINISTRATIVE LAW: CASE AND COMMENTS 173–76, 213–229 (11th ed. 2011).

[77] See infra, Section III.F and III.G.

context may not rise to full judicial recourse. It may simply mean that individual beneficiaries have some procedural avenue for demanding the promised justification such that they are plausibly considered rights-holders as distinct from incidental beneficiaries.

If we can establish rights-like protection for freedom from paperwork, why not for human health?

The Paperwork Reduction Act (PRA)

I start by examining the Paperwork Reduction Act (PRA), 44 U.S.C. §3501 et seq, and walking through its rights-forming mechanics. This legislation prohibits regulatory action that imposes information collection without a procedural review of the paperwork burden. The procedural review required under the PRA must be cleared through the powerful Office of Management and Budget (OMB) in the Executive Office of the President.

The PRA, like many RIA measures, advances important hidden purposes that are not reflected in the outward-facing title of the measure. For instance, the PRA accomplishes the important task of authorizing the Office of Information and Regulatory Analysis (OIRA) within OMB. This entity, which serves as a clearinghouse for regulations and certain other administrative actions, has roots in a deregulatory agenda.[78] Whether it retains this cast today is in some dispute,[79] but the creation of OIRA, if nothing else, centralizes a presidential administration's control over regulations, a policy goal that does not necessarily coincide with paperwork reduction. As we will see, hidden policy goals are a common feature among the measures instituting RIAs.

Scope
Each RIA demands additional procedure and heightened justification beyond background cost-benefit judgments. To differentiate the especially encumbered

---

[78] See, e.g., Nestor M. Davidson & Ethan J. Lieb, Regleprudence at OIRA and Beyond, 103 GEO. L. J. 259, 280, n. 95 and n.76 (2015) (describing Nixon's deregulatory agenda as crucial in the history of regulatory review). See also, Jim Tozzi, OIRA's Formative Years: The Historical Record of Centralized Regulatory Review Preceding OIRA's Founding, 63 ADMIN. L. REV. 37 (2011). See also Thomas O. McGarity, Regulatory Analysis and Regulatory Reform, 65 TEX. L. REV. 1234, 1249 (1987) (recounting the origins of regulatory analysis in the Nixon, then Ford, Carter and Reagan administrations).

[79] See Elena Kagan, Presidential Administration, 114 HARV. L. REV. 2245 (2001) (describing how the Clinton administration used OMB and OIRA in a pro-regulatory way, including through the use of "prompt letters" and other presidential directives). See also Cass R. Sunstein, The Office of Information and Regulatory Affairs: Myths and Realities, 126 HARV. L. REV. 1838 (2013). But see Lisa Heinzerling, Inside EPA: A Former Insider's Reflections on the Relationship Between the Obama EPA and the Obama White House, 31 PACE ENVTL. L. REV. 325, 332 (2014) (discussing how the Obama White House used OIRA to block regulatory action).

actions from background governmental action normally subject to ordinary CBA, RIAs must supply some standard for determining when the heightened scrutiny applies. Thus RIA procedures are only triggered when there is some threshold burden to the chosen value. The fact that RIAs in their very name foreground the impact assessment function derives in part from the necessary assessment of threshold impact before the right to heightened justification is triggered. Each RIA is characterized by its threshold trigger, or scope of application.

The PRA's requirements are not triggered by paperwork per se, but by regulatory action imposing "information collection," whether paper or electronic. Information collection is defined in the regulations as "the obtaining, causing to be obtained, soliciting, or requiring the disclosure to an agency, third parties or the public of information . . . imposed on ten or more persons" and "includes any requirement or request for persons to obtain, maintain, retain, report, or publicly disclose information."[80]

This condition upon agency information collection applies not only to Cabinet-level agencies but independent regulatory agencies as well.[81]

The provisions of the PRA impose a presumption against this type of burden which must be surmounted by means of a special justification with the rights-as-proportionality features we identified.

Sufficiency of Purpose and Fit

Under 44 U.S.C. § 3506(c), "[E]ach agency shall . . . establish a process . . . to review each collection of information . . . for "an evaluation of the *need* for the collection of information."[82] The need must be articulated in terms such as whether "the information has practical utility," according to the certification requirement under § 3506(c)(3)(A), and the claim of "practical utility" must be subjected to public comment.[83] Thus, a declaration of utility and need, or in other words, "sufficient purpose," must be produced.

Meanwhile, under 44 U.S.C. §3506(c)(2)(A) and (3)(A), the agency must "certify that . . . the proposed collection of information is *necessary* for the proper performance of the functions of the agency."[84] This requirement of necessity demands a level of means-ends fit between the action imposing the burden and the purpose which it is meant to serve.

---

[80] 5 C.F.R. § 1320.3(c).

[81] Carey, *supra* n.75 at 14 (saying that "independent agencies, as well as independent regulatory agencies" fall within the PRA's coverage. By contrast, executive orders, including those that impose default cost-benefit analysis requirements, do not always reach independent or independent regulatory agencies).

[82] 44 U.S.C. § 3506(c)(1)(A)(i) (2012); 5 C.F.R. § 1320.5(d)(1)(iii).

[83] 44 U.S.C. § 3506(c)(2)(A)(i).

[84] 44 U.S.C. § 3506(c)(2)(A), (3)(A) (emphasis added).

Section 3506(2)(A) tasks the agency with certifying whether it has "minimize[d] the burden of the collection of information on those who are to respond," ostensibly demanding the least-restrictive means.

The fit requirement is even more rigorous should the paperwork burden fall on members of a special protectorate, small business. Section 3506(c)(3) obliges the agency not merely to "certify . . . that each collection of information . . . (C) reduces . . . the burden of information collection on persons . . . including with respect to small entities." It also proceeds to list specific mitigation measures for small businesses that could be used to achieve this "reduction to the extent practicable and appropriate." The suggested mitigation methods include different compliance standards, timetables, or exemptions, prodding special treatment of small entities in the collection of information.[85] This apparatus further illustrates the hidden purposes and privileging of groups that may not be apparent from the outward framing of the RIA measure.[86]

PRA also contains a rather strict mechanism forcing lookback tailoring of even *prior* approved information collections. Under §3507(g), the OMB Director "may not approve a collection of information for a period in excess of 3 years." Any extension would then require another process of review. Meanwhile, under §3513, the OMB Director "shall periodically review selected agency information resource management activities," thus serving as another channel of accountability for continual adjustment of fit while monitoring for continued sufficiency of purpose.[87]

Claiming

Under §3508, the Director of OMB may provide "the agency and other interested persons an opportunity to be heard, or to submit statements in writing." This hearing provision serves as one way for beneficiaries to enlist someone, namely the OMB Director, to hold the agency to account for the PRA requirements. Section 3508 admonishes that "[t]o the extent, if any, that the Director determines that the collection of information by an agency is unnecessary for any reason, the agency may not engage in the collection of information." The necessity determination "includ[es] whether the information shall have practical utility." Thus, insufficient purpose or lack of means-ends rationality can be claimed by a rightsholder in a hearing to invalidate the measure imposing a paperwork burden.

Another provision, §3517(b) provides that "[a]ny person may request the Director to review any collection of information conducted by or for an agency

---

[85] 44 U.S.C. § 3506(c)(3)(c)(i)-(iii).

[86] I will later suggest that one "hidden" or "complementary" purpose of HIAs is equity and will show how that can be built into the HIA. *See infra* text accompanying n.253.

[87] I will also later suggest that lookback monitoring for continued justification should be built into HIAs so that existing arrangements can be subjected to HIA as well.

to determine, if, under this subchapter, a person shall maintain, provide or disclose the information to or for the agency. Unless the request is frivolous, the Director shall . . . respond to the request within 60 days . . . and take appropriate remedial action if necessary."[88]

Moreover, persons can claim individualized immunities under §3512, the "Public Protection" provision of the PRA. The section stipulates that "No person shall be subject to any penalty for failing to comply with a collection of information that is subject to this subchapter" if the agency has not received OMB approval of its compliance with the PRA in the form of a valid OMB control number. Under §3512(b), "The protection provided by this section may be raised in the form of a complete defense, bar, or otherwise at any time during the agency administrative process or judicial action applicable thereto." The PRA implementing regulations also apply this section to benefits that are conditioned upon the information collection: "[T]he agency shall not treat a person's failure to comply in and of itself as grounds for withholding the benefit or imposing the penalty. The agency shall instead permit respondents to prove or satisfy the legal conditions in any other reasonable manner."[89]

Apart from the normal administrative law requirement to take comments into account,[90] the PRA statute also insists under §3507(d)(2) that in the final rule, an agency "shall explain how any collection of information contained in the final rule responds to the comments, if any, filed by the Director or the public, or the reasons such comments were rejected."[91] In totality, the heightened justification requirement triggered by paperwork burdens is arguably held and enforceable by individual members of the public, rather than consisting of a mere duty to uphold the collective good.

History

Freedom from paperwork was not a value suddenly elevated to this privileged status without prior groundwork. It was originally recognized as a concern in the Federal Reports Act of 1942,[92] but this legislation was criticized in the 1970s as ineffectual, and was finally superseded by the PRA in 1980.[93] Stuart Shapiro and Deanna Moran observe that the interest groups supporting the PRA were principally businesses and state and local governments.[94] Meanwhile, the diffuse

---

[88] 44 U.S.C. § 3517 (b)(1) and (2). 5 C.F.R. § 1320.14(c).

[89] 5 C.F.R. § 1320.6(c).

[90] *See* United States v. Nova Scotia Food Products, 568 F.2d 240 (1977).

[91] 44 U.S.C. § 3507(d)(2).

[92] Pub. L. No. 77-841, 56 Stat. 1078 (1942).

[93] Paperwork Reduction Act of 1980, Pub. L. No. 96-511, 94 Stat. 2812 (1980).

[94] *See* Stuart Shapiro & Deanna Moran, *The Checkered History of Regulatory Reform Since the APA*, 19 N.Y.U. J. Legis. & Pub. Pol'y 141, 161–162 and n. 115 and 124 (2015).

nature of the benefits from paperwork meant that no interest group came forward and supported its collection.[95]

The PRA itself was followed by the Paperwork Reduction Reauthorization Act of 1986,[96] then further amended in the Paperwork Reduction Act of 1995,[97] the Economic Growth and Regulatory Paperwork Reduction Act of 1996,[98] Government Paperwork Elimination Act of 1998,[99] and the Small Business Paperwork Relief Act of 2002.[100] This history suggests that many of the RIAs that are not now easily classifiable as a form of subconstitutional "right" may still be "rights-in-the-making," thus modeling a pathway for "normalizing" an analogous RIA to protect health.

Regulatory Flexibility Act (RFA) as Amended by the Small Business Regulatory Enforcement Fairness Act (SBERFA)

The Regulatory Flexibility Act (RFA), like the PRA, was shaped iteratively by Congress, most notably in the form of SBERFA in 1996.[101] RFA enshrines the favored value of small business freedom from economic burden. Agencies imposing such a burden must make a special showing of heightened justification, and this justification is expressly subject to judicial review.

Scope
For the justification requirements to attach, though, a rule must reach the threshold of having a "significant economic impact" on a "substantial number of small entities."[102] Because these terms are malleable, an agency head must certify if she finds that a rule does *not* meet those standards and is therefore not subject to the analysis requirements.[103] As we will see, this certification, which must be accompanied by statement of factual basis, is subject to judicial review.[104]

---

[95] *Id.* at 161 n. 113. President Carter himself signed the PRA over the objections of his Cabinet. *See* Tozzi, *supra* n.78.

[96] Paperwork Reduction Reauthorization Act of 1986, Pub. L. No. 99-500, 100 Stat. 335 (1986) (Title VIII, §§801-820 of the Continuing Appropriations Resolution).

[97] Paperwork Reduction Act of 1995, Pub. L. No. 104-13, 109 Stat. 163.

[98] Economic Growth and Regulatory Paperwork Act of 1996, Pub. L. No. 104-208, 110 Stat. 3009 (codified in scattered titles of the U.S. Code).

[99] Government Paperwork Elimination Act of 1998, Pub. L. No. 105-277, §§1701-1710, 112 Stat. 2681, 2749-51 (codified at 44 U.S.C. § 3504 (2012)) (involving electronic submissions).

[100] Small Business Paperwork Relief Act of 2002, Pub. L. No. 107-198, 116 Stat. 729 (codified in scattered sections of 44 U.S.C.).

[101] 5 U.S.C. § 601–612.

[102] 5 U.S.C. § 605(b).

[103] 5 U.S.C. § 605 (b),

[104] 5 U.S.C. § 611(a)(2)

The RFA also applies to "interpretative rules" of the IRS, so long as they are published in the Federal Register, and "only to the extent that such interpretative rules impose on small entities a collection of information requirement."[105] The concerns of the PRA and the RFA intertwine once more, suggesting that many of these RIAs are part of an interconnected agenda.

Sufficiency of Purpose and Fit

As with other RIAs, the RFA clearly demands justification in the form of sufficient purpose and fit. The initial regulatory analysis that must accompany the proposed rule is called the initial "reg-flex."[106] In it, an agency must describe "reasons why action by the agency is being considered."[107] The agency must also supply "a succinct statement of the need for, and the objectives of the proposed rule."[108]

The initial reg-flex must also describe "any significant alternatives to the proposed rule which accomplish the stated objectives . . . and which minimize any significant economic impact of the proposed rule on small entities."[109] The statute then lists the mitigating alternatives that "shall be discussed," including "differing compliance or reporting requirements or timetables," "clarification, consolidation, or simplification of compliance," "use of performance rather than design standards," and "exemption."[110] Agencies are therefore subject to a fairly stringent least-restrictive means analysis. When the final rule is promulgated, each final reg-flex must also include:

> [A] description of the steps the agency has taken to minimize the significant economic impact on small entities . . . including a statement on the . . . reasons for selecting the alternative adopted . . . and why each one of the other significant alternatives to the rule . . . was rejected.[111]

The measure also imposes a lookback requirement. Each agency must review its rules every ten years to see if they fall within the scope of the RFA and whether they must be changed or rescinded "to minimize any significant economic impact of the rules upon a substantial number of such small entities."[112]

---

[105] 5 U.S.C. § 603(a). *See also,* Thomas O. Sargentich, *The Small Business Regulatory Enforcement Fairness Act,* 49 ADMIN L. REV. 123, 128 (1997).

[106] Richard J Pierce, Jr., *Small is Not Beautiful: The Case Against Special Regulatory Treatment of Small* Firms, 50 ADMIN. L. REV. 537, 546 (1998).

[107] 5 U.S.C. § 603(b)(1) and (2).

[108] 5 U.S.C. § 604(a)(1). *See also,* 5 U.S.C. § 603(b)(2).

[109] 5 U.S.C. § 603(c).

[110] 5 U.S.C. § 603(c) (1)–(4).

[111] 5 U.S.C. § 604(a)(5).

[112] 5 U.S.C. § 610.

Claiming

Initially, the RFA did not expressly authorize judicial review of agency actions. However, courts would consider the contents of the reg-flex analysis in determining whether the rule was "arbitrary and capricious" through ordinary administrative law challenges.[113] SBERFA, passed by the Gingrich Congress in 1996,[114] added a special judicial review provision. Small entities can go to court under that provision to challenge an agency's RFA analysis for final rules, an agency's threshold certification of no significant impact, and the agency's ten-year lookback review outcomes.[115] SBERFA also authorizes small entities to recover attorneys' fees,[116] and stipulates a right of intervention for the Chief Counsel for Advocacy of the Small Business Administration in any such action.[117]

The Chief Counsel for Advocacy of the Small Business Administration acts as a representative for small businesses, whom any agency promulgating a rule must also consult at key points.[118] With respect to two particularly villainized agencies, EPA and OSHA,[119] the role of the Chief Counsel is enlarged. She must convene a review panel for each EPA or OSHA rule,[120] identifying individual representatives of affected small entities[121] to review the initial reg-flex and proposed rule.[122] The language stipulates that "where appropriate, the agency shall modify the proposed rule, the initial regulatory flexibility analysis or the decision on whether an initial regulatory flexibility analysis is required."[123] This mechanism of tasking a representative with vindication of designated rights exists alongside ordinary judicial review.

History

The RFA was enacted in 1980, itself a deregulatory moment.[124] Then in 1996, it was, as described, substantially amended to favor small business even further.[125] The political significance of SBREFA's passage in 1996 extends beyond small business, gesturing toward the entire political agenda of the anti-regulatory

---

[113] See e.g., Michigan v. Thomas, 805 F.2d 176, 187–8 (6th Cir. 1986).

[114] See Shapiro and Moran, supra n.94.

[115] 5 U.S.C. § 611(a)(2) (giving jurisdiction "to review any claims of noncompliance with §§ 601, 604, 605(b), 608(b) and 610").

[116] SBERFA, Pub. L. No. 104-121 § 231, 110 Stat. at 862–3 (1996) amending 5 U.S.C. § 504(a).

[117] 5 U.S.C. § 612.

[118] See e.g., 5 U.S.C. § 606(b) (notifying Chief Counsel of any certification of "lack of significant economic impact on a substantial number of small entities."); 5 U.S.C. § 603(a) (requiring transmittal of initial reg-flex to the Chief Counsel).

[119] 5 U.S.C. § 609(b) (applying additional requirements for initial reg-flex by "covered agencies" and § 609(d) defining covered agency).

[120] 5 U.S.C. § 609(b) (2) and (3).

[121] 5 U.S.C. § 609(b)(2).

[122] 5 U.S.C. § 609(b)(4).

[123] 5 U.S.C. § 609(b)(6).

[124] See Paul Verkuil, A Critical Guide to the Regulatory Flexibility Act, 1982 DUKE L.J. 213 (1982).

[125] Pub. L. No. 104-121, 110 Stat. 864 (1996).

Gingrich-led Republican Revolution then dominating US politics. A crucial part of the agenda of the new Republican majority in that highly charged time was regulatory reform,[126] including measures that would have imposed a supermandate for cost-benefit analysis.[127] Despite the significant political energy that the Gingrich Congress expended, their omnibus regulatory reform bills failed to overcome the opposition of Democrats, including then-President Clinton.[128] SBREFA was among the only pieces of the Republican agenda that did ultimately wend its way to completion. This capsule history showcases how RIAs have served as vehicles for the popular struggle to inscribe conceptions of rights in extraconstitutional space.

National Environmental Policy Act (NEPA)

To fully understand the RIA template as it might be applied to human health, we must look at NEPA, the godparent of all regulatory analysis requirements.[129] Passed in 1969 and signed by Richard Nixon on January 1, 1970, it requires agencies to "include in every recommendation or report on proposals for legislation and other major Federal actions significantly affecting the quality of the human environment, a detailed statement ... on ... the environmental impact of the proposed action."[130] In effect, it made "environmental protection a part of the mandate of every federal agency and department."[131]

Scope
As noted, the requirement of a detailed statement applies to "every recommendation or report on proposals for legislation and other major Federal actions significantly affecting the quality of the human environment."[132]

While "significantly affecting" is not defined in the statute, NEPA regulations do contain a clever device for making this threshold determination. Agencies

---

[126] See BARBARA SINCLAIR, UNORTHODOX LAWMAKING: NEW LEGISLATIVE PROCESSES IN THE U.S. CONGRESS 110 (1997).

[127] See also Pierce supra n.106 at 546.

[128] See Sinclair, supra n.126 at 110–113.

[129] 42 U.S.C. §4321 et seq. See also McGarity supra n.78 at 1247 (noting that "[t]he idea that agencies should prepare a separate regulatory analysis document describing the costs and benefits of proposed and final rules and credible rule-making alternatives probably originated with the National Environmental Policy Act of 1969").

[130] NEPA § 202(1)(C), 42 U.S.C. § 4332(1)(C).

[131] CalvertCliff's Coordinating Comm. v. Atomic Energy Comm'n, 449 F.2d 1109, 1112 (D.C. Cir. 1971).

[132] 42 U.S.C. § 4332(1)(C) (2000). Lookback review might not be available in the sense that previously approved major federal actions do not continue to be subject to this procedural burden for continued effect even if the environmental circumstances of those prior actions have changed. See Norton v. Southern Utah Wilderness Alliance, 542 U.S. 55 (2004).

must conduct Environmental Assessments (EAs) which "briefly provide sufficient evidence and analysis for determining whether to prepare an environmental impact statement or a finding of no significant impact."[133] Thus, some
minimal environmental assessment is necessary in order to determine whether a
full Environmental Impact Statement (EIS), that is, the special justification step,
must be conducted. The device of the "finding of no significant impact" (FONSI)
is the flip-side of the EIS in the sense that if an EA concludes in a FONSI, then
an EIS need not be conducted.[134] Sometimes substantive environmental mitigation commitments are made at this stage to obtain what is called a "mitigated
FONSI," and thereby avoid the EIS process.[135] This process illustrates how negative liberties are not entirely separable from affirmative commitments insofar as
the possibility of mitigation results in affirmative government promises to promote the value otherwise shielded by the impact assessment. EAs and FONSIs
are also subject by statute to judicial review.[136]

Sufficiency of Purpose and Fit

Unlike its RIA progeny, the NEPA statute does not require an analysis of sufficiency of purpose in so many words. The regulations interpreting NEPA however do. A decision contrary to the most environmentally preferable alternative
must be described in terms of the other "economic and technical considerations
and agency statutory missions . . . including any essential considerations of national policy" that weighed against the environmentally preferable alternative.[137]
This language insists that the countervailing factors be weighty.

The NEPA statute does specifically demand a showing of fit. The agency must
include in its detailed statement under § 4332(1)(C) "any adverse environmental effects which cannot be avoided should the proposal be implemented."[138]
Moreover, it must describe "alternatives to the proposed action."[139] This language
has been interpreted as a procedural requirement to consider, though not necessarily adopt, less environmentally damaging alternatives.[140] The regulations
interpreting NEPA also require that the decision-maker *record* the environmentally preferable alternative, and even articulate how the agency decided against
this alternative based on the weighty purposes described above.[141]

---

[133]   40 C.F.R. § 1508.9.
[134]   40 C.F.R. § 1508.13.
[135]   Bradley Karkkainen, *Toward a Smarter NEPA: Monitoring and Managing Government's
Environmental Performance*, 102 COLUM L. REV. 903 (2002).
[136]   Save Our Ten Acres (SOTA) v. Kreger, 472 F.2d 463 (5th Cir. 1973).
[137]   *See* 40 CFR § 1505.2.
[138]   NEPA § 202(1)(C)(ii), 42 U.S.C. § 4332(1)(C)(ii).
[139]   NEPA § 202(1)(C)(iii), 42 U.S.C. § 4332(1)(C)(iii).
[140]   *See, e.g.*, Vermont Yankee v. NRDC, 435 U.S. 519 (1978).
[141]   40 CFR §1505.2 (requiring a "Record of Decision," or ROD).

Claiming

While NEPA did not include an express judicial review provision, courts have reviewed for NEPA compliance using ordinary measures of administrative rationality when invoked under § 702 of the Administrative Procedure Act (APA).[142] Courts apply a "hard look" standard to judge an agency's execution of its obligations under NEPA,[143] and a regulation can be enjoined if the agency's performance of these functions is so inadequate as to render regulation arbitrary and capricious.[144] Moreover, the mitigation measures that may have been adopted as a condition of the FONSI are judicially enforced.[145]

History

NEPA has proven surprisingly enduring. Congressional amendment has remained fairly minor,[146] although many new laws that Congress passes contain NEPA exemptions.[147] The administration promulgated binding NEPA regulations in the late 1970s, but oddly on the authority of President Carter's Executive Order 11514, rather than on the basis of statutorily delegated rulemaking authority.[148] These regulations have operated through the decades, despite "such a shaky legal foundation."[149] NEPA, which declares a Congressional policy of "recognize[ing] that each person should enjoy a healthful environment,"[150] has managed to achieve such a degree of entrenchment that one observer notes, "If environmental law has a superstatute, it is the procedural NEPA."[151]

---

[142] See, e.g., Salmon River Concerned Citizens v. Robertson, 32 F.3d 1346, 1353-4. (9th Cir. 1994) (where the justiciability of compliance with NEPA was conceded precisely on the question of whether the consideration of human health effects—albeit measured by methods other than HIA—were adequate to satisfy NEPA requirements).

[143] Kleppe v. Sierra Club, 427 U.S. 390, 410 (1976), Robertson v. Methow Valley Citizen's Council, 490 U.S. 332, 338 (1989).

[144] See, e.g. Coeur D'Alene Lake v. Kiebert, 790 F. Supp. 998 (D. Idaho 1992), Baltimore Gas & Electric Co. v. Natural Resources Defense Council, Inc. 462 U.S. 87 (1983). See generally, Nicholas C. Yost, The Background and History of NEPA, THE NEPA LITIGATION GUIDE (Ferlo et al., eds., 2nd ed. 2012)

[145] Tyler v. Cisneros, 136 F. 3d 603 (9th Cir. 1998).

[146] Bradley Karkkainen, Whither NEPA, 12 N.Y.U. ENVTL. L.J. 333, n.14 (2004).

[147] See, e.g. Lynton K Caldwell, Beyond NEPA: Future Significance of the National Environmental Policy Act, 22 HARV. ENVTL. L. REV. 203, 205 n.9 (counting the number of exceptions to NEPA authorized by Congress by the year 1997, and finding 28). See also, William H. Rodgers, Jr., NEPA at Twenty: Mimicry and Recruitment in Environmental Law, 20 ENVTL. L. 485, 496 (1990).

[148] 3 C.F.R. § 531 (1971). The EO directs agencies to "comply with the regulations issued by [CEQ] except where such compliance would be inconsistent with statutory requirements."

[149] See Karkkainen supra n.147 at 335.

[150] NEPA § 101(c), 42 U.S.C. § 4331(c).

[151] See, e.g., Jedidiah Purdy, Coming into the Anthropocene, 129 HARV. L. REV. 1619 (April 7, 2016) https://harvardlawreview.org/2016/04/coming-into-the-anthropocene/; Arthur W. Murphy, The National Environmental Policy Act and the Licensing Process: Environmentalist Magna Carta or Agency Coup de Grace?, 72 COLUM. L. REV. 963 (1972) (describing NEPA as an 'environmentalist Magna Carta").

Unfunded Mandates Reform Act (UMRA)

The Unfunded Mandates Reform Act (UMRA) was passed in 1995 and imposes heightened scrutiny for the uncompensated economic burdens that subnational governments shoulder because of federal mandates.[152] A "federal intergovernmental mandate," the target of UMRA, is defined as "any provision in legislation, statute, or regulation that would impose an enforceable duty upon State, local or tribal governments . . . or would reduce or eliminate the amount of authorization of appropriations for . . . the purpose of complying with any such previously imposed duty."[153] What is notable about UMRA is that it applies to all legislative action as well as regulatory.[154] Title I of the Act addresses legislation and Title II concerns regulatory action. I will discuss Title II only briefly, as it resembles the earlier examples of the PRA and RFA, and then focus mainly on Title I.

The scope of UMRA Title II extends to rulemaking "likely to result in promulgation of any rule that includes any Federal mandate that may result in the expenditure by State, local, and tribal governments, in the aggregate, or the private sector, of $100 million or more (adjusted annually for inflation) in any one year."[155] We are by now familiar with the devices used here: a required statement of the measure's beneficial purpose, required consideration of the least burdensome alternative, consultation requirements, and APA-based judicial review.

Legislative Sufficiency of Purpose and Fit

I now turn to the portion of UMRA that applies to legislative action. Under Title I, when a Congressional committee reports out legislation "that includes any Federal mandate," regardless of magnitude, the legislation must be accompanied by a reporting of not only costs anticipated in the first five fiscal years, but also the "benefit anticipated from the Federal mandates (including the effects on health and safety and the protection of the natural environment)."[156] Such declaration

---

[152] 2 U.S.C. § 1501 and scattered sections.

[153] 2 USC § 658(5). This definition is simplified for exposition purposes here. The definition features certain economic thresholds and a number of exclusions as well, including a complex partial exclusion of conditions placed on spending, which the statute differentiates from conditional provisions attached to entitlement programs. Statutes imposing federal intergovernmental mandates trigger reporting requirements, but these are only enforceable above a certain economic threshold. *Id.* Also in the process of bill passage, an amendment was added such that federal mandates upon the *private sector* (rather than just upon subnational governments) would also trigger scrutiny. 2 U.S.C. § 658(6) and (7). *See infra* n.184.

[154] UMRA § 202 et seq (Title I).

[155] UMRA § 202(a), 2 USC § 1532(a).

[156] Congressional Budget and Impoundment Control Act of 1974 (Budget Act) § 423(c)(2) (as amended by the Unfunded Mandates Reform Act of 1995), 2 USC § 658d(c)(2). Budget Act § 423(f), 2 USC § 658d(f) assigns a duty to the Congressional Budget Office (CBO) to estimate the cost of federal mandates in proposed legislation.

of benefit could be understood as a requirement to state a sufficient purpose for the imposition of the federal mandate.

What leaps out about this § 423(c) committee reporting duty is that no point of order is available to enforce this requirement.[157] In legislating UMRA, Congress amended a two-decade old law, the Congressional Budget and Impoundment Control Act of 1974, often referred to as the Budget Act. UMRA therefore inserted many of its requirements directly into the framework of the Budget Act.[158]

As a general matter, Congress' overall budgeting framework is enforced by an elaborate system of points of order as we noted in Chapter 2.[159] After all, for Congress' budget to have meaning, it must encumber the passage of laws that exceed the budget.[160] The Budget Act thus subjects such budget nonconforming legislation to a point of order that any member of Congress can raise.[161] To proceed with the legislation once such an objection has been raised, the relevant house must waive the implicated rule,[162] a step which, according to the Budget Act framework, requires a supermajority vote.[163]

However, the UMRA committee reporting requirement under § 423 is not subject to a point of order.[164] Even if it were, the regular committee process is now somewhat of a relic as many bills in our hyperpolarized political context are steered by leadership directly to the floor.[165]

This situation does not mean that UMRA is unenforceable as applied to legislation. UMRA contains a second tier of requirements apart from § 423. Recall that § 423 applies to "any Federal mandate" regardless of magnitude. On the other hand, § 425 of the UMRA-amended Budget Act imposes an even stronger

---

[157] The Budget Act § 423(f) requirement for a CBO estimate to accompany the committee reported bill is protected by point of order. Budget Act § 425(a)(1) says "It shall not be in order in the Senate or the House of Representatives to consider (1) any bill or joint resolution that is reported by a committee unless the committee has published a statement of the Director on the direct costs of Federal mandates in accordance with section 423(f) before such consideration." But this section does not mention the need to accord with § 423(c), which contains the other committee reporting requirements.

[158] Congressional Budget and Impoundment and Control Act of 1974 is often referred to as the "Budget Act" (Pub. L. 93–344, 88 Stat. 297, 2 U.S.C. §§601–688).

[159] Christina S. Ho, *Budgeting on Autopilot*, 50 TULSA L. REV. 695, 716 (2015).

[160] *Id.* at 716-7.

[161] 2 U.S.C. § 633 (f)(1) and (2).

[162] BILL HENIFF, JR., CONG. RES. SERV., RS20371, OVERVIEW OF THE AUTHORIZATION-APPROPRIATIONS PROCESS (2012), http://www.senate.gov/CRSReports/crs-publish.cfm?pid='0DP%2BPLW%3C%22%40%20%20%0A.

[163] While usually only a majority vote is required to override the ruling of a chair when such ruling is appealed to the whole Senate, some points of order under the budget process require 60 votes to waive. 2 U.S.C. § 621 note, Pub. L. No. 93-344 § 904(c) and (d). *See* Elizabeth Garrett, *Enhancing the Political Safeguards of Federalism? The Unfunded Mandates Reform Act of 1995*, 45 KANSAS L. REV. 1113, 1161–1168 (1997).

[164] UMRA §425(a)(1), 2 U.S.C. § 658d(a)(1) (by contrast subjecting the CBO reporting requirement, as opposed to the committee reporting requirement, to a point of order).

[165] Garrett *supra* n.164 at 1142.

condition, but only upon significant mandates exceeding an economic threshold of roughly $50 million in direct costs. This condition, if not met, *does* trigger a point of order.[166] This point of order only needs a mere majority to overcome, a point to which I will return momentarily.[167] Various aspects of the § 425 condition are discussed below, but it requires, roughly speaking, some indication that the mandate's burdens will be mitigated through one of the suggested mitigations, a matter to which I will return.[168] While this point of order does not apply expressly to the absence of sufficient purpose for the mandate, one could view a vote to overcome the point of order as a legislative determination that the purpose of legislation containing the unfunded mandate *is* sufficiently important to overcome the presumption.[169] In other words, forcing a separate vote on this issue alone can be viewed as a requirement of extra clarity on the sufficiency of purpose to infringe on the favored value of states' economic freedom.[170]

At first glance, the articulation of fit, by means of identifying and justifying choices that depart from the least burdensome alternative, is not a condition placed on legislative intergovernmental mandates. However, this initial impression gives way once one realizes that the principal means by which the intergovernmental burden is to be minimized is through federal funding. UMRA requires either funding or other mitigation for legislation to constitute a "funded" rather than "unfunded" mandate and thereby escape the point of order. For instance, § 425(a)(2)(A) and (B) list conditions exempting legislation from the point of order, such as new budget authority, or an automatic circuit-breaker that kicks in whenever appropriations fall short to "implement a less costly mandate or mak[e] such mandate ineffective for the fiscal year."[171] Thus UMRA, in effect, requires mitigation to render the burden less restrictive on states and localities.

Lookback review is also built into UMRA. If within ten years, the implementing agency re-estimates the mandate's costs and they prove to be higher, the agency must notify Congress with recommendations for either mitigation or lapse of the mandate's burdens.[172] Garrett also notes that "Congress has the authority under the Act to request CBO to perform follow-up studies."[173]

---

[166] Budget Act § 425(a)(2) (as amended by UMRA), 2 U.S.C. § 658d(a)(2).

[167] Garrett *supra* n.164 at 1161–1168 (explaining that a majority vote is needed to sustain a ruling of the chair to overrule the point of order, or to appeal a ruling of the chair sustaining the point of order, or voting on the point of order even if the Chair has declined to rule). *Id.* at 1161–2.

[168] *See infra* text accompanying n.174.

[169] Garrett, *supra* n.164 at 1165–6, 1172–3.

[170] *See generally,* William Eskridge & Philip Frickey, *Quasi-Constitutional Law: Clear Statement Rules as Constitutional Lawmaking,* 45 VANDERBILT L. REV. 593 (1992).

[171] Budget Act § 425(a)(2)(A) and (B)(iii) (bb); 2 USC § 658d(a)(2)(A) and (B)(iii) (bb).

[172] Budget Act § 425(a)(2)(B)(iii), 2 U.S.C. § 658d(a)(2)(B)(iii).

[173] Garrett, *supra* n.164 at 1160.

Legislative Claiming

The point of order serves as the accountability mechanism for the heightened legislative criteria of § 425, and those criteria can in turn be understood as requirements for extra clarity by Congress with respect to sufficiency of purpose and fit. If the legislation contains no funding or express funding mitigation for a federal mandate above the threshold, a point of order can be raised, requiring the *clarity* of a vote on the sufficiency of the mandate's purpose to overcome the unfunded mandate objection.[174]

Any state can therefore have its representative delegation make a claim on its behalf, if one subscribes to the "political safeguards of federalism" view of how elected Senators relate to their states.[175] The point of order can only be overcome by majority vote, but that requirement arguably remains politically consequential insofar as it forces a separate roll call vote requiring Members of Congress to take a visible stance on that isolated issue.[176] The Senate has even on occasion voted to raise that threshold to sixty votes.[177] While that threshold reverted back to a simple majority in subsequent fiscal years, the threat of elevation in any given year remains.[178]

History

In the floor debates over UMRA, Democratic politicians voiced "concerns that the legislation would impede the federal government's ability to protect public health"[179] while the allies of the so-called intergovernmental lobby were vocal in support.[180] But business groups were also strong UMRA proponents, condemning environmental laws such as the Clean Air Act as examples of

---

[174] Garrett, *supra* n.164 at 1161–1168 (detailed description of the mechanics and incentive structure behind points of order generally and UMRA points of order in particular). Budget Act § 424(a)(1), 2 USC § 658c(a)(1) (imposing a $50 million per fiscal year threshold for intergovernmental mandates).

[175] Herbert Wechsler, *The Political Safeguards of Federalism: The Role of the States in the Composition and Selection of the National Government*, 54 COLUM. L. REV. 543 (1954). JESSE H. CHOPER, JUDICIAL REVIEW AND THE NATIONAL POLITICAL PROCESS: A FUNCTIONAL RECONSIDERATION OF THE ROLE OF THE SUPREME COURT 184 (1980).

[176] Garrett, *supra* n.164 at 1161 and 1163–4. *See also*, Elizabeth Garrett, *Framework Legislation and Federalism*, 83 NOTRE DAME L. REV. 1495, 1496 and 1503–4 (2008).

[177] H. Con. Res. 95, 109th Cong. (2005) (enacted), https://www.congress.gov/bill/109th-congress/house-concurrent-resolution/95 (the fiscal year 2006 budget resolution). The Senate also included a supermajority threshold in an early version of the fiscal year 2010 budget resolution, S. Amdt. 819 (Enzi) to S. Con. Res. 13, 111th Cong. (2009), https://www.congress.gov/amendment/111th-congress/senate-amendment/819?s=a&r=162. However, this change dropped out before the budget was finalized.

[178] *See id. See also*, ROBERT JAY DILGER & RICHARD S. BETH, CONGRESSIONAL RESEARCH SERVICE, UNFUNDED MANDATES REFORM ACT: HISTORY, IMPACT, AND ISSUES (January 25, 2011), https://www.everycrsreport.com/reports/R40957.html#_Toc478474110.

[179] Shapiro & Moran, *supra* n.94 at 167, *citing* Dilger & Beth, *supra* n.179. Senator Frank Lautenberg protested that OSHA and EPA would be hampered in their ability to set minimum standards to address the collective action problems of a patchwork regime. *Id.*

[180] Garrett, *supra* n.164 at 1136.

unfunded federal mandates.[181] The constituency favoring UMRA (states and small business, supported by big business) was quite similar to the constituency backing the RFA.[182] It is perhaps not so surprising then that non–federalism-related purposes burrowed their way into UMRA by amendment, imposing "private-sector cost impact statements when the economic burdens [exceed] 100 million USD."[183] UMRA thus elevates *private* economic freedom as well.

Noncanonical Examples of RIAs

Here I wish to argue for the similarity of a few additional measures imposing heightened justification requirements. By now I hope it is evident that these heightened justification requirements exist on some kind of quasi-rights continuum, and I make the case here for these other examples as points on the same spectrum.

Endangered Species Act (ESA)

ESA § 7(a)(2) commands: "Each Federal agency shall, in consultation with . . . the Secretary, insure that any action . . . by such agency . . . is not likely to jeopardize the continued existence of any endangered species or threatened species or result in the destruction or adverse modification of habitat of such species which is determined . . . to be critical." Any agency action that burdens species preservation in this way can only proceed if it has been granted an exemption, which in turn depends on sufficiency of purpose and fit.

The ESA actually features two thresholds of burden. Section 7(a)(3) requires consultation with the Secretary over "prospective agency action . . . if the applicant has *reason to believe* that an endangered species or a threatened species *may be present in the area affected* by his project and that implementation of such action *will likely affect such species*."[184]

By contrast, the previously mentioned § 7(a)(2) has a higher threshold; namely, "agency action [that] is *likely to jeopardize the continued existence of* any endangered [or threatened] species . . . *or result in the destruction or adverse modification of habitat* of such species."[185] But this paragraph also places a correspondingly

---

[181] Shapiro and Moran *supra* n.94 at 168.

[182] *Id.* at 169.

[183] *See* S. Amdt. 19 (Kempthorne) to S. 1, 104th Cong. (1995) (enacted), https://www.congress.gov/amendment/104th-congress/senate-amendment/19/all-info.

[184] ESA § 7(a)(3), 16 U.S.C. § 1536(a)(3) (emphasis added).

[185] ESA § 7(a)(2), 16 U.S.C. § 1536(a)(2) (emphasis added).

heavier requirement, beyond mere consultation, upon agency actions that reach the higher threshold of impingement upon the favored value. Such impingement forces an agency to obtain an "exemption" from the § 7(a)(2) prohibition through prescribed procedures. Exemption involves formal hearing and vote of the multi-member committee,[186] colloquially known as the "God Squad,"[187] and hinging upon substantive showings such as sufficiency of purpose and fit.[188]

Sufficiency of Purpose and Fit

Section 7(h)(A) provides that voting committee members may grant exemptions on the basis of determinations that "the action is of regional or national significance,"[189] that "such agency action is in the public interest,"[190] and that "the benefits of such action clearly outweigh the benefits of alternative courses of action." These formulations all amount to a finding that the purpose of the action is sufficiently important to justify an exemption.

Section 7(h)(A)(i) also lists a fit requirement as one of the determinations necessary for the committee member to vote in favor of an exemption. Specifically, the impingement upon endangered species by the agency must be justified by a Committee determination that "there are no reasonable and prudent alternatives to the agency action."[191] Section 7(h)(B) goes on to require that the Committee granting the exemption

> establish such reasonable mitigation and enhancement measures, including, but not limited to, live propagation, transplantation, and habitat acquisition and improvement, as are necessary and appropriate to minimize the adverse effects of the agency action upon the endangered species, threatened species, or critical habitat concerned.[192]

Claiming

Section 7(n) grants "judicial review under [the APA], of any decision of the Endangered Species Committee under subsection (h),"[193] though this

---

[186] ESA § 7(e), 16 U.S.C. § 1536(e) (listing in subparagraph (3) the seven members of the "God Squad"); ESA § 7(h), 16 U.S.C. § 1536(h); ESA §7(h) (listing the requirement that "the Committee shall make a final determination whether or not to grant an exemption . . . by a vote of not less than 5 of its members" and then articulating the determinations that must be made to support such a vote).
[187] Jared des Rosiers, *Exemption Process under the Endangered Species Act: How the God Squad Works and Why*, 66 NOTRE DAME L. REV. 825 (1991).
[188] ESA § 7(h)(A) and (B), 16 U.S.C. § 1536(h)(A) and (B).
[189] ESA § 7(h)(A)(iii), 16 U.S.C. § 1536(h) (A)(iii).
[190] ESA § 7(h)(A)(ii), 16 U.S.C. § 1536(h)(A)(ii).
[191] *Id.* (emphasis added).
[192] ESA § 7(h), 16 U.S.C. § 1536(h).
[193] ESA § 7(n), 16 U.S.C. § 1536(n).

enforcement tool has since been saddled with notorious standing limitations.[194] The court has nevertheless waded in on occasion to enforce these species-preservation norms, with *TVA v. Hill* serving as a vivid reminder.[195] The Court held there that the statute forbade cost-benefit balancing in a way that prompts Sunstein to muse that "perhaps the [ESA] is best taken to be rooted in a theory of rights, one that rebuts the presumption in favor of cost-benefit balancing."[196] The God Squad has rarely found occasion to overcome the ESA's protections,[197] but occasionally agencies engage in negotiation over discretionary decisions such as whether to designate or list a relevant species or habitat, or whether "jeopardy" to the relevant species is found.[198]

History

This anomalously stringent subconstitutional provision was, like other quasi-rights on this list, the result of a decades-long struggle to entrench biodiversity as a favored value. The Endangered Species Preservation Act enacted in 1966 merely provided a means of listing native species with limited protections.[199] It was amended in 1969, and only assumed its current form in 1973. The provisions were then weakened five years later with the allowance of exemptions from the ESA's protections through the "God Squad" process described above.[200] Major amendments have since passed and Congress has periodically intruded to grant relief for those who sought to overcome this presumptive protection of endangered species without prevailing in the God Squad process.[201]

Religious Freedom Restoration Act of 1993 (RFRA)

RFRA arose in response to the Supreme Court's decision in *Employment Div., Dept. of Human Resources of Ore. v. Smith*.[202] Prior to *Smith*,[203] the Supreme

---

[194] Lujan v. Defenders of the Wildlife, 504 U.S. 555 (1992).

[195] 437 U.S. 153, 194–95 (1978).

[196] Cass Sunstein, The Cost-Benefit State 68 (2002). *See also*, Amy Sinden, *In Defense of Absolutism, Combating the Power of Politics in Environmental Law*, 90 Iowa L. Rev. 1405 (2005) (also characterizing the absolutism of the ESA as a rights-approach).

[197] *See* Sinden, *id.* at 1504.

[198] *Id.*

[199] U.S. Fish and Wildlife Service, Endangered Species Act: A History of the Endangered Species Act of 1973 (last updated November 1, 2017), https://www.fws.gov/endangered/laws-policies/esa-history.html.

[200] Sinden, *supra* n.197 at 1505.

[201] *Id.*

[202] 42 U.S.C. §§ 2000bb *et seq. See also* 494 U.S. 872 (1990) (refusing to apply strict scrutiny to neutral, generally applicable laws that impose a substantial burden on the practice of religion). 42 U.S.C. §§ 2000bb(a) (2)–(4) and 2000bb-1(a).

[203] 485 U.S. 439 (1988).

Court applied strict scrutiny under the Free Exercise Clause of the Constitution, not just to laws targeting religion but also to laws that are "neutral toward"[204] and only incidentally burden religion.[205] By analogy, I argue in this chapter that generally applicable laws that do not target human health per se, but which burden health nonetheless, should receive HIA scrutiny.

The *Smith* decision in 1990 was a pivot for the Supreme Court.[206] Two individuals were fired for ceremonially ingesting peyote, thereby violating employer and state-imposed drug restrictions. Because Smith was fired for misconduct defined without regard to religion, just as Sherbert was fired for refusal to work on Saturday, he did not qualify for unemployment benefits. The general prohibition on drug use and possession was deemed neutral to religion and applied to all individuals regardless of creed. Therefore, according to Justice Scalia writing for a 6–3 majority, the compelling interest and least restrictive means test were not triggered.[207] Religious minority interests could seek protection in the general horse-trading of the political process and would not otherwise be singled out for special justification of any incidental burden.[208]

Congress in RFRA reimposed strict scrutiny, requiring a showing of compelling governmental interest and least restrictive means for generally applicable laws that substantially burdened "a person's exercise of religion," in a manner paralleling the RIA requirements we have seen.[209]

RFRA, like UMRA, covers both legislative and regulatory activity, self-declaring, "This chapter applies to all Federal law, and the implementation of that law, whether statutory or otherwise, and whether adopted before or after November 16, 1993."[210] RFRA evidently contemplates lookback application as well.[211]

But not every regulation or statute is captured insofar as the law must still qualify as one that "substantially burdens a person's exercise of religion." This parameter calls to mind other RIA threshold requirements. NEPA kicks in only

---

[204] This phrase is used in the Congressional findings for RFRA, 42 U.S.C. § 2000bb(a)(2) and (4).

[205] Sherbert v. Verner, 374 U.S. 398 (1963). *See also* Wisconsin v. Yoder, 406 U.S. 205 (1972).

[206] 374 U.S. 398 (1963). The decision was presaged by *Lyng v. Northwest Indian Cemetery Protective Association*, 485 U.S. 439 (1988).

[207] 499 U.S. 872, at 879.

[208] *Id.* at 980.

[209] 42 U.S.C. § 2000bb-1(a), (b). Though *City of Boerne v. Flores*, 521 U.S. 507 (1997) partially invalidated RFRA insofar as Congress' Fourteenth Amendment power was deemed insufficient to authorize the imposition of RFRA upon the states, Congress restored some state applications of RFRA in the form of the Religious Land Use and Institutionalized Persons Act (RLUIPA), relying on Congress' Commerce and Spending Powers instead. Pub. L. No. 106-274, 114 Stat. 803 (2000), codified as 42 U.S.C. § 2000cc *et seq.*

[210] 42 U.S.C. § 2000bb-3(a).

[211] Some would argue that the "lookback" application is the only portion of RFRA on sound constitutional footing. *See, e.g.*, Branden Lewiston, *RFRA as Legislative Entrenchment*, 2017 PEPPERDINE L. REV. 26 (2017).

when a "major federal action significantly affects the quality of the human environment," and the RFA is triggered if a rule will have "a significant economic effect on a substantial number of small entities."

The threshold term in RFRA, "exercise of religion," is defined in the statute as "any exercise of religion, whether or not compelled by or central to, a system of religious belief."[212] However, the threshold term "substantial burden" is not further specified in statute and has been contested in court.[213]

The "sufficiency of purpose" that a law must display in order to justify substantial burden on religious exercise is manifestly required. The statute prevents such burden unless "that application of the burden to the person ... is in furtherance of a compelling government interest."[214] RFRA's demand for fit in the event of government action countervailing religious liberty is also readily apparent. The government must demonstrate that the burdening measure is "the least restrictive means of furthering that compelling governmental interest."[215]

The government can be called to account for nonconformance with RFRA by the putative individual rights-holders. The statute allows an aggrieved person to assert "violation of this section ... as a claim or defense in a judicial proceeding and obtain appropriate relief against a government."[216]

Through this discussion it should be apparent that RFRA contains the same structural elements as the other regulatory analysis statutes: (1) a trans-substantive law passed by Congress, (2) imposing requirements upon federal action across jurisdictional bounds, (3) triggered by a threshold impact upon a favored value, (4) when that value is not otherwise protected by the Constitution, and (5) imposing a condition of heightened justification for that burden (6) consisting of a showing of sufficiency of purpose and fit. "Impact assessment," in terms of a showing of "substantial burden," is required in order to make the threshold showing for the heightened scrutiny to apply. The only differences lie in, first, the mechanism of enforcement and second, the timing of when the justification must be produced, a matter which is related to the mode of enforcement. According to UMRA, any member of Congress can raise a point of order to prevent the statute from going forward for failure to fulfill the heightened justification requirement. Under RFRA, the power of the courts can be harnessed to

---

[212] 42 U.S.C. § 2000bb-2(4) *referring to* § 2000cc-5(7).

[213] Burwell v. Hobby Lobby 573 U.S. __ (2014); 134 S. Ct. 2751 (concluding that the condition that for-profit employers coverage but not direct financing of all contraception options if they wish to enjoy tax-exemption for electing to offer health benefits was not so attenuated as to fail the "substantial burden" threshold). Observers have noted that the substantial burden test was thereby defined down to virtually nothing. *See, e.g.,* Elizabeth Sepper, *Free Exercise Lochnerism*, 115 COLUM L. REV. 1453, 1497 (2015) (the substantial burden test required merely that "plaintiff's assert ... that a law imposes a substantial burden").

[214] 42 U.S.C § 2000bb-1(b)(1).

[215] 42 U.S.C. § 2000bb-1(b)(2).

[216] 42 U.S.C. § 2000bb-1(c).

strike the rule or statute for failure to fulfill the heightened justification require-ment. Of course, because of the nature of judicial review as opposed to points of order, the justification need not be tendered *ex ante* as it would be under UMRA, before the measure is issued. Court action, after all, will usually occur *post hoc*.

Private Property/Takings Executive Order

In the late 1980s, Reagan signed EO 12630, "Governmental Actions and Interference with Constitutionally Protected Property Rights." It has not since been revoked.[217] Under this EO, before any agency undertakes regulation of pri-vate property to protect public health or safety, it must "anticipate, and account for" a number of considerations in its internal deliberations and submissions to OMB.

This heightened justification requirement clearly extends to subconstitutional burdens on private property. Even without examining the case law on regulatory takings, this point is evident from the language of the EO. Part of the statement of heightened justification required before the agency takes action is an "estimate, to the extent possible, [of] the potential cost to the government in the event that a court later determines that the action constituted a taking."[218] Thus, the set of actions to which the EO is expected to apply exceeds the actions that will later be found a taking.

The agency must first, "[i]dentify clearly, with as much specificity as possible, the public health or safety risk created by the private property use that is the sub-ject of the proposed action."[219] Thus, the purpose of the regulatory action must be specifically articulated.

The EO next requires agencies to "[e]stablish that such proposed action sub-stantially advances the purpose of protecting public health and safety against the specifically identified risk."[220] The agency must show the aspect of fit that Robert Alexy might call "suitability," namely that the means does advance the important justifying purpose identified above.[221] Also, the agency must "[e]stablish to the extent possible that the restrictions imposed on the private property are not dis-proportionate to the extent to which the use contributes to the overall risk." This

---

[217] Exec. Order No. 12630, 53 Fed. Reg. 8859 (March 15, 1988). *See* recent regulations complying with its requirements, *e.g.* Department of Health and Human Services' 340B Drug Pricing Program Ceiling Price and Manufacturer Civil Monetary Penalties Regulation, 82 Fed. Reg. 14332 (March 20, 2017) (to be codified at 42 C.F.R. pt. 10), https://www.gpo.gov/fdsys/pkg/FR-2017-03-20/pdf/2017-05491.pdf.

[218] Exec. Order No. 12630 § 4, 53 Fed. Reg. 8859 (March 15, 1988).

[219] Exec. Order No. 12630 § 4(d)(1), 53 Fed. Reg. 8859 (March 15, 1988).

[220] *Id.*

[221] ROBERT ALEXY, A THEORY OF CONSTITUTIONAL RIGHTS (1985).

provision advances a different aspect of fit, "necessity," prohibiting excess burden that is not sufficiently linked with, and therefore cannot draw sufficient justification from, the important purpose.

Though executive orders may lack private enforcement, many of the other measures that now feature mature claiming mechanisms also started out in weaker, precursor form. The Paperwork Reduction Act was preceded by the Federal Reports Act.[222] The Unfunded Mandates Reform Act succeeded the State and Local Government Cost Estimates Act of 1981 which had existed for thirteen years but lacked the accountability provided by points of order.[223] Similarly, the extraconstitutional protection of private property from regulatory burden may now take the form of a mere executive order, but bills have been introduced since to codify it.[224] Indeed, H.R. 925 passed the House during the Gingrich-led Republican revolution, though it later died in the Senate.[225] This bill would have triggered agencies to compensate property owners for the regulatory burdens on their private property use if that federal agency action reduced the property's fair market value by a certain threshold percentage (eventually set at 20 percent).[226] Meanwhile, the executive order itself has enjoyed significant longevity,[227] continuing to elevate the protection of private property rights above the constitutional baseline, just as RFRA does for the protection of free exercise, and as UMRA does for the protection of federalism-related values.

Other Impact Assessments Established by the Executive Branch

Other EOs on the continuum may or may not yet merit the label of "rights." Some constitute duties to the public at large, rather than duties with corresponding rights. For instance, George W. Bush issued EO 13211, "Actions Concerning Regulations that Significantly Affect Energy Supply, Distribution or Use," which required federal agencies to prepare a "Statement of Energy Effect" (SEE).[228] This SEE is triggered only when federal actions may have "significant adverse effect"

---

[222] Shapiro and Moran, *supra* n.94.

[223] *See* Garrett *supra* n.164 at 1153, 1160–63. 2 U.S.C. § 653(a)(2), repealed by Unfunded Mandates Reform Act of 1995, Pub. L. 104-4 § 104, 109 Stat. 48, 62 (1995).

[224] The Private Property Rights Act, S. 50, 102nd Cong. (1992) (introduced by Senator Steven Symms).

[225] The Private Property Protection Act, H.R.925, 104th Cong. (1995). This provision was also included in The Job Creation and Wage Enhancement Act of 1995, H.R. 9 § 201–210, 104th Cong. (1995) (a component of the Republicans Contract with America). *See* SINCLAIR, supra n.126 at 113–133. *See also,* THOMAS O. MCGARITY, FREEDOM TO HARM 78 (2013) (explaining that Senate Republicans failed to overcome filibusters on various omnibus regulatory reform efforts).

[226] Sinclair, *id.* at 122–5.

[227] U.S. Gen. Accounting Office, GAO-03-1015, *Regulatory Takings: Implementation of Executive Order on Government Actions Affecting Private Property Use* (September 2003).

[228] Exec. Order No. 13211, 66 Fed. Reg. 28355 (May 22, 2001).

on "supply, distribution, and use of energy." OMB issued a memorandum in 2001 listing circumstances that would constitute "a significant adverse effect," including reductions in crude oil supply in an amount of ten thousand barrels per day or more, reductions in coal or natural gas production of a certain amount, and increases in the cost of energy production and distribution in excess of 1 percent.[229] Some environmental advocates warned this EO could "curtail critical habitat designation or other environmental protection,"[230] and therefore urged Obama to repeal it in his first hundred days.[231] He declined to do so, and this EO remains in effect today.[232]

This EO illustrates how some impact assessment requirements may depart from the structured, individuated analysis that characterizes rights. For example, whom does the energy order protect? Certain energy interests? The general public who pay energy bills and depend on energy supplies? This EO might be fairly characterized as duty to the public-at-large, like Alexy's protectionist tariff from Chapter 2, rather a duty with corresponding rights-bearers.

Rectifying the Glaring Omission of Health

Thus far, our discussion reveals a field of contest over conceptions of rights. A picture emerges of ongoing struggle to elevate certain protected interests to rights status. Moreover, this struggle is taking place in the legislative and administrative domains.

How would we characterize the state of play? By this snapshot, we enjoy a panoply of negative rights, namely, freedom from government-imposed paperwork, small business freedom from economic burdens, and religious freedom beyond constitutional levels of protection. State interests are shielded from economically burdensome federal mandates and property owners assert freedom from subconstitutional regulatory takings. But are we free from government action that burdens people's health? In some politically motivated instances, we virtually ban health impact assessment, as was the case for a long time with respect to

---

[229] OFFICE OF MGMT. & BUDGET, EXECUTIVE OFFICE OF THE PRESIDENT, OMB MEMORANDUM M01-27, GUIDANCE FOR IMPLEMENTING EXEC. ORDER 13211 (July 13, 2001), https://www.whiteho use.gov/omb/memoranda_m01-27.

[230] Elizabeth Glass Gettleman et al., Inquiry into the Implementation of Bush's Executive Order 13211 and the Impact on Environmental and Public Health Regulation, 27 FORDHAM ENV. L. REV. 225, 228 (2015).

[231] Rebecca Bratspies et al., Center for Progressive Reform, Protecting Public Health and the Environment by a Stroke of a Presidential Pen: Seven Executive Orders for the President's First 100 Days (2008), http://www.progressivereform.org/CPR_ExecOrders_Stroke_of_a_Pen.pdf.

[232] Elizabeth Glass Gettleman et al., Impact of Executive Order 13211 on Environmental Regulation: An Empirical Study, 89 ENERGY POLICY 302 (2016), http://academicworks.cuny.edu/cgi/ viewcontent.cgi?article=1068&context=sph_pubs.

guns and their effect on health.[233] We have indirect claims to health or sustainability under NEPA and the ESA, in the form of designated interests in environmental protection. Environmental entitlements are unquestionably urgent, but classic environmental exposure is not the only threat to health. There is a glaring gap in the protection of basic human well-being. Therefore, I propose we institute an HIA requirement as a foundational assertion of the right to health.

The selective imposition of accounting and justification requirements provides a familiar procedural means of institutionalizing substantive norms. Selectively procedural and therefore "semi-substantive" means of protecting background rights have been noted by numerous scholars, including Matthew Stephenson.[234]

Here I present options to consider for an HIA requirement that I believe should be enacted by Congress. I offer these features as a starting point for policy debate.

Scope

The requirement should apply to both legislative action and agency action, just as UMRA and RFRA do. The HIA could also apply to both regulatory and deregulatory government action. This symmetry already characterizes other RIAs as well as judicial scrutiny of administrative action.[235] Because this HIA would be imposed by statute, not executive order, it would also cover independent regulatory agencies.

---

[233] Language from the so-called Dickey Amendment had been inserted into appropriations bills each year since 1996, "prevent[ing] funds from being used to advocate for or promote gun control." This language, while not strictly forbidding research or data-gathering on the health effects of gun policies, has chilled such conduct and remained in effect through the FY 2018 Appropriations bill. *See* Consolidated Appropriations Act of 2018, Pub. L. No. 115-141 (2018), https://www.congress. gov/bill/115th-congress/house-bill/1625/text. For another example of statutory language that, although not yet enacted, seeks to prohibit impact assessment, *see* Local Zoning Decisions Protection Act H.R. 482, 115th Cong. (2017), http://gosar.house.gov/sites/gosar.house.gov/files/Local%20Zon ing%20Decisions%20Protection%20Act%202017.pdf (declaring "Notwithstanding any other provision of law, no Federal Funds may be used to design, build, maintain, utilize, or provide access to a Federal database of geospatial information on community racial disparities or disparities in access to affordable housing").

[234] *See, e.g.,* Matthew C. Stephenson, *The Price of Public Action: Constitutional Doctrine and the Judicial Manipulation of Legislative Enactment Costs,* 118 YALE L.J. 2, 6, 39 (2008). *See also,* Eskridge and Frickey *supra* n.171.

[235] *See* Jonathan Masur, *The Regulatory Accountability Act, Or: How Progressives Learned to Stop Worrying and Love Cost-Benefit Analysis,* NOTICE & COMMENT (May 4, 2017), http://yalejreg.com/ nc/the-regulatory-accountability-act-or-how-progressives-learned-to-stop-worrying-and-love-cost-benefit-analysis-by-jonathan-masur/. *But see* Reagan's Exec. Order No. 12630 § 2(1), 53 FR 8859 (1988) (specifically defining "policies that have takings implications" in such a way to "not include: (1) Actions abolishing regulations, discontinuing governmental programs, or modifying regulations in a manner that lessens interference with the use of private property"). For the general principle that judicial review of agency action applies symmetrically, *see* Motor Vehicle Manufacturers Assn. v. State Farm Mutual Ins. Co., 463 U.S. 29 (1983).

The statute would need to specify an HIA-triggering condition based on the nature of a policy's effect on health. This threshold question has been crucial in each of the RIA measures we have examined.[236] One could assign the duty to either an agency head or a designated health official. This approach draws from the example set by RFA, whereby the agency head must decide and certify whenever government action avoids a threshold impact on "a substantial number of small entities."[237] A determination of "no substantial impact on health" would be subject to judicial review, just as a certification of insignificant impact is under RFA, or FONSI is under NEPA.[238]

Alternatively, we could adapt the NEPA mechanism, whereby the impact analysis and detailed statement condition would apply to "major Federal actions significantly affecting" human health, and the agency would have to perform some kind of preliminary HIA to see if this threshold is met. This two-step process parallels the mechanism of the preliminary EA under NEPA, which concludes in either a FONSI or proceeds to a full EIS. This example illustrates how a trigger mechanism could be designed such that an early, smaller HIA might be required for *all* government action. Meanwhile, the desire to avoid full HIAs might encourage health commitments across sectors as various government organs sought the HIA equivalent of "mitigated FONSIs."[239] I discuss below what form those mitigating actions might take.[240] NEPA's implementation also proves that a trigger threshold need not be specified in advance and can be elaborated case-by-case.

For HIAs to empower beneficiaries *as rights-holders*, we should consider adding a mechanism for individuals or their representatives to initiate or call for the HIA heightened justification procedure. The availability of judicial review for the determination of "no trigger" under RFA or FONSI under NEPA, would represent one avenue. One could also establish a Chief Counsel for Health Advocacy along the lines of the Chief Counsel for Advocacy of the Small Business Administration, which would institutionalize representation of community health interests.[241]

---

[236] *See* Shapiro and Moran, *supra* n.94 at 171–72 (observing, "Much as the vague definition of 'significant impact' in the [Regulatory Flexibility Act] was a source of agency discretion, the term 'economically significant' in the UMRA was largely left open to interpretation by individual agencies. Critics of the Act noted that the vague definition allows agencies to evade assessments and benefit-cost analysis by determining that rules do not qualify as economically significant. The GAO supported this criticism, stating that the Act gave agencies too much discretion in complying with the requirements").

[237] *See supra* text accompanying n.102.

[238] *Id. See also* text accompanying n.137.

[239] *See supra* text accompanying n.136.

[240] *See infra* text accompanying n.264–65.

[241] *See infra* text accompanying n.118–23. I thank Alan Morrison for this insight.

UMRA requires CBO to judge a bill's projected costs to subnational governments against the triggering threshold to determine whether a point of order would lie against it.[242] Similarly, GAO or some other entity designated by Congress could be tasked with calculating whether a bill "significantly affects human health."[243] Alternatively, we could piggyback on existing RIA thresholds such that any action meeting the UMRA threshold as calculated by CBO would also be subject to full HIA. For instance, the National Historic Preservation Act (NHPA) has piggybacked on NEPA such that any "major federal action" under NEPA also garners some process under NHPA.[244]

Alternatively, "significantly affecting human health" could be construed as adversely affecting key health indicators for a numerical threshold of persons by a certain magnitude. I do not believe this approach requires an optimal set of thresholds. Some initial proxies could be set, just as in Bush's EO 13211, the effect on energy supply was established as adversely affecting energy prices by more than 1 percent, or a drop in crude oil production by ten thousand barrels a day or more. Similarly, the Gingrich Congress' attempt to legislate regulatory takings identified an arbitrary trigger of 20 percent reduction in the property's fair market value.[245] The difficulty of setting a perfect threshold should not block the development of a provisional mechanism, just as those difficulties did not impede the establishment of RIAs protecting other values.

Participatory

HIAs should follow NEPA in promoting participation.[246] This commitment would enhance an emerging feature of HIAs insofar as they are taken up by disadvantaged communities and their supporting coalitions. For instance, HIAs have been wielded by Native Alaskan tribal groups to assert their interests in health and well-being when oil and gas permits are granted near their lands.[247]

---

[242] See supra n.157.

[243] This idea takes inspiration from NEPA's creation of CEQ and the Science Advisory Board, and PRA's authorization of OIRA. However, the HIA proposal could authorize a Congressional agency like CBO rather than an executive entity. For just such a proposal from a former Congressman, see, T. J. Cox et al., Reconceptualizing Congressional Decision-making Around Well-being: A Health in All Policies Approach, HARVARD JOURNAL ON LEGISLATION ONLINE (2021), https://harvardjol.com/ (accessed June 16, 2021).

[244] 16 U.S.C. § 470 (2018) (current version of Act in scattered sections of 54 U.S.C.); 36 C.F.R. § 800 (2019).

[245] See supra n.228.

[246] See NEPA Litigation Guide, supra n.145 at 25.

[247] See National Petroleum Reserve-Alaska Final Integrated Plan/ Environmental Impact Statement (2012), https://eplanning.blm.gov/epl-front-office/projects/nepa/5251/41004/43154/ Vol2_NPR-A_Final_IAP_FEIS.pdf (constituting an EIS process where the Alaskan Inter-Tribal Council participated heavily).

In Los Angeles, communities at risk of being dislocated by stadium development also used HIAs successfully to block the proposal.[248] Causa Justa's community organizers meanwhile recruited the Alameda County public health department to conduct an HIA surveying the health harms of foreclosure.[249] In San Francisco, HIAs likewise contributed to the successful campaign for a living wage.[250]

Under my proposal, any member of Congress could call for an HIA for legislative measures through a point of order. Arguably, this mechanism allows democratic participation through lobbying, though this approach also renders the tool more accessible to powerful interests.

Equity

The measure that I am proposing would embed a preference for health equity even more deeply into the HIA methodology. HIAs should impose justificatory burdens not just on actions with direct and indirect effects on human health, but also on actions exacerbating health inequality.

A landmark British report on health disparities in 1998 declared that "[a]ll policies likely to have a direct or indirect effect on health should be evaluated in terms of their impact on health inequalities, and should be formulated in such a way that by favouring the less well-off they will, wherever possible, reduce such inequalities."[251] The HIA could at a minimum require that "all policies likely to have a direct or indirect effect on health must report their impact on health inequalities."

The "fit" requirements, which I discuss below, should then proceed to encourage the formulation of policies to favor the less well-off and reduce such inequalities.[252] Mimicking the NEPA regulations which require the agency decision-maker to "record" the environmentally preferable alternative and justify how the agency rejected this alternative,[253] the decision-maker could be required to record the most health equity-promoting alternative. If the agency chose otherwise, then it would have to describe the reasons and explain by way of the specific "economic and technical considerations and agency statutory

---

[248] See RWJF supra n.61.
[249] Victoria Colliver, *Foreclosures Can Make You Sick, Report Says*, SFGATE (September 2, 2010), https://www.sfgate.com/health/article/Foreclosures-can-make-you-sick-report-says-3254499.php.
[250] Id.
[251] D. ACHESON ET AL., INDEPENDENT INQUIRY INTO INEQUALITIES IN HEALTH (1998).
[252] For a recent proposal along these Rawlsian lines, see Alicia Ely Yamin and Ole Frithjof Norheim, *Taking Equality Seriously: Applying Human Rights Frameworks to Priority Setting in Health*, 36 HUM. RTS. Q. 296 (2014).
[253] 40 C.F.R. § 1505.2.

missions . . . including any essential considerations of national policy," mirroring NEPA implementing language.[254]

For those who believe that attention to equity represents an interjection of additional favored values into the HIA mechanism apart from health, there are a few responses. One is that identification of health impacts necessarily includes identification of the *distribution* of health impacts as discussed earlier.[255] Furthermore, social and economic inequality are major determinants of population health, with effects independent of those caused by poverty.[256] Because the health gradient is steeper at lower SES levels, SES distribution must flow downward to have salutary effects on population health. Promoting equity is closely congruent with the protection of health.

Moreover, we can argue that other RIAs also include ideologically clustered secondary values. UMRA sneaks in concern not just for burdens on States and localities, but costs to private entities too. The PRA includes extra protection for small business.

Impact Analysis

The legislative and regulatory proposals that fall within the HIA measure's scope of application must be accompanied by reporting on the burdens they place on health and its distribution. Again, some impact analysis and reporting would already exist by virtue of the threshold determination of the HIA measure's applicability, just as some environmental impact analysis is done in the form of an EA to determine whether there is sufficient effect on the quality of the human environment to warrant a full EIS.[257]

Sufficiency of Purpose

These health-affecting measures must also clearly declare the purpose and need for that action. As with the PRA, an agency must describe the "need" for the action being considered.[258] Borrowing again from NEPA, I would suggest that need must be framed in terms of "economic and technical considerations and agency statutory missions . . . including any essential considerations of national policy."[259]

[254] *Id.*
[255] *See supra* text accompanying n.49–55.
[256] *See supra* text accompanying n.19–21.
[257] *See supra* n.134–35.
[258] 44 U.S.C. § 3506(c).
[259] 40 C.F.R. § 1505.2.

As with UMRA, any legislative action would be subject to a showing of sufficiency of purpose insofar as a separate vote to overcome the point of order would be required, thereby demonstrating Congress' conclusion that the non–health sector policy furthers a sufficiently important purpose to justify the burden on health.

Fit

Just as we earlier contemplated the incorporation of equity considerations by requiring a recording of the alternative that favors the least well-off,[260] we could apply that same recording requirement to the least health-restrictive alternative.

A point of order could be available for any health-affecting policy that, as we mention above, reduced major health indicators of a population by a certain threshold magnitude. Just as unfunded mandates could avoid the point of order if funded, HIA points of order could be avoided if the health-burdening legislation included certain designated health-promoting measures. We could deliberate over and devise what those might be, and I assume our judgments on the appropriate mitigation policies would change with changing circumstances. For instance, PRA specifies certain mitigation strategies such as different compliance timetables and exemptions that must be considered when small businesses are burdened.[261] ESA does the same for endangered species.[262] The set of must-consider health mitigation and improvement strategies could be specified to included investment in early childhood education, housing and other social determinants of health, or some other action that would reduce the Gini coefficient, a well-known metric of inequality.[263]

Enforcement/Claiming

Beyond enforcement by point of order, compliance with regulatory as well as legislative HIA requirements could also be subject to judicial review. Even if not specifically authorized, courts might still, as they have with NEPA, construe APA-based judicial review to be available for whether agency action is arbitrary and capricious in light of inadequacies in health impact assessment.[264]

---

[260] *Supra* text accompanying n.253–58.
[261] *See supra* text accompanying n.110.
[262] *See supra* text accompanying n.193.
[263] *See, e.g.*, DAVID BUCK & SARAH GREGORY, IMPROVING THE PUBLIC'S HEALTH: A RESOURCE FOR LOCAL AUTHORITIES (2013) (for nine recommendations to improve public health and reduce inequalities).
[264] *See supra* n.144.

Lookback Review of Existing Federal Laws

A true Ungerian destabilization[265] right would affect existing policies as well as new policies. Thus, any policy might be analyzed and challenged on the basis of its adverse effects on health and health equity. While this notion may sound extreme, many of the examples I describe contain precisely such lookback and ongoing tailoring requirements that affect all existing policies, rather than new policies alone.[266]

A recent example of lookback scrutiny is former President Obama's EO 13563, Improving Regulations and Regulatory Review. Section 6 requires agencies to plan for periodic review of existing "significant" rules.[267] Other examples also come to mind. For instance, a five-year sunset was proposed by the Gingrich Congress for all regulations subject to other types of RIAs.[268]

Any already-approved legislation would be subject to judicial review, just as any measure is now subject to RFRA challenge.[269] Prior legislation would also be vulnerable to a point-of-order certainly upon reauthorization or amendment, but could also be draw a point of order at designated re-evaluation points as well.

I argue that we should move from sporadic to general use of HIAs to foster a rights-based approach to health. This chapter demonstrates that a negative procedural right to health could be enunciated in the form of an HIA requirement and circumvent the bias against recognizing positive social and economic rights in the US legal tradition, even as they supply the predicate for demanding affirmative provision for health in the form of mitigation measures. Neoliberal rights "deflect consideration of how we are systemically connected to one another globally, irrespective of our choices."[270] HIAs would seed a right that pushes back on that view.[271]

Meanwhile the illusion of a distinction between positive and negative rights is ever more difficult to maintain. The entitlements of the "haves" are so blatantly non-neutral and involve choices to affirmatively allocate state resources in their

---

[265] How do we unwind states of the world that are damaging? How do we combat the inertia and the power of incumbents as they affect future humanity? For these goals we need destabilization rights. ROBERTO MANGABEIRA UNGER, FALSE NECESSITY: ANTI-NECESSITARIAN SOCIAL THEORY IN THE SERVICE OF RADICAL DEMOCRACY 530 (1987) (explaining that "destabilization rights protect the citizen's interest in breaking open the large-scale organizations or the extended areas of social practice that remain closed to the destabilizing effects of ordinary conflict and thereby sustain insulated hierarchies of power and advantage"). Scott Burris provided the insight that my proposal for HIAs resembles a call for destabilization rights.

[266] See supra n.87, 112, 173, and 212.

[267] Exec. Order No.13563, 76 Fed. Reg. 3821 (January 21, 2011).

[268] See also Stuart Shapiro and Deanna Moran, supra n.94 at 172.

[269] See supra text accompanying n.212-13.

[270] See O'Keefe, supra n.43 at 736.

[271] See also West, supra n.34 at 91-102 (arguing that we should revitalize rights in forms that recognize relational aspects of human nature).

favor. The increasing circumstances of scarcity also emphasize choice. We are so interconnected with one another and these interconnections are now hypertrophic, as evidenced by climate change, infectious disease, 360-degree surveillance,[272] pervasive social media, and algorithmic use of big data. Coercion (or unconsented for harms or appropriations at the hands of others) occur routinely yet our traditional lines and bulwarks of liberty rights cannot contain the spillover. We need a complementary right to insulate people from systemic harm as well.

Our freedom is not the only thing we can claim against one another. Kantian rights of liberal autonomy protect a person in the abstract, stripped of all specific character. A right to health, by attending to our embodied selves, could serve as a useful corrective. Our liberal tradition sharply divides the right from the good, while a right to health presupposes continuity between rights and human flourishing. At least we may start with a negative right to health as a baseline integrity from harm, checking and supplementing traditional liberty and property rights by marking another place to toe the line, an additional index of justice.

---

[272] *See, e.g.,* SHOSHANA ZUBOFF, THE AGE OF SURVEILLANCE CAPITALISM: THE FIGHT FOR A HUMAN FUTURE AT THE NEW FRONTIER OF POWER (2019).

6

How Reinsurance Is a Right

I have shown in the previous chapter how a right to health could be constituted even within the classic negative liberty tradition, noting that in operation, such a right could also leverage affirmative commitments of material resources by way of mitigation.

However, let us now turn to face squarely the question of how we in the US might be able to lay claim to the state's affirmative commitment of health resources without those preconditions.

We take the same comparative sectoral methodology that we used in Chapter 5 and apply it to the question of what to propose as a plausible and achievable "affirmative" right to affordable healthcare in the United States. How have claimants in other sectors created and then redeemed on entrenched expectations—their sense of entitlement—to affirmative material backing from the state?

Here I lay out the evidence that government has been guaranteeing other material interests apart from health by serving as "reinsurer" in those arenas. Following scholars across numerous disciplines, I contend that one longstanding but underappreciated government function in the United States is the state's role as reinsurer of primary insurers and other private supply-side financiers. By this "reinsurance function," I refer to the state's function in absorbing catastrophic costs when losses exceed what these primary private institutions could be expected to bear. When the state serves in this way, it does so in order to stabilize these private institutions and shore up their ability to extend access to goods and services to the public. Despite a professed aversion to "entitlements,"[1] the United States has regularly furnished a robust material safety net against catastrophic risk, if not to the individual beneficiaries, then to the primary private insurer or financier who provides access to those goods or services. In this chapter, I advance the argument that that these guarantees, even if diverse in form and label,

---

With permission, Chapter 6 adapts material from Christina S. Ho, *With Liberty and Reinsurance for All: The Deep Case for a Government Backstop in Health Care*, 100 Denv. L. Rev. ____ (forthcoming 2023).

[1] Jamelle Bouie, Opinion, *Joe Manchin Should Stop Talking About 'Entitlement.'* N.Y. Times (October 8, 2021), https://www.nytimes.com/2021/10/08/opinion/joe-manchin-biden.html, (accessed June 13, 2022) (discussing pivotal 50th Democratic Senate vote-holder, Senator Joe Manchin and his public stance objecting to "entitlement" culture). *See generally* David Super's account as laid out in Chapter 2, *supra* and drawing principally from David A. Super, *The Political Economy of Entitlement*, 104 Columbia L. Rev. 633 (2004).

should be understood as examples of state performance of the reinsurance function. This federal reinsurance helps assure the public's access to goods and services that we collectively deem vital, including not just banking, but also housing, agricultural goods, higher education, and pensions.

Public reinsurance amounts to a state precommitment to absorb catastrophic loss. And when provided in some domains and not others, it can function as inscriptions of rights would—announcing upfront binding constraints that guide how our polity prioritizes among competing values and interests. The state, through reinsurance, is declaring at time one which material interests it will privilege at time two, and articulating the threshold conditions for that assistance.[2]

By examining reinsurance as a state function deeply anchored in US politico-legal bedrock, I seek first to argue that healthcare lags insofar as it fails to rank among the interests we expressly reinsure. However, haphazard suggestions of health reinsurance abound as I will also show in the next chapter. In laying out the picture of comprehensive reinsurance everywhere but health, my argument bears on the case for reinsurance in healthcare by implication. Healthcare, I contend, should be on at least equal footing. But even beyond that story line, the tale of reinsurance and its development in other sectors suggests a playbook for how reinsurance for healthcare could become a right, first seeded and then fortified with specific rights-like features, and then ever more entrenched to the point that it could potentially underpin state-sponsored universal healthcare, as I argue by the end of the next chapter.

Basics of Reinsurance and Some Health Sector Illustrations

In this section, I introduce the features of reinsurance using latent, scattered health sector examples to suggest its promise as a health policy tool before plunging headlong into the use of reinsurance across other domains.

Through this chapter and the next, I will contend that when the government provides a backstop against high losses in order to stabilize the underlying private risk market, the state is furnishing a form of government-sponsored reinsurance even if it is not technically labeled as such.[3] State-sponsored reinsurance in this sense establishes a risk ceiling above which supplier-mediated risks are transferred to the government to be distributed or spread publicly in some way.

---

[2] *See* Chapters 3 and 4, discussing the structure of rights as laying the set of entitlements R, and qualifying traits in set S.

[3] Christina S. Ho, *Health Reinsurance as a Human Right, in* INSURANCE AND HUMAN RIGHTS (Margarida Lima Rego & Birgit Kuschke, eds., forthcoming). Some commentators have observed that this is not true reinsurance if the private risk market does not consist of actual insurers providing insurance products. I will show how the underlying primary financiers or providers can function as insurers, even if they are banks, mortgage lenders, employers, or hospitals.

What is reinsurance? Primary insurers seek out reinsurance when loss exposure outpaces insurers' willingness to carry risk.[4] One common reason an insurer might desire reinsurance is in situations of unwanted exposure to correlated (covariant) loss. For instance, crop insurers might draw on reinsurance when weather or other localized events pose a primary source of crop failure. Weather events can impose losses upon many enrollees at the same time. Those losses are not statistically independent of one another as most farms in a region experience the same weather.[5] Health insurance is also afflicted by this kind of correlated loss. Indeed, Medicare's financing woes testify to how an aging society can generate cost exposures that are not stochastically independent.[6] More recently, the task of insuring a new population, such as that now enrolled in the Affordable Care Act (ACA), poses correlated risk insofar as all new enrollees might share a higher risk propensity. This type of "insurance for insurers" can of course be state-sponsored, but it is also commercially available for private purchase.[7] In this book, my aim is to flesh out a public right, and I therefore focus on state-sponsored measures.

Government-sponsored reinsurance can perform the same functions by collecting assessments (in lieu of commercial premiums) and pooling them in a state-organized fund that shields the primary insurer from risks beyond a designated "attachment point." Apart from organizing such a fund, government can also subsidize that fund from sources such as general tax revenue.[8]

The attachment point marks a threshold condition that triggers reinsurance coverage. An attachment point is thus analogous to a deductible under a primary insurance policy. Both represent the threshold expenditure that the insured must

[4] KATHERINE SWARTZ, *Reinsurance: How States Can Make Health Coverage More Affordable for Employers and Workers* vi (2005), https://www.commonwealthfund.org/publications/fund-reports/2005/jul/reinsurance-how-states-can-make-health-coverage-more-affordable (discussing Healthy New York, a state reinsurance program).

[5] Joseph W. Glauber, *Crop Insurance Reconsidered*, 86, AM. J. OF AGRIC. ECON. 1179–1195 (2004), https://onlinelibrary.wiley.com/doi/abs/10.1111/j.0002-9092.2004.00663.x (accessed April 1, 2021).

[6] *See*, THEODORE R. MARMOR, THE POLITICS OF MEDICARE (2nd ed. 2000). *See also*, MEDICARE TRUSTEES, 2020 ANNUAL REPORT OF THE BOARDS OF TRUSTEES OF THE FEDERAL HOSPITAL INSURANCE AND FEDERAL SUPPLEMENTARY MEDICAL INSURANCE TRUST FUNDS (2020), https://www.cms.gov/Research-Statistics-Data-and-Systems/Statistics-Trends-and-Reports/ReportsTrustFunds.

[7] Mark A. Hall, *The Three Types of Reinsurance Created By Federal Health Reform*, 29 HEALTH AFF. 1168–1172 (2010), https://www.healthaffairs.org/doi/abs/10.1377/hlthaff.2010.0430 (accessed March 24, 2021).

[8] M. KENT RANSON & SARA BENNETT, *Role of Central Governments in Furthering Social Goals through Microinsurance Units*, *in* SOCIAL REINSURANCE: A NEW APPROACH TO SUSTAINABLE COMMUNITY HEALTH FINANCING 245–61, 258 (David M. Dror & Alexander S. Preker, eds., 2002), http://documents.worldbank.org/curated/en/425661468779093475/pdf/265280PAPER0Social0reinsurance.pdf (noting that "Government may set up a reinsurance scheme (or solidarity fund). Participating [insurers may] contribute to this pool . . . , [g]overnment may establish this fund but not contribute to the pooled resources or establish the fund and make some contribution to the pooled resources (a combination of reinsurance and subsidy)").

incur before the third party's payment obligations take effect. The Medicare prescription drug benefit, added by George W. Bush in 2003, provides a useful example for illustrating these features. Unlike traditional Medicare benefits, which were covered by the federal government as a single public payer, the Bush administration and Republican Congressional sponsors of the Medicare prescription drug (Part D) benefit insisted that prescription drugs were covered by private plans, albeit subsidized by the government. Government did prescribe certain benefit parameters though. The standard benefit featured a deductible of $480, meaning that the Medicare senior receiving a standard benefit from a stand-alone private prescription drug policy in the 2022 policy year must first spend $480 in drug costs out of her own pocket before her plan begins to pay claims.[9]

However, the private prescription drug plan itself also enjoys a measure of reinsurance—in this case, the proverbial insurance for insurers. Once the Medicare enrollee's *total* pharmaceutical expenditures including their out-of-pocket costs reach an attachment point of roughly $10,000, qualifying as catastrophic, the private prescription drug plan is partially shielded from claims. The federal government absorbs 80 percent of the drug costs that the enrollee incurs above that catastrophic threshold.[10] Thus the fraction of the loss that the reinsurer agrees to pay above the attachment point is 80 percent in this Medicare Part D example. The fraction that remains to be paid by the original insurer is called coinsurance. The coinsurance retained by the private prescription drug plan under contract with the government would be 20 percent by implication. Indeed this 20 percent coinsurance level is slated to take effect in 2024 as part of the package of health measures in the Biden Administration's Inflation Reduction Act that recently passed into law.[11] Until then, the Part D design retains a small oddity. The primary insurer's coinsurance share is currently still 15 percent, with the other 5 percent of costs allotted back to the Medicare beneficiary herself to pay out-of-pocket.

Some reinsurance, once triggered, does not extend to the absorption of costs above an upper bound. In addition to an attachment point and coinsurance, many reinsurance policies feature some type of cap or ceiling beyond which loss reverts from the reinsurer back to the primary insurer. For instance, the ACA, taking a page from the Medicare prescription drug playbook, also authorized a reinsurance program to cushion any program start-up road bumps. Unlike the permanent Medicare Part D reinsurance program, the ACA's program expired

---

[9] *An Overview of the Medicare Part D Prescription Drug Benefit*, KFF (October 13, 2021), https://www.kff.org/medicare/fact-sheet/an-overview-of-the-medicare-part-d-prescription-drug-benefit/ (accessed March 24, 2022).

[10] *Id.*

[11] The Inflation Reduction Act of 2022, Pub. L. No. 117-169, 136 Stat. 1818, 1878 § 11201(b) (codified as amended in 42 U.S.C. § 1395w–115(b)) (August 16, 2022).

after three years, leaving states scrambling to restabilize their Exchange markets after year three, as we will see in the next chapter. In the first year of the ACA's implementation, the reinsurance program was slated to reimburse private health plans 80 percent of the cost of claims exceeding a per beneficiary attachment point of $45,000, leaving 20 percent for the primary ACA plan to coinsure.[12] But the promised 80 percent federal absorption of these costs was not open-ended. It capped out when a given beneficiary's claims reached $250,000.

In the health insurance world, reinsurance can take the form of an "aggregate" stop-loss policy, or an "excess of loss" policy (also called a "specific" excess policy).[13] Aggregate policies define the attachment point by the "total amount of benefits paid to *all* participants or beneficiaries beyond which the insurance company will indemnify the loss," whereas specific policies define the attachment point by "the level of benefits paid to *individual* beneficiaries beyond which the insurance company will indemnify the plan."[14]

Examples of both abound in the United States, particularly in the context of employer-sponsored coverage. Employer health benefits are, as we recall from Chapters 3 and 4, governed by a federal law called the Employee Retirement Income Security Act (ERISA). We will return to discuss various aspects of ERISA in greater depth later both in this chapter and the next. Under ERISA case law, some employers can elect to "self-insure" their workforce. They would do so by foregoing the purchase of outside health insurance policies, and instead undertaking to pay their beneficiaries' medical claims from the employers' own coffers. By choosing this arrangement, employers enjoy a valuable regulatory loophole. These so-called self-insured or self-funded plans are exempted from

---

[12] AMERICAN ACADEMY OF ACTUARIES ISSUE BRIEF, DRIVERS OF 2015 HEALTH INSURANCE PREMIUM CHANGES 4 (June 2014), https://www.actuary.org/sites/default/files/files/2015_Premium_Drivers_Updated_060414.pdf (estimating that "[r]einsurance program payments for 2014 generally reduced projected net claim costs by about 10 to 14 percent"). *See also,* DEPARTMENT OF HEALTH AND HUMAN SERVICES, CENTER FOR MEDICARE AND MEDICAID SERVICES, TRANSITIONAL REINSURANCE PROGRAM: PRO RATA ADJUSTMENT TO THE NATIONAL COINSURANCE RATE FOR THE 2014 BENEFIT YEAR LTR. (June 2015), https://www.cms.gov/CCIIO/Programs-and-Initiatives/Premium-Stabilizat ion-Programs/The-Transitional-Reinsurance-Program/Downloads/RI-Payments-National-Prorat ion-Memo-With-Numbers-6-17-15.pdf. In the latter years of the program the attachment point rose (to $90,000 for FY 2016), and the federal share of the claims above the attachment point dropped to 50 percent. *See* Patient Protection and Affordable Care Act; HHS Notice of Benefit and Payment Parameters for 2016; Final Rule, 80 Fed. Reg. 10750, 10752 (February 27, 2015).

[13] *Id.* at 105 (also describing another form, quota loss (or quota share) reinsurance, as "not as prevalent in connection with health insurance"). *See also,* THE ROLE OF REINSURANCE UNDER HEALTH REFORM, 20 RECORD OF SOCIETY OF ACTUARIES 741–59, 746 (1994), https://www.soa.org/globalass ets/assets/library/proceedings/record-of-the-society-of-actuaries/1990-99/1994/january/rsa94v 20n3b14.pdf. The policy rationale for this type of specific excess reinsurance is that it sharpens the effect of reinsurance against the "primary insurer's" strong incentives to engage in risk selection. *See,* Emmett B. Keeler et al., *Insurance aspects of DRG outlier payments,* 7 J. HEALTH ECON. 193–214 (1988). *See also,* OUTLIER PAYMENTS, CMS WEBPAGE, https://www.cms.gov/Medicare/Medicare-Fee-for-Service-Payment/AcuteInpatientPPS/outlier (accessed March 24, 2021) (hereinafter Outlier Payments CMS).

[14] Am Medical Security, Inc. v. Barlett, 111 F.3d 358 (1997) (emphasis added).

many state regulations and relieved from key ACA-related standards as well. But few businesses, particularly smaller employers, can comfortably absorb the risk that in any given year, covered beneficiaries might meet with more medical catastrophes and incur losses far exceeding the employer's budgeted estimate. Thus, many of these purportedly self-insured employers also purchase what is called commercial "stop-loss" insurance, as the 7th Circuit explained in *Edstrom v. Companion Life Insurance:*

> If an organization utilizes a cost-plus or self-insured method of financing, it may choose to limit its potential aggregate medical claims exposure by purchasing insurance that would make payment if claims exceeded a certain predetermined amount for the entire group. This insurance coverage for capping the total claims experience of the group is known as aggregate stop loss. A firm might also limit its liability using specific stop loss. Specific stop loss sets a limit on the amount that a plan sponsor will pay for an individual case. If a catastrophic medical case occurs, the employer will only be responsible for paying covered medical costs on that individual case up to the stop-loss amount.[15]

In elaborating the circumstances of that case, the Seventh Circuit focused in on the specific stop-loss policy that Edstrom secured: "Edstrom ... sponsors a group health insurance plan for its employees and their dependents [and] pays claims under the plan out of its own pocket—up to $65,000. Above that, an insurance company, the defendant, Companion, which has sold Edstrom what is called a 'stop-loss' insurance policy, pays ... Companion's policy specifies an aggregate as well as a specific stop-loss amount, but the former is not involved in this case and we can therefore ignore it."[16]

Contrast this type of $65,000 per beneficiary attachment point with the alternate design of aggregate attachment points at issue in *Bank of Louisiana v. Aetna.* Here, the Bank of Louisiana's self-insured health plan purchased an "aggregate stop-loss" policy from Aetna whereunder Aetna would take on the claims liabilities once total claims across all beneficiaries in the plan reached $600,000.[17]

Both kinds of stop loss are commonplace. In its 2020 Employer Health Benefits Survey, Kaiser Family Foundation reported that roughly two-thirds of workers with employer-sponsored coverage were enrolled in self-insured plans. Out of all workers in larger firms (over 50 employees), 62 percent were

---

[15] Edstrom Indus., Inc. v. Companion Life Ins. Co., 516 F.3d 54, 548 (7th Cir. 2008) quoting JERRY S. ROSENBLOOM, THE HANDBOOK OF EMPLOYEE BENEFITS: DESIGN, FUNDING AND ADMINISTRATION, 98 (2nd ed., 2005).

[16] *Id.* at 548.

[17] Bank of Louisiana v. Aetna U.S. Healthcare Inc., 468 F.3d 237, 239–40 (5th Cir. 2006).

in self-insured plans that had some stop-loss backing.[18] Then of that 62 percent, "87% are in plans where the stoploss insurance limits the amount the plan must spend on *each* worker or enrollee [specific per-beneficiary stop-loss], 57% are in plans where the stoploss insurance limits the *overall* amount the plan must pay [aggregate stop-loss]."[19] The two percentages add up to more than 100 percent because many health plans are availing themselves of *both* specific and aggregate attachment points.

The use of both designs simultaneously occurs in part because these two devices have slightly different functions. Medicare's Inpatient Prospective Payment System (IPPS) helps illustrate. Under the IPPS system, Medicare pays a preset average payment to any given hospital for every episode of illness that the hospital treats. Because the average payment is offered without regard to the actual medical resources consumed in any patient's case, this system forces the hospital to act as a partial insurer against the risk that any given Medicare case will prove unusually costly.[20] Medicare however also backs that hospital with two kinds of reinsurance. When transitioning to this type of payment system, Medicare typically builds in a period during which they limit the *total* annual hospital losses across all Medicare beneficiaries under the new payment system.[21] This protection amounts to an aggregate stop-loss policy.

Medicare additionally makes "specific loss" payments to hospitals for individual "outlier" cases exceeding some fixed loss, set at roughly $27,000 per case for fiscal year 2021.[22] Emmett Keeler explains:

> In addition to reducing financial risk to hospitals, outlier payments . . . make payments more equitable by giving additional money to hospitals that treat sicker and more expensive patients than average . . . reduc[ing] the problems of access for patients who can be identified by hospitals as likely to need very expensive treatment. . . . These other goals explain why the government [] has kept outlier payments on a case-by-case basis, even though hospital risk . . . is minimized by payments that set a limit on annual hospital losses.[23]

---

[18] This figure leaves out workers in firms below 50 employees, as some states bar the sale of stop-loss to smaller employers.

[19] Kaiser Family Foundation, *2020 Employer Health Benefits Survey—Section 10: Plan Funding*, KFF (2020), https://www.kff.org/report-section/ehbs-2020-section-10-plan-funding/ (accessed December 21, 2021) (emphasis added).

[20] Keeler, *supra* n.13.

[21] *E.g.*, CMS, Medicare Claims Processing Manual, Chapter 3—Inpatient Hospital Billing § 190.4.2.1(2) Budget Neutrality Components, Rev. 10369, (September 24, 2020), https://www.cms.gov/Regulations-and-Guidance/Guidance/Manuals/downloads/clm104c03.pdf.

[22] Hospital Inpatient Prospective Payment Systems for Acute Care Hospitals, 85 Fed. Reg. 58432 (September 8, 2020), https://www.federalregister.gov/documents/2020/09/18/2020-19637/medicare-program-hospital-inpatient-prospective-payment-systems-for-acute-care-hospitals-and-the (setting the outlier payment at $27,195 for fiscal year 2021).

[23] *See* Keeler, *supra* n.13.

Thus these two devices, aggregate versus specific stop-loss, draw from a slightly different mix of public policy justifications. Commentators have explained that a reinsurance threshold defined in terms of an anomalously expensive individual case is better suited to the policy goal of reducing discrimination against sicker patients. But in addition to reducing potential risk selection or discrimination of this sort, reinsurance can also serve at least two other purposes. It can reduce premiums (or in the Medicare example, the overall financial load that the hospital must carry to cover risk volatility), while also boosting private insurer participation (in this case hospital participation) in "new government programs that alter basic market conditions").[24] These latter two reasons—reducing premiums and inducing market participation—are the public policy justifications more directly implicated in Medicare's *aggregate* stop loss measure described above.

These three public policy functions operate to help not only the most visible beneficiaries. While they certainly help the insurers themselves, and even secondarily the catastrophically ill patients who rack up medical bills, what is striking is how these functions also benefit *lower-risk* members of the pool more broadly, those who never reach the catastrophic threshold:

> Reinsurance [helps low-risk individuals] in at least five distinct ways. First, if the government injects funds for reinsurance, the low-risk enrollees shed some of the economic burden of subsidizing the highest medical costs. Second, reinsurance reduces volatility for primary insurers so they need not load on an additional risk premium, making health coverage more affordable. Third, by eliminating the advantages of risk selection, reinsurance helps primary insurers trim the expense of aggressive risk selection activities. Fourth, to the extent that reinsurance blunts incentives for risk selection, it benefits not only high-risk individuals who might otherwise be excluded from coverage, but also the low-risk consumer who has access to a better product. According to the famous Rothschild-Stiglitz model, reducing risk selection benefits healthier low-risk individuals insofar as they might otherwise be offered only bare-bones products on the insurance market.[25] Finally, to the extent that more private insurers are encouraged to enter the market, price competition can exert downward pressure on premiums.[26]

By addressing the claims of the most medically expensive patients, reinsurance has the potential to systemically improve the stability, affordability, and appeal of

---

[24] Hall, *supra* n.7 at 1169.

[25] Michael Rothschild & Joseph Stiglitz, *Equilibrium in Competitive Insurance Markets: An Essay on the Economics of Imperfect Information*, 90 Q. J. OF ECON. 629–649 (1976), https://www.uh.edu/~bsorense/Rothschild&Stiglitz.pdf.

[26] Ho, *supra* n.3.

health coverage for all Americans, an argument that becomes important in the concluding section of this chapter.

To accomplish these goals, reinsurance characteristically reimburses *post hoc* for *actual* expenses that the insurer incurs, as compared to other types of risk stabilization programs that distribute money based on insurers' *predicted* losses.[27] High-risk pools, for instance, offer coverage to those who have been classified as high risk, thus serving enrollees who are predictably high-cost and thereby excluded or priced out of other products even before they have incurred any claims. However, some of the most recent policy proposals in this health policy space have been referred to interchangeably as reinsurance programs or "invisible high-risk pools."[28] Some may complain that health sector observers use the term "reinsurance" too loosely, eliding the distinction between these two risk stabilization tools. On this view, there is arguably one type of so-called reinsurance program, where the cession of claims is based on an attachment point defined by the beneficiary's high-cost diagnosis, that should be called an "invisible" high-risk pool instead.[29]

Take Alaska as an illustrative case. Alaska and a number of other US states sought waivers of otherwise applicable federal requirements in order to experiment with their administration of the ACA.[30] Remarkably, the vast majority of these so-called Section 1332 waivers that states sought were for reinsurance programs to stabilize the ACA exchanges.[31] In Alaska's waiver, though, the reinsurance program is structured to pay 100 percent of the cost of claims associated with any of 33 health conditions.[32] These "attachment point" conditions flag those illnesses that are significant cost-drivers, including cystic fibrosis, hemophilia, bone marrow disorders, and end-stage renal disease.[33]

Under this design, where *diagnosis* rather than a claims total triggers payment, the program could technically be said to be based on *ex ante* risk rather actual *post hoc* loss. Therefore, what Alaska and others refer to as "health reinsurance"

---

[27] Katherine Swartz, Reinsuring Health Why More Middle-Class People Are Uninsured and What Government Can Do 102 (2006).

[28] *See* Chapter 7 describing the proposals debated in "Health Reinsurance in the Recent Policy Landscape."

[29] Govind Persad, *Expensive Patients, Reinsurance, and the Future of Health Care Reform*, 69 Emory L. J. 1153 (2020), at 26, n. 131 *citing* Joel Allumbaugh et al., *Invisible High-Risk Pools: How Congress Can Lower Premiums And Deal With Pre-Existing Conditions*, Health Affairs Blog, Following the ACA (2017), https://www.healthaffairs.org/do/10.1377/hblog20170302.059003/full/ (accessed April 2, 2021).

[30] *See* Chapter 7 describing the proposals debated in "Health Reinsurance in the Recent Policy Landscape."

[31] *Resource: State-Based Reinsurance Programs via 1332 State Innovation Waivers*, SHADAC (August 10, 2020), https://www.shadac.org/publications/resource-state-based-reinsurance-progr ams-1332-state-innovation-waivers (accessed April 2, 2021).

[32] Persad, *supra* n.29 at 29, n. 131 *citing* Allumbaugh et al., *supra* n.29.

[33] Persad, *id.*

in this context is perhaps more akin to an invisible high-risk pool. However, the distinction matters little if indeed the conditions, like end-stage renal disease, are certain to be medically costly. I will in these two chapters follow the common usage in health policy circles of the term "reinsurance" to include programs whose attachment points are defined by diagnosis.[34] I argue that these policies, though they might fall outside the strictest sense of the term, perform the function of reinsurance, whereby catastrophic losses beyond a certain threshold are offloaded to stabilize the primary private risk market.

Chapter Approach

Domain by domain, I will identify examples of government reinsurance, revealing how policies that may appear under different names have recognizably similar structures. It is hardly an exaggeration to say that whenever we in the United States have sought to guarantee the availability of a crucial service, we turned to reinsurance.

In identifying these examples, I show the ubiquity and deep entrenchment of the role of the US government in establishing risk ceilings above which private risks are spread to the public, thereby stabilizing the private risk market for a critical good or service.

This account exposing reinsurance as a device operating in the background across so many domains accomplishes three tasks:

1) One goal is to "normalize" the case for health reinsurance. Why is it not feasible to commit to the provision of reinsurance for human health if it has proven feasible for these other interests?[35] By revealing the similarities in the guarantees offered for other material interests, we render its absence in the health sector less a matter of prudent government reluctance to commit to an expensive, discretionary privilege. The kneejerk, yet false characterization of health backstopping as a "privilege, not a right" places the burden on health proponents to justify an expensive payout. By contrast, the fact of across-the-board assurances in other material sectors and a conspicuous deprivileging of the value of human health shifts the burden back to those who are obliged to explain why we backstop these other areas, but not human health in any comprehensive manner.

---

[34]   *Id.* at 29 (describing the vernacular use).
[35]   "The cost of 'emergency' agricultural subsidies could fund the expansion of Medicaid to many uninsured low-income parents, yet the cost of the two interventions are rarely compared, even when Congress enacts farm 'emergencies' several years in a row." Super, *supra* n.1 at 647, n. 55.

2) A second goal through this discussion is to persuade that a government guarantee of resources in the form of health reinsurance would resemble a rights-like guarantee. At the most basic level, if a right is a tool for "vindicat[ing] the priority" of a value, then rights are the appropriate tool to correct the problem depicted in this account, which lays plain the specter of reinsurance for every catastrophe *but* the most fundamental risks of morbidity and mortality.[36] Of course, not all forms of prioritization are rights. As we recall, rights must be claimable to be distinguished from other kinds of norms, such as obligations to the public at large. Our discussion will show that reinsurance programs in these non–health sectors deploy the chief mechanisms of prioritization that David Super says characterizes U.S. statutory entitlements: they feature legal causes of action for claiming on the entitlement (positive entitlement) and they feature mandatory budget allocations ("budgetary entitlement").[37] These features alone flag reinsurance as a state commitment entrenched to a degree "beyond" ordinary legislation that is subject to appropriations caps. But what is even more surprising is that time and again, even when reinsurance has not yet been promised as a matter of positive statutory enactment, various constituencies harbor and make good on their implicit expectations of government reinsurance, thus frequently satisfying Super's properties of "functional," "responsive," and "subjective" entitlement. I will show where expressions of those expectations have come to lodge successfully for material provision from the federal government under the norm of reinsurance. These examples of government satisfaction of implicit reliance serve to demonstrate that the government's past actions with respect to catastrophic risk exposure in other contexts create a public expectation of affirmative government backing for analogous risks in the future. And medical coverage is one of the areas where we should press the claim.

3) Third and finally, apart from the above two payoffs, this cross-sectoral examination also allows us to identify parallel techniques across sectors, picking up strategic lessons for health advocacy. Such lessons include templates for how entrenchment was achieved step-wise, as well as examples of what has worked or not in these other sectors, including measures like single-lender, insurance mandates, premium subsidies, conditional risk mitigation standards, public fallback options, upside

---

[36] Gregoire Webber & Paul Yowell, *Introduction*, Securing Human Rights through Legislation 10 (Gregoire Webber & Paul Yowell, eds., 2018)

[37] *Accord* Bd. of Regents v. Roth, 408 U.S. 564 (1972); Perry v. Sindermann, 408 U.S. 593 (1972); Goldberg v. Kelley, 397 U.S. 254 (1970); Mathews v. Eldridge, 424 U.S. 319 (1976. *See also* Blessing v. Freestone, 520 U.S. 329 (1997); Gonzaga v. Doe, 536 U.S. 273 (2002). The statutory language must, among other requirements, be sufficiently mandatory to admit of individual enforcement.

gain recoupment and more. Various interest groups in these non–health domains started by marshaling ad hoc assistance, later building up more regularized aid programs, and finally securing a degree of fiscal guarantee on the mandatory side of the federal budget. Some programs have even morphed from reinsurance to more direct government provision over time. Advocates in these other arenas have leveraged informal expectations of government reinsurance to cash out claims to robust government guarantees against catastrophic risk. The same should be done to satisfy our no less compelling health care needs.

Reinsurance as a Right in Non–Health Domains

Now I turn to the task itself and look for reinsurance-like structures protecting access to crops, housing, higher education, banking, pensions, and disaster-relief.

Crop Insurance

Our inquiry begins with aid to farmers to protect against catastrophic threats, especially to food crops.

Step-Wise Entrenchment
In the late 1930s, Franklin Delano Roosevelt instituted crop insurance for "selected crops in selected counties."[38] But the program did not assume its modern form until 1980, and its development over time marks out a pathway to entrenchment. Weather events, pests, or other threats to agricultural production have long been treated as disasters, prompting government aid. Over time that aid became a standing and increasingly regularized response to public expectations:

> The Federal Crop Insurance Improvement Act of 1980 . . . replac[ed] a standing disaster assistance program with subsidized crop insurance. To encourage sales, private companies were enlisted to deliver the product. . . . Almost overnight, the crop insurance program was converted from a pilot program offering limited coverage to a limited number of crops . . . to a nationwide program covering most major field crops in most major growing regions.[39]

[38] DAVID MOSS, WHEN ALL ELSE FAILS: GOVERNMENT AS THE ULTIMATE RISK MANAGER 261 (2004).

[39] Joseph W. Glauber, Crop Insurance Reconsidered, 86 AM. J. AGRIC. ECON. 1179–1195 (2004).

Description of the Government Reinsurance Role

Under this nationwide program, whose institutionalization remains relatively recent, farmers growing insurable crops purchase the level and type of insurance that they choose within a framework that is standardized, subsidized, and reinsured by an agency incorporated within the US Department of Agriculture (USDA). This government corporation is known as the Federal Crop Insurance Corporation (FCIC).[40] In the mid-1990s, the purchase of at least minimum catastrophic (CAP) coverage was made compulsory in order to combat adverse selection in the crop insurance market, mirroring the rationale behind the individual mandate in the ACA with respect to the health insurance markets.[41] Under FCIC, the farmer pays a portion of the premium, depending on coverage level. If the farmer selects CAP coverage only, the government then covers 100 percent of the premium with the farmer owing merely an extra flat fee. Should the farmer "buy up" to a higher level of coverage, the government's share of the premium declines. Government premium subsidies averaged 62 percent of the premium cost in 2014.[42] ACA subsidies by contrast averaged 86 percent of premiums prior to the pandemic for those eligible for premium tax credits.[43] As with ACA plans, the FCIC insurance policies are sold and serviced through private insurance companies, called Approved Insurance Providers (AIPs). Finally, and this is the point of this section, USDA reinsures the AIPs' losses under terms laid out in a Standard Reinsurance Agreement (SRA).[44] This government "[r]isk sharing was seen as an inducement to encourage companies to participate in the program."[45] The loss-sharing takes the form of a layered quota share reinsurance contract. Assume that an insurer's loss ratio lies between 1 and 1.60, meaning that the insurer pays out more in claims than it collects in premiums, to the point where the insurer faces 60 percent more in payouts than in collected premium revenue. Under the SRA, the insurer does not have to bear the entire loss. The federal government will reimburse 35 percent of the loss and sometimes more depending on the particular state at issue. Insurers with higher aggregate losses above that layer are reinsured by government to an ever-greater extent. The final layer of reinsurance kicks in if the loss ratio exceeds 5. All losses above that level are fully reimbursed by the federal government.[46]

---

[40] 7 U.S.C. § 1501 *et seq.*

[41] Glauber, *supra* n.39 at 1182 (stating that participation was mandatory between 1994 and 1996, 1989 and 1990 for everyone who had received prior relief payments).

[42] DENNIS A SHIELDS, Congressional Research Service, *Federal Crop Insurance: Background* 27 (2015), https://fas.org/sgp/crs/misc/R40532.pdf.

[43] CENTER FOR MEDICARE AND MEDICAID SERVICES, EARLY 2020 EFFECTUATED ENROLLMENT SNAPSHOT 2 (2020), https://www.cms.gov/CCIIO/Resources/Forms-Reports-and-Other-Resources/Downloads/Early-2020-2019-Effectuated-Enrollment-Report.pdf.

[44] 7 C.F.R §§ 400.161-400.176. SHIELDS, *supra* n.42 at 2.

[45] Glauber, *supra* n.39 at 1187.

[46] Reinsurance Agreements Archive, UNITED STATES DEPARTMENT OF AGRICULTURE, RISK MANAGEMENT AGENCY WEBSITE, https://www.rma.usda.gov/en/Topics/Reinsurance-Agreements/

Federal Financing and Budgetary Entitlement

Government organized risk corridors that narrow the range of downside losses and upside windfalls, as we will see in the next chapter, have been used in health policy to smooth the launch of potentially volatile new insurance markets, like the ones for the Medicare prescription drug benefit, or the new ACA private health plans. Aggregate reinsurance can therefore resemble a one-sided risk corridor, a structural equivalence that we will return to later to help us excavate cross-applicable insights that we might otherwise miss. Crop insurance is structured as a two-sided risk corridor. It provides not only for the sharing of downside loss with the government, thus reinsuring and thereby cushioning the AIPS; it also requires some measure of upside gain-sharing with the government. Private insurers must pay *in* to the FCIC some of their unexpectedly large underwriting gains. This two-sided risk corridor is not designed for perfect symmetry; the amount that insurers receive from government for underwriting losses is larger than the amount the government recoups by way of gain-sharing.[47] The difference therefore represents a federal subsidy. This system of crop insurance cost the government $14.1 billion in FY 2012 alone and totaled $72 billion from 2007 to 2016 "making crop insurance the most significant cost component of the farm safety net."[48] This substantial sum is moreover funded on the mandatory side of the budget.[49] As Joseph Glauber has observed, the experience of crop insurance "suggests an alternative role for government as regulator and reinsurer of catastrophic risks rather than as a provider of individual risk protection through the sale of retail risk products."[50]

Legal Enforceability as a Positive Entitlement

Private crop insurers are not the only ones who can hold FCIC accountable to pay out under the standard reinsurance agreement; legal rights run between the FCIC and farmers as well under the "cut through clauses" of the standard primary crop insurance agreements.[51] In *Olsen v. U.S.*, for example, the primary insurance policy between farmers and the AIP stated in the first paragraph that

---

SRA-Archive-1998-2018 (accessed April 15, 2021) (described in the 2020 Standard Reinsurance Agreement).

[47] Alan R. Jung & Cyrus A. Ramezani, *Insurance and Reinsurance Contracts as Complex Derivatives: Application to Multiple Peril Policies*, 3 J. OF RISK 89 (2001), https://www.risk.net/node/2161167 (accessed April 15, 2021).

[48] SHIELDS, *supra* n.42. *See also*, CONGRESSIONAL RESEARCH SERVICE, *Federal Crop Insurance: Program Overview for the 115th Congress* 15 (2018), https://www.everycrsreport.com/reports/R45193.html (accessed April 15, 2021).

[49] 7 U.S.C. §1516. *See* USDA's MANDATORY FARM PROGRAMS—CBO's BASELINE AS OF MARCH 6, 2020, 46 (2020), https://www.cbo.gov/system/files/2020-03/51317-2020-03-usda.pdf.

[50] Glauber, *supra* n.39 at 1192.

[51] Olsen v. U.S., 665 F.Supp.2d 1225, 1229–1230 (2009).

"[in] the event we cannot pay your loss, your claim will be settled in accordance with the provisions of this policy and paid by FCIC."[52]

Subjective Entitlement

The explicit promise of crop reinsurance does not exhaust the scope of farmers' entitlement to the public fisc. Despite the history of how FCIC and its scheme of regularized assistance arose to replace the ad hoc emergency aid that Congress would grant farmers, in recent years the ad hoc claims that farmers made upon the public purse extended far beyond the express promises grounded in positive statute and contract terms. With the climate-related increase in wildfire and hurricane threats, farmers have petitioned Congress regularly for additional emergency appropriations, further realizing their claims on the implicit backing America offers to reinsure against catastrophe.[53]

The Ultimate Beneficiary

Another type of reinsurance for farmers, beyond crop insurance or even prices supports, takes the form of government backing for farmers' mortgages. This indirect supply-side support dates back to at least the Progressive Era and represents the peculiarly roundabout way that Americans use government to secure material provision in a crucial sector. These land finance supports arose not from concern for mortgage lenders, the most immediate beneficiaries of this government backstop, but out of "[c]oncerns about the social well-being of rural America [which] drew . . . attention to the problem of farm credit. . . . Mounting food prices further reminded a burgeoning middle class that the decline of the countryside came at the expense of the entire nation."[54]

What could be seen as a bailout for lenders or insurers was partially motivated by a desire to assure the supply of food for Americans, another layer of "cut-through."

Homeownership and Mortgages

This same approach prompted affirmative government support for housing more broadly as well. We thus turn from the government's backstopping of risk relating to mortgages for farmland to risk backstopping as applied to residential housing.

---

[52] *Id.* at 1230.

[53] Megan Stubbs, CONGRESSIONAL RESEARCH SERVICE, *Agriculture Disaster Assistance* RS21212 (April 23, 2020), https://sgp.fas.org/crs/misc/RS21212.pdf (noting that farmers secured in excess of $5 billion more for disaster assistance in Fiscal Years (FY) 2017–2019).

[54] SARAH L. QUINN, AMERICAN BONDS 71 (2019) (hereinafter, S. QUINN).

Description of the Government Reinsurance Role

Support for homeownership looms large in the history of government-backed risk management. Institutional creditors pool the risk of bad loans, performing an insurance-like function, and mortgages themselves constitute a primary safeguard. With respect to the creditor, the security interest in the real property shields her from the debtor default, and for the debtor at risk of default, nonrecourse mortgages have made foreclosure a fallback means of discharging the debt.[55] But government has always had a hand in shaping and supporting mortgages as private risk management devices.[56]

Here I focus on the major federal programs that backstop mortgages. The basic infrastructure of these programs grew out of the Great Depression. Home lending had cratered, and default risks overflowed the capacity of existing institutions. From the late 1920s to 1933, homes lost 30 to 40 percent of their value.[57] The government surveyed a subset of cities in 1934 and "found that 45 percent of owner-occupied mortgaged homes were in default."[58] Debtors could not pay, and creditors froze lending. Congress responded with multiple measures, chief among which was the National Housing Act (NHA).

The 1934 NHA created the Federal Housing Authority (FHA) to provide lenders with the assurance they needed to re-extend and expand credit to Americans purchasing homes. The FHA, now a part of the Department of Housing and Urban Development (HUD), did so by furnishing *mortgage insurance* to approved lenders when they offered qualifying mortgage products. The FHA placed conditions on the mortgages they would insure, essentially setting a product standard resulting in the prevailing template of low down-payment thirty-year mortgages with amortized repayment of capital.[59] Short-term mortgages had left American families vulnerable during the Depression, and the structure of the FHA mortgage obviated the need for multiple stacked

---

[55] As a result of the Great Depression, some states passed anti-deficiency statutes that restricted the lenders' recourse to deficiency judgments for any debt in excess of the proceeds of the foreclosure, but these cover a relatively small share of mortgages. *See generally*, John Mixon & Ira B. Shepard, *Antideficiency Relief for Foreclosed Homeowners: ULSIA Section 511(b)*, 27 WAKE FOREST L. REV. 455 (1992); John Mixon, *Fannie Mae/Freddie Mac Home Mortgage Documents Interpreted as Nonrecourse Debt (with poetic comments lifted from Carl Sandburg)*, 45 CALIF. WEST. LAW REV. 35 (2008). *See also*, Danielle D'Onfro, *Limited Liability Property*, 39 CARDOZO LAW REV. 1365 (2018).

[56] *See generally*, S. QUINN, *supra* n.54.

[57] Steven D. Levitt, *Economist Price Fishback: The Real Facts About the Original Home Owners' Loan Corporation (and What They Mean for a Modern Incarnation)*, FREAKONOMICS (2008), https://freakonomics.com/2008/10/17/economist-price-fishback-the-real-facts-about-the-original-home-owners-loan-corporation-and-what-they-mean-for-a-modern-incarnation/ (accessed April 15, 2021).

[58] S. QUINN *supra* n.54 at 139, *citing* PRICE V. FISHBACK, THE NEW DEAL, GOVERNMENT AND THE AMERICAN ECONOMY: A NEW HISTORY 394–5 (new ed. 2007).

[59] S. QUINN *supra* n.54 at 142.

mortgages to cope with high down-payments and the prospect of balloon balances coming due.

Then, after World War II, "the G.I. Bill authorized the VA [Department of Veterans Affairs] to guarantee mortgages for veterans . . . By 1955, 41 percent of the nation's mortgages were backed by the FHA or VA."[60]

The Ultimate Beneficiary

FHA mortgage insurance casts its benefits widely. The insurance pays out to reimburse lenders for "deficiencies" or shortfalls when the value of the foreclosed property does not cover the debt.[61] These deficiencies typically proliferate during market downturns when property values crash systemically, which in reinsurance terms suggests covariant or correlated loss. Unless the loans are stipulated as "non-recourse" either by contract or statute, mortgage lenders can generally pursue the borrowers for such deficiencies, but often to little avail, since a homeowner facing foreclosure likely cannot pay off any additional sums.[62] This mortgage insurance payout thus protects the homeowner-borrower from these deficiency judgments that compound the catastrophe of default and foreclosure. It also protects lenders from the risk of uncollectible debt which can arise from the correlated risk environment of a market collapse. It also benefits many other homeowners by encouraging greater mortgage lending so that more households can purchase homes.[63]

And the policy conditions that we chose to attach to the offer of this reinsurance—namely the terms of the standard low-downpayment thirty-year FHA mortgage—also reach multiple constituencies. As Sarah Quinn observes:

> For families, a longer repayment period and a lower down payment lessened the risk of foreclosure during market crises and eliminated the need for second or third mortgages. For lenders, insurance managed the risk of default. For the Roosevelt administration, it was a low-cost way to promote lending for new homes and repairs for the estimated 13 million homes in need of improvements in 1934.[64]

[60] *Id.* at 159.

[61] Chad Chirico & Susan Mehlman, Congressional Budget Office, *How FHA's Mutual Mortgage Insurance Fund Accounts for the Cost of Mortgage Guarantees* (October 22, 2013), www.cbo.gov, https://www.cbo.gov/publication/44634.

[62] *See* Kimbriell Kelly, *Lenders seek court actions against homeowners years after foreclosure,* Washington Post (June 15, 2013), https://www.washingtonpost.com/investigations/lenders-seek-court-actions-against-homeowners-years-after-foreclosure/2013/06/15/3c6a04ce-96fc-11e2-b68f-dc5c4b47e519_story.html (accessed April 15, 2021).

[63] Swartz, *supra* n.27 at 142.

[64] *Id.*

Federal Financing and Partial Mandatory Budgetary Entitlement

The funds for FHA mortgage insurance are held in a dedicated fund, the Mutual Mortgage Insurance Fund (MMIF). A portion of the MMIF is devoted to the budgetary accounting of a different program, Home Equity Conversion Mortgage (HECM) program, but the portion we are focusing on holds cash reserves and financial flows for the FHA single-family mortgage guarantee program. The MMIF is financed in part by fees (functionally premiums) that borrowing homeowners pay into a dedicated fund over part of the course of the mortgage. It is also replenished by recoveries from sales of the homes of defaulting borrowers. Additionally, according to the Congressional Budget Office (CBO), "When the MMI fund has insufficient funds to cover losses on its programs, the fund receives an . . . infusion of funds from the general fund of the Treasury."[65] This funding infusion is classified as mandatory spending for any obligations arising under previously issued FHA mortgage insurance.[66] The United States has not, however, taken on any mandatory budget obligations with respect to any future applicant's expectation of qualifying for FHA insurance. Such funding remains subject to the ordinary appropriations process. Thus, we have yet to stand behind a prospectively responsive entitlement that would rise to meet the needs of any homeowner applicant that could meet the stated FHA mortgage insurance eligibility criteria of homeowner insureds in years past. The Congressional Budget Office labels the prospective FHA mortgage guarantees as "discretionary credit programs" even as student loan guarantees are by contrast listed among the sixteen federal credit programs that the CBO classifies as "mandatory credit programs."[67]

Legal Enforceability as a Positive Entitlement and the Ultimate Beneficiary

The National Housing Act nevertheless speaks of the lender-mortgagee's "entitlement" to insurance benefits, again presumably referencing entitlements generated under prior commitments. Indeed courts and Attorney General rulings have long taken the position that mortgage insurance benefits are backed "by the full faith and credit of the United States," claimable under the Tucker Act even if the MMIF fund runs out.[68] Moreover, as under FCIC, the government in

---

[65] CHAD CHIRICO & SUSAN MEHLMAN, CONGRESSIONAL BUDGET OFFICE, *How FHA's Mutual Mortgage Insurance Fund Accounts for the Cost of Mortgage Guarantees* (October 22, 2013), www.CBO.GOV, https://www.cbo.gov/publication/44634 (accessed October 21, 2021) (citing the Federal Credit Reform Act of 1990, under which all federal credit programs, unless otherwise exempted, are provided with budgetary resources to cover the cost of loans and loan guarantees that have been made in prior years).

[66] *Id.*

[67] CONGRESSIONAL BUDGET OFFICE, ESTIMATES OF THE COST OF FEDERAL CREDIT PROGRAMS IN 2022 (2021), https://www.cbo.gov/publication/57537 (accessed May 6, 2022).

[68] *See* Nat'l State Bank of Newark v. U.S., 357 F.2d 704 (1966). *See also* Slattery v. U.S., 635 F.3d 1298, 1318–19 (2011) citing Attorney General rulings regarding similar programs (*citing* "41 Op. A.G. 424 (1959) (loan guarantees issued by the Secretary of Defense under the Armed Services housing

administering FHA mortgage insurance has claimable legal duties not only to the primary insurer, namely, the mortgage holder who has legal claim to MMIF funds, but often duties to the homeowner-mortgagor themselves. Homeowners with FHA-insured mortgages have in the past successfully sued HUD to aid homeowners directly in the form of payments on their behalf so they might avoid foreclosure. Indeed these demands spurred Congress to pass authorization for similar measures to help homeowners avoid foreclosure through assignment.[69] In the disposition of benefits under assignment, the relationship with HUD cuts through the mortgage holder to the homeowner. As the Court of Federal Claims explained recently, one possible outcome when foreclosure looms is HUD taking title to the property:

> If a loan covered by FHA mortgage insurance defaults, the mortgage holder or servicer generally will either foreclose on the property or obtain a deed-in-lieu of foreclosure. The mortgage holder or servicer will then usually make an insurance claim to FHA for [the unpaid principal balance of the defaulted mortgage] and convey title to the property to HUD in return. "HUD will then generally dispose of any collateral it receives in exchange for paying an insurance claim from the MMI fund in order to recoup the losses due to paying the insurance claim."

However, as the court notes, there are other methods of disposition: "FHA can also accept assignment of the mortgage in exchange for an insurance payout."[70] In these cases of assignment, the state's material backing of an intermediary financier, namely the mortgage lender, establishes a trigger whereupon the FHA ultimately assumes a direct financing relationship with the homeowner as well.

In Super's taxonomy, there remains one measure along which the FHA program fell gravely short: the program was never a fully responsive entitlement.

---

mortgage insurance program are obligations of the United States); Op. A.G. 363 (1958) (contracts entered by Secretary of Commerce to insure loans and mortgages pursuant to the Merchant Marine Act of 1936 are binding obligations of the United States, despite need for future appropriations)").

[69] See Ferrell v. Pierce, 743 F.2d 454, 455–56 (7th Cir.1984). Now, see generally, National Housing Act Section 230, 12 U.S.C. § 115u. See also Ferrell v. U.S. Dep't of Hous. & Urb. Dev., 186 F.3d 805, 808 (7th Cir. 1999) ("[temporary mortgage assistance payments] differed from the mortgage assignment program in that it allowed HUD to take over temporarily part or all of the mortgagor's payments and to make those payments to the mortgagee directly, rather than paying off the entire mortgage and taking assignment of the mortgage.") See also Lee v. Kemp, 731 F. Supp. 1101 (D.D.C. 1989) (plaintiffs are within the "zone of interest" under the National Housing Act to qualify for standing as persons aggrieved able to bring suit under the APA).

[70] Associated Mortgage Bankers Inc. v. U.S., 153 Fed. Cl. 189, 192 (2021). 12 U.S.C. § 1710(a)(1)(A). See also, 12 U.S.C. § 1710(g) ("Notwithstanding any other provision of law, the Secretary shall also have power to pursue to final collection, by way of compromise or otherwise, all claims against mortgagors assigned by mortgagees to the Secretary as provided in this section").

The FHA did *not* purport to perform the mortgage insurance function for every homeowner who satisfied funding standards. FHA policies as to the lenders and loans that it would back instead encoded racial segregation. The FHA's system of redlining excluded Black families from homeownership opportunities. Meanwhile, the *Underwriting Manual* of the Federal Housing Administration declared that "incompatible racial groups should not be permitted to live in the same communities."[71] The government decided whose risks to backstop based on race, while selectively abandoning others to the consequences of their bad bets. This grave breach joins the lack of responsiveness that stems from the extension of mandatory budget status only to *prior commitments* of mortgage insurance.[72]

Mantled in what FHA insurance was available then, lenders in the 1930s still found the risk environment intractable given the overall context of the Great Depression. I will discuss two further aspects of mortgage risk that required government safety nets.

Step-Wise Entrenchment of the Secondary Market

While the FHA could improve matters for the newly standardized FHA loans going forward, what about non–FHA loans? The Great Depression, after all, was characterized by a flood of troubled mortgages issued prior to the FHA. Who would mop up their risks? The federal government stepped in through a different program to buy those non–FHA loans. In 1933, the Home Owners' Loan Corporation (HOLC) was created as a short-term emergency relief measure and funded with $200 million in government-backed bonds.[73] HOLC then traded those bonds for troubled mortgages to refinance, leaving borrowers with easier terms.[74] Multiple constituencies benefited while some were invidiously excluded. HOLC notoriously deployed its soft power of standard-setting and norm-building to map home-lending risk,[75] creating the redlined maps whose influence rippled through FHA and beyond to "reproduce[] a set of racist underwriting standards that benefited white families in white neighborhoods."[76]

HOLC was a temporary program, supplying proof of concept for the idea of a secondary market. But this idea had yet to be more durably institutionalized. The private mortgage landscape continued to lack a secondary market to buy the broader spectrum of mortgages on an ongoing basis. As Quinn observes,

---

[71] RICHARD ROTHSTEIN, THE COLOR OF LAW (2017).

[72] CHAD CHIRICO & SUSAN MEHLMAN, CONGRESSIONAL BUDGET OFFICE, *How FHA's Mutual Mortgage Insurance Fund Accounts for the Cost of Mortgage Guarantees | Congressional Budget Office* (October 22, 2013), WWW.CBO.GOV, https://www.cbo.gov/publication/44634 (accessed October 21, 2021).

[73] Pub. L. No. 74-43 (June 13, 1933).

[74] S. QUINN *supra* n.54 at 141.

[75] KENNETH T. JACKSON, CRABGRASS FRONTIER: THE SUBURBANIZATION OF THE UNITED STATES (1987).

[76] S. QUINN *supra* n.54.

"FHA insurance protected against credit risks, but its long-term mortgages tied up funds for 15 or so years. This created a significant liquidity problem, and it heightened the need for a working secondary market where investors could off-load their mortgages."[77]

Description of the Government's Reinsurance Role By Way of the Secondary Market

The assurance that the lender could sell mortgages to the government thus added another reinsurance-like backstop. In 1934, Congress still harbored hope that the private sector could perform this function and wrote specific authority into the NHA to charter private national associations for this purpose. The government offered tax exemptions and other flexibilities, even promising investment. Congress authorized the Reconstruction Finance Corporation, a Roosevelt vehicle for jolting the country out of the Depression, to buy stock in these associations. However, "[t]he market was too broken and conservative investors too wary."[78] Finally, the government had to amend the NHA in 1938 to create the Federal National Mortgage Association (FNMA or "Fannie Mae") as a government entity at the outset to furnish some kind of secondary market for mortgages.[79]

One might say that Fannie and its later siblings served as a quasi-public option to absorb mortgage risk regardless of private market participation. Fannie Mae, Freddie Mac, and Ginnie Mae were endowed with the capacity to issue bonds to attract even more private funding to the credit market. Quinn explains, "Fannie and Freddie don't issue mortgages. Instead, they buy loans from lenders and package the debt into bonds [mortgage-backed securities) that are sold to investors with guarantees of interest and principal. The process makes housing more affordable, while keeping the mortgage market humming."[80] The guarantees behind these mortgage-backed securities are funded by guarantee fees that all lenders pay to the government. This fund helps assure the timely payment of principal and interest to the security holders in the event that too many underlying borrowers miss payments on their mortgages.[81] Fannie, which Congress spun off the government's balance sheet into a fully for-profit shareholder-owned company in 1968,[82] now serves this function for conventional mortgages

---

[77] *Id.*

[78] *Id.* at 143.

[79] *Id.*

[80] *Id.*

[81] DIVISION OF MISSION & GOALS FEDERAL HOUSING FINANCE AGENCY, *Fannie Mae and Freddie Mac Single-Family Guarantee Fees in 2016* 2–3 (2016).

[82] US GOVERNMENT ACCOUNTABILITY OFFICE (GAO), *Fannie Mae and Freddie Mac: Analysis of Options for Revising the Housing Enterprises' Long-Term Structures* 12 (September 2009), https://www.gao.gov/products/gao-09-782.13, GAO-09-782.

issued by the larger commercial banks while Freddie performs as its counterpart for smaller thrift savings banks and credit unions.[83] Ginnie Mae (Government National Mortgage Administration) guarantees the payment of principal and interest on mortgage-backed securities for FHA loans, VA and USDA loans, and unlike the pre-2007–8 Fannie and Freddie, did so with the express backing of the US Treasury.[84]

Federal Budgetary Entitlement and Subjective Entitlement

Ginnie Mae was backed by the government on a mandatory, nonappropriated basis.[85] Curiously, the solvency of Fannie and Freddie, though not explicitly guaranteed by the government, remained tinged with vague government associations. This implicit government backing in fact materialized during the mortgage crisis of 2007–8.[86] With too few mortgage payments incoming and inadequate fees to make good on all the guarantees to investors, Fannie Mae was bailed out by the Federal Treasury and placed under conservatorship in September of 2008.[87] Thus, "[i]nvestors consider Fannie and Freddie securities to be as safe as Treasuries, partly because as long as the companies remain in conservatorship, most bondholders assume the government would make good on any losses."[88] As of now, CBO lists Fannie Mae and Freddie Mac mortgage guarantees as "mandatory" credit programs.[89]

Lessons for Policy Design

These government reinsurance entanglements also come with the opportunity, and indeed duty, to set policy with care. FHA cultivated certain mortgage terms as benchmarks while constructing racist conditions for mortgage insurance eligibility. HOLC encoded those conditions in the form of redlining maps.

---

[83] FEDERAL HOUSING FINANCE AUTHORITY, OFFICE OF THE INSPECTOR GENERAL, *A Brief History of the Housing Government-Sponsored Enterprises* 13 (2011), https://www.fhfaoig.gov/Content/Files/History%20of%20the%20Government%20Sponsored%20Enterprises.pdf.

[84] 12 U.S.C. § 1721(g) ("In the event the issuer is unable to make any payment of principal of or interest on any security guaranteed under this subsection, the Association shall make such payment as and when due in cash").

[85] *Id.*

[86] NICHOLAS F. BRADY, *Report of the Secretary of the Treasury on Government Sponsored Enterprises* 1 (May 1990), https://budgetcounsel.files.wordpress.com/2016/11/u-s-dept-of-the-treasury-report-of-the-secretary-of-the-treasury-on-government-sponsored-enterprises-may-311990.pdf ("The government sponsored enterprises are entities established by Congress to perform specific credit functions but are privately owned. The market perception of Federal backing for GSEs [Government Sponsored Enterprises] weakens the normal relationship between the availability and cost of funds to the GSEs and the risk that these enterprises assume").

[87] *See,* Jonathan G. Katz, *Who Benefited from the Bailout?,* 95 MINN. L. REV. 1568 (2011).

[88] Austin Weinstein, *Fannie-Freddie May Be Freed Without Congress, Calabria Says,* BLOOMBERG. COM (May 8, 2019), https://www.bloomberg.com/news/articles/2019-05-08/fannie-freddie-may-be-released-without-congress-calabria-says (accessed April 16, 2021).

[89] CONGRESSIONAL BUDGET OFFICE, ESTIMATES OF THE COST OF FEDERAL CREDIT PROGRAMS IN 2022, *supra* n.67.

These examples show the opportunity as well as the peril of government reinsurance, which is too often transacted behind the scenes and obscured from public view. Indeed, the goal of this chapter and the next is in large part to foreground the stakes and subject these government interventions to public justification of priorities. We should account for our elevation of some material interests through reinsurance. We should account for our use of backstops to effect standards. When the NAACP, the Urban League, and others in the 1950s revealed these racist standards and pressed FHA to "withdraw its support for redlining and racial covenants," they ultimately prevailed, in some sense drawing on our implicit sense that the entitlement should be "responsive" such that similarly situated applicants could qualify on equal footing. But norms and patterns had already been inscribed into the riskscape.[90]

The government's selective decision-making about whom to bail out is precisely what is concealed by the fragmentation of these analogous programs across different policy arenas with different names. What I seek to do here is ask why certain kinds of risks, heretofore ignored, do not merit bailout as well. In 1954, the NAACP-Urban League coalition demanded the creation of a Voluntary Home Mortgage Credit Program to provide loans for prospective borrowers who had twice been denied.[91] This embryonic, but visionary program points to the road not taken. Rather than treat the fallout of race-based underwriting as a given, we could have decided to build a guaranteed floor under Black prospective homeowners to protect them against the risks of systemic racism—limiting the extent of suffering and the opportunities they could be denied on account of the correlated risk of societal racism.[92] This program, however, was time-limited from its inception, sunsetting on June 30, 1957. Though extended several times, the program terminated in 1965.[93]

Higher Education

We in the United States have enabled access to higher education through government backing of student loans. By 1981–1982, loans dominated the student financing landscape and they remain the "the largest category of consumer debt

---

[90] S. QUINN *supra* n.54 at 165.
[91] Home Financing is Accelerated; Voluntary Home Mortgage Credit Program Aids Small Town Buyers, N.Y. TIMES (April 1, 1956), at 227, https://www.nytimes.com/1956/04/01/archives/home-financing-is-accelerated-voluntary-home-mortgage-credit.html (accessed April 16, 2021). Housing Act of 1954, Pub. L. No. 83-560 § 607(b), 68 Stat. 590, 637; 12 U.S.C. § 1750gg(b).
[92] S. QUINN *supra* n.54 at 165.
[93] Housing Act of 1961, Pub. L. No. 87-70, § 903, 75 Stat. 149,191 (1961); 12 U.S.C. § 1750jj.

other than home mortgages."[94] Any loan carries default risk, but because education can be understood a component of "human capital," that default risk can never be mitigated through collateralization by mortgage. The student-side risk that our higher education policies purport to manage is the risk that "the returns to their education [in the labor market] will not justify the investment."[95] Given the positive public externalities that education generates, government has repeatedly taken it upon itself to intervene.[96] Some of the risk-management methods used suggest parallels with our health care policies. For instance, government-backed student loans are not underwritten for risk factors like a student's major or their school, just as individual insurance cannot be underwritten based on health status.[97]

Description of the Government's Reinsurance Role

The student loan system evolved over time, with the government providing aid first to veterans through the GI Bill of 1944 and later extending this benefit to civilians.[98] The structure of education assistance bore strong overtones of government reinsurance all the while. Like ACA coverage and crop insurance, federal student loans were offered through private entities, at least until 2010, and these creditors served to pool the risk of the fraction of higher education loans that would eventually sour. Just like insurers, they charge financing, much as insurers would charge premiums, to absorb this risk. Yet private banks proved insufficiently willing to lend for the purpose of higher education, in part because the debt could not be collateralized.[99] Therefore in 1965 a suite of inducements was introduced, including federal guarantees on the loans.[100] Family Federal Education Loan (FFEL) loans thereafter came with a federal promise that under certain catastrophic conditions, like borrower default or permanent disability,

---

[94] John Brooks & Adam Levitin, *Redesigning Education Finance: How Student Loans Outgrew the "Debt" Paradigm*, 109 GEORGETOWN L.J. 5 (2020). *See also* WILLIAM ZUMETA ET AL., FINANCING AMERICAN HIGHER EDUCATION IN THE ERA OF GLOBALIZATION 24, 77 (2012).

[95] Jan Libich & Martin Macháček, *Insurance by Government or Against Government? Overview of Public Risk Management Policies*, 31 J. OF ECON. SURVEYS 436–462 (2017).

[96] *Id.*

[97] Brooks & Levitin, *supra* n.94 at 6. The health equivalent can be found in the ACA, Pub. L. No. 114-148 §1201 (2010), amending Public Health Service Act §§ 2701-2706, codified at 4 U.S.C. §§ 300gg *et seq.*

[98] Servicemen's Readjustment Act of 1944, Pub. L. No. 78-346, 58 Stat. 284 (1944). *See*, SUZANNE METTLER, THE SUBMERGED STATE 71 (2011). John Brooks, *Income-Driven Repayment and the Public Financing of Higher Education*, 104 GEORGETOWN L.J. 229 (2016) at 245, and 247 n. 100 ("The Hope and Lifetime Learning Credits were added by the Taxpayer Relief Act of 1997, Pub. L. No. 105-34, § 201, 111 Stat. 788, 799-806 (1997)").

[99] S. QUINN *supra* n.54 at 157.

[100] *Id.*

the federal government would take over the loan and pay off virtually all the remaining principal to the lender.[101]

Legal Enforceability as a Positive Entitlement and the Ultimate Beneficiary

This reinsurance-like guarantee amounted to affirmative state provision by bank shot. The government ostensibly backed only the lenders, but the relationship frequently "cut through" the lender and established direct obligations from the state to the borrower. For instance, our federal dockets brim with former students suing the government to argue that because they met the "attachment point" standards for permanent disability, they can claim by right a government payoff of their loans.[102] Courts do not as a general matter read the Higher Education Act itself as granting student borrowers a private right of action to enforce its provisions against violating lenders.[103] However, claims against the government for its determinations of default or disability can be brought under the Administrative Procedure Act or the Tucker Act.[104] Courts have even found that the mandatory language regarding government disability discharge creates a protected property interest sufficient for the purposes of Due Process claims.[105] These guarantees accordingly qualify as "positive entitlements" under Super's schema.

Federal Financing and Budgetary Entitlement

The FFEL program's somewhat misleading and roundabout mode of subsidy also proved expensive. One measure of the steep cost is evident in the flip-side savings that were expected when in 2009, President Barack Obama finally proposed to end FFEL. He replaced these subsidies with direct government lending instead and CBO projected that this historic swap would save $61 billion over ten years.[106]

---

[101] Higher Education Act of 1965, Pub. L. No. 89-329, §§ 430-35, 79 Stat. 1244 (1965). *See also,* ALEXANDRA HEGJI, *The Higher Education Act (HEA): A Primer* 14, CONG. RES. SERV. (2016), https://www.wisconsin.edu/government-relations/download/the_washington_view_blog/The-Higher-Education-Act-(HEA)---A-Primer.pdf.

[102] *See generally* Lankster v. U.S., 87 Fed.Cl. 747 (2009); Kalfountzos v. Duncan, No. 2:12-CV-529-MCE-EFB, 2012 WL 2450713 (E.D. Cal. June 26, 2012); Labickas v. Ark. St. Univ., 78 F.3d 333, 334 (8th Cir.1996) (no HEA right of action for borrowers against private lenders). *See* Riddles v. Sallie Mae, No. 08-CV-1499 (NG), 2009 WL 3734302, at *3 (E.D.N.Y. November 4, 2009) (government determinations concerning the loan guarantee program can be challenged under the Administrative Procedure Act or the Tucker Act).

[103] Labickas v. Ark. St. Univ., 78 F.3d 333, 334 (8th Cir.1996).

[104] Riddles v. Sallie Mae, No. 08-CV-1499 (NG), 2009 WL 3734302, at *3 (E.D.N.Y. November 4, 2009).

[105] Higgins v. Spellings, 663 F. Supp. 2d 788 (W.D. Mo. 2009) (finding that students have a due process interest in discharge based on meeting the preliminary eligibility criteria for government relief from loan repayment for those who are "totally and permanently disabled").

[106] METTLER, *supra* n.98, at 76 and 83.

But what can we say about the federal student loan guarantee prior to its hard-won reform? What did it represent in our collective understanding of the governmental role? Quinn flatly states that "[i]n the 1970s, student loans shifted from an antipoverty program to a middle-class entitlement," and part of that shift took place through the Higher Education Act of 1972, which established Pell Grants, and the Student Loan Marketing Association, otherwise known as Sallie Mae, upon which Congress initially conferred government backing.[107] Pell Grants are another model of government provision: they are a form of direct grant to students that Obama tried unsuccessfully to convert into a budgetary entitlement in 2010.[108] The costs of FFEL guarantees, by contrast, have long ranked among the mandatory spending items that do not require annual congressional appropriations, thereby satisfying Super's criteria for "budgetary entitlements."[109]

Step-Wise Transition Between Private and Public Provision

The history of higher education lending is marked by transition pathways between privately and publicly organized modes of provision. Like Fannie Mae, Sallie Mae was created initially to provide a secondary market for government-insured education loans.[110] The government guaranteed Sallie Mae's obligations until 1984.[111] Sallie also enjoyed Congressional authority to undertake "other activities," a permission which it construed liberally when it began issuing loans itself. Now a fully private entity, its functions have departed from secondary market services, and it has morphed into just another private issuer of student loans.[112]

---

[107] Pub. L. No. 92-318, § 133(a), 86 Stat. 235, 265-69 (1972).

[108] The failures have to do in part with the need to pass the education reform provisions in the same reconciliation vehicle as the ACA, which was not budget neutral, and the need to find sufficient savings to meet the budget caps necessary for the bill to pass under the filibuster-proof reconciliation rules. That tale is well told in METTLER, *supra* n.98, at 83-4.

[109] UNITED STATES DEPARTMENT OF EDUCATION, FY 2009 BUDGET JUSTIFICATION, STUDENT LOANS OVERVIEW (2008), Q-5, https://www2.ed.gov/about/overview/budget/budget09/justificati ons/q-loansoverview.pdf (classifying the FFEL guarantees among the "mandatory programs whose costs are largely driven by student loan demand, fueled by increases in the price of postsecondary education and prevailing interest rates. Defaults are also a key component of program costs. The programs are funded by indefinite budget authority and do not require annual congressional appropriations").

[110] H.R. Rep. 92-554, 92nd Congress, 2nd Sess. (1972). *See also*, 20 U.S.C. § 1087-(a) (articulating the purpose "to establish a private corporation which will be financed by private capital and which will serve as a secondary market and warehousing facility for student loans, including loans which are insured by the Secretary under this part or by a guaranty agency, and which will provide liquidity for student loan investments.") *See*, US Government Accountability Office (GAO), SECONDARY MARKET ACTIVITIES OF THE STUDENT LOAN MARKETING ASSOCIATION, REPORT TO THE SENATE COMMITTEE ON LABOR AND HUMAN RESOURCES (1984), https://www.gao.gov/assets/150/141 563.pdf.

[111] PHILIP QUINN ET AL., *Lessons Learned from the Privatization of Sallie Mae-DRAFT* 3, U.S. DEPARTMENT OF TREASURY OFFICE OF SALLIE MAE OVERSIGHT (2006), https://www.treasury.gov/ about/organizational-structure/offices/Documents/SallieMaePrivatizationReport.pdf.

[112] S. QUINN *supra* n.54 at 157. *See also* PHILIP QUINN ET AL, *supra* n.111, Appendix 1 at 1.

Prior to the 2010 student loan reforms, the division of labor was such that private banks, including the repurposed Sallie Mae, took the lead in issuing student loans while the federal government acted as their guarantor. Now, the government now issues 90 percent of higher education loans directly, a model that closely approximates the single-payer model in health care and which we might think of as "single-lender."[113]

Even today under the direct public lending model, the government's role still bears a reinsurance imprint. Students can presently opt for fulfillment of their obligations under the terms of an income-driven repayment (IDR) program. Under these IDR programs, including Income-Based Repayment (IBR) and Pay-As-You-Earn (PAYE), students are protected against monthly repayments higher than 10 percent of discretionary income. Any balance after a maximum of twenty years under that repayment structure is forgiven.[114] That period reduces by half if the student undertakes public interest work.

It is not hard to see how this structure protects the student against the risk of "the returns to their education [in the labor market]" falling short of the repayment obligations.[115] The labor market is in one sense the payer of first resort, but only up to a certain threshold. The government-as-reinsurer protects the student from *post hoc* risks once the graduate's income, taking into account the benefits of higher education, is realized.[116]

What is particularly interesting about the education story is that it demonstrates that the government's affirmative provision of an indirect guarantee can pave the way to a more direct subsidy, backstopping the end-user directly, rather than the private intermediary.[117] Obama himself explained his agenda thus in April of 2009:

> Under the FFEL program, lenders get a big government subsidy with every loan they make. And these loans are then guaranteed with taxpayer money, which means that if a student defaults, a lender can get back almost all of its money from the government.[118]

---

[113] Brooks, *supra* n.98 at 251, n. 125 ("For the 2013–2014 academic year, private lenders originated only $10 billion out of $106 billion in all student loans; the federal government thus originated over 90% of all student loans"). *See also id.* at 251 n. 124 (describing how the legislation "ended the government subsidy for private student loans, increased the amount of public loans available, and expanded and redefined the IBR program") *citing* the Health Care and Education Reconciliation Act of 2010, Pub. L. No. 111-152, §§ 2201-13, 124 Stat. 1029, 1074-81 (2010).

[114] 34 C.F.R. § 685.209(a)(1)(v), 34 C.F.R. § 685.209(a)(6). *See* Brooks, *supra* n.98 at 253.

[115] Libich & Macháček, *supra* n.95.

[116] Brooks, *supra* n.98.

[117] METTLER, *supra* n.98 at 69–87.

[118] *Id.* at 69, *citing* Barack Obama, "Remarks by the President on Higher Education," WHITE HOUSE, OFFICE OF THE PRESS SECRETARY (April 24, 2009), http://www.whitehouse.gov/the_press_office/Remarks-by-the-President-on-Higher-Education/.

While students received loans from private lenders in name, those loans would likely have been more expensive without government guarantees. [119] Obama lamented the cost of such an approach, "[W]e could be investing the same money in our students, in our economy, and in our country [rather than] paying banks a premium to act as middlemen."[120]

On March 23, 2010, in the same fraught vehicle as the ACA, Obama finally succeeded in achieving this phase-change from loan-guarantees to direct lending and using the savings from this de-privatization to increase Pell Grants and furnish the income-linked options that protected borrowers from repayments exceeding 10 percent of income.

The realm of higher education finance remains troubled, even as its history reveals the possibility of policy development to meet the ongoing challenges.

Bank Reinsurance for Money Risk

The domains I have discussed so far are all adjacent to the domain of banking, which lends itself to similar treatment.

Description of the Federal Reinsurance Role Through FDIC

Banking and money supply are deemed crucial services whose availability has long required a program of federal government guarantees. The transition from precious metal specie to paper money, as David Moss explains, had a basic structure, which gave rise to risks:

> When people stored gold coins in their pockets and purses, they gained liquidity (that is, the ability to spend their wealth anytime or anywhere they pleased) but they also immobilized precious capital. No one else could use this wealth for productive purposes if it was rattling around in someone's pocket. Bank notes were quite different, however. So long as individuals held onto these notes, banks could lend out most of the underlying funds to worthy borrowers. It was a neat trick. Although the notes were technically redeemable in specie, the real backing was the loans themselves.[121]

This arrangement posed certain risks: banks face both default risk from making bad loans, and liquidation risk, which Moss describes as the risk that "note holders and depositors would occasionally demand specie for their notes . . . far

---

[119] John Brooks, *Quasi-Public Spending*, 104 GEORGETOWN L.J. 1057, 1090 (2016).
[120] METTLER, *supra* n.98 at 69, citing Obama, *supra* n.118.
[121] MOSS, *supra* n.38 at 88.

beyond [the bank's] ability to pay."[122] Nowadays, liquidation risk is addressed by a number of institutions, one of which is the Federal Deposit Insurance Corporation (FDIC), an independent agency created during the New Deal to collect premiums from banks that are then used to insure deposits.[123]

Budgetary Entitlement and Legal Enforceability as a Positive Entitlement
FDIC is backed by a trust fund, the Deposit Insurance Fund, which adheres to a minimum reserve ratio of 1.35.[124] But this dedicated trust fund does not exhaust the federal resources devoted to meeting FDIC obligations. FDIC expenditures are classified on the direct spending side by CBO, and further backed by both the authority to borrow from the Treasury, and by the permanent, mandatory resources of the Judgment Fund.[125] Meanwhile, the FDIC has the capacity "[t]o sue and be sued, and complain and defend, by and through its own attorneys, in any court of law or equity, State or Federal."[126]

Banking institutions are not the only ones to bring suit to make good on the FDIC's backing; depositors have also sued FDIC to assert their claims. 12 U.S.C. § 1821(f)(4) authorizes review of FDIC insurance claim determinations in accordance with the Administrative Procedure Act.[127] The banks that enjoy this insurance are subject to required capital levels and other matters of financial soundness in part to protect depositors as the ultimate beneficiaries.[128]

[122] *Id.* at 89.
[123] FDIC: FEDERAL DEPOSIT INSURANCE CORPORATION WEBPAGE, https://www.fdic.gov/ (accessed April 17, 2021).
[124] Dodd-Frank Wall Street Reform and Consumer Protection Act, P.L. 111-203, § 334, 124 Stat. 1376, 1539 (2010) (codified as 12 USC §1817(b)), *cited in* FY2022 BUDGET, ANALYTICAL PERSPECTIVES, *Ch. 15 Credit and Insurance* 181, 189 (2021), https://www.govinfo.gov/app/details/BUDGET-2022-PER/context.
[125] *See, e.g.*, CBO, AN UPDATE TO THE BUDGET AND ECONOMIC OUTLOOK: 2016 TO 2026 (August 2016), https://www.cbo.gov/publication/51129. For borrowing authority, *see* 12 U.S.C. § 1824(a) and for how even this authorized line of credit can be increased, *see* 12 U.S.C. § 1824(a)(3)(A). *Slattery v. United States*, 635 F.3d 1298 (2011) (confirming Tucker Act jurisdiction for FDIC cases, citing Comptroller General's letter concluding the same for FDIC's counterpart with respect to savings and loan institutions: "[W]e are of the opinion that FSLIC's promissory notes and assistance guarantees are obligations of the United States, backed by its full faith and credit." 68 Comp. Gen. 14, 1988 WL 223985 (October 11, 1988)).
[126] 12 U.S.C. § 1819(a) (Fourth); *See also id.* at 1819(b)(2)(a).
[127] 12 U.S.C. § 1821 (f)(4) ("A final determination made by the [FDIC] regarding any claim for insurance coverage shall be a final agency action reviewable in accordance with [5 U.S.C. § 708] by the United States district court for the Federal judicial district where the principal place of business of the depository institution is located." For claims against FDIC when FDIC is a receiver, *see* 12 U.S.C. § 1821(d)(6)(A) ("the claimant may . . . file suit on such claim . . . in the district or territorial court of the United States for the district within which the depository institution's principal place of business is located"). (12 U.S.C. § 1821(d)(7)(A) ("If any claimant requests review under this subparagraph in lieu of filing or continuing any action under paragraph (6) . . . , the [FDIC] shall consider the claim after opportunity for a hearing on the record. The final determination of the [FDIC] with respect to such claim shall be subject to judicial review under [5 U.S.C. § 706]."
[128] Statement of Sheila C. Bair, *On the Causes and Current State of the Financial Crisis before the Financial Crisis Inquiry Commission* (January 14, 2010), https://www.fdic.gov/news/speeches/chairman/spjan1410.html.

Description of the Government Reinsurance Role Through the Federal Reserve Bank

The FDIC performs this oversight function even for those state-chartered banks outside the Federal Reserve System.[129] For Reserve system member banks however, the Federal Reserve itself is the crucial backstop for depositor risk, serving as the "lender of last resort" so that commercial banks can meet the demands for liquidity.[130] Indeed, the Fed has authority in unusual or exigent circumstance to perform that same backstopping function for numerous other entities as well under the notorious § 13(3) of the Federal Reserve Act.[131]

I argue here that the lender of last resort (LLR) function is an instance of the broader reinsurance function, and indeed one that belongs distinctively to government.[132] This argument about the comparative advantage of government as LLR should be comfortable and familiar. Long associated with nineteenth-century British businessman Walter Bagehot, this allocation of duties has even garnered arch-free-marketeer Milton Friedman's support.[133]

According to Moss, "The notion of banks as insurers was first formalized [by] Douglas W. Diamond and Philip H. Dybvig."[134] Part of the interest that borrowers pay to banks is a *premium* for the banks to pool and spread default risk. Part of the return foregone when depositors place their money with the bank is a *premium* for certainty and liquidity. Not only were banks acting as insurers, but the Federal Reserve, as the banker to the banks, was providing the proverbial "insurance for insurers," with all the too-big-to-fail pathologies that this backing entailed.[135] One commentator quips, "The practice of a state-sponsored LLR function became institutionalized and by extension moral hazard was systemically inscribed in the financial and monetary sphere. *Effectively this function acted as insurance.*"[136]

The Federal Reserve, alongside numerous other arms of government, reinsured systemically significant banks in both implicit and explicit ways in

---

[129] BOARD OF GOVERNORS OF THE FEDERAL RESERVE SYSTEM (U.S.). *Supervising and Regulating Financial Institutions and Activities,* THE FEDERAL RESERVE SYSTEM: PURPOSES AND FUNCTIONS 72, 74–80 (2016), https://www.federalreserve.gov/aboutthefed/files/pf_5.pdf.

[130] Gary Gorton & Andrew Metrick, *The Federal Reserve and Panic Prevention: The Roles of Financial Regulation and Lender of Last Resort,* 27 J. ECON. PERSPECT. 45–64 (2013).

[131] 12 U.S.C. § 343(A) (2006).

[132] Marie-Laure Djelic & Joel Bothello, *Limited liability and its Moral Hazard Implications: The Systemic Inscription of Instability in Contemporary Capitalism,* 42 THEOR SOC 589, 595 (2013), https://doi.org/10.1007/s11186-013-9206-z (accessed March 23, 2021) (ascribing the LLR function as "a term attributed to English merchant banker turned Member of Parliament, Henry Thornton").

[133] *Id. citing* Xavier Freixas et al., *Lender of Last Resort: What Have We Learned Since Bagehot?* 18 J. OF FINANCIAL SERVICES RES. 63 (2000). *Id.*

[134] Moss, *supra* n.38 at 361, n. 4 *citing* Douglas W. Diamond & Philip H. Dybvig, *Bank Runs, Deposit Insurance, and Liquidity,* 91 J. OF POL. ECON. 401–419 (1983).

[135] Moss, *supra* n.38 *citing* Gregory Moore, *Solutions to the Moral Hazard Problem Arising from The Lender-of-last-resort Facility,* 13 J. OF ECON. SURVEYS 443–476 (1999).

[136] Moore, *supra* n.135 at 444 (1999) (emphasis added).

order to keep them humming. It is notable that for William Eskridge and John Ferejohn, the history of our "independent central bank presiding over a national paper currency" exemplifies the emergence "by fits and starts" of a superstatutory framework, consistent with my story of step-wise entrenchment.[137]

The Ultimate Beneficiary

The justification for state provision of this reinsurance invoked not just supply-side protection of the banks themselves, but ultimately, the protection of individual depositors. In the debate over FDIC and bank backstopping during the Great Depression, Representative Robert Luce of Massachusetts importuned:

> I have seen insurance extended in every direction . . . and I fail to understand why the depositors in a bank, persons who have no opportunity to know, who have in fact no knowledge about the interior affairs of the bank . . . should not be insured against mischance that they cannot guard against and prevent.[138]

Former Obama administration Treasury Secretary Timothy Geithner attempted the modern equivalent of this argument. In his book, he defends his bailout of the banks, whom he calls the "arsonists" of the last financial crisis, as ultimately intended to "protect the innocent" Americans whose deposits, credit, jobs, were at stake in the systemic risk cyclone that was the Great Recession.[139] Geithner's mistake was to assume that the backstopping role did not then give him leverage to discipline the financial institutions he was propping up.

His justification rings somewhat hollower in the financial sector than in other sectors, such as health. With the increasingly hermetic clientelism of the financial sector, some of the indirect beneficiaries were not broader depositors, but merely other banks. Jonathan Katz describes how "[t]he real beneficiaries of the government's [financial crisis] actions were AIG creditors and counterparties to open AIG positions," first among whom was Goldman Sachs.[140] Katz says:

---

[137] Eskridge & Ferejohn, A REPUBLIC OF STATUTES; THE NEW AMERICAN CONSTITUTION 313. For perspectives on the soft entrenchment of the central bank as an anchor institution whose lack of Constitutional stature belies its power, independence, and durability, *see also*, David Zaring, *Law and Custom on the Federal Open Market Committee*, 78 LAW CONTEMP. PROBL. 157–188 (2015). Kathryn Judge, The Federal Reserve: A Study in Soft Constraints, 78 LAW & CONTEMP. PROBS., no. 3, 2015, at 65. Adrian Vermeule, *Conventions of Agency Independence*, 113 COLUM. L. REV. 1163, 1168–81 (2013). Peter Conti-Brown, The Structure of Federal Reserve Independence 42 (STANFORD UNIV. ROCK CTR. FOR CORPORATE GOVERNANCE, Working Paper Series No. 139, 2013).

[138] Moss, *supra* n.38 at 118

[139] Marilyn Geewax, *It's Geithner Vs. Warren in Battle of the Bailout*, NPR.ORG (2014), https://www.npr.org/2014/05/25/315276441/its-geithner-vs-warren-in-battle-of-the-bailout (accessed April 19, 2021).

[140] Katz, *supra* n.87.

[O]ne must recognize that much of the total cost of the AIG intervention could have been avoided, or reduced if government officials had acted prudently (in negotiating the original terms of the AIG loan and in monitoring AIG bonuses), had [they] insisted on shared sacrifice from . . . counterparties in its negotiations, and had [they] not used AIG as a disguised funding conduit to other institutions.[141]

He continues, "There is a widespread perception that the decision to bail out AIG without demanding concessions was designed to save its counterparties, such as Goldman Sachs."[142]

Subjective Entitlement

Some might contend that these implicit guarantees of government bailout in times of crisis differ from the explicit guarantees laid out in reinsurance policies. But any differentiation in kind would depend on how widely and strongly held the expectation was that government would step in. Some data suggests that this belief was so pervasive in banking that the implicit promise was nearly as good as explicit. "The belief in an implicit government guarantee of the largest banks dramatically reduces the cost of capital for [those] banks. This study concludes that today the eighteen largest banks borrow at rates 0.78 percent lower than smaller banks," and they enjoyed lower rates even before the 2008 recession as well.[143] The beneficiaries of government banking reinsurance were in no small part these banks who could borrow at lower rates, reaping the benefits of what Super might have understood to be a shared subjective understanding of what these too-big-to-fail banks would be entitled to. The key question is whether banks were passing these benefits of subjective entitlement onto their depositors or instead pocketing the gains. Health insurers, by contrast, are required to pass on savings in the form lower premiums or rebates because of the medical loss ratio limits established by the ACA.[144] These limits ensure that government subsidies to insurance companies are used primarily on medical services for enrollees. Patient

---

[141] *Id.*

[142] *Id.* at 1593, *citing* SIMON JOHNSON & JAMES KWAK, 13 BANKERS: THE WALL STREET TAKEDOWN AND THE NEXT FINANCIAL MELTDOWN (2011), and ANDREW ROSS SORKIN, TOO BIG TO FAIL 532–33 (2010). For the account that Goldman then received more money from the AIG special purpose vehicle (SPV) than it received from TARP, and for the crowning detail that shortly after Goldman received that SPV money, it repaid its TARP loan, thereby escaping the TARP conditions on executive compensation, *see* Katz, *supra* n.87 at 1594.

[143] JOHNSON AND KWAK, *supra* n.142 at 180–181. *See also* FIN. CRISIS INQUIRY COMM'N, PRELIMINARY STAFF REPORT, GOVERNMENTAL RESCUES OF 'TOO-BIG-TO-FAIL' FINANCIAL INSTITUTIONS 12–13 (2010), https://fcic-static.law.stanford.edu/cdn_media/fcic-reports/2010-0831-Governmental-Rescues.pdf.

[144] PHSA § 2718(b), codified as 42 U.S.C. § 300gg-18(b) (setting medical loss ratio at no less than 85% in the large group market, and no less than 80% in the small group and individual markets, with any smaller percentage triggering the duty to rebate a portion of premiums to the enrollees).

medical claims must represent at least 85 percent of earned premiums in the case of large group insurers and at least 80 percent in the case of individual and small group insurers. Corresponding profit margins that are greater than 15 percent (or 20 percent for individual and small group plans) and are not spent on medical claims must be rebated to the subscribers.

Though banking institutions enjoyed significant ad hoc bailouts and implicit guarantees, we should not overlook the additional sums channeled through preestablished automatic stabilizers, each another paving stone in the stepwise entrenchment of bank reinsurance.[145] Some have argued that these non–TARP (Troubled Assets Relief Program) bailouts were more important than the ad hoc bailout that was TARP itself.[146] For example, FDIC and FHA mortgage insurance both performed their intended roles while institutions like Ginnie Mae mopped up some of the spiraling mortgage debt and the Department of Education absorbed student loan fallout.[147]

We have entrenched the expectation that federal government will furnish material aid to secure an elaborate network of institutions against systemic money risk that would far exceed any individual bank's capacity to manage. This safety net was defended not only in the name of the individual depositor but even more broadly on behalf of any individual participant in the US market economy. Why then would we spurn health risk?

Pensions

ERISA was first introduced in 1964 by Indiana Senator Vance Hartke as the Federal Reinsurance of Private Pensions Act,[148] with the aim of authorizing the

---

[145] Lael Brianard, *Monetary Policy Strategies and Tools When Inflation and Interest Rates are Low* (2020), https://www.federalreserve.gov/newsevents/speech/brainard20200221a.htm (accessed April 19, 2021).

[146] Katz, *supra* n.87 at 1569 (contending that "the money trail reveals that the funds expended by TARP were in fact merely one component of a much larger government intervention"). *See also, Id.* at 1585 (observing that "when compared to other government loan guarantee programs and secondary market interventions, it was a small piece of a very large pie . . . overall federal support for the national financial system [was] $3.7 trillion in actual expenditures and guarantees. Most of that amount was assumed or spent without direct congressional action.") The size of this sum should help cast entitlements like Medicare, which in total represents less than a trillion USD a year in annual spending, as less unrealistic than we may have been led to believe. *See* NHE Fact Sheet (December 2021) https://www.cms.gov/Research-Statistics-Data-and-Systems/Statistics-Trends-and-Reports/NationalHealthExpendData/NHE-Fact-Sheet#:~:text=Historical%20NHE%2C%202020%3A&text=Medicare%20spending%20grew%203.5%25%20to,16%20percent%20of%20total%20NHE.

[147] Katz, *id.* at 1585–7.

[148] James Wooten, *"The Most Glorious Story of Failure in the Business": The Studebaker-Packard Corporation and the Origins of ERISA*, 49 BUFF. L. REV. 683, 686 (2001). Wooten later says, "When Senator Jacob Javits introduced comprehensive pension-reform legislation in 1967, his bill contained a termination-insurance proposal that drew many of its provisions from a later version of Hartke's

Pension Benefit Guaranty Corporation (PBGC). The idea of the PBGC arose out of union advocacy in the face of employer defaults on pension obligations. Unions had negotiated for pensions through private bargaining.[149] Yet these promises were repeatedly broken due to underfunding and plant closures.[150] Pensions themselves serve as insurance against the risks of income loss due to old age. Yet unions and workers continued to seek further forms of security to back this insurance, especially against the risk that the employer's financing would fall short of the plan's obligations. As the United Auto Workers (UAW) actuary lamented in 1958, "Vested rights ... were hailed as a great achievement when they were won. ... But ... [t]hey must be made to stick, even in the event of a plan termination."[151] UAW proposed "establishing something like the Federal Deposit Insurance Corporation to backstop private pension plans."[152] This quote suggests the rights-like propagation of the idea of government reinsurance from banking to pensions even as the creation of FDIC for banks was, in Representative Luce's words above, justified by previous examples of government "insurance extended in every direction." This cross-sector extension comports with the implicit rights thesis I argue should obtain for health, namely, the thesis that government's past action backstopping catastrophic risk in other circumstances lays the groundwork for those in similar circumstances to press claims for like provision. This logical progression evinces an understanding that government aid in the event of loss beyond a certain threshold is a matter of *principle*, or, in other words, a rights-amenable norm.

The Ultimate Beneficiary

Notably, UAW chose government reinsurance rather than attempting to bargain collectively for more employer protection against pension default risk, which might have resulted in lower wages for active employees. The benefit of reinsurance as compared to other policies lay in how it would redound not just to the highest-risk individuals, but to broader low-risk constituencies, as each of

---

bill." *Id.* at 736. *See*, The Pension and Employee Benefit Act of 1967, S. 1103, 90th Cong. (1967) (introduced by Sen. Javits).

[149] Wooten, *supra* n.148, at 686. Though Social Security existed, "public retirement benefits were thought to be inadequate" especially by higher wage workers, which led to supplementation through privately bargained pensions. *Id.*

[150] *Id.* at 704 ("The tax laws allowed an employer to fund past-service liability created by a plan amendment over the same term—about twelve years—that applied to the initial liability when a plan was created. UAW contracts commonly called for a firm to amortize the liability on a thirty-year schedule from the date of the benefit increase").

[151] *Id.* at 717–8, *quoting* Memorandum from Max Bloch to James Brindle 4 (June 17, 1958) (UAW Social Security Department Collection, Unprocessed Materials, Accession Date March 23, 1978, Box 4 of 7, Staff Collective Bargaining Folder, Archives of Labor and Urban Affairs, Wayne State University).

[152] *Id.* at 720.

the above examples illustrate. And like other reinsurance efforts, PBGC was intended to induce private primary insurers, the employers in this case, to continue "offering voluntary retirement plans in the first place."[153] This goal appears in the PBGC authorizing language[154] and is baked into ERISA jurisprudence.[155]

Description of the Federal Reinsurance Role
PBGC's policy design bore certain reinsurance features, by now familiar to us, such as premiums and a cap on benefits.[156] Employers pay into the fund at premium rates set by Congressional formula.[157] In addition to benefits paid by PBGC on behalf of a terminated plan, the companies formerly responsible for the pension obligations must make payments to pensioners according to the applicable recovery ratio, much like coinsurance.[158] The benefit structure also features what is functionally an attachment point, whereupon PBGC pays out the benefits promised. This point is based on findings made in the terminations process.[159] In a termination, PBGC must declare the presence of certain conditions, including whether the plan can pay benefits currently due, in order to trigger PBGC responsibility.[160]

Legal Enforceability as a Positive Entitlement
Like FDIC, PBGC is subject to suit under its authorizing statute. Claimants, as listed, include retirees and participants, the ultimate beneficiaries:

> any person who is a plan sponsor, fiduciary, employer, contributing sponsor, member of a contributing sponsor's controlled group, *participant, or beneficiary*, and is adversely affected by any action of the corporation with respect to a plan in which such person has an interest, or who is an employee organization

---

[153] Brendan Maher & Paul Secunda, *Pension De-risking*, 93 WASH. U. L. REV. 733, 737 (2016).

[154] 29 U.S.C. § 1302(a) (stating, "The purposes of this subchapter, which are to be carried out by the corporation, are (1) to encourage the continuation and maintenance of voluntary private pension plans for the benefit of their participants").

[155] *See, e.g.*, Pilot Life Ins. Co. v. Dedeaux, 48 U.S. 41, 42 (1987) (declaring in the context of ERISA's civil enforcement scheme, that the statute "represents a careful balancing of the need for prompt and fair claims settlement procedures against the public interest in encouraging the formation of employee benefit plans").

[156] Wooten, *supra* n.148 at 725. 29 U.S.C. § 1322(b)(3). Pension Benefit Guaranty Corporation, *Maximum Monthly Guarantee Tables*, PBGC.GOV, https://www.pbgc.gov/wr/benefits/guaranteed-benefits/maximum-guarantee (accessed April 20, 2021) (listing the maximum monthly guarantees set by formula tied to a Social Security index. The 2021 maximum for a sixty-five-year-old retiree is $6034.09 per month, for instance). There is also an aggregate limit on benefits imposed in 29 U.S.C. § 1322(b)(3)(B).

[157] 29 U.S.C. § 1306.

[158] 29 U.S.C. § 1322(c).

[159] 29 U.S.C. §§ 1341, 1341A, 1342.

[160] PENSION BENEFIT GUARANTY CORPORATION, *Pension Plan Termination Fact Sheet*, PBGC. GOV, https://www.pbgc.gov/about/factsheets/page/termination (accessed April 20, 2021).

representing such a participant or beneficiary so adversely affected for purposes of collective bargaining with respect to such plan.[161]

Any of these parties "may bring an action against the [PBGC] for appropriate equitable relief [in federal district court]."[162]

Subjective Budgetary Entitlement

PBGC benefits, while ostensibly paid for out of premiums and resources contributed by employer plans, have nevertheless enjoyed periodically bailout by the taxpayers, thereby constituting an implicit or subjective entitlement.[163] While the fund for single-employer pension guarantees is currently in surplus, the multi-employer fund has confronted significant challenges recently. Congress has intervened more than once. "In December 2019, the enactment of the Bipartisan American Miners Act of 2019, Pub.L. No. 116-94, div. M, 133 Stat. 2534, provided additional funding for future annual Treasury transfers to the 1974 United Mine Workers of America Pension Plan (included in PBGC's multiemployer program)."[164] Just recently, the March 2021 American Rescue Plan coronavirus relief omnibus plugged in $86 billion to enable the multiemployer fund to "cover full pension benefits for workers in ailing plans over the next three decades. The relief measure would also reinstate any benefits that had been suspended for recipients."[165]

Natural Disasters: Floods

We now turn to what is perhaps the core case for government reinsurance to backstop catastrophic risk, namely, natural disaster.

Description of the Federal Reinsurance Role

One of the leading disaster law experts, Jim Chen, explains government flood reinsurance in the following terms, which by now have a familiar ring:

---

[161] 29 U.S.C. § 1303(f) (emphasis added).

[162] Id.

[163] Pension Protection Act of 2006, P.L. No. 109-280 (2006).

[164] U.S. General Accounting Office, *The Nation's Fiscal Health: Action is Needed to Address the Federal Government's Fiscal Future*, An Annual Report to Congress 46, n. 52, GAO-20-403SP (March 2020), https://www.gao.gov/assets/710/707107.pdf.

[165] Greg Iacurci, *Covid relief bill gives $86 billion bailout to failing union pension plans*, CNBC (March 8 2021), https://www.cnbc.com/2021/03/08/covid-relief-bill-gives-86-billion-bailout-to-failing-union-pension-plans.html.

Private insurance . . . represents the first and arguably most important layer of financial preparedness for disaster. . . . But many disasters pose special trouble, even for the largest, most financially secure insurers. . . . Modern portfolio theory sheds clarifying light on what is perhaps the most insidious factor undermining the financial integrity of private insurance for catastrophic risk: private insurers are extremely loath to cover risks that are highly correlated to each other. . . . For this reason insurers routinely exclude coverage for flood damage (or even water damage more generally), even in policies that purport to cover all risks.[166]

Here I discuss flood disasters as an entry point to examining the federal role in disaster coverage and relief more generally. Indeed, the risk of flood damage is backed by federal funds, to the point of nigh full risk absorption following the precise logic Chen articulates.

In the aftermath of the great Mississippi flood of 1927, every flood insurer left the market.[167] Floods continued to be excluded from homeowners' or other policies throughout the 1950s, prompting calls for public intervention. There was a general consensus that the studies to map and identify flood risk exceeded private capacity and required the Federal Army Corps of Engineers.[168] Thus in 1968, Congress created the National Flood Insurance Program (NFIP). NFIP used federal resources to spur flood coverage, while simultaneously requiring communities who gained such coverage to institute zoning, building codes, and other hazard mitigation measures.[169] Part A of the NFIP was structured as a public-private partnership with government reinsuring the private primary insurers, though gradually phasing-out the government subsidy.[170] However, because participation of both insurers and insureds remained voluntary, many property owners and communities continued to opt out.

Step-Wise Transition Between Public and Private Provision
Congress responded by passing the Flood Disaster Protection Act of 1973, which mandated the purchase of flood insurance for any property in a designated risk zone that received federal assistance or a federally backed mortgage.[171] On the

[166] Jim Chen, *Modern Disaster Theory: Evaluating Disaster Law as a Portfolio of Legal Rules*, 25 EMORY INT'L L. REV. 1121, 1133–5 (2011).

[167] *Id.*

[168] Edward T. Pasterick, *The National Flood Insurance Program: A U.S. Approach to Flood Loss Reduction in* FLOOD ISSUES IN CONTEMPORARY WATER MANAGEMENT (J. Marsalek et al., eds., 2000), *cited in* SWARTZ, *supra* n.27 at 139.

[169] Moss, *supra* n.38 at 263.

[170] COMPTROLLER GENERAL U.S. GENERAL ACCOUNTING OFFICE, *Examination of the Financial Statements of the National Flood Insurance Program as of December 31, 1977* 2 (1979), https://www.gao.gov/assets/ced-79-70.pdf. 42 U.S.C. §§ 4051-57.

[171] 42 U.S.C. § 4012a. Moss, *supra* n.38 at 262–3.

supply side, many private insurers still elected not to participate, continuing to exclude floods from property and casualty policies, even as they included tornado coverage.[172] Those insurers who did join the consortium of participating companies did not always cooperate with government financial oversight.[173] The National Flood Insurance Act happened to have been designed with a Part B apparatus, which authorized HUD to administer a type of "public fallback option" in the event that the Part A industry partnership proved unworkable.[174] Part B provides:

> If at any time, after consultation with representatives of the insurance industry, the Administrator determines that operation of the flood insurance program as provided under part A cannot be carried out, or that such operation, in itself, would be assisted materially by the Federal Government's assumption, in whole or in part, of the operational responsibility for flood insurance under this chapter (on a temporary or other basis) he shall promptly undertake any necessary arrangements to carry out the program of flood insurance authorized under subchapter I through the facilities of the Federal Government, utilizing, for purposes of providing flood insurance coverage, either—
>
> (1) Insurance companies and other insurers, insurance agents and brokers, and insurance adjustment organizations, as fiscal agents of the United States,
> (2) such other officers and employees of any executive agency . . . as the Secretary and the head of any such agency may from time to time agree upon.[175]

I quote this section of statute so extensively in order to show its functional similarity to another program. Part B describes an arrangement whereby the government contracts with private insurance companies to act as fiscal agents of the government, in the place of or alongside federal officers and employees. The fiscal agents would serve under these contracts in order to administer the insurance that the government provides by processing claims, making payments, and otherwise servicing policies. This relationship resembles the full risk-bearing relationship that Medicare has cultivated with the Medicare Administrative Contractors (MACs)—formerly called "fiscal intermediaries" or "carriers"—who administer "single-payer" traditional Medicare benefits.[176] Medicare is

---

[172] *Id.* at 262.
[173] U.S. GENERAL ACCOUNTING OFFICE, *supra* n.170 at 3–4.
[174] 42 U.S.C. §§ 4071–72.
[175] 42 U.S.C. § 4071.
[176] 42 U.S.C. § 1395kk-1(a)-(d). "Fiscal intermediaries" for Medicare Part A hospital benefits are explained further under 42 U.S.C. §1395h, "Carriers" for Medicare Part B benefits are explained under 42 U.S.C. §1395u. 42 C.F.R. § 400.202 ("Carrier means an entity that has a contract with CMS to determine and make Medicare payments for Part B benefits payable on a charge basis and to perform other related functions").

similarly authorized by statute to contract with MACs to determine and make payments, conduct education, outreach, and communication and other services to carry out the Medicare program.[177]

In 1977, the government, having struggled to audit or negotiate new terms with the flood insurance industry partners, judged that the government would save money by direct provision. HUD therefore activated Part B and assumed the insurance of flood risk directly, contracting with private intermediaries solely to administer the policies on HUD's (and later FEMA's) behalf.[178] Since 1983, private insurers have taken on an increased role administering the NFIP, "including selling and servicing policies and adjusting claims, but they largely have not been underwriting flood risk themselves."[179] Government actually holds the risk and private entities "sell and service" the policies as hired agents, keeping a whopping 32 percent of the premium.[180]

Legal Enforceability as a Positive Entitlement

FEMA prescribes a Standard Flood Insurance Policy (SFIP) and the National Flood Insurance Act supplies original, exclusive jurisdiction for actions based on SFIP claims without regard to amount in controversy, sounding once again in the properties of Super's "positive" entitlements.[181]

Federal Financing: Budgetary Entitlement and Subjective Entitlement

As with the MMIF and the FDIC deposit insurance fund, the NFIP has a direct line of credit from the US Treasury. The cap on this borrowing authority expanded to an additional $30 million after a recent spate of hurricanes, including Hurricane Katrina and Sandy.[182] Even this degree of explicit financial backing has not exhausted the implicit government guarantee on offer in the flood context.[183] The Government Accountability Office (GAO) cites the following recent history:

---

[177] 42 U.S.C. § 1395kk-1(d).

[178] U.S. GENERAL ACCOUNTING OFFICE, *supra* n.170.

[179] DIANE P. HORN & BAIRD WEBEL, *Private Flood Insurance and the National Flood Insurance* 6, CONG. RES. SERV. R45242 (April 2020). *See also*, Pecarovich v. Allstate Ins. Co., 272 F. Supp. 2d 981 (C.D. Cal. 2003) ("All flood claims are paid from the United States Treasury, regardless of whether the policy is issued by FEMA or by a WYO insurer" *citing* 44 C.F.R., § 62, App. A44, C.F.R., Pt. 62, App. A Art. III(D)(1)).

[180] SWARTZ, *supra* n.27 at 139.

[181] 42 U.S.C. § 4072. For SFIP, *see* 44 C.F.R. Section 61.13 and 44 C.F.R. § 61, App. A(1)-(3).

[182] FY2022 BUDGET, *see supra* n.124 at 181, 192.

[183] This recent history has also prompted FEMA to experiment with bringing in a layer of private reinsurance to absorb mounting risks, reminding us that the degree of public and private risk-bearing remains adjustable. *Id.*

Congress [has] demonstrated its willingness to fund the implicit exposure of policyholder claims that exceeded the amount NFIP was authorized to borrow from the Treasury. In October 2017, when NFIP was about to exhaust its borrowing authority, Congress passed a supplemental appropriation which the President signed into law, that cancelled $16 billion of NFIP debt to the Treasury.[184]

A recent legislative reversal signals the degree to which this implicit expectation—or subjective entitlement—of continued federal assistance is entrenched. Congress tried in 2012 to reduce its assistance for flood insurance through the Biggert-Waters Flood Insurance Reform Act of 2012, but after outcry, Congress promptly restored premium relief again by passing the Homeowners Flood Insurance Affordability Act of 2014.[185]

Lessons for Policy Design

Jim Chen concludes that "[d]espite these shortcomings, the NFIP retains value as the one policy tool that has shown even modest historical success in 'guid[ing] development away from floodplains.' "[186] Reinsurance has thus served as leverage for conditional federal standards to address or prevent the underlying causes of risk. And as with the education example, the phase-change of flood insurance to a Medicare-like administrative contractor model shows that government reinsurance can serve as a stepping stone to more direct public provision.

Natural Disasters: Beyond Floods

Related dynamics characterize our treatment of natural disasters more generally.

Description of the Federal Reinsurance Role

Apart from flood disasters, the federal government's role in responding to major disasters can be said to consist of the "provision of *de facto* reinsurance for the insurers that sell the policies in the first place."[187]

---

[184] GAO April 2020, *infra* n.204 at 24, citing GAO, *Fiscal Exposures: Federal Insurance and Other Activities That Transfer Risk or Losses to the Government* (March 27, 2019), https://www.gao.gov/products/gao-19-353, GAO 19-353.

[185] Jennifer Wriggins, *Flood Money: The Challenge of U.S. Flood Insurance Reform in a Warming World*, 119 PENN. STATE L. REV. 361 (2014).

[186] Chen, *supra* n.166 at 1135–6, *citing* Oliver A. Houck, *Rising Water: The National Flood Insurance Program and Louisiana*, 60 TUL. L. REV. 61, 160 (1985).

[187] SWARTZ, *supra* n.27 at 101.

One example lies in the structure of the Robert T. Stafford Relief and Emergency Assistance Act (1988).[188] The Stafford Act, which succeeded the Disaster Relief Act, first passed in 1950,[189] is a major pillar of federal disaster response.[190] Stafford relief is triggered upon presidential declaration of a major disaster.[191] If the president declares a national emergency, additional categories of assistance become available even beyond those slated for major disasters.[192]

Notably, the structure of Stafford assistance maps recognizably onto the features we have come to associate with reinsurance. Stafford Act policies are structured to reinsure rather than insure, insofar as the relief contemplates that states and localities will respond first. The federal aid depends on a declaration to trigger and even then becomes available typically only after a Preliminary Damage Assessment (PDA) to evaluate whether the incident has reached a threshold of "unusual severity and magnitude."[193] This type of attachment point is set by guidance, some of which is published as the Preliminary Damage Assessment Guide (PDA).[194] The PDA threshold is defined as damage that exceeds the states' capacity to respond without assistance from the federal government, an expression of the states' primary insurer role. The factors considered in making that threshold determination include matters such as the amount of insurance coverage already in place and the state's total taxable resources, positioning the federal government as the insurer of last resort.[195]

The aid once triggered includes not only Individual Assistance (IA) but also Public Assistance (PA) and PA encompasses mitigating and preventive action as well, intended to protect lives, property, public health, and safety.[196]

---

[188] Disaster Relief and Emergency Assistance Amendments of 1988, Pub. L. No. 100-707, 102 Stat. 4689 (1988), 42 USC §§ 5121 et seq.

[189] The Federal Disaster Relief Act of 1950, Pub. L. No. 81-875, 64 Stat. 1109 (1950).

[190] BRENNAN CENTER FOR JUSTICE, A Guide to Emergency Powers and Their Use 1–2 (2020), https://www.brennancenter.org/our-work/research-reports/guide-emergency-powers-and-their-use (accessed April 19, 2021) (identifying four major framework statutes in our current legal landscape for federal disaster relief, including the Stafford Act, 42 U.S.C. §§ 5121 et seq., the National Emergencies Act, 50 USC §§ 1601-1651, the Public Health Service Act, 42 U.S.C. §§ 201 et seq., including 42 U.S.C. § 247d, as well as 22 U.S.C. § 2318(a)(1) for drawdown of resources from the Department of Defense).

[191] Daniel Farber, Presidential Power in a Pandemic, CPRBLOG (THE CENTER FOR PROGRESSIVE REFORM) (2020), http://progressivereform.org/cpr-blog/presidential-power-pandemic/ (accessed April 19, 2021) (explaining, "A major disaster authorizes the government to distribute supplies and emergency assistance, unemployment assistance, emergency grants to assist low-income migrant and seasonal farmworkers, food coupons and distribution, relocation assistance, community disaster loans, and emergency public transportation").

[192] Id.

[193] 44 C.F.R. § 206.33(b). See generally, BRUCE R LINDSAY & ELIZABETH M WEBSTER, Congressional Primer on Responding to and Recovering from Major Disasters and Emergencies 26, CONG. RES. SERV. R41981 (2020), https://fas.org/sgp/crs/homesec/R41981.pdf.

[194] Federal Emergency Management Agency (FEMA) Individual Assistance Declarations Factors Guidance, 84 Fed. Reg. 10521 (March 21, 2019). See, FEMA Preliminary Assessment Guide (May 2020), https://www.fema.gov/disasters/preliminary-damage-assessment-reports/guide.

[195] Id.

[196] Farber, supra n.191.

Step-Wise Entrenchment

Michelle Landis Dauber's work reveals that "Congress' role in disaster relief dates as far back as the earliest days of the American republic with some of the first private bills enacted."[197] This federal role, seemingly ad hoc, was actually so deeply entrenched that by 1887, precedent was routinely invoked "as a powerful argument both for and against the enactment of particular relief."[198] A capsule example of this reasoning was voiced by Texas Democratic Senator, Richard Coke, sponsoring a relief bill for drought in his state:

> Coke . . . argued that although his wealthy state did not need the aid . . . it was entitled to receive the federal largess because "[t]here is not a session of Congress that money for the relief of people somewhere in the United States is not expended. We ask for no departure from any precedents established by the Government . . . we are not asking [for anything] except for that which has always been freely granted to others having no greater rights or equities than ourselves."[199]

Disaster relief was plainly understood as rights-like in nature, claimable in like cases as a matter of principle. It has since been regularized, institutionalized under FEMA, codified not only in the Stafford Act but through at least one hundred other statutes, according to the Brennan Center for Justice.[200]

Terrorism-Related Disasters

The federal backstop for terrorism-related disasters merits its own mention.

Description of the Federal Reinsurance Role and Step-Wise Extension

In the wake of 9/11, the insurance market for terrorism coverage collapsed. Congress responded by passing the Terrorism Risk Insurance Act of 2002 (TRIA) to furnish government reinsurance in case of a certified terrorist attack.[201] This coverage is available for insurance lines such as commercial property, business interruption, workers' compensation and general liability, though notably not life or health.[202] It was originally slated to last three years, just as HOLC was,

---

[197] MICHELE LANDIS DAUBER, THE SYMPATHETIC STATE 18 (2012).

[198] Id.

[199] Id. at 27.

[200] BRENNAN CENTER FOR JUSTICE, A Guide to Emergency Powers and Their Use 1–2 (2020), https://www.brennancenter.org/our-work/research-reports/guide-emergency-powers-and-their-use (accessed April 19, 2021).

[201] Pub. L. No. 107-297, 116 Stat. 2322 (2002).

[202] 15 U.S.C. § 6701 note, Terrorism Risk Insurance Act of 2002 § 102(11), Pub. L. 107–297 (November 26, 2002).

but TRIA has since been extended with the most recent reauthorization effective through 2027.[203]

Consistent with its reinsurance design, TRIA's purpose was to spur private provision of a service through hefty government assumption of catastrophic losses. The parameters of coverage are more complex and have changed over time, generally in the direction of "increas[ing] insurers' share of the losses and thus decreas[ing] explicit federal fiscal exposure."[204] Accordingly, Treasury now pays 80 percent of "insured losses" above the insurer's individual attachment point, which is currently set at 20 percent of that insurer's direct-earned premiums from the prior calendar year.[205] The coverage only triggers if aggregate losses exceed certain thresholds, and extends only to a particular ceiling.[206]

As with many state insurance guaranty funds, TRIA is based on industry contribution to its collective financing. Here the payment is collected not as a prepayment premium but as a *post hoc* "recoupment."[207] The recoupment consists of an *ex post* premium surcharge, capped at 3 percent, that insurers would collect from the insureds to remit to the government.[208] All issuers of commercial policies would potentially owe recoupment, even on policies without terrorism risk coverage. However, they only pay when the specific recoupment threshold is met, and only until total insurers' payments compensate fully for the federal loss with an additional margin for the federal government risk-bearing and incidentals.[209]

Budgetary and Positive Entitlement

To give a rough sense of the proportion of losses to be borne by the government under TRIA, Treasury ran a hypothetical scenario for a 2018 terrorist event in San Francisco. They estimated nearly $40 billion in overall losses out of which the government would foot $4.4 billion in explicit reinsurance. Meanwhile, insurers would pay $17 billion in claims to policyholders.[210] To the extent that

---

[203] Terrorism Risk Insurance Extension Act of 2005, Pub. L. No. 109-144, 119 Stat. 2660 (2005). *See,* Terrorism Risk Insurance Program Reauthorization Act of 2007, Pub L. No. 110-160, 121 Stat. 1839 (2007). *See,* Clay Hunt Suicide Prevention for American Veterans Act, Pub. L. No. 114-2, 129 Stat. 30 (2015). *See also,* Further Consolidated Appropriations Act 2020, Pub. L. No. 116-94 § 502, 133 Stat. 3026 (2019).

[204] U. S. GOVERNMENT ACCOUNTABILITY OFFICE, *Terrorism Risk Insurance: Program Changes Have Reduced Federal Fiscal Exposure* 11 (April 20, 2020), GAO-20-348, https://www.gao.gov/produ cts/gao-20-348 (accessed April 19, 2021) (hereinafter "GAO April 2020").

[205] 31 C.F.R. § 50.4(p).

[206] GAO April 2020, *supra* n.204 at 7.

[207] 15 U.S.C. § 6701 note, Terrorism Risk Insurance Act of 2002 § 103(e)(7), Pub. L. 107–297 (November 26, 2002).

[208] 15 U.S.C. § 6701 note, Terrorism Risk Insurance Act of 2002 § 103(e)(8)(C), Pub. L. 107–297 (November 26, 2002).

[209] 15 U.S.C. § 6701 note, Terrorism Risk Insurance Act of 2002 § 103(e), Pub. L. 107–297 (November 26, 2002).

[210] *Id.* at 13–4.

TRIA would affect the federal budget, its impact would sound in mandatory or "direct" spending.[211]

Section 107 of TRIA provides an exclusive federal cause of action for "property damage, personal injury, or death arising out of or relating to such act of terrorism," and preempting otherwise available state causes of action "arising out of or resulting from an act of terrorism."[212] However, it also seeks to bar claimants from suing for federal share in the loss above the attachment point because of the following preclusive language: "Any determination of the Secretary under this subsection [providing Federal shared compensation for insured loss] shall be final, unless expressly provided, and shall not be subject to judicial review."[213]

Subjective and Functional Entitlement

The US Government Accountability Office (GAO) has been tasked with periodically review[ing] potential taxpayer exposure under TRIA and reporting to the Senate Banking Subcommittee on Financial Institutions and Consumer Protection. GAO has repeatedly voiced its concern over what it calls the government's "implicit fiscal exposure" beyond the explicit terms of TRIA. Industry has, after all, expressed confidence that Congress would step in ad hoc to cushion them from "recoupment" should a large terrorist event occur.[214] GAO publicly worries that federal action in past disasters has created an "expectation that the government would provide financial assistance to businesses for uninsured or underinsured losses . . . regardless of whether a loss-sharing program existed."[215] For instance, terrorism insurance ordinarily excludes terrorist attacks involving nuclear, biological, chemical, or radiological (NCBR) weapons. Moreover, stand-alone insurance for NBCR events is either unavailable or prohibitively expensive. These losses would therefore remain uninsured and as such, would never count toward an individual insurer's deductible thereby never triggering TRIA reinsurance.[216] These arbitrary exclusions are hard for a layperson to anticipate or understand as part of reasonable fulfilment of TRIA's function. It is therefore commonly presumed that government would step in to relieve businesses in an NBCR event, perhaps through other disaster relief channels described above, or as Congress did for the financial and auto

---

[211]   Perry Beider & David Torregrosa, Congressional Budget Office, *Federal Reinsurance for Terrorism Risk and Its Effects on the Budget* 9, Working Paper (June 2020), www.cbo.gov/publication/56420 (classifying the costs of TRIA as "direct" spending).

[212]   15 U.S.C. § 6701 note, Terrorism Risk Insurance Act of 2002 § 107, Pub. L. 107–297 (November 26, 2002).

[213]   15 U.S.C. § 6701 note, Terrorism Risk Insurance Act of 2002 § 103(e)(5), Pub. L. 107–297 (November 26, 2002), 116 Stat. 2322.

[214]   GAO April 2020, *supra* n.204 at 20.

[215]   *Id.* at 22.

[216]   *Id.* at 22–23.

industries after the 2008 financial crisis.[217] This confidence that despite the positive law exclusion of certain terrorist events, insurers would receive reinsurance nonetheless bespeaks TRIA's status as what in Chapter 2, David Super calls a "functional" entitlement, namely, a program that would satisfy a salient function in the world regardless of the technical limitations and cutoffs.

Why Not Health?

The question that lingers after surveying the immense government infrastructure for collective risk absorption is, why not reinsure healthcare risk? Why should the state "de-risk" banking conditions and not de-risk the human condition by assuring the institutional resources for healthcare response? The single loss that is arguably of most immediate felt concern is somehow excluded from this curated riskscape. In the era of the "de-risking state," as Daniela Gabor has dubbed it, this differential underinvestment in health is emphatically not a given, but a matter of collective choice.[218]

Some might argue that the case for reinsurance is less compelling in circumstances of predictable, stochastically independent loss, rather than catastrophic, systemically correlated loss.[219] But can anyone in year 2023 deny that high-cost ruinous health events are systemically correlated? This correlation exists not just in times of pandemic. Countless studies demonstrate that the inflationary, often wasteful conditions affecting national health expenditure are not mere happenstance—they are constituted by collective policy. High-cost healthcare covaries to the extent that Medicare's deferential payment policies led to the inflation of price, volume, and the technological character of end-of-life care.[220] It covaries because everyone faces increased medical cost risk from the pharmaceutical industry's profiteering, a situation enabled by the FDA's enfeebled approval standards, coupled with lavish grants of exclusivity. It covaries because our choices to fragment health finance through devolution, through ERISA, and the public-private divide, mean that payers cannot negotiate effectively

---

[217] *Id.* at 22–24.

[218] *See,* Daniela Gabor, *Critical Macro-Finance: A Theoretical Lens,* 6 FINANCE AND SOCIETY 45, 51 (2020), http://financeandsociety.ed.ac.uk/article/view/4408 (accessed April 21, 2021) ("the most notable post-Lehman institutional change is the rise of central banks as market-makers of last resort (MMLR) for a set of collateral securities. While initially restricted to large central banks, the COVID-19 pandemic has seen central banks of emerging countries adopt it too"). *See also,* S. QUINN, *supra* n.54 at 203 (urging that we look for the social contract in these hidden choices, reminding us that "[u]nderstandings of the limits and possibilities of what people owe to each other and can expect from the state are written into the designs of financial instruments,").

[219] *See e.g.,* J. David Cummins et al., *The Costs and Benefits of Reinsurance,* (February 10, 2021), http://dx.doi.org/10.2139/ssrn.1142954

[220] *See generally,* JILL QUADAGNO, ONE NATION, UNINSURED (2006).

on price. Everyone experiences these increased risks of high medical cost on a community-wide basis, rather than as individual events.

How Reinsurance Constitutes a Right

So far I have recounted how certain expectations become encoded, and encoded durably, open to principled claims that depend on and engender the kinds of binding legal reliance, pathways to suit, embedded institutionalism, mandatory funding, and subjective political entitlement that constitute entrenchment in our policy landscape. Let us recount how these features might render these reinsurance programs tantamount to affirmative socioeconomic rights.

One recognizable hallmark of entitlements is claimability. This property of rights is called the property of "positive entitlement" in Super's taxonomy insofar as positive entitlements give rise to legal claims in court.[221] As we noted throughout our discussion, these examples of reinsurance typically (though not universally) feature individual rights to sue, often empowering not just the primary insurer but also the ultimate beneficiary.

Some of these causes of action are artifacts of statutory authorization, but even absent these grants, the reinsurance provisions are commonly drafted in such a way that they are "sufficiently choate to constitute a property interest for purposes of the Due Process Clause."[222] We examined each program above for their formal reinsurance traits such as triggering attachment points and clearly delimited coinsurance and caps. It so happens that these traits peculiarly fit the model of sharply outlined eligibility and benefit commitments that afford claimants purchase under the prevailing right of action doctrines. Many are familiar with the procedural due process jurisprudence effected by the *Goldberg v. Kelly* and the *Board of Regents v. Roth* line of cases. These cases find constitutionally protected property interests in statutorily conferred benefits like those in our welfare and disability programs. However, such benefits must be crisply mandated such that there are "mutually explicit understandings that support [one's] claim of entitlement to the benefit."[223] Again, reinsurance programs are well positioned to satisfy such tests as they are designed to provide guarantees that are more explicitly articulated than mere subjective expectation of a governmental benefit.

---

[221] Super, *supra* n.1 at 638. He later calls these "positive entitlements."

[222] *Id.* at 649 citing Rosado v. Wyman 397 U.S. 397, 408-420 (1970) and King v. Smith 392 U.S. 309, 333-334 (1968) for the ability to sue under the statute (permitting claims by AFDC beneficiaries to challenge NY benefits reduction even under the admittedly slippery language of § 402(a)(23)). Also citing Goldberg v. Kelly, 397 U.S. 254, 261-2 & n. 8 (1970) and Perry v. Sindermann, 408 U.S. 602-03 (1972) for the doctrine that such statutory entitlements constitute property which then triggers constitutional Due Process protection.

[223] Board of Regents v. Roth 408 U.S. 564 (1972); Perry v. Sindermann 408 U.S. 602-03 (1972).

The judicial enforceability of these expectations of eligibility and benefit is partly what leads to the mandatory funding status that is the hallmark of Super's budgetary entitlements. The court-enforced requirement that concomitant benefits be provided *in each case* that is similarly situated relative to stated eligibility requirements means that Congress's funding must follow the qualifications that it previously authorized. Any actions to the contrary, such as imposing a hard ceiling on appropriations, would prove, and have indeed proven, inoperative for the above programs.[224] After all, many of these reinsurance funds featured additional borrowing authority as well as access to the permanent Claims and Judgments fund of the Court of Federal Claims. Thus rather than limiting the amount spent each year at its discretion, Congress is instead bound by its prior statutory authorization to supply sufficient funds to meet the number of beneficiaries that satisfy eligibility standards each year. This obligation is not only what gives mandatory funding its name, but also what renders these reinsurance programs instances of Super's "responsive entitlement," where the funding rises or falls to meet the number of beneficiaries who fulfill prior eligibility parameters. This type of responsive program contrasts with those that must trim eligibility to fit prior funding caps.

And as we recall from Chapter 2, due process is not the only positive law that underwrites the mandatory status of the funding. US suits under well-specified statutory terms are also governed by remarkably similar principles in a few other settings. One setting critical to the claimability of a number of the reinsurance provisions above is that of the Tucker Act, whose governing doctrine also favors reinsurance-like claims. The Tucker Act makes the United States liable for any "express or implied contract" claims that could be sourced in "the Constitution, or any Act of Congress or any regulation of an executive department."[225]

Again, the properties of reinsurance lend themselves to satisfying the legal standards in this area. To avail oneself of the Court of Federal Claims under the Tucker Act, a claimant must meet the so-called *Mitchell* test which is as follows: "[A] statute or regulation is money-mandating for jurisdictional purposes [for the Tucker Act] if it can fairly be interpreted as mandating compensation for damages sustained as a result of the breach of the duties [it] impose[s]."[226] Indeed, reinsurance obligations are typically memorialized in contract or follow from statutory commitments that are specific and mandatory in their terms, thus fulfilling the "money-mandating" requirement under the Tucker Act. I have accordingly noted above where insureds and

---

[224] Matthew Lawrence, *Disappropriation*, 120 COLUM. L. REV. 1, 16 n.36, 23 and 73 (2020). David A. Super, *The Political Economy of Entitlement*, 104 COLUM. L. REV. 633, 652 n. 80 (2004).

[225] 28 U.S.C. § 1491.

[226] United States v. Mitchell, 463 U.S. 206, 217 (1983). *See also*, Fisher v. United States, 402 F.3d 1167, 1173 (Fed. Cir. 2005).

beneficiary-assignees have brought suits under the Tucker Act to enforce promised state reinsurance eligibility and benefit parameters.

Thus even if Congress were to attempt to cap appropriations for a reinsurance
program, as long as a claimant satisfied the *Mitchell* standard under the Tucker
Act in the Federal Court of Claims, a further reservoir of "permanent unlim-
ited funding" would remain available to meet these judgments. As the Federal
Circuit has said, "failure [of Congress] to appropriate funds to meet statutory
obligations prevents the accounting officers of the Government from making
disbursements, but such rights [remain] enforceable in the Court of Claims."[227]
As we examined in previous chapters, rights are at bottom a form of prioritization, and the reinsurance programs are able to achieve resource priority in part
through the mandatory funding mechanism of budgetary entitlement.

Moreover, this ability for aggrieved beneficiaries to sue under the Tucker Act
brings the affected programs into conformity with true "responsive" entitlements
in Super's language, and further undergirds the funding assurance afforded these
various reinsurance-like programs in the prioritization and certainty of provision against Congressional appropriations vicissitudes.[228]

The claimability (positive entitlement), the characteristic entitlement
funding (budgetary entitlement), and the property of responsiveness (responsive entitlement) in no way exhaust the mechanisms of priority that these
reinsurance programs enjoy when competing against other programs for material resources. So many of these reinsurance programs, from those for crops,
banking, mortgage, flood, disaster, and terrorism loss have also attained recognition by means of subjective entitlement. Primary insurers and their insureds
have staked out and vindicated their claims to funding far beyond what was
spelled out in positive law. When dealing with TRIA, for example, insurers are
prepared to seek pay outs even if the relevant terrorism events are nuclear, biological, chemical or radiation-based. They will stand on their claims given that
these catastrophes that are functionally analogous, even if technically excluded
under the statute. These examples illustrate how the politico-legal reinsurance principle operating here has endowed these reinsurance efforts with the
properties that Super finds characteristic of functional, responsive, and subjective entitlements.

---

[227] Greenlee County, Ariz. v. U.S., 487 F.3d 871, 877 (Fed. Cir. 2007) *citing* N.Y. Airways, 369 F.2d
at 748.

[228] Further evidence of prioritized funding status for these reinsurance programs can even be seen
in the budget sequestration mechanisms, from which many of these programs are exempt. 2 U.S.C. §
905, exempting FCIC, Fannie Mae and Freddie Mac, FDIC, NFIP, the Terrorism Insurance Program,
PBGC, FEMA and NFIP, various Federal Reserve budgetary accounts. *See* Ryan Rosso, *Medicare and
Budget Sequestration*, CONG. RES. SERV. R45106, 1 n.3 and 9 (March 29, 2020), https://crsreports.
congress.gov/product/pdf/R/R45106.

I mention here a third doctrinal sphere that favors the claimability of reinsurance programs and becomes more relevant for the next chapter, where Medicaid looms large. Federal law is generally stingy when it comes to finding private rights of action to enforce federal standards, but if the reinsurance-like program takes the form of a joint federal-state cooperative spending program like Medicaid, or even some of the state-federal disaster grant-in-aid programs, the governing doctrine for whether a beneficiary has a right of action for monetary damages is often analyzed under 42 U.S.C § 1983. Section 1983, passed as a Reconstruction-era civil rights law, grants individuals a federal right of action for redress, including damages, if any state official or person acting "under color of" state law deprives the individuals of "any rights, privileges, or immunities secured by the Constitution and laws" of the United States.[229] Thus any Congressionally authorized reinsurance program that is administered by the states—should it rise to the level of a "right, privilege or immunity secured by the . . . laws"—might be enforceable in federal court.

The courts have devised standards for such claims, as articulated by the *Blessing v. Freestone* and *Gonzaga v. Doe* line of cases. The three-factor *Blessing* test asks (1) whether Congress intended that the provision in question benefit the plaintiff; (2) whether the right protected by the statute is so "vague and amorphous" that its enforcement would strain judicial competence; and (3) whether the statute unambiguously imposes a binding obligation on the States.[230] Classic express reinsurance with its concrete definition of insureds, its mandatory promises to pay as well as its crisp triggers and terms, is therefore eminently suited for judicial administration. *Gonzaga* focused the *Blessing* test more squarely on the first factor of Congressional intent, now requiring that Congress' intent to create enforceable rights is evinced in its use of "clear and unambiguous terms."[231] One strand of the Court's focus in assessing the clarity of Congress's "rights-creating language," pushes us to look at whether those provisions have an "aggregate" or an "individual" focus, a rights-distinguishing inquiry that we introduced in Chapters 1 and 2, and which again plays to reinsurance's strengths as an individuated benefit with salutary systemic effects.[232]

[229] 42 U.S.C. § 1983.

[230] *See* Blessing v. Freestone, 520 U.S. 329, 340–41, 117 S.Ct. 1353, 137 L.Ed.2d 569 (1997).

[231] Gonzaga v. Doe, 536 U.S. 273, 291 (2002).

[232] *Id.* at 288 ("FERPA's nondisclosure provisions further speak only in terms of institutional policy and practice, not individual instances of disclosure. . . . Therefore, as in Blessing, they have an 'aggregate' focus, 520 U.S., at 343 . . . , they are not concerned with 'whether the needs of any particular person have been satisfied . . .'").

Combining the Rights Form with State Duties to Foster
Systemic Background Conditions

This aspect of what I consider a sympathetic interplay between the features of re-insurance and the features of our legal doctrine around implied and other cross-cutting rights of action in the federal judiciary invites a final word on an aspect of the peculiarly rights-like nature of reinsurance. As we explained in Chapters 1 and 2, the argument for a right to health has been persistently dogged by the fact that many important health measures may look more like duties to the public-at-large, rather than rights redounding to particular beneficiaries. Consider for instance, the importance of the government role in regulating the private insur-ance market,[233] or the state's oft-exhorted duty to control against prescription drug or other healthcare cost inflation, or the public focus on market stabiliza-tion tools like the individual mandate and community rating, which enable com-prehensive risk pooling.[234] These are all important cornerstones of healthcare access in a mixed public-private health sector like the one we have in the United States. But the campaign for fulfillment of these regulatory duties has sometimes defied rights treatment because of the diffuse systemic nature of their benefits.

Reinsurance, however, is peculiarly fit-for-purpose because it does double duty. It constitutes a type of state duty that is comparatively easy to frame as an individually claimable legal right, as I sought to document above.[235] Yet it also manages to serve an important systemic function within the health system. It is remarkably well-suited for framing as a right while not running afoul of John

---

[233] *See, e.g.*, Everaldo Lamprea, *Colombia's Right-to-Health Litigation in a Context of Health Care Reform*, in THE RIGHT TO HEALTH AT THE PUBLIC/PRIVATE DIVIDE: A GLOBAL COMPARATIVE STUDY 131–158 (C. Flood & A. Gross, eds., 2014) (describing how the pharmaceutical industry and the upper socioeconomic strata's interests were served by the constitutional health rights claiming pathway of the *tutela*: "The escalation of health litigation in a context of deregulation of pharma-ceutical prices transformed Colombia's hyper-individualized right-to-health litigation into a fiscal trap with detrimental effects on the financial stability of the health sector." The relatively privileged won lawsuits forcing government to finance new high-end pharmaceuticals and procedures, many of which lacked strong evidence of cost-effectiveness even as services such as human papillomavirus vaccines or preventive health screenings were left with insufficient funding. These *tutela* lawsuits might not have skyrocketed if the state could have curbed unjustified claim denials by private insurers. But Colombia "proved ineffectual in chastising health insurance companies that custom-arily deny . . . health services"). *Id.*

[234] *See Minister of Health v. New Clicks South Africa Pty Ltd.* (CCT 59/2004) [2005] ZACC 14, par. 514. In New Clicks, the South African Constitutional Court Justice Albie Sachs stated that the fulfilment of health rights requires government to engage in coordinating overall market conditions. In a case where the Constitutional Court declared that the right to health included the right to gov-ernment regulation of pharmaceutical pricing as a necessary condition for access to medicines, Sachs wrote: "Preventing excessive profit-taking from the manufacturing distribution and sale of medicines is more than an option for the government. It is a constitutional obligation flowing from its duties under Section 27(2)." *See also id.* at par. 706 (J. Moseneke, declaring, "Prohibitive pricing of medicine . . . would in effect equate to a denial of the right of access to health care").

[235] Cruz v. Zucker, 116 F.Supp.3d 334, 347 (S.D.N.Y. 2015) quoted approvingly in Davis v. Shah, 821 F.3d 231, 247 (2nd. Cir. 2016).

Tasioulas's and others' complaints about the overloading of "health rights" to include health governance obligations that nevertheless sit uncomfortably with the key property of rights as political norms that focuses on the role of the claimant, the *bearer* of the rights.[236]

This is because, as noted at the outset of this chapter, reinsurance helps more than just the most visible beneficiaries, even as it can be "attributed to individuals one by one."[237] Why not press the priority of health care needs then, capitalizing on this lucky confluence, and using the venerated tool of rights? Health reinsurance as a right can be happily reconciled with our accumulated wisdom about what should be provided by the state to foster human health, much of which, it turns out, is collective in nature.

A government's obligations should include the creation of stable background conditions for individuals to come together to organize collective financing for health provision and protection. Health reinsurance would be one of those basic government duties, similar to the provision of stable currency, basic safety, security, and national defense. As I have written before, "Certainly, governments could and should provide more coverage beyond mere reinsurance within their available resources. But my argument here is that at a minimum, they have a duty to provide something that performs the reinsurance function as the groundwork that brings organized affordable health care within reach."[238]

The Playbook

If we are convinced that this cluster of entitlement features suffices to qualify reinsurance programs as partially if not yet fully entrenched rights, then the examples discussed in this chapter also suggest an instructive playbook. Their histories fill in a picture of how rights come into being through a step-wise process of development, drawing from a reservoir of political moral norms and sending shoots throughout the legal corpus that later grow strong trunks, and deep roots.

The Stafford Act, like crop insurance, aims to take what had been a formerly ad hoc relief effort and over time, regularize and codify it so that it could be predicted, relied upon, institutionalized under FEMA, rendered a matter of principle, open to claiming, and ever more entrenched in the financial resources and

---

[236] *See* Joel Feinberg, *The Nature and Value of Rights* 145, 155 reprinted in RIGHTS, JUSTICE, AND THE BOUNDS OF LIBERTY (1980).

[237] *See* Jeremy Waldron, *Rights in Conflict*, 99 ETHICS 503, 507 (1989) (describing the distinctive, individuate nature of rights in this way).

[238] Christina S. Ho, *Health Reinsurance as a Human Right, in* INSURANCE AND HUMAN RIGHTS 85 (Margarida Lima Rego & Birgit Kuschke, eds., 2022).

legitimacy it commands. Health rights advocates among us should take comfort from these examples: rights need not arrive fully formed like Athena from Zeus's head. As we noted in Chapter 2, "Entrenchment . . . refers not only to a condition but to a process, and it is always a matter of degree."[239] Every day we pose and answer the questions of what to preserve, what is of lasting value, what to hold dear; our commitment to these collective choices is wrought in the mandatoriness of funding, the durability of institutions like the Federal Reserve and Fannie Mae, and even in the repeated renewal of TRIA in the face of statutory sunset dates. In the next chapter I proceed to apply some of the more specific lessons to the health sector to sketch out the policy prescriptions for how to inscribe a right to reinsurance for health.

---

[239] PAUL STARR, ENTRENCHMENT 2 (2019).

7

Health Reinsurance as an Affirmative Right to Health

The introduction of reinsurance to the health sector would not be a "foreign" graft, nor feel unfamiliar, as I explain in this chapter. In fact, the development of our patchwork system of laws in healthcare could arguably be understood as a history of implicit reinsurance, as yet incomplete. Medicaid was established in part for persons who fit the labels of "aged, blind and disabled" and those who were institutionalized, given that these groups were often the most-costly health-care utilizers whom no one would insure. The fight for Medicare was supported by unions and employers to off-load the cost of retiree health insurance onto the government. Many of the groups later added to Medicare also exemplified the reinsurance principle whereby high-cost risks that would skew insurance risk pools were ceded to the state. For instance, in 1972, the United States gave Medicare eligibility to workers who qualify for Social Security Disability Insurance for at least two years. At the same time, end-stage renal disease patients were added and in 2001, Medicare was extended to patients with amyotrophic lateral sclerosis (ALS). Even ERISA's effect on the health sector sounds in reinsurance: its displacement of state laws with its own scant remedial scheme functions as limited liability for employer-sponsored health plans.[1] It constitutes a government-sponsored risk ceiling that distributes the risks of benefit denial across patient-beneficiaries rather than employers.

With permission, Chapter 7 adapts material from Christina S. Ho, *With Liberty and Reinsurance for All: The Deep Case for a Government Backstop in Health Care*, 100 Denv. L. Rev. ____ (forthcoming 2023).

[1] Aetna Health Inc. v. Davila, 542 U.S. 200 (2004), Pilot Life Ins. Co. v. Dedeaux, 481 U.S. 41 (1987) (declaring that ERISA's limited remedies displace state remedial regimes). For demonstration that this type of limited liability serves as an insurance scheme for employer health plans, *see* David Moss, When All Else Fails: Government as the Ultimate Risk Manager 83, 83–84 (2004), "limited liability is actually a remarkably simple risk management device. All that it does is shift a portion of default risk from shareholders to creditors—in many ways mimicking an insurance policy." Marie-Laure Djelic & Joel Bothello, *Limited Liability and its Moral Hazard Implications: the Systemic Inscription of Instability in Contemporary Capitalism*, 42 Theor Soc 589 (2013) (arguing that "the emergence through time of elective affinities between" [limited liability] and some of the features of insurance, namely moral hazard. "This leads us . . . to argue that the two notions have become structurally connected over time in the particular form of capitalism that dominates our contemporary world and that this is having highly significant consequences."

As Jeanne Lambrew, one of the architects of the ACA, has observed, "Reinsurance was the only proposal in both the Republicans' 2017 'repeal and replace' bills and the Democratic alternatives."[2] Could these elements be reconfigured and extended to provide a uniform substrate of true reinsurance across all segments of our currently fragmented health sector? If the United States were finally to turn to health rights as part of the social compact, could the affirmative right to healthcare be constituted consistent with our deeply rooted affinity for government backstopping roles, by assuring a right to reinsurance of health coverage?[3] I start by describing the depth and extent of the heretofore unacknowledged rootstock that might support the growth of reinsurance across our healthcare terrain. I then conclude with suggestions for how to further nurture that development, recognizing it openly for what it is, extending its scope, and incorporating the lessons we have learned from our accumulated experience with state-sponsored reinsurance across health and non–health domains, as described in both this and the previous chapter.

Health Reinsurance in the Recent Policy Landscape

Health reinsurance has reared its head frequently in recent US health policy debates.

At the Federal Level

The ACA itself featured a reinsurance provision designed to serve a classic reinsurance function, namely, the enticement of private plan entry into what was then an uncharted market. Because the ACA inaugurated a new breed of private health plan—one that covered a slate of essential health benefits available to virtually all purchasers in the individual market regardless of health status—the implementation of the ACA exchanges came with irreducible uncertainty. By ending exclusions based on health status and preexisting conditions, the ACA might uncork a flood of high-cost enrollees onto these new Exchanges. To reassure private insurers and encourage them to offer exchange plans nonetheless, the ACA included three premium stabilization programs: a risk-adjustment measure, a risk-corridor provision, and a temporary transitional reinsurance

---

[2] Ellen Montz & Jeanne Lambrew, *The Next Big Thing in Health Reform: Where to Start?* THE AMERICAN PROSPECT (2018), https://prospect.org/health/next-big-thing-health-reform-start/ (accessed March 17, 2021).

[3] Moss, *see supra* n.1. MICHELE LANDIS DAUBER, THE SYMPATHETIC STATE (2012).

provision.[4] Under this temporary reinsurance program, primary insurers owed per-enrollee assessments to a fund that was statutorily set to total $10 billion in 2014, $6 billion in 2015, and $4 billion for 2016.[5] This assessment was pejoratively nick-named the belly-button tax and calculated at $63 per covered life for 2014, $44 for 2015, and $27 for 2016.[6]

The funds were used in turn to reimburse ACA plans 80 percent of the cost of claims exceeding the per beneficiary attachment point of $45,000.[7] Federal absorption of these costs capped out when the beneficiary's claims reached $250,000. In the latter years of the program, the attachment point rose, reaching $90,000 in FY 2016, and the federal share of the claims above the attachment point dropped to 50 percent.[8]

Though the reinsurance provision in the ACA lasted just three years, federal and state officials alike have found ways to extend it. For instance, § 1343 of the ACA authorized risk adjustment, another premium stabilization program, and did so without any statutory time limitation. Therefore, once the ACA reinsurance provision expired, the Obama administration modified risk adjustment to incorporate the Centers for Medicare & Medicaid (CMS) provision described earlier, assuring government payment of 60 percent of costs when an enrollee's claims exceed $1 million.[9] This provision rolls a layer of reinsurance into the permanent risk adjustment infrastructure of the ACA.

In 2016, when Republicans gained control of both Congress and the presidency, efforts to undermine the ACA took the form of "repeal-and-replace" legislation.[10]

---

[4] Patient Protection and Affordable Care Act (ACA), Pub. L. No. 111-148, § 1341, 124 Stat. 193, 208 (2010) (hereinafter "ACA"). The other two premium stabilization programs were ACA §1343 risk adjustment provisions and the ACA § 1342 risk corridors program.

[5] ACA Pub. L. No. 111-148, § 1341(b)(3)(B)(iii) (2010).

[6] HHS Notice of Notice of Benefit and Payment Parameters for 2014, 77 Fed. Reg. 73,118, 73,120, 73,152, 73,157 (proposed December 7, 2012) (proposed NBPP for 2014) (to be codified at 45 C.F.R. § 153.220) (applying the assessment to all commercial lines of business and even when the health plan is acting as a third-party administrator to employer self-insured plans).

[7] AMERICAN ACADEMY OF ACTUARIES ISSUE BRIEF, DRIVERS OF 2015 HEALTH INSURANCE PREMIUM CHANGES 4 (June 2014), https://www.actuary.org/sites/default/files/files/2015_Pre mium_Drivers_Updated_060414.pdf (estimating that "[r]einsurance program payments for 2014 generally reduced projected net claim costs by about 10 to 14 percent"). See also, Department of Health and Human Services, Center for Medicare and Medicaid Services, Transitional Reinsurance Program: Pro Rata Adjustment to the National Coinsurance Rate for the 2014 Benefit Year Ltr. (June 17, 2015), https://www.cms.gov/CCIIO/Programs-and-Initiatives/Premium-Stabilization-Programs/The-Transitional-Reinsurance-Program/Downloads/RI-Payments-National-Proration-Memo-With-Numbers-6-17-15.pdf.

[8] Patient Protection and Affordable Care Act; HHS Notice of Benefit and Payment Parameters for 2016; Final Rule, 80 Fed. Reg. 10750, 10752 (February 27, 2015).

[9] Kevin Counihan, Building on Premium Stabilization for the Future, The CMS Blog (August 11, 2016), https://ccf.georgetown.edu/wp-content/uploads/2016/08/Building-on-Premium-Stabilizat ion-for-the-Future-_-The-CMS-Blog.pdf (accessed May 21, 2020).

[10] The American Health Care Act of 2017 (AHCA) H.R. 1628, 115th Cong. (2017) (serving as the main legislative vehicle for repeal-and-replace. The bill passed the House but not the Senate). During Senate consideration of H.R. 1628, leadership sought to replace the language of H.R.1628 with various substitutes, including the Better Care Reconciliation Act of 2017 (BCRA), https://www.budget.

Reinsurance featured prominently in these Republican proposals, though in the end, none of them mustered enough support to pass the Senate. Even the pared-down "skinny repeal" effort ultimately failed on the strength of Republican Senator John McCain's dramatic, middle-of-the-night, thumbs-down vote.

But it is still noteworthy that H.R. 1628, the Republican House-passed version of the repeal-and-replace legislation, contained a Patient and State Stability Fund in § 132, providing up to $15 billion a year to support reinsurance and invisible high-risk pooling, or other related state programs.[11] Any states who did not establish such a program could rely on a federally administered fallback paying 75 percent of claims above a $50,000 attachment point up to a $350,000 claims ceiling.[12] An additional $15 million would be available for the Federal Invisible Risk Sharing Program which would cover claims above an attachment point for individuals with certain conditions who would be ceded to the program.[13]

On the Senate side, the Republican Health Education Labor and Pensions Committee Chair, Senator Lamar Alexander, championed a provision that he called "Alaska for All."[14] It was incorporated into the Better Care and Reconciliation Act text which never reached a Senate vote. This provision grew to total $132 billion for grants to states to undertake stabilization programs like reinsurance.[15] Senator Susan Collins of Maine, whose state had instituted a successful reinsurance-like program, was a vocal proponent.[16]

Democrats have also favored reinsurance. In 2020, Representatives Angie Craig and Scott Peters introduced a stand-alone ACA reinsurance bill,

---

senate.gov/imo/media/doc/BetterCareReconcilistionAct.6.26.17.pdf. BCRA was not introduced as stand-alone legislation, but a version of BCRA was dubbed "skinny repeal," and introduced as an amendment to AHCA, S. Amdt No. 667, otherwise known as the Health Care Freedom Act of 2017, https://www.congress.gov/amendment/115th-congress/senate-amendment/667 (defeated 49–51).

[11] *See,* H.R. 1628 § 132. *See also,* Joel Allumbaugh et al., *Invisible High-Risk Pools: How Congress Can Lower Premiums and Deal with Pre-Existing Conditions | Health Affairs Blog,* HEALTH AFFAIRS BLOG, FOLLOWING THE ACA (2017), https://www.healthaffairs.org/do/10.1377/hblog20170302.059 003/full/ (accessed April 2, 2021).

[12] H.R. 1628 § 132.

[13] FREDERICK BUSCH & PAUL R. HOUCHENS, *Reinsurance and High-Risk Pools: Past, Present, and Future Role in the Individual Health Insurance Market* (2017), https://us.milliman.com/en/insi ght/reinsurance-and-highrisk-pools-past-present-and-future-role-in-the-individual-health-i# (accessed April 22, 2021).

[14] *Obamacare Stability Plan,* BNA, (October 2017), https://www.bna.com/obamacare-stability-plan-n57982089948/ (referring to a public summary of the proposal available at http://src.bna.com/ w5r). An earlier version of this provision was filed officially as S. Amdt. No. 649 to AHCA, H.R. 1628, https://www.congress.gov/amendment/115th-congress/senate-amendment/649?s=a&r=19.

[15] BRCA discussion draft § 103 (July 13, 2019), https://www.budget.senate.gov/imo/media/doc/ BetterCareJuly13.2017.pdf.

[16] KATHLEEN ELY ET AL., *The Federal Invisible High Risk Pool Effect on Premium Rates, Individual Marketplace Enrollment and Use of Federal Funds* 4 (2017), https://thefga.org/wp-content/uploads/ 2017/04/The-Federal-Invisible-High-Risk-Pool.pdf. *See also,* Mark Hall & Nicholas Bagley, *Making Sense of 'Invisible Risk Sharing',* HEALTH AFFAIRS BLOG, FOLLOWING THE ACA (April 12, 2017), https://www.healthaffairs.org/do/10.1377/hblog20170412.059601/full/ (accessed April 2, 2021).

proposing $10 billion a year for state reinsurance programs.[17] The funds were fully federal and projected to reduce premiums by about 10 percent.[18] The bill, like AHCA, contained a default federal fallback. H.R. 1425 later became the underlying vehicle for an entire slate of ACA enhancements, dubbed "ACA 2.0," that the Democratic House passed 274–179 and which prominently featured reinsurance.[19]

While the Senate failed to take up ACA 2.0 enhancements or any further repeal-and-replace bills, Congress had by the end of 2017 passed President Trump's Tax Cuts and Jobs Act (TCJA), stripping the individual mandate which had functioned as a key ACA risk stabilization device.[20] In the aftermath, various constituencies espoused reinsurance to fill in the gap. Former Wisconsin governor Scott Walker, staunchly conservative, signed into law a $200 million reinsurance measure even as he authorized continued challenge to the ACA in the ultimately unsuccessful case to strike the law on constitutional grounds.[21] Republican Senator Susan Collins initially demanded reinsurance as a condition of her vote in favor of the Trump tax bill.[22] Fifteen states as of the writing of this chapter have since sought and received the flexibility to institute their own reinsurance programs, a point to which I return below.[23]

---

[17] Patient Protection and Affordable Care Enhancement Act, H.R. 1425, 116th Congress § 106 (2020) (placed on calendar in the Senate), https://www.congress.gov/bill/116th-congress/house-bill/1425. *See also*, Charles Gaba, *#ACA2.0 gets a vote at last: A Deep Dive into #HR1425, the Affordable Care Enhancement Act*, ACA Signups (June 23, 2020), https://acasignups.net/20/06/24/aca20-gets-vote-last-deep-dive-hr1425-affordable-care-enhancement-act (accessed April 2, 2021).

[18] H.R. 1425, 116th Congress § 106 (2020). *See also, strengthening our Health Care System: Legislation to Lower Consumer Costs and Expand Access: Hearing on H.R. 1425, H.R. 1386, and H.R. 1385*, Before the Health Subcomm. of the H. Comm. on Energy and Commerce, 116th Cong. (2019), https://energycommerce.house.gov/committee-activity/hearings/hearing-on-strengthening-our-health-care-system-legislation-to-lower (describing the provision as authorizing $10 billion so that states, or CMS can, on behalf of states, establish a state reinsurance program or other cost-reducing initiatives).

[19] ACA *supra* n.17.

[20] Tax Cuts and Jobs Act of 2017 (TCJA), Pub. L. No. 115–97 § 11081, 131 Stat. 2054 (2017).

[21] *California v. Texas*, 141 S. Ct. 2104, 2112–13 (2021). *Update: Wisconsin Gov. Signs Health Reinsurance Bill; State Joins "Obamacare" Suit*, Insurance Journal (February 28, 2018), https://www.insurancejournal.com/news/midwest/2018/02/28/481836.htm (accessed April 3, 2021) (relating that "this year, as he faces re-election in November, Walker has pushed the reinsurance proposal as a way to stabilize the market and lower premium costs for the state's roughly 200,000 people who purchase insurance under the law. Wisconsin Democratic Party chairwoman Martha Laning called the bill an election-year attempt to disguise how damaging years of fighting the Affordable Care Act have been").

[22] Prior to passage of the TCJA Act of 2017, *supra* n.20, Senator Susan Collins proposed some conditions for her support for the tax proposal, including passage of Alexander-Murray and her own Collins-Nelson proposal containing reinsurance provisions. *See, e.g.*, Dwyer Gunn, *Can the Collins Compromise Save the Affordable Care Act?*, Pacific Standard (November 29, 2017), https://psmag.com/news/can-the-collins-compromise-save-the-affordable-care-act (accessed April 3, 2021).

[23] SHADAC Resource: State-Based Reinsurance Programs via 1332 State Innovation Waivers, SHADAC (2020), https://www.shadac.org/publications/resource-state-based-reinsurance-programs-1332-state-innovation-waivers (accessed April 2, 2021).

These efforts have stalled due to Biden's American Rescue Plan (ARP) COVID-relief bill that extended eligibility for ACA tax subsidies to nearly all Americans and was renewed through the end of 2025 in the Inflation Reduction Act.[24] Because these federally financed subsidies are structured to cap how much any American individual or family could be asked to pay for insurance, any policy like reinsurance that would reduce premiums will hold little political salience for American consumers or states in the near term.

Even with the appeal of premium-reduction in abeyance because of this temporary dynamic, the New Democrat Coalition of centrists in the House listed national reinsurance first in their letter to President Biden outlining healthcare priorities.[25]

At the State Level

While federal reinsurance proposals worked themselves to this strange impasse, states had long ago forged ahead. Prior to the most recent state reinsurance boom, "[s]even states [] had established mandatory reinsurance pools [for small group plans] and 19 [had] voluntary reinsurance pools...."[26]

In the 1990s, New Jersey tried a conditional reinsurance scheme under the auspices of its Individual Health Coverage Program, designed to leverage insurers into selling policies on the individual market. If an insurer decided not to participate in this regulated individual market, it was required to pay assessments that would then be redistributed to the participating carriers who had claims overruns. However, the gaming of this system by small carriers led to its demise.[27]

New York had considered state reinsurance as far back as 1989, with the Universal New York Health Care plan which was ultimately shelved.[28] The idea

[24] *See* American Rescue Plan Act of 2021, Pub. L. No. 117–2, § 9661, 135 Stat. 183 (2021). *See also* Inflation Reduction Act of 2022, Pub. L. No. 117-169, 136 Stat. 1818, § 12001(b) (codified as amended in the Internal Revenue Code of 1986 § 36B(c)(1)(E)) (2022) (extending these subsidies through the end of 2025).

[25] Kim Schreir et al., *New Democrat Coalition letter to President Joe Biden outlining health care priorities* (April 21, 2021), https://newdemocratcoalition.house.gov/imo/media/doc/21AP R21_NDC%20HC%20Priorities%20Letter%20vF.pdf.

[26] Furrow et al., Health Law: Cases, Materials and Problems 649 (7th ed. 2013) *citing* Blue Cross Blue Shield Association, State Legislative Health Care and Insurance Issues: 2012 Survey of Plans (2012). *See also,* Joel Cantor & Alan Monheit, State Health Insurance Market Reform: Toward Inclusive and Sustainable Health Insurance Markets (2012).

[27] Katherine Swartz, Reinsuring Health Why More Middle-Class People Are Uninsured and What Government Can Do 95 (2006).

[28] *Id.* at 178, n. 23, *citing* Dan E. Beauchamp & Ronald L. Rouse, *Universal New York Health Care— A Single-Payer Strategy Linking Cost Control and Universal Access,* 10 New England J. of Med. 644 (1990).

re-emerged a decade later, when Healthy New York launched using tobacco settlement funds to provide subsidized reinsurance to those private plans offering affordable insurance for uninsured lower-income individuals and small business employees.[29] The state required all HMOs to participate and participating small employers had to subsidize at least 50 percent of premiums.[30] The program halved premiums in this risk-selection-plagued segment of the pre-ACA market and inspired John Kerry to feature reinsurance in his healthcare presidential platform, a proposal discussed later in this chapter.[31]

Maine's program, like New York's earlier example, has also been invoked frequently by national policymakers.[32] In 2011, Maine's legislature authorized the Maine Guaranteed Access Reinsurance Association (MGARA), a private nonprofit entity, to operate a reinsurance (or technically, invisible high-risk pool) program for Maine's pre-ACA individual health insurance market.[33] MGARA collected $4 per member per month from all health insurers, including those merely processing claims for employer self-insured plans. It then paid for high-risk enrollees, identified as having one of eight diagnoses (like rheumatoid arthritis) or as otherwise determined through a medical questionnaire.[34] For cumulative claims within the $7,500 to $32,500 range, MGARA would pay 90 percent on behalf of "ceded" individuals. The rate dialed up to 100 percent once claims hit $32,500.[35] But the insurers also had to turn over 90 percent of the premiums they collected for these individuals that they ceded to MGARA.

Maine sought through this program to offer affordable individual market options to enrollees with preexisting conditions in the period before the ACA went live. And it achieved notable premium savings, though perhaps not from reinsurance alone.[36]

When the ACA's primary insurance market reforms switched on in 2014, two provisions addressed reinsurance as a health policy tool. The first was the transitional federal reinsurance provision, § 1341, described above.[37] The second was

[29] Individuals making up to $34,000 a year, adjusted annually, were eligible. Small employers were eligible where 30 percent of the payroll earned $34,000 a year or less. Swartz, *supra* n.27 at 178, n.23.

[30] RANDALL R BOVBJERG, *How Have States Like New York and Arizona Used Reinsurance to Help Businesses Control the Cost of Health Insurance?* 19–27 (2007), https://wisfamilyimpact.org/wp-content/uploads/2014/10/s_wifis24c03.pdf.

[31] *Id.*

[32] *E.g.,* Patty Wight, *Secret to Maine's Touted High-Risk Pool? Enough Money,* ALL THINGS CONSIDERED (May 17, 2017), https://www.npr.org/sections/health-shots/2017/05/17/527960631/the-idea-the-gop-s-health-care-bill-borrows-from-maine (accessed April 3, 2021).

[33] Hall & Bagley, *supra* n.16.

[34] *Id.*

[35] Scott Harrington, *Stabilizing Individual Health Insurance Markets with Subsidized Reinsurance,* 21 PENN LEONARD DAVIS INST. HEALTH ECON. (2017), https://ldi.upenn.edu/brief/stabilizing-individual-health-insurance-markets-subsidized-reinsurance (accessed April 3, 2021).

[36] *See* Hall & Bagley, *supra* n.16.

[37] ACA § 1341.

§ 1332, which allowed states to apply for waivers from major ACA requirements in order to undertake state-specific innovation. Such waivers are granted subject to assurances that the state waiver plan would achieve at least as much coverage as the unaltered ACA scenario and that the coverage would be as comprehensive and affordable as it would have been otherwise while not adding to the federal deficit.[38]

Reinsurance became a key pillar of many § 1332 waiver proposals. Once the Trump administration and Republican Congress neutered the individual mandate, reinsurance proved a handy tool to restabilize state exchanges as Governor like Scott Walker recognized. The idea also gained traction because Tom Price, Trump's first Secretary of Health and Human Services, and his CMS Director, Seema Verma, "invit[ed] states to pursue approval of waiver proposals that include high-risk pool/state-operated reinsurance programs." These Trump administration officials specifically trumpeted Alaska's proposal as a model.[39]

Alaska had used reinsurance to bring its ACA market back from the brink.[40] Individual market premiums had been rising 30–40 percent per year and in 2017, only Premera remained as the sole ACA plan.[41] Premera faced a skewed enrollee pool, with just 37 patients consuming a quarter of claims costs. At that point, Alaska's reinsurance/high-risk pool program stepped in. The program raised $55 million, which it devoted to paying the costs of any enrollee who had one of 33 high-cost conditions, including hemophilia, HIV/AIDS, and multiple sclerosis.[42] Following this intervention, premiums actually fell for 2020 and 2021, and an additional plan rejoined the market.[43]

As mentioned above, fifteen states have instituted their own reinsurance plans under § 1332 authority.[44] Beyond those fifteen, two additional states (Iowa and

[38] ACA § 1332.
[39] DHHS Press Release, *Secretary Price and CMS Administrator Verma Take First Joint Action: Affirm Partnership of HHS, CMS, and States to Improve Medicaid Program* (March 14, 2017), https://www.hhs.gov/about/news/2017/03/14/secretary-price-and-cms-administrator-verma-take-first-joint-action.html. Thomas E. Price, *The Secretary of Health and Human Services Letter To the Governors on Section 1332 State Waivers* (March 13, 2017), https://www.cms.gov/CCIIO/Programs-and-Initiatives/State-Innovation-Waivers/Downloads/March-13-2017-letter_508.pdf.
[40] SHADAC Resource, *supra* n.23.
[41] Louise Norris, *Alaska health insurance marketplace: history and news of the state's exchange*, HEALTHINSURANCE.ORG (December 16 2020), https://www.healthinsurance.org/health-insurance-marketplaces/alaska/ (accessed April 3, 2021).Tim Jost, *Alaska Reinsurance Plan Could Be Model For ACA Reform, Plus Other ACA Developments*, HEALTH AFFAIRS BLOG, FOLLOWING THE ACA (June 16, 2016), https://www.healthaffairs.org/do/10.1377/hblog20160616.055420/full/ (accessed April 3, 2021).
[42] ALASKA SECTION 1332 STATE INNOVATION WAIVER APPLICATION 3 (2017), https://www.commerce.alaska.gov/web/Portals/11/Pub/Headlines/Alaska%201332%20State%20Innovation%20Waiver%20June%2015%202017.pdf
[43] Louise Norris, *Alaska State Health Insurance Marketplace Guide 2023*, HEALTHINSURANCE.ORG (September 19, 2022) https://www.healthinsurance.org/alaska-state-health-insurance-exchange/ (accessed December 6, 2022).
[44] SHADAC Resource, *supra* n.23.

Oklahoma) submitted but later withdrew their applications. Some suggest that their waivers faltered for the crudest of political expediencies.[45] One rumor was that the Trump administration delayed Oklahoma's and Iowa's approvals because of its desire to undermine Obamacare to help make the case for repealing what would then be characterized as a poorly functioning regime.[46] A handful of additional states (Idaho, Louisiana, Connecticut, and Wyoming) have publicly considered reinsurance waivers but have yet to submit proposals.[47]

Because these § 1332 reinsurance programs often reduce premiums, they save the US Treasury from paying more in tax credits on behalf of subsidized enrollees.[48] Under the §1332 waiver terms, the federal government then "passes those savings through" to the waiver states.[49] States may reinvest those funds into the reinsurance programs that generated those savings in the first place. Alaska has received more enough in pass-through funds to finance its reinsurance program while some other states have had to kick in additional financing.[50] Many states rely on insurer assessments to fund their contributions to the reinsurance funds.[51] Other states collect funds from providers.[52] New Jersey generated revenue by imposing a state individual mandate penalty to replace the federal penalty that was zeroed out in the Trump TCJA. Delaware, Colorado, and Maryland raised funds from a premium tax, taking advantage of the expiration of the federal premium tax.[53]

---

[45] See Joel Ario, *Failure to Approve Oklahoma Waiver Undermines Trust Between HHS and States,* Health Affairs Blog, Following the ACA (September 30, 2017), https://www.healthaffairs.org/do/10.1377/hblog20170930.062255/full/ (accessed April 3, 2021).

[46] Alison Kodjak, *Administration Sends Mixed Signals on State Health Insurance Waivers,* NPR. org (October 19, 2017), https://www.npr.org/sections/health-shots/2017/10/19/558310690/adm inistration-sends-mixed-signals-on-state-health-insurance-waivers (accessed April 3, 2021).

[47] SHADAC Resource, *supra* n.23. *See also* Govind Persad, *Expensive Patients, Reinsurance, and the Future of Health Care Reform,* 69 Emory L. J. 1153 (2020), at 26, n.125.

[48] ACA § 1401.

[49] CBO's March 2018 score of the last-ditch Bipartisan Health Care Stabilization Act projected that 60 percent of the federal cost of extending reinsurance would be offset by reductions in other costs, mainly premium tax credits. Bipartisan Health Care Stabilization Act of 2018 As Provided to CBO on March 19, 2018 (version TAM18347), (2018), https://www.cbo.gov/publication/53666 (accessed April 5, 2021).

[50] Persad, *supra* n.47.

[51] Justin Giovannelli, JoAnn Volk, Rachel Schwab, & Emily Curran, *The Benefits and Limitations of State-Run Individual Market Reinsurance,* Commonwealth Fund (Nov. 11, 2020), https://www.commonwealthfund.org/publications/issue-briefs/2020/oct/benefits-limitations-state-run-individual-market-reinsurance.

[52] Lynn Blewett, *Minnesota's 1332 Reinsurance Waiver Dilemma,* Health Affairs Blog, Following the ACA (December 7, 2017), https://www.healthaffairs.org/do/10.1377/hblog20171 204.352539/full/ (accessed April 5, 2021). *See also,* Marianne Goodland, *Last-minute negotiations shake up reinsurance bill,* Colorado Politics (June 13, 2020), https://www.coloradopolitics.com/legislature/last-minute-negotiations-shake-up-reinsurance-bill/article_e9e1a704-ad17-11ea-a8e5-3f177a158267.html (accessed April 5, 2021).

[53] Norris, *supra* n.43. *See also,* Giovannelli et al., *supra* n.51.

Many states have adopted a specific excess-of-claims attachment point with a few states following Alaska's condition-based system. To give a sense of the range of program features, Delaware pays 75 percent of claims between $65,000 and $215,000, while Minnesota pays 80 percent between $50,000 and $250,000.[54] Oklahoma's program would have kicked in at just $15,000 in per beneficiary claims.[55] Idaho, in its aborted waiver plan, proposed a condition-specific attachment point. Idaho was notable insofar as it sought a dual ACA/Medicaid waiver that proposed to offload the top twenty most costly conditions, amounting to 2,500 cases, onto Medicaid. This risk ceding would have decreased premiums by 20 percent for the remaining 94,000 Idahoans in the ACA market.[56] Idaho's program would have flopped anyway, because it included a Medicaid work requirement of the kind that has been struck down by courts.[57] As it turned out, the deal was scuttled by pharmaceutical interests who did not want to accept the discounted Medicaid rate for high-cost drugs.[58] Idaho's example suggests the ready-made role that Medicaid could play in reinsurance.

Other states also considered extending government reinsurance, but only at government-set pricing. For instance, Colorado originally proposed to limit the reinsurance payments that it made to providers on behalf of the ceded claims to a ceiling of somewhere between 150–200 percent of Medicare rates. However, provider opposition and Trump administration hostility squelched that initiative.[59] Instead, providers agreed to offset the increased cost of de-linking from Medicare prices by paying assessed fees to finance the reinsurance fund.[60]

By implementing reinsurance, Alaska famously reduced premiums by over 30 percent.[61] Maryland's rates fell by nearly 40 percent in the first year of operation.[62] Oregon saw 7–8 percent reductions, Montana cut 9 percent, and Rhode

---

[54] Christopher Snowbeck, *Minnesota extends "reinsurance" program*, STAR TRIBUNE (June 3, 2019), https://www.startribune.com/minnesota-extends-reinsurance-program/510776452/   (accessed April 5, 2021). *See also*, Blewett, *supra* n.52.

[55] OKLAHOMA SECTION 1332 STATE WAIVER APPLICATION (2017), https://www.shadac.org/sites/default/files/1332ResourcePage/Oklahoma/1332%20State%20Innovation%20Waiver%20Final.pdf

[56] Idaho Department of Health and Welfare and Department of Insurance, *Idaho Health Care Plan Dual Waiver Strategy, Idaho Legislative Session* (2018), https://doi.idaho.gov/DisplayPDF?ID=DualWaiver&Cat=OtherDocs.

[57] *Accord*, Gresham v. Azar, 950 F.3d 93 (2020). William L. Spence, *Health committee revives "dual-waiver" plan*, THE LEWISTON TRIBUNE (March 20, 2018), https://lmtribune.com/northwest/health-committee-revives-dual-waiver-plan/article_7f48540c-6507-5b80-95b6-83b2c1ce39ca.html (accessed April 5, 2021) (describing Idaho's waiver plan).

[58] Remarks by Pat Kelley, Executive Director of HealthIdaho, HIX conference, University of Pennsylvania, March 5–6, 2019.

[59] Marianne Goodland, *Colorado House Committee Approves "Reinsurance" Bill Intended to Lower Health Premiums*, COLORADO POLITICS (February 27, 2019), https://www.coloradopolitics.com/news/colorado-house-committee-approves-reinsurance-bill-intended-to-lower-health-premiums/article_a9769748-3b02-11e9-9376-e7273614913b.html (accessed April 5, 2021). *But see* GIOVANNELLI ET AL., *supra* n.51, for Trump administration opposition.

[60] Goodland, *id.*

[61] GIOVANNELLI ET AL., *supra* n.51.

[62] *Id.*

Island, 4 percent.[63] In New Jersey, "[i]nstead of increasing by 12.6% ... ave[rage] premiums dropp[ed] by 9.3% ... or around $1,500 per unsubsidized enrollee for the year. Nearly $1,000 of that average drop is thanks to the reinsurance program; the other $470 is due to reinstating the mandate penalty."[64] In its first year of operation, people across Colorado saved 22 percent on insurance premiums on the individual market.[65]

The Unacknowledged History of Reinsurance in US Healthcare

This flurry of recent activity should not deflect our attention from how pervasive, even deeply rooted, this hidden reinsurance principle is throughout the history of the US health system.

In the story of America's quest for national health insurance, President Harry Truman looms large. Truman sought to complete Franklin Delano Roosevelt's unfinished project by adding compulsory health insurance to the protections afforded by Social Security. His famous defeat at the hands of a galvanized, Red-baiting American Medical Association (AMA), in concert with the insurance and business lobbies, led national health insurance advocates to revise their strategy. They turned to focus on particular groups like elderly and disabled Americans whom no private insurer wished to enroll.[66]

The History of Eisenhower's Health Reinsurance Proposal

But the historic Truman defeat also led to an effort by Dwight Eisenhower, proposing health reinsurance as the alternate conservative path. In his 1954, State of the Union, Eisenhower explained it thus:

> I am flatly opposed to the socialization of medicine.... The Federal Government can do many helpful things and still carefully avoid the socialization of medicine.... A limited Government reinsurance service would permit the private

---

[63] *Id.*

[64] Charles Gaba, *New Jersey: Does Seema Verma have a point for once?? Nah, probably not*, ACA SIGNUPS (January 30, 2019), https://acasignups.net/19/01/30/new-jersey-does-seema-verma-have-point-once-nah-probably-not (accessed April 2, 2021).

[65] GIOVANNELLI ET AL., *supra* n.51.

[66] This story has been well told. *See, e.g.,* THEODORE R. MARMOR, THE POLITICS OF MEDICARE (2nd ed. 2000), https://www.routledge.com/The-Politics-of-Medicare/Marmor/p/book/9780202304 250 (accessed April 1, 2021).

and non-profit insurance companies to offer broader protection to more of the many families which want and should have it.[67]

The mid-century hegemony of the employer-sponsored coverage system, along with the political coalition of AMA with insurer and business interests, combined to center private insurance as the dominant source of health coverage. But this reliance upon private insurance left unavoidable gaps in the system corresponding to the groups that private insurers found unavailing. Persons who were elderly or disabled were simply the most visible examples of those whom insurers wished to either leave off their rolls or add only grudgingly at higher rates to reflect their medical risk. Elderly and disabled applicants were doubly disadvantaged by their lower rates of participation in the formal employment sector, constraining their finances and access to job-based coverage.[68]

Other groups lacking resources for private insurance included lower-income Americans and dependent children with their caregivers.[69] When commercial insurers entered the health insurance market mid-century to compete with the provider-organized Blue Cross Blue Shield plans, they brought with them actuarial tables from their accumulated expertise offering life insurance.[70] Using these techniques, they could medically "underwrite" their coverage products; that is, use demographic and other predictive factors to identify when to reject applicants, when to limit or exclude coverage for preexisting conditions, and when to charge higher rates commensurate with the applicant's risk.[71] Blue Cross Blue Shield (BCBS) initially lacked this expertise. Later, as a condition of the various tax and regulatory exemptions associated with their quasi-public status, BCBS plans were prohibited from pursing these strategies anyway, as they were often required to offer flat community rating and guaranteed issue to all members, regardless of health risk.[72] Thus, the lion's share of high-loss health claims gravitated to BCBS. A savvy Blue Cross Blue Shield executive proposed government reinsurance so that their plans might not succumb to a destabilizing

---

[67] President Dwight D. Eisenhower, State of the Union Address, 1 Pub. Papers 6 (January 7, 1954).

[68] ROBERT STEVENS & ROSEMARY STEVENS, WELFARE MEDICINE IN AMERICA: A CASE STUDY OF MEDICAID 6 (2003) at 27–28 (explaining that "[f]or the elderly, rising costs were of special concern or at least of special interest. In view of the fact that they frequently had fixed incomes").

[69] *Id.* at 19–22.

[70] John A. Cogan, Jr., *Does Small Group Health Insurance Deliver Group Benefits: An Argument in Favor of Allowing the Small Group Market to Die*, 93 WASH. L. REV. 1121, 1145–6 (2018).

[71] JILL QUADAGNO, ONE NATION, UNINSURED: WHY THE U.S. HAS NO NATIONAL HEALTH INSURANCE 55–6 (2006).

[72] *Id.* at 56 (describing how Blue Cross executives importuned government to relax or address these structures "complain[ing] that Blue Cross was rapidly losing business to commercial insurers who experience-rated their premiums to attract young, healthy customers, leaving the Blue Cross plans with the older, sicker individuals. Some plans were forced to raise their rates. Others abandoned community rating, where all policyholders would pay the same rate (regardless of health risk) and started basing premiums on health risk.")

cost spiral due to these effects.[73] The Rockefeller Foundation, along with Nelson Rockefeller and other key government figures, lent their support, and Eisenhower jumped aboard.[74]

Eisenhower's proposed legislation offered private insurers a deal. It set certain minimum standards for health plans to qualify for reinsurance. It barred age restrictions and assorted other exclusions from coverage. It also demanded more comprehensive benefits such as increased hospital days or relaxed benefit caps "in order to reach more effectively into the areas of catastrophic illness."[75] The proposal also required enrollment of certain groups "now considered uninsurable" by private plans.[76] In exchange, government would protect the plans from high and unmanageable losses resulting from this broadened coverage.[77] This bargain bears more than an echo of the Dworkinian principle we traced through Chapters 3 and 4. Yet the House of Representatives tabled the proposal with a resounding 238–134 vote, a surprise defeat that the *New York Times* laid at the hands of the AMA.[78]

This episode did not mark the end of reinsurance as a policy theme in US healthcare.

History of Medicaid

Leading up to the passage of Medicaid's precursor program, the Kerr-Mills Act of 1960, certain populations were identified as special concerns, including children, those who are blind, and the elderly. Certainly one reason for the salience of these groups is that they represented the traditional categories of eligibility for

---

[73] Jacob Hacker, *Boundary Wars: The Political Struggle over Public and Private Social Benefits in the United States* 310, Doctoral Dissertation, Yale University, 2000, *cited in* QUADAGNO, *supra* n.71 at 45–49.

[74] *See* Oveta Culp Hobby papers, MS 459 box 35 (pp. 10–14) Woodson Research Center Fondren Library, Rice University.

[75] *Id.*

[76] Jordan M. Graham, "We Are Against Socialized Medicine, But What Are We For?: Federal Health Reinsurance, National Health Policy, and the Eisenhower Presidency," 69–84 Graduate Student Theses, Dissertations, & Professional Papers 4492, University of Montana-Missoula (2015), https://scholarworks.umt.edu/etd/4492 (quoting Oveta Culp Hobby).

[77] *Id.* (describing how at the Congressional hearing on the proposal, the administration's special assistant of Health and Medical Affairs Division of HEW was Dr. Chester Keefer, and he described the proposal as one that would "guarantee, for a premium, insurance companies against losses from broadened benefits and broadened coverage"). *See also, To Your Health*, THE HARVARD CRIMSON (February 21, 1955), https://www.thecrimson.com/article/1955/2/21/to-your-health-pmany-of-our/ (accessed April 6, 2021) (stating that "Insurance companies would reject no-one as a 'poor risk' under the administration medical bill. Fiscal hocus-pocus called 'reinsurance' will enable them to sell policies even to the victims of cancer, diabetes, and polio").

[78] John D. Morris, *Eisenhower Plan for Health Funds Rejected in House*, N.Y. TIMES (July 14, 1954), https://www.nytimes.com/1954/07/14/archives/eisenhower-plan-for-health-funds-rejected-in-house-in-surprise-move.html (accessed April 6, 2021).

cash assistance welfare in the United States, a taxonomy grounded in notions of which among us were "deserving" of assistance. Robert and Rosemary Stevens traced the ideological lineage thus:

> Impoverished old people, underfed children, and the unemployable blind could scarcely be blamed for their condition nor envied for being recipients of relief. . . . These early categorical programs are important because the divisions were carried over into the Social Security Act of 1935 to become—with the addition of a further category for the totally and permanently disabled in 1950—the framework on which Medicaid was drafted.[79]

This heritage remains discernible in Medicaid today.

But another throughline runs alongside and explains the persistence of these categories as the subjects of collective health aid: these categories make sense according to a *reinsurance* and not just a *welfare medicine* rationale. As evident in the Eisenhower history above, the rise of employer-sponsored health coverage (which at its peak covered 80 percent of Americans under the age of sixty-five) successfully papered over the uninsured problem to such an extent that comprehensive universal healthcare as a policy goal receded from view.[80] The problem of health coverage could instead be reframed as that of addressing those specific groups *who were not privately insurable.* The situation of elderly Americans acquired special prominence in this context, as they represented an especially risky population that private insurance would not take on.[81] Less than 15 percent of the elderly had any form of health insurance in the late 1950s, the inverse of the situation for working-age Americans.[82]

This concern over the extreme medical needs of particular populations characterizes nearly all of the traditional categories for cash assistance that were eventually folded into Medicaid. Of the categories of the elderly, the blind, the totally and permanently disabled, and dependent children with their families, all but the last draws not just from a welfare story of "deserving" status among the poor, but also from the reinsurance rationale that some medical needs would exceed ordinary expectations within the insurable range.

---

[79] STEVENS & STEVENS, *supra* n.68 at 6.

[80] *See generally*, ROBIN A. COHEN ET AL., CDC, NATIONAL HEALTH STATISTICS REPORT: HEALTH INSURANCE COVERAGE TRENDS, 1959–2007: ESTIMATES FROM THE NATIONAL HEALTH INTERVIEW SURVEY (2009), https://www.cdc.gov/nchs/data/nhsr/nhsr017.pdf.

[81] STEVENS & STEVENS, *supra* n.68 at 39, n.26 (stating that the reason is that "because of their high medical risk [they] were unable to buy health insurance at prices they could afford."), *citing* U.S. Public Health Service, Health Statistics from the U.S. National Healthy Survey: Older Persons, Selected Health Characteristics, July 1957–June 1959, Public Health Service Pub. No. 584-c4 (1960).

[82] Thomas Bodenheimer & Kevin Grumbach, *Paying for Health*, 272 JAMA 634 (1994).

This line of reasoning drove other early characteristics of Medicaid as well. In Medicaid's forerunner, the Kerr-Mills program,[83] a new eligibility category had emerged, that of the "medically needy."[84] The medically needy represented a new concept of need, separate from "deserving" poverty. "Medically indigent" beneficiaries "were defined as elderly or blind persons or totally disabled persons . . . who were not on public assistance and whose incomes might be above state eligibility levels for cash assistance but who nevertheless had incomes insufficient to meet their medical bills."[85] What was notable was not how poor they were, but how crushing their medical costs were. In practice, these individuals were often those whose medical conditions led to institutionalization. Medical need or indigence, a concept Medicaid employs even today, captures the intuition that catastrophic medical circumstances, without regard to poverty per se, should trigger the responsibility of the state. Unfortunately, Congress trimmed back some of the implications of this policy in 1967. Afraid of unexpectedly high state spending on an open-ended promise of federal match, it decided for a period of time to limit the category of medically needy to those whose incomes fell below 133.3 percent of the welfare eligibility level.[86]

Medicaid as a government program has historically shouldered costly institutional care, regarded implicitly as provision beyond any ordinary family's means. Under the Kerr-Mills program, leading states such as California prioritized the provision of this expensive outlier care even ahead of more basic medical services.[87] Medicaid seemed to fill in by affirmatively providing government support along lines like age, disability, and institutionalization, many of which were the categories identified for Dworkinian preclusion, as we saw in Chapters 3 and 4.

Medicaid also took on a reinsurance function amid Medicaid's managed care revolution. While Medicaid initially contemplated direct state payment for

---

[83] STEVENS & STEVENS, *supra* n.68 at 28–9.

[84] *Id.* at 29 (explaining the addition in 1960 of medically needy beneficiaries under Kerr-Mills Act's Medical Assistance to the Aged, followed by the 1962 extension of this concept to blind and disabled recipients in Title XVI.) *Id.* at 62–5 (describing the optional eligibility category of the "categorically related medically needy" as defined by both high medical bills and membership in one of the traditional eligibility categories, despite income otherwise exceeding the prevailing means-test level. The authors go on to explain that this concept was expanded by the state option category of "non-categorically related medically needy" and by the Ribicoff Amendment to all children, regardless of whether they were categorically qualified. The mechanism that states used to operationalize and define this threshold of "medical indigence" was the spend-down provision, which sweeps individuals into the ambit of eligibility despite their higher incomes if their medical bills "spend-down" so much of their income that the remaining portion falls at or below the means threshold. *See,* Social Security Act (SSA) § 1902(a)(17), 42 U.S.C. § 1396a(a)(17).

[85] STEVENS & STEVENS, *supra* n.68 at 62.

[86] *Id.*

[87] *Id.* at 3.

health services,[88] it has since become a program that operates largely through state payments to intermediary managed care organizations that organize healthcare provision on Medicaid's behalf.[89] Kaiser Family Foundation counts that as of July 2019, 40 states used capitated managed care models to deliver services in Medicaid, and "more than two-thirds (69%) of all Medicaid beneficiaries received their care through comprehensive risk-based [managed care organizations] (MCOs)."[90] With this transformation, many state Medicaid programs instituted formal reinsurance for the private risk-bearing entities that they had contracted with to deliver care.[91] Medicaid itself sometimes serves as the stop-loss insurer,[92] but "[m]any states that began providing public reinsurance to Medicaid managed care plans ended by allowing plans to buy private [reinsurance] coverage instead."[93]

We have long used Medicaid to backstop catastrophic risks in other ways as well. Because of its open-ended matching structure, it serves as automatic countercyclical fiscal stabilizer in economic downturns.[94] We also turned to Disaster Relief Medicaid after catastrophic events like 9/11 and major hurricanes.[95] Medicaid may, more than any other aspect of our healthcare system today, exemplify the reinsurance impulse.

---

[88] *Id.* at 90–100 (recounting the example of New York's original program).

[89] SSA § 1915(g), 42 U.S.C. § 1396n(g).

[90] *See, e.g.*, Elizabeth Hinton et al., *10 Things to Know about Medicaid Managed Care*, KFF (October 29, 2020), https://www.kff.org/medicaid/issue-brief/10-things-to-know-about-medicaid-managed-care/ (accessed April 6, 2021).

[91] 42 C.F.R. § 438.1-438.7 (2020) (requiring that "payments to Medicaid MCOs must be actuarially sound. Actuarial soundness means that "the capitation rates are projected to provide for all reasonable, appropriate, and attainable costs that are required under the terms of the contract and for the operation of the managed care plan for the time period and the population covered under the terms of the contract").

[92] For examples of state reinsurance provisions, *see* Reinsurance for Medicaid contactors, State-by-State, George Washington University Health Policy Department, https://publichealth.gwu.edu/departments/healthpolicy/CHPR/nnhs4/GSA/Subheads/gsa246.html (accessed April 3, 2021). *See, e.g.*, Stop Loss Program, New York State Department of Health Website, https://www.health.ny.gov/facilities/hospital/reimbursement/stoploss/ (accessed April 6, 2021) (New York Medicaid's stop loss website, offering state-based reinsurance that Medicaid managed care plans can purchase from the state).

[93] Randall R. Bovbjerg & Elliot Wicks, *Implementing Government-Funded Reinsurance in the Context of Universal Coverage* 19 (2006), https://www.urban.org/sites/default/files/alfresco/publication-pdfs/1000983-Implementing-Government-Funded-Reinsurance-in-the-Context-of-Universal-Coverage.pdf.

[94] Moira Forbes & Chris Park, *A Countercyclical Medicaid Financing Adjustment: Moving towards Recommendations*, MACPAC presentation (December 10, 2020), https://www.macpac.gov/publication/a-countercyclical-medicaid-financing-adjustment-moving-towards-recommendations/ (accessed May 5, 2021).

[95] Christina S. Ho, *To Stop the Coronavirus, We Need to Cover More Than Just the Coronavirus*, Slate Magazine (March 6, 2020), https://slate.com/technology/2020/03/we-must-give-medicaid-to-all-who-face-coronavirus.html (accessed May 5, 2021).

History of Medicare

Yet Medicare exhibits strong signs of a reinsurance frame as well. Wilbur Cohen, one of the architects of Medicare, understood the entire project of the Social Security Act along the lines of government responsibility for catastrophic risks. According to Marmor:

> [Cohen] actively campaigned for disability insurance covering workers over the age of 50. He did so on the assumption that by slowly expanding the number of impoverishing conditions insured against by social security, the risk of catastrophic health expenses would be left as the obvious major omission within the social insurance program requiring remedial legislation.[96]

When Truman's advisors regrouped after 1950, they narrowed their sights to focus on the elderly first.[97] They did so because the incidence of high-cost claims concentrated among the elderly who therefore struggled to find private insurers willing to offer affordable coverage.[98] Even the decision by the Johnson administration to prioritize hospital costs first (ultimately Medicare Part A) signaled that their primary concerns were the catastrophic episodes that resulted in large hospital bills.[99] Political support for Medicare legislation was bolstered by the benefits that reinsurance would bring to unions and employers. Those bedfellows favored relief from the increasing burden of retiree health insurance, and they were happy to off-load these costs onto the government.[100]

As we know now, the version of Medicare that eventually passed addressed more than just large hospital bills. Having taken that portion of the administration's proposal and called it Medicare Part A, House Ways and Means Chairman Wilbur Mills co-opted two competing proposals and, in a strategic flourish, appended them to the Medicare package. The result was the proverbial "three-layer cake," comprised of Medicare Part A, Medicare Part B, and Medicaid. The two co-opted proposals had been intended by opponents of Medicare as narrower substitutes for Medicare. The Republican ranking member, John Byrne advocated Bettercare, a proposal for premium subsidies that the elderly could use to purchase voluntary insurance. Wilbur Mills mimicked that structure and applied it to seniors' physician and other outpatient costs to constitute Medicare Part B. The AMA-backed Eldercare proposal, which would have devolved the

---

[96] MARMOR, *supra* n.66.

[97] *Id.* at 10–11.

[98] *Id.* at 11.

[99] *Id.* at 24–6 (attributing these views to Wilbur Cohen, and the House Ways and Means sponsor, Rep. Aime Forand).

[100] *See, e.g.*, QUADAGNO, *supra* n.71 at 55–62. *Id.* at 148–9 (making this point regarding employers). TOM DASCHLE ET AL., CRITICAL: WHAT WE CAN DO ABOUT THE HEALTH-CARE CRISIS 47 (2008).

problem of coverage gaps to states by merely expanding the existing Kerr-Mills state grants-in-aid, was added to the bill as Medicaid. The efforts of Medicare's opponents to sidetrack the proposal ended up expanding it even beyond what the Johnson administration dared ask for.

After Medicare's passage, additional eligibility categories were approved from time to time, and virtually all of these groups exemplified the principle of re-insurance. These populations represented high-cost patients who would skew insurance risk pools. Medicare eligibility allowed these risks to be off-loaded onto the government. For instance, the workers who qualified for Social Security Disability Insurance for at least two years were added regardless of age to the Medicare rolls in 1972, as were end-stage renal disease patients who needed expensive dialysis.[101] In 2001, Medicare was extended to patients with amyotrophic lateral sclerosis (ALS).[102] According to Marmor, this pattern of prioritization distinguishes the United States from all other industrialized countries, who covered their formal working sectors first.[103]

Because of unsustainable growth in hospital charges, Medicare in the 1980s sought to curb inpatient spending by switching to an inpatient prospective payment system (IPPS) which we described briefly in the last chapter. Instead of paying a la carte for each service delivered to a Medicare patient, the government switched to "essentially pay[ing] hospitals the national average cost . . . for each patient admitted to the hospital" for that particular diagnosis-related group (DRG) or patient case.[104] This form of payment shifts some of the risk of a Medicare beneficiary's high service use from the government insurer to the hospital instead, which, as we noted last chapter, renders the hospital a quasi-insurer. The hospital would in theory now face an incentive to control its spending and conserve resources. From the very outset, the formula for these averaged DRG payments contained the aforementioned adjustment for "outliers."[105] These outlier payments function as insurance that the hospitals "purchase" to protect against high-cost cases:

---

[101] See Social Security Act of 1972, Pub. L. 92-603 §§ 201 and 299I, 86 Stat. 1329, 1373 and 1463; see also SCOTT SZYMENDERA, Social Security Disability Insurance (SSDI) and Medicare: The 24-Month Waiting Period for SSDI Beneficiaries Under Age 65, CONGRESSIONAL RESEARCH SERVICE REPORT RS22195 (January 7, 2009), https://greenbook-waysandmeans.house.gov/sites/greenbook.waysandmeans.house.gov/files/2012/documents/RS22195_gb_0.pdf. See also Paul W. Eggers, Medicare's End Stage Renal Disease Program, 22 HEALTH CARE FINANC. REV. 55–60 (2000).

[102] See Consolidated Appropriations Act of 2001, PL 106-554. See also, SWARTZ, supra n.27 at 4–5 (stating that ALS patients' costs can put them in the "top 1 percent of the distribution for health spending").

[103] Theodore Marmor & Kip Sullivan, Medicare at 50: Why Medicare-for-all Did Not Take Place, 15 YALE J. HEALTH POLICY LAW ETHICS 141 (2015).

[104] See, Emmett B. Keeler et al., Insurance aspects of DRG outlier payments, 7 J. HEALTH ECON. 193–214 (1988).

[105] See Chapter 6.

Outlier payments can be viewed as insurance against excessive losses on a case. They are intended to cover the marginal costs of care beyond the outlier threshold (a deductible on losses), and are financed by a tax on reimbursement of non-outlier patients (a per-case premium).[106]

The "per-case premium" takes the form of an overall reduction in each DRG payment by 5 percent to finance the outlier payments.[107] Generally that payment is structured to cover 80 percent of costs above the deductible, which we earlier noted as roughly $27,000 per case in FY 2021.[108] This structure mirrors the coinsurance and attachment points that feature commonly in reinsurance policies.[109] A study from the early days of outlier payments showed who in the end benefited from this policy, namely,

individuals with end-stage renal disease or diabetes as secondary complications to their current stay . . . [who] were more apt to generate large losses. Being [B]lack also predict[ed] large losses, but this effect [was] substantially reduced when we control[led] for the hospital. These characteristics could easily be known to the hospital at admission time, and thus the hospitals could discriminate against these patients if they choose to do so.[110]

This quote reveals that outlier payments reinsure insofar as they function not merely to smooth volatility and thereby reduce overall costs; they also follow the justification for our nation's favored reinsurance policies by functioning to increase beneficiaries' access to the institutions that absorb risk, especially for those groups vulnerable to risk discrimination. This anti-discrimination, anti-risk-selection function remains relevant, even under Biden's current American Rescue Plan-Inflation Reduction Act premium tax credit regime, which otherwise dulls the premium reduction incentives to pursue reinsurance.

Starting as early as the 1980s, Medicare was buffeted by the same forces that pushed Medicaid toward greater managed care intermediation.[111] In its current incarnation, Medicare incorporates managed care by paying private "at-risk"

---

[106] Id.

[107] Id. at 197.

[108] See Chapter 6, n.20. Hospital Inpatient Prospective Payment Systems for Acute Care Hospitals, 85 Fed. Reg 58432 (September 8, 2020), https://www.federalregister.gov/documents/2020/09/18/2020-19637/medicare-program-hospital-inpatient-prospective-payment-systems-for-acute-care-hospitals-and-the (setting the outlier payment at $27,195 for fiscal year 2021).

[109] SWARTZ, supra n.27 at 132 (describing how "Medicare pays a hospital 80 percent of its costs above the threshold that defines an outlier case").

[110] Keeler supra n.104.

[111] See, e.g., James C. Beebe, An Outlier Pool for Medicare HMO Payments, 14 HEALTH CARE FINANC REV 59–63, 59 (1992), https://www.ncbi.nlm.nih.gov/pmc/articles/PMC4193317/ (accessed April 13, 2021).

plans a prospective capitated lump sum to provide comprehensive Medicare services (usually Parts A, B, and D) for any given enrollee. This mode of furnishing Medicare is now referred to as Medicare Advantage, though it previously went by the names Medicare Part C and Medicare+Choice.[112] Medicare does not provide reinsurance to the private plans, arguably because the statute requires these Medicare Advantage Organizations (MAOs) to "assume full financial risk . . . for the provision of [] health care services."[113] But nearly all MAOs purchase their own reinsurance.[114]

Medicare Advantage, in its own perverse way, however, enjoys a de facto government high-risk pool. The healthiest seniors are skimmed by private plans, and traditional Medicare with full government risk-absorption, catches the residual pool.[115] Indeed this dynamic was well-known and widely expected at the time these programs were designed:

> In 1996, for example, the most expensive 10 percent of program beneficiaries averaged $37,000 in medical expenditures and accounted for 75.5 percent of all program costs. In the new Medicare market, private insurers could be expected to compete aggressively to avoid enrolling such costly patients, leaving them for the public Medicare program.[116]

In 2003, after decades of political clamoring for Medicare to add prescription drug coverage, the Bush administration finally did so by creating Medicare Part D.[117] However, this $400 billion benefit came with the stipulation that such coverage could only be delivered by private plans, either through the MAOs described above, or by private stand-alone prescription drug plans, which did not yet exist as a product.[118] Unlike Medicare Parts A and B, the Medicare Part D deal that the Bush Administration struck expressly prohibited the government from financing patient costs directly. The government could only contract with private

---

[112] YASH M. PATEL & STUART GUTERMAN, *The Evolution of Private Plans in Medicare* (2017), https://www.commonwealthfund.org/publications/issue-briefs/2017/dec/evolution-private-plans-medicare (accessed April 13, 2021).

[113] 42 U.S.C. § 1395w-25(b); SSA § 1855(b).

[114] Bruce Fried & John R. Russell, IV, *CMS: Quota share reinsurance "not permissible" for Medicare Advantage plans*, DENTONS INSIGHTS (2017), https://www.dentons.com/en/insights/alerts/2017/february/13/cms-quota-share-reinsurance-not-permissible-for-medicare-advantage-plans (accessed April 13, 2021).

[115] MARMOR, *supra* n.66 at 143, 180.

[116] *Id.*

[117] Medicare Prescription Drug Improvement and Modernization Act of 2003, Pub. L. 108-173 (December 8, 2003).

[118] *See, e.g.,* the so-called noninterference clause, SSA § 1860D-11(i), 42 U.S.C. § 1395w-111(i). For the near $400 billion over ten year price tag, *see Estimating the Cost of the Medicare Modernization Act: Hearing Before the Comm. On Ways & Means*, 108th Cong. 1–2 (2004) (statement of Douglas Holtz-Eakin, Director, Cong. Budget Off.), https://www.cbo.gov/sites/default/files/108th-congress-2003-2004/reports/03-24-medicare.pdf.

plans to provide coverage instead. In other words, the primary insurer was never the government, but always private plans from the outset. However, government faced the challenge of inducing private actors to offer an unprecedented category of insurance in an entirely new market. As one commentator recounted, "When the Medicare Modernization Act of 2003 (MMA) created an outpatient prescription drug benefit, there was doubt about whether a viable insurance market would form because drug-only insurance was not offered commercially; uncertainty arising from the lack of credible data on Medicare beneficiary drug utilization and spending put insurers at high risk."[119] Therefore Congress braided reinsurance into the design of Medicare Part D to reassure and thereby entice insurers to participate in the new Medicare Part D program. This reinsurance had no built-in sunset and offered greater backstopping to private insurers compared to the ACA's three-year transitional reinsurance measure described earlier this chapter.[120] Part D reinsurance was and remains comparatively generous. For instance, the FY 2021 out-of-pocket threshold for beneficiaries clocked in at $6,550 ($10,048 in *total* prescription drug expenditures). For prescription drug costs above that point, the federal government would directly cover 80 percent of costs, and the private Part D plans would pay only 15 percent in coinsurance.[121] Beneficiaries remained responsible for the remaining 5 percent of prescription drug costs.[122] This government relief proved so ample that MedPAC has warned that it may fuel excessive pricing by pharmaceutical companies for their specialty drugs.[123] Federal support has even increased under the recently passed Inflation Reduction Act of 2022, which eliminated the 5 percent beneficiary coinsurance, and lowered the out-of-pocket cap from the aforementioned $6550 to $2000 by 2025.[124] To counterbalance this effect, the Inflation Reduction Act also introduces new requirements that manufacturers provide Medicare rebates

---

[119] Steven M. Lieberman, *Adapting Medicare Advantage Bidding For COVID-19–Related Uncertainty On Claims: A Proposal*, HEALTH AFFAIRS BLOG (2020), https://www.healthaffairs.org/do/10.1377/hblog20200513.916922/full/ (accessed April 13, 2021).

[120] *See supra*, text accompanying n. 6–9.

[121] Kaiser Family Foundation, *An Overview of the Medicare Part D Prescription Drug Benefit*, KFF (October 13, 2021), https://www.kff.org/medicare/fact-sheet/an-overview-of-the-medicare-part-d-prescription-drug-benefit/ (accessed May 6, 2022).

[122] Joshua Cohen, *New Reinsurance Model in Medicare Part D*, FORBES (February 11, 2019), https://www.forbes.com/sites/joshuacohen/2019/02/11/new-reinsurance-model-in-medicare-part-d/ (accessed April 13, 2021).

[123] MEDPAC, *Chapter 6: Sharing Risk in Medicare Part D*, *in* MEDPAC JUNE 2015 REPORT (2015), http://www.medpac.gov/docs/default-source/reports/chapter-6-sharing-risk-in-medicare-part-d-june-2015-report-.pdf.

[124] The Inflation Reduction Act of 2022, Pub. L. No. 117-169, 136 Stat. 1818, 1878 § 11201(a) and (b) (codified as amended in 42 U.S.C. § 1395w–102(b) and 42 U.S.C. § 1395w–115) (August 16, 2022).

on drugs whose prices rise faster than inflation, and new authority for the federal government to negotiate drug prices on select high-priced medications.[125]

One Medicare episode might defy this characterization of Medicare as re-insurance; namely, the failure of the Medicare Catastrophic Coverage Act of 1988. The legislation, championed by then-Democratic House Ways and Means Chairman Dan Rostenkowski, would have established caps on Medicare patients' payments to hospitals and doctors, apparently backstopping seniors' exposure to high medical costs.[126] But upon examination of the benefits and burdens, the policy seems less like loss-spreading reinsurance, and more like forced contribution to supplemental coverage, especially concentrating the burdens on affluent seniors. Rather than drawing from general funds and payroll taxes, the proposal ended up requiring Medicare recipients themselves (already on a fixed income and bearing the risk exposure that justified Medicare in the first place) to pay extra premiums to self-fund additional benefits. Those benefits included not only catastrophic insurance, but a number of other items oppor-tunistically added to this legislation, including prescription drugs long before the Bush administration eventually succeeded in adding a Part D benefit. This financing source was not original to the proposal's conception but forced upon Rostenkowski by the hardline anti-spending Reagan administration. Reagan had telegraphed that he would not block catastrophic coverage for seniors per se. However, he would oppose any additional commitments of federal spending.[127] This constraint forced Representative Rostenkowski to raise pay-fors from the Medicare recipients themselves. Rostenkowski managed to get the bill passed, but the backlash was legendary, producing indelible footage of Rostenkowski fleeing his car pursued by angry senior mobs.[128] Congress repealed the measure within 18 months of passage. As Marmor explains, the true objection was not to the capping of seniors' medical financial exposure above a certain threshold, but to where the burden fell for financing that policy. Rather than spreading risk, the legislation surcharged those most at risk of catastrophic health events, espe-cially those seniors who were affluent and needed government reinsurance the least, since many already had private secondary coverage. In 1986, for instance, 80 percent of all seniors were covered under supplemental Medigap policies which were either paid for by the seniors themselves, or enjoyed as a retirement

[125] The Inflation Reduction Act of 2022, Pub. L. No. 117-169, 136 Stat. 1818, 1833-1877, §§ 11001 et seq, 11101 et seq, 11201(c)–(g) (codified in scattered sections of 42 U.S.C. § 1320f, 1395w) (August 16, 2022).

[126] MARMOR, supra n.66 at 110–13 (capping beneficiary payments for hospital and physician care at $2146 per year). See QUADAGNO, supra n.71 at 153.

[127] MARMOR, supra n.66 at 112.

[128] CBS NEWS, Washington Unplugged, "Buried In The Archives," The Original Town-Hall Battle (August 10, 2009), https://www.youtube.com/watch?app=desktop&v=qre7DzEtxyc&feature=emb_logo (accessed April 13, 2021).

benefit accruing from their previous employers.[129] Moreover, the proposed benefits swelled to include prescription drugs, which were at the time considered more routine than catastrophic, even as the legislation failed protect against the costs of needed long-term care, which seniors dreaded as a ruinous expense.[130] Arguably the backlash was not to the concept of reinsurance itself, but instead to the ways that the policy design departed from true reinsurance. Meanwhile the addition of pharmaceutical benefits to the bill not only added to the bill's expense but also galvanized the pharmaceutical industry to spend $3 million lobbying against the prospect of government leverage.[131]

Jill Quadagno sums up the reinsurance significance of Medicare best: "Politically, Medicare filled the remaining gap that negotiated plans could not cover, removing all pressure for national health insurance. Immediately, as the burden of the older, otherwise uninsured population was removed, Blue Cross began lowering its rates across the country."[132]

The History of ERISA in Healthcare

ERISA, as we learned last chapter, is a pension guaranty statute that also sets federal standards governing other fringe benefits like employer-sponsored health coverage. It has been a recurring presence throughout this book, hinting at its outsize role in shaping US healthcare. Yet the drafters of ERISA gave far less thought to the effects on health benefits than they did to traditional pensions. As Bill Sage so memorably noted in 1996, "Although in its text 'hospital' appears only once and 'physician' not at all, ERISA may be the most important law affecting health care in the United States."[133]

Though ERISA's role in the US health sector has always posed something of a puzzle, I will argue here that understanding ERISA as an imperfect reinsurance measure for employer-sponsored health benefits may supply the key.

We begin with the observation that the federal health-related protections in ERISA have been scant, devoid of "substantive federal requirements for private health care plan coverage and benefits."[134] Background state laws governing pension annuities generally offer less protection than federal ERISA standards. But in the health context, the situation is reversed: state substantive and remedial

---

[129] QUADAGNO, *supra* n.71 at 150.
[130] *Id.* at 150–159.
[131] *Id.* at 155.
[132] *Id.* at 75.
[133] William M. Sage, *"Health Law 2000": The Legal System and the Changing Health Care Market*, 15 HEALTH AFF. (MILLWOOD) 9–27 (1996).
[134] Colleen E. Medill, *HIPAA and Its Related Legislation: A New Role for ERISA in the Regulation of Private Health Care Plans*, 65 TENN. L. REV. 485, 488 (1998).

protections actually surpass the federal protections of ERISA. This imbalance is evident in the statute's structure. As Colleen Medill observes, ERISA's Title I is divided into parts and the substantive coverage and benefits standards of Parts 2 and 3 apply to pension plans alone.[135] Only Parts 1, 4, and 5 extend to health benefit plans as well. These health-pertinent provisions, however, originally contained no substantive benefit standards, speaking only to procedural and formal matters, such as annual reporting, disclosure, documentation, the handling of plan assets, and the assignment of fiduciary responsibility to plan administrators.[136] Even this last protection is illusory as the plan administrator, working on behalf of the employer, is unavoidably conflicted.[137] Part 5 establishes a federal enforcement scheme and most notably, *with strong preemption provisions.*[138] Thus, without providing any substantive federal health standards, ERISA still operates to displace virtually all state governance. The effect of this "most important law affecting health" has therefore been largely deregulatory, as we flagged in Chapters 3 and 4, but explain more fully now.

The scope of preemption has proven extraordinary. The express preemption terms are themselves broad, as some recent commentators note:

> When state laws conflict with federal . . . preemption doctrine generally displaces the state law in favor of the federal. But the express . . . preemption in ERISA [§ 514(a)] sweeps even further, purporting to invalidate "any and all" state laws that "relate to" an employee benefit plan, not merely those which unavoidably conflict.[139]

To be sure, the express preemption provision features an exception that purports to "save" state laws that "regulate insurance" from the force of ERISA's sweeping preemption clause.[140] However, this savings clause is in turn limited by the "deemer clause."[141] Under the deemer clause, insurance regulations might be saved, but any employer health plans that are self-insured (rather than backed by insurance purchased from a third-party insurer) cannot be deemed to be

---

[135] *Id.* at 487–90.

[136] 29 U.S.C. §§ 1106-8, 1102-1105, 1109-1112.

[137] Brendan Maher & Paul Secunda, *Pension De-risking*, 93 Wash. U. L. Rev. 733, 760 (2016) (observing, "It has long been recognized that many ERISA fiduciaries are, in practice, conflicted because they are employed, controlled, or beholden to the plan sponsor), *citing* Metro Life Ins. Co. v. Glenn, 554 U.S. 105. 120 (2008) (conceding that in most ERISA cases, fiduciaries are under a conflict of interest, though that fact does not automatically undercut the deference granted to their judgments).

[138] Gobeille v. Liberty Mut. Ins. Co., 577 U.S. 312, 323 (2016) (Thomas, J., concurring).

[139] Erin Fuse Brown & Elizabeth Y McCuskey, *Federalism, ERISA, and State Single-Payer Health Care*, 168 Univ. Pa. Law Rev. 389, 392 (2020).

[140] ERISA § 514(b)(2)(A), 29 U.S.C. § 1144(b)(2)(A).

[141] ERISA § 514(b)(2)(B), 29 U.S.C. § 1144(b)(2)(B).

insurance, or, in other words, cannot be treated as coming under the purport-edly saved state regulations.[142] This provision dangles in front of employers the promise of federal exemption from state insurance laws (and now many ACA standards) if they opt to self-insure, rather than paying premiums to a third-party insurer to cover all medical claims arising under the employer-sponsored health plan. Self-insuring would presumably involve employers paying the cov-ered claims themselves and thereby "bear[ing] the risk that the cost of claims may exceed estimates."[143] However, as we introduced in the previous chapter, these self-insured employers frequently offload their excess risk to other commercial insurers by buying commercial stop-loss policies. These stop-loss policies are hard to distinguish from off-the-shelf health insurance policies; they "can look very much like a regular high-deductible insured plan [as there] is little practical difference between a self-insured plan with an individual stop-loss attachment point of $10,000 and a normal insurance plan with a high $10,000 deductible."[144] Thus employers can claim self-insured status to enjoy the regulatory exemptions, but still escape most of the actual risk of absorbing stochastic loss.

The force of ERISA preemption does not end there with the deemer clause's reclamation of the deregulatory preemption shield for these ostensibly self-insured plans. The Supreme Court has found that ERISA effectuates, in Justice Thomas's words, a "still stronger" preemption than mere conflict or express.[145] A "complete" field preemption is posited by the Court and does not arise from the text of the § 514 preemption clause. Instead, the Court reasons that the struc-ture of the list of remedies available in ERISA under § 502 *implies* that any addi-tional state remedies, regardless of whether they conflict with the text of ERISA or relate to an employee benefit plan, are displaced. As Justice O'Connor argues, "The six carefully integrated civil enforcement provisions found in § 502(a) of the

---

[142] Russell B. Korobkin, *The Battle Over Self-Insured Health Plans, or "One Good Loophole Deserves Another,"* 1 YALE J. HEALTH POLICY LAW ETHICS 89 (2005). FMC Corp. v Halliday, 498 U.S. 52 (1990).

[143] Timothy Stoltzfus Jost & Mark A. Hall, *Self-Insurance for Small Employers Under the Affordable Care Act: Federal and State Regulatory Options,* 86 NYU ANN. SURV. OF AM. L. 539, 546 (2013).

[144] *Id.*

[145] Aetna Health Inc. v. Davila, 542 U.S, 200, 201 124 S.Ct. 2488, 2491 (2004) (declaring:

"The pre-emptive force of ERISA § 502(a) is still stronger. In *Metropolitan Life Ins. Co. v. Taylor,* 481 U.S. 58, 65-66 (1987), the Court determined that the similarity of the language used in the Labor Management Relations Act, 1947 (LMRA), and ERISA, combined with the 'clear intention' of Congress 'to make § 502(a)(1)(B) suits brought by participants or beneficiaries federal questions for the purposes of federal court jurisdiction in like manner as § 301 of the LMRA,' established that ERISA § 502(a)(1)(B)'s pre-emptive force mirrored the pre-emptive force of LMRA § 301. Since LMRA § 301 converts state causes of action into federal ones for purposes of determining the propriety of removal, so too does ERISA § 502(a)(1)(B). Thus, the ERISA civil enforcement mechanism is one of those provisions with such "extraordinary pre-emptive power" that it 'converts an ordinary state common law complaint into one stating a federal claim for purposes of the well-pleaded complaint rule.' Metropolitan Life, 481 U.S., at 65–66").

statute as finally enacted . . . provide strong evidence that Congress did not intend to authorize other remedies that it simply forgot to incorporate expressly."[146]

This unfortunate strong-form preemption blocks state remedies when often what is at stake in these suits is precisely the level of relief. The federal enforcement scheme under § 502 includes a federal cause of action for denial of benefits under employee benefit plans, stripped of compensatory or punitive damages.[147] Section 502(a)(1)(B) merely allows the "participant or beneficiary to recover benefits due him under the terms if the plan."[148] "Put another way, if a patient were to die from a brain tumor following a routine denial of a diagnostic procedure, the patient's survivors could recover no more than the value of the [diagnostic] test itself."[149]

Employers effectively enjoy a limit on their liability for administering employee health benefits.[150] This government-assured risk ceiling is a form of reinsurance. Writing of ordinary limited liability for corporations, David Moss explains, "[L]imited liability is actually a remarkably simple risk management device. All that it does is shift a portion of default risk from shareholders to creditors—in many ways mimicking an insurance policy."[151] He goes on to describe how limited liability, like reinsurance, helps lure greater participation in the private risk market, just as the body of ERISA doctrine embraces the goal of encouraging employers to offer health benefits.[152] As a final parallel to reinsurance, the excess risk transferred by limited liability is spread broadly to backstop private capital: "[T]he only real losers from [the introduction of] limited liability law were involuntary creditors, who were forced to assume additional default risk without compensation of any kind. This meant that a tiny bit of additional risk fell on every member of society, since just about anyone could become the victim of a corporation in one way or another."[153]

---

[146] Pilot Life Ins. Co. v. Dedeaux, 48 U.S. 41, 54 (1987) (declaring, "The six carefully integrated civil enforcement provisions found in § 502(a) of the statute as finally enacted . . . provide strong evidence that Congress did not intend to authorize other remedies that it simply forgot to incorporate expressly").

[147] Sara Rosenbaum & Joel Teitelbaum, *Law and the Public's Health*, 119 PUBLIC HEALTH REPORTS 510, 510 (2004), https://www.ncbi.nlm.nih.gov/pmc/articles/PMC1497659/pdf/15313115.pdf. *See also*, Mass. Mut. Life Ins. v. Russell, 473 U.S. 134 (1985).

[148] ERISA § 502(a)(1)(B), 29 U.S.C. § 1132(a)(1)(B).

[149] Rosenbaum & Teitelbaum, *supra* n.147 at 511.

[150] *Id.* at 512 (2004) (stating "ERISA plan fiduciaries are shielded from any serious financial consequences for what might be an arbitrary and capricious denial of coverage.")

[151] DAVID MOSS, WHEN ALL ELSE FAILS: GOVERNMENT AS THE ULTIMATE RISK MANAGER 83 (2004).

[152] *Id. See also*, Pilot Life Ins. Co. v. Dedeaux, 48 U.S. 41, 42 (1987) (declaring in the context of ERISA's civil enforcement scheme, that the statute "represents a careful balancing of the need for prompt and fair claims settlement procedures against the public interest in encouraging the formation of employee benefit plans").

[153] Moss, *supra* n.151 at 83–4.

Under ERISA, the "tiny bit of additional risk" is the possibility that inability to finance medical expenses can spiral into grave health and real-world consequences. ERISA takes this risk, which employers would otherwise absorb by furnishing health benefits as contracted, and instead distributes it among all employee-beneficiaries.

History of John Kerry's Failed Presidential Campaign Proposal for Health Reinsurance

Our accidental health governance regime, propped up by Medicare, Medicaid and ERISA, left major gaps and distortions. However, state governments, hobbled by scale and ERISA preemption, were limited in what they could do to patch the holes as ever more Americans lost employer-sponsored private coverage. John Kerry, in his ill-fated 2004 presidential run, proposed to address some of these coverage gaps through health reinsurance for employers. Reinsurance would serve to entice employers to provide and maintain health benefits for all their workers.[154]

The Kerry campaign website described the plan thus:

> Under this proposal, the pool would reimburse . . . employer and group health insurance plans that meet certain qualifications for a portion of catastrophic costs. "Catastrophic costs" would be defined as the annual claims for an individual that exceed a certain threshold. This catastrophic threshold would be set so that the average estimated savings would be approximately 10 percent for qualifying plans nationwide.[155]

This constraint translated into an attachment point of roughly $30,000 in 2006, and an estimated $50,000 by 2013. If a beneficiary ran costs above that point, the government would absorb 75 percent of those, leaving the employer to pay only 25 percent.[156] This approach would shave an estimated $1,000 a year off the cost of employer-based family coverage.[157]

[154] John Kerry for President: John Kerry's Plan To Make Health Care Affordable To Every American, KERRY-EDWARDS PRESIDENTIAL CAMPAIGN WEBSITE (2004), http://web.archive.org/web/20040828055342/http:/www.johnkerry.com/issues/health_care/health_care.html (accessed April 15, 2021) (hereinafter Kerry Campaign Website).

[155] Kerry Campaign Website, Id.

[156] Ceci Connolly, Kerry Plan Could Cut Insurance Premiums, WASHINGTON POST (June 5, 2004), at A01, https://www.washingtonpost.com/wp-dyn/articles/A16748-2004Jun4.html (accessed April 15, 2021).

[157] Kerry Campaign Website, supra n.154.

An employer "pay-or-play" model, one of the leading approaches to health reform for over a decade by that point,[158] would have employed a tax penalty as a stick against those employers failing to cover their workers. The Kerry reinsurance policy instead offered a carrot to employers to extend coverage. Much like the Eisenhower proposal, Kerry's policy also laid out certain qualifying standards for health plans as a condition for receiving reinsurance. If the employer plans met these standards, they would receive the benefit of this government backstop for each employee. It was estimated that "less than half of 1 percent of private insurance claims hit Kerry's $50,000 catastrophic threshold. Yet this small fraction devoured 15 percent of all medical services provided in 2000."[159]

Kerry's reinsurance-based proposal was crafted for its broad acceptability and smooth fit with the existing social and political landscape, showing once again how the concept of reinsurance is a heretofore unremarked throughline in our nation's healthcare history. In the end, George W. Bush proceeded to win a second term, defeating John Kerry and cutting off prospects for this next incremental step in the health reinsurance project.

Issues and Lessons

Across the non–health sectors described in the previous chapter, we recognize many themes native to the health domain as well. In the health arena, like in housing and education, we have similarly continued to struggle over whether certain risks can be "redlined" out of health coverage. Through the ACA, we have, as in crop insurance, also chosen not to provide direct government services but to channel the power of private insurers. And we have struggled with whether to institute a public option, even as public fallbacks arose in other contexts, such as Fannie Mae in the secondary market for mortgages, direct lending in higher education, or even government-borne flood risk. We can also draw lessons from the missteps and experience accumulated in these other domains. I will only touch on three lessons here by way of indication: (1) Conditioning the Offer of Reinsurance, (2) Upside Recoupment, and (3) Reinsurance as a Common Substrate across the fragments of our health system. And I will peg these discussions to historical precedents in the health system to show that the roots and trunks are there upon which such lessons could be grafted.

---

[158] See, e.g., DASCHLE ET AL., supra n.100 at 76–7 (2008) ("As the 1992 election drew closer, the pay-or-play model emerged as the most promising approach"). Id at 77.

[159] Connolly, supra n.156 (attributing the finding to research by Stuart Altman).

Conditioning the Offer of Reinsurance

In the previous chapter, we observed repeatedly that the offer of government re-insurance was used as leverage to standardize an area of private transaction. We should take a page from this playbook and use reinsurance as leverage to bring disparate segments of the health system under one common regulatory frame.[160]

In his ultimately unsuccessful presidential bid, John Kerry proposal promised government reinsurance to employers on the condition that employers provide coverage to their employees. Eisenhower proposed to offer reinsurance to private health plans if they met certain qualifying standards. Recently, Sherry Glied and Katherine Swartz have proposed conditional reinsurance to create a more uniform coverage approach to COVID-19-associated care. For instance, they propose that reinsurance be given to state Medicaid plans if states agree to cover all the COVID costs for the uninsured, and that reinsurance for COVID-related healthcare be made available to private plans only on condition that they waive cost-sharing.[161] Reinsurance can serve as leverage for system-wide, salutary re-form and has routinely performed that function in other sectors.

FHA insurance was by design available only for thirty-year, low down-payment mortgages for the purpose of seeding new industry standards.[162] The Federal Reserve imposes prudential regulation on the institutions that enjoy its backing, thus using its leverage to mitigate risk in the financial system.[163] The post-Depression Glass-Steagall Act safeguarded all bank deposits under FDIC and as a condition required the separation of commercial and investment banking to "prevent[] banks from using government-insured deposits to engage in high-risk business."[164] More recently, the 2014 Farm Bill conditioned crop in-surance premium subsidies on compliance with conservation of wetlands and highly erodible land.[165]

Thus, the provision of health reinsurance should be tied to requirements that reduce the systemic risks and exposures that plague our health system. Indeed, part of the appeal of reinsurance lies in its ability to align the inci-dence of high medical costs with the state, which is the entity that arguably

---

[160] John D. Morris, *Eisenhower Plan for Health Funds Rejected in House*, N.Y. TIMES (July 14, 1954), https://www.nytimes.com/1954/07/14/archives/eisenhower-plan-for-health-funds-rejected-in-house-in-surprise-move.html (accessed April 6, 2021).

[161] Sherry Glied & Katherine Swartz, *Using Federal Reinsurance to Address the Health Care Financial Consequences of COVID-19*, HEALTH AFFAIRS BLOG (2020), https://www.healthaffairs.org/do/10.1377/hblog20200401.505998/full/ (accessed April 22, 2021).

[162] SARAH L. QUINN, AMERICAN BONDS 142, 170–76 (2019) (hereinafter S. QUINN). *See supra* text accompanying.

[163] *See*, Gary Gorton & Andrew Metrick, *The Federal Reserve and Panic Prevention: The Roles of Financial Regulation and Lender of Last Resort*, 27 J. ECON. PERSPECT. 45–64 (2013).

[164] Jonathan G. Katz, *Who Benefited from the Bailout?*, 95 MINN. L. REV. 1568, 1597–98 (2011).

[165] S. QUINN, *supra* n.162.

qualifies as the "least cost avoider" given its unique capacity to control systemic medical cost conditions.[166] Our initial failure to impose pharmaceutical cost control as a condition of reinsurance in the profligate Medicare Part D design proves a cautionary tale.[167] The result is "that in 2016, 3.2 million beneficiaries reached the Part D catastrophic phase [and] [t]he costs for reinsurance have almost quadrupled to $37.4 billion in 2016 from $9.4 billion in 2008."[168] Government backing for prescription drug spending should have carried government price controls, as the recent Inflation Reduction Act drug cost provisions begin to address. This logic is recognized in some of the recent state reinsurance proposals, such as Colorado's, which originally limited the government reinsurance paid to a set percentage of the Medicare reference price.[169] Although Colorado and other states have flinched from cost-control conditions in the face of political pushback the policy logic remains compelling.[170] Once the government is a fiscal stakeholder in high-cost medical cases, it should be both well-incentivized and well-positioned to address cost drivers. Why indeed should we grant monopolies or license government patents[171] to the pharmaceutical industry only for industry to turn around and charge high rates that the taxpayer must reabsorb?[172]

[166] On the concept of the "least cost avoider," proposing that the costs should be imposed generally on whoever is best positioned to prevent those costs, *see generally*, Guido Calabresi & Jon T. Hirschoff, *Toward a Test for Strict Liability in Torts*, 81 YALE L.J. 1055, 1060–67 (1972).

[167] MEDPAC, *supra* n.123 at 167. These runaway costs are not inevitable with reinsurance. The American Academy of Actuaries have proposed a number of policy designs that would blunt the inflationary effects of reinsurance, including well-designed ceilings on reinsurance, and use of Hierarchical Condition Categories (HCC's) to dampen moral hazard effects. See, 76 Fed. Reg. No. 136 41935 (July 15, 2011). See, American Academy of Actuaries, *Potential Approaches for Identifying High-Risk Individuals and Determining Payments Under the Temporary Reinsurance Program* (2010), https://www.actuary.org/sites/default/files/pdf/health/Reinsurance%20Options%209%2022%202 010.pdf.

[168] Joshua Cohen, "New Reinsurance Model in Medicare Part D," Forbes (February 11, 2019), https://www.forbes.com/sites/joshuacohen/2019/02/11/new-reinsurance-model-in-medicare-part-d/?sh=3fad3391452d. Standards Related to Reinsurance, Risk Corridors and Risk Adjustment, 76 Fed. Reg. No. 136 41935 (July 15, 2011). *See also* American Academy of Actuaries, Letter from Mita Lodh & Robert Bachler, Risk Sharing Work Grp., Am. Acad. of Actuaries, to Dr. Melinda Buntin, Director, Off. of Econ. Analysis & Modeling (Sept. 22, 2010), https://www.actuary.org/sites/default/files/pdf/health/Reinsurance%20Options%209%2022%202010.pdf. (outlining 4 approaches).

[169] *See* Goodland, *supra* n.59. Charles Gaba, *Colorado: Reinsurance Waiver Would Reduce Premiums 23%...Using Medicare-Based Reimbursement??*, ACA SIGNUPS (2019), https://acasignups.net/19/03/25/colorado-reinsurance-waiver-would-reduce-premiums-23using-medicare-based-reimbursement (accessed April 22, 2021). (reinsured claims would be paid at no more than 150 percent of Medicare. Some note, however, that it is hard to identify when reinsured claims begin and when the spending counts as below the reinsurance threshold.)

[170] *See supra* text accompanying n.59–60.

[171] Hall, *supra* n.16 at 476.

[172] Amy Kapczynski & Aaron S. Kesselheim, *'Government Patent Use': A Legal Approach to Reducing Drug Spending*, 35 HEALTH AFF. (MILLWOOD) 791–797 (2016).

Upside Recoupment

Chief among the conditions that any proposal should build in would be that the *upside* financial gains of government reinsurance be captured for the public. Any reinsurance design must ensure that "subscribers receive the full benefit of the subsidy rather than [allowing it] to cover corporate overhead and profits."[173] For instance, a medical loss ratio like that already legislated in the ACA would trigger rebates to individual or small group consumers whenever the ratio of claims payments to earned premium revenue falls short of 80 percent.[174] This type of provision ensures that the premiums and state subsidies are used primarily on medical services for enrollees, and does so by limiting the amount that individual and small group insurers can reap in profits or lavish on administrative costs to 20 percent. Any additional amounts that are not spent on medical claims must be rebated to the subscribers.

A similar mechanism to assure that benefits flow to the public benefit would be a two-sided risk corridor where the premiums and subsidies that exceed claims above a certain threshold are recaptured by the government. Crop insurance as we saw in Chapter 6, contains just such an upside gain-sharing risk-corridor provision.[175] Some analogous type of device would be necessary to protect against reinsurance programs becoming yet another vehicle for socializing the risks while privatizing the gains, as Obama lamented of the federal student loan guarantee program.[176]

Reinsurance as a Common Substrate

As I suggested earlier, reinsurance could be leveraged to impose standardized requirements across all private health plans and state Medicaid plans. It could thus help foster a common substrate across our fragmented health system, bringing employer-sponsored insurance, Medicaid, and the ACA exchanges into closer integration. Right now, one fragment of our health system that has sheared sharply off the rest of the health coverage landscape is that of self-insured employer plans, to which nearly two-thirds of employees with employer-sponsored

---

[173] Hall, *supra* n.16 at 476.
[174] PHSA § 2718(b), codified as 42 U.S.C. § 300gg-18(b) (setting medical loss ratio as no less than 85 percent in the large group market, and no less than 80 percent in the small group and individual markets, with any smaller percentage triggering the duty to rebate a portion of premiums to the enrollees).
[175] *See* Chapter 6.
[176] QUINN, *supra* n.162 at 13.

coverage are now subject.[177] These plans are exempt not only from state insurance regulation, as detailed in our ERISA preemption discussion, but relieved also from important ACA standards. These bypassed standards include the requirement to cover standardized essential health benefits (EHB), the requirement to participate in the risk pool with risk adjustment alongside other plans, the minimum medical loss ratio requirements we discussed above, the requirements to justify unreasonable rate increases, and the most stringent rules against annual and lifetime limits.[178]

As I suggest in the ERISA discussion, we already provide employer-sponsored health plans with a type of implicit limited liability protection that is a close cousin to reinsurance.[179] We should take what is now quasi-reinsurance for the risks of benefit denial and rationalize it into an offer of express reinsurance redirected toward the actual risk of concern—high medical expenses. Just as we forbade the sale of unauthorized Medicare supplemental plans when we introduced the federally regulated Medigap plans, we could swap in Kerry-like strictly conditioned federal reinsurance to displace the sale of the private stop-loss coverage that currently allows plans to masquerade as self-insured and thereby escape state insurance regulation as well as ACA standards.

Thus, federal reinsurance might be offered instead of ERISA preemption of state claims and would be conditioned upon reforms like regulatory parity between insured and self-insured plans on the provision of essential health benefits, participation in risk adjustment, medical loss ratio requirements and more. Even under the expired ACA reinsurance provision, or under some state reinsurance programs, like Maine's, third-party administrators for self-insured employer-sponsored plans paid the "belly-button tax" that financed the reinsurance pool, one tiny signal of the policy impulse to use reinsurance to knit the fragments of our health system into some relationship of common mutuality.[180] Meanwhile federal reinsurance, essentially a 100 percent federal matching percentage, could be offered conditionally to state Medicaid programs, perhaps to bring them into greater standardization.

The measures sketched here are but incremental and specific policy suggestions await further development; there are many different ways of embodying and perfecting the reinsurance principle in the health sector, as I have tried to show. These are just initial steps whose significance could snowball. John Jacobi has

---

[177] *See, e.g.*, Gobeille v. Liberty Mut. Ins. Co., 136 S.Ct. 936, 952 (2016) (J. Ginsburg, dissenting) ("About half of Americans with health insurance receive coverage from their employers . . . and 61% of such persons are covered by an employer's self-insured plan) (citations omitted).

[178] Jost & Hall, *supra* n.143, at 550–551 and 564.

[179] *See supra* text accompanying n.145–153.

[180] *See supra* n.6.

argued that reinsurance, by establishing a foothold for broadly pooled health risk, could place us on the path to more comprehensive reform.[181] After all—and here I steal a quip from health economist Henry Aaron—what would we call government reinsurance with an attachment point of zero? We would call it single-payer.[182]

[181] John V. Jacobi, *The Present and Future of Government-Funded Reinsurance*, 51 St. Louis Univ. L.J. 369, 381 and 395–6 (2007), *quoting* Alan Weil, *Increments Toward What?*, 20 Health Aff. 68, 81 (2001), https://doi.org/10.1377/hlthaff.20.1.68 (accessed April 22, 2021) (proposing, "we can judge incremental reform proposals not only on the basis of who they cover today, but whether they move us in the right direction for the future").

[182] Hall, *supra* n.16 at 478, *citing* Randall Bovbjerg et al., *Reform of Financing for Health Coverage: What Can Reinsurance Accomplish?* 29 Inquiry 158, 168 (1992) (recounting, "Noted health economist Henry Aaron once proposed a government reinsurance program as a way to transition to a single-payer system, explaining that 'if the [stop-loss] limit were lowered, directly or by erosion due to inflation, the scope of private coverage would shrink, ultimately to the point of disappearing'").

8

Epilogue

This book was written amid a bungled collective response to a global pandemic, in full view of the exhaustion of our public institutions, while steeped in a political culture poisoned by the drip of disinformation-laced despair. It was conceived even as we march straight toward climate change, it was edited in the wake of the violent insurrection of January 6, 2021, and it was completed despite the outbreak of war in Ukraine. This process was accompanied all the while by the delegitimization of the Supreme Court and its turn against reproductive, sex, and gender freedoms, and punctuated by a barrage of mass shootings and border atrocities. And yet—or maybe even because of—this context, this book bears a message of good news. My purpose seems to me even more urgent perhaps because it arrives at a time when good news may be hard to receive.

This book tells a story by way of hypothetical. It asks the reader to consider the explanatory value and normative pay-off of a hypothesized health right. Other scholars have sought to explain health jurisprudence by postulating a *Lochner*-style or libertarian right to bodily autonomy operating across our health case law.[1] Indeed the influence of a crude libertarian ideology on our collective health decisions has been much deplored. Some noted that "the importation of libertarian norms into structural analyses . . . is the feature of the ACA litigation that has proven most rankling to the legal academy."[2] Recent cases striking government pandemic measures have drawn keening outrage.[3] The hostile judicial attitude toward gun regulation and the hardball refusal by private employers to even file a simple certification to allow their employees to access insurer-funded

---

With permission, Chapter 8 adapts minor material from Christina S. Ho, *Are We Suffering from an Undiagnosed Health Right*, 42 AM. J. OF L. AND MED. 743 (2016).

[1] *See* Jessie Hill, *The Constitutional Right to Make Medical Treatment Decisions: A Tale of Two Doctrines*, 86 TEX. L. REV. 277 (2007); Moncrieff, *supra* n.17 (characterizing this right to freedom of health as liberty with respect to disposition of one's body). *See also* Abigail R. Moncrieff, *Safeguarding the Safeguards: The ACA Litigation and the Extension of Indirect Protection to Nonfundamental Liberties*, 64 FLA. L. REV. 639 (2012) (hereinafter Moncrieff, *Safeguarding*); Eugene Volokh, *Medical Self-Defense, Prohibited Experimental Therapies, and Payment for Organs*, 120 HARV. L. REV. 1813 (2007). Although not focusing on health law, others have discussed commercial speech doctrine, as driven by neo-*Lochner* economic libertarianism. *See, e.g.*, Jeremy Kessler, *The Early Years of First Amendment Lochnerism*, 116 COLUM. L. REV. (2016); Jedediah Purdy, *Neoliberal Constitutionalism: Lochnerism for a New Economy*, 77 LAW & CONTEMP. PROBS. 195 (2014).

[2] Moncrieff, *Safeguarding, supra* n.1, at 643.

[3] Luke Herrine et al., Seven Reactions to NFIB v. Department of Labor, LPE PROJECT BLOG (January 26, 2022), https://lpeproject.org/blog/seven-reactions-to-nfib-v-department-of-labor/.

contraception at no cost to the employer—these and many other U.S. health phe-
nomena are hard to read as anything other than extreme privileging of individual
and business prerogatives over health.[4]

At this point I need hardly reassure the reader that my project is not to purge
the law of background norms or "ideological" influence. I seek rather to disturb
the false sense that any background ideology must necessarily be *Lochner*ian in
content.[5] There are other strands within our jurisprudential inheritance available
for extrapolation and the neoliberal story is not the only account we can give
of ourselves. If we wish to posit background rights to help map our health law
terrain, we have a wider range of political options to choose from and possibly
reconstruct. Why assume that economic laissez-faire is the political principle
motivating and extending our body of positive law, but deny such possibility
for other values like human health? The acceptance of canonical property and
liberty interests as the sole point of tangency between community norms and
the law continues to fuel the disregard for health rights that I hope to contest.
The weaponized denial of any other possibility may be what forces the judges in
Chapter 4 who might otherwise build a rights-like norm of Dworkinian preclusion into contorted all-or-nothing postures, forever deflecting frank consideration of whether we should require certain baseline provision of health. Perhaps
it is our indoctrination in this half-truth that is at work—the easy lie that health
measures are only bestowed by grace rather than due by right—whenever we
hide our strong normative commitment to responding to health need under the
ill-fitting label of nondiscrimination.

This book offers a story about who we are, and I deliver it at a moment when
we have come not to recognize ourselves in what we have collectively wrought.
We may need this telling now more than ever as a reminder that our deeper ideals
and values are there in our works yet. And why wouldn't they be? Roberto Unger
teaches that "law . . . is the product of real collective conflict, carried on over a
long time, among many different wills and imaginations, interests and visions."[6]

---

[4] New York State Rifle & Pistol Association, Inc. v. Bruen, 597 U.S. __, 142 S.Ct. 2111 (2022)
(striking New York state's "concealed-carry" gun permitting law); Zubik v. Burwell 578 U.S. __
__ (2016) (remanding a case that challenged an Obama Administration attempt to accommodate
employers with religious objections by allowing them to opt out of the ACA requirement for mandatory contraceptive health coverage by means of employer self-certification which would then trigger
insurance issuers to make separate payments for those affected employees. Religious employers had
argued that such certification still burdened their religious freedom, and the parties were directed on
remand to work out an accommodation that did not impose such a burden.). Little Sisters of the Poor
Saints Peter and Paul Home v. Pennsylvania, 591 U.S. ___, 140 S. Ct. 2367 (2020) (allowing Trump
Administration's interim final rule to stand, providing exemption from the contraceptive mandate
to all religiously or morally objecting employers, including for-profit and publicly traded employers,
without certification or any other mechanism of assuring separate coverage for employees needing
contraception).

[5] Roberto Mangabeira Unger, False Necessity: Anti-Necessitarian Social Theory in
the Service of Radical Democracy 530 (1987).

[6] Roberto Unger, What Should Legal Analysis Become 65 (1996).

To deny that conflict, to unsee the many visions, to abandon the projects built faithfully over decades, one of which I have traced here, is a kind of nihilism. Let us reject the learned impulse to extinguish those moments, some of which might spark us and our inheritors to recover our best selves. Susan Marks rightly reminds the rights cynics in her audience: "Fatalism is a politics because, and to the extent that, by treating actuality as though it were fate, activists help to make it become so."[7]

Throughout this book, we have documented examples of successful advocacy to "navigate the perilous crossing from interests to rights."[8] Recall the statutory elevation of religious liberty beyond constitutional levels of protection, the coinage of "the unfunded mandate" and its associated enforcement mechanisms, the entrenchment of the banking backstops in the form of near-constitutional independence for the Federal Reserve, the federalization of flood insurance, and the build-out of a nigh ineradicable financing infrastructure for housing and higher education.

Rights are not, and have never been either given or not. They can instead be made and unmade with the work of making them passing from one generation to another. Legitimate expectations arise if nurtured and acknowledged, rather than frustrated and squelched, which is what the current knee-jerk dismissal of health-as-a-right functions to achieve. If this space for dynamic discourse and patient cultivation of our social compact and anchor institutions is available for other interests, why not health?

This dynamic discourse happens both within the courtrooms and without; it is as I have tried to show a dialogue among different actors. The Reagan administration, in its disdain for the courts permissive Takings Doctrine, crafted executive orders to protect private property more aggressively. Congress took corresponding action to protect religious liberty when Justice Scalia failed to scrutinize generally applicable laws with sufficient vigor in *Smith*. Franklin Delano Roosevelt and subsequent Congresses entrenched an infrastructure of reinsurance for housing finance. Meanwhile, courts used various reason-vetting tools to scrutinize age-based distinctions even as Congress feinted and left the arena. Federal courts simultaneously took an open-textured Congressional instruction like ERISA and construed employee healthcare rights down to a vanishing point, a gambit they tried for the ADA too. In the ADA battles, however, the EEOC put up resistance and Congress countered with the ADA Amendments Act of 2000. Agencies and legislatures may act to thwart a conception proffered

---

[7] Susan Marks, *Four Human Rights Myths* 217, 228, *in* HUMAN RIGHTS: OLD PROBLEMS, NEW POSSIBILITIES (David Kinley, Wojciech Sadurski, and Kevin Walton, eds., 2013).

[8] John Tasioulas & Effy Vayena, *Just Global Health*, THE OXFORD HANDBOOK OF GLOBAL JUSTICE (2020), https://www.oxfordhandbooks.com/view/10.1093/oxfordhb/9780198714354.001.0001/ oxfordhb-9780198714354-e-7 (accessed September 23, 2021).

by the courts. At the end of Chapter 4, we mentioned Washington State's 2022 state benefit mandate for medically necessary gender-affirming care, curbing *Smith v. Rasmussen* and its permission to states to carve out such surgeries. Recall also the *DeSario* letter, where in the aftermath of a Second Circuit decision permitting tightly closed Medicaid formularies for DME, HHS restored the requirement that states allow exceptions for off-list DME if medically necessary.

How can one scoff at proposals for frank inclusion of the right to health as one project amid this rights-wrangling discourse, especially when these efforts are happening already? Why accede to the project of sidelining health rights, a project that has assumed mythic status, untethered from real events? But myths can be made or busted. Which do we choose each time we tell ourselves that expansive readings of health statutes "lack historical precedent," or each time we label broad legislative grants for public health as "no 'everyday exercise of federal power'"?[9] These phrases were deployed by the Supreme Court majority to strike down the recent COVID-19 workplace vaccine-or-test requirement, forcibly maintaining the neoliberal no-right-to-health-myth.

An alternative tradition once seeded can grow. We have excavated just some of the pathways along which shoots and runners already criss-cross the terrain. Dworkin the constructivist explains how rights principles accumulate their own momentum and vital force pressing for extension in the next case.[10] I have always found it highly suggestive that the cases involving health and the body are the sites of some of the most glaringly raw exercises of judicial political fiat in recent years. Why can we trace the development of the "major questions doctrine," through our successive efforts to protect the people from benzene, tobacco, and particulate matter, high premiums in state ACA exchanges, and now COVID-19?[11] Why is the elaboration of substantive due process and its limits carried out through landmark health cases involving physician-assisted suicide, abortion, and contraception?[12] Perhaps the violence of these decisions hints at the fecund power of this hidden tradition of health values. What is so forceful and compelling that it requires such emphatic judicial concealment and vicious pruning? Why, in Chapters 3 and 4, was the presumptive force of health as a value so available as a matter of intuitive justice, yet so absent from our doctrinal toolkit? This story speaks not just of wider possibilities for alternative ideas; it also tells a history of effective suppression.

---

[9] NFIB v. Department of Labor, OSHA, 595 U.S. ___ (2022) *per curiam* (slip op. p. 3 and 5) (citations omitted).

[10] RONALD DWORKIN, TAKING RIGHTS SERIOUSLY 111–122 (1978).

[11] Indus. Union Dept. v. Amer. Petroleum Inst. 448 US 607 (1980), FDA v. Brown & Williamson Tobacco Corp., 529 U.S. 120 (2000), Whitman v. American Trucking Ass'ns 531 U.S. 457 (2001), King v. Burwell 576 U.S. 473 (2015), NFIB v. Department of Labor, OSHA, 595 U.S. ___ (2022).

[12] Griswold v. Connecticut, 381 U.S. 479 (1965), Roe v. Wade, Washington v. Glucksberg 521 U.S. 702 (1997), Planned Parenthood of Southeastern Pa. v. Casey, 505 U.S. 833 (1992).

Health rights would help shift us from the political economy of neoliberalism to the political economy of the body, a correction that is particularly urgent right now. Robin West has long warned us that we neglect at our peril the basic Hobbesian insight that the body's vulnerability, the threats of morbidity and mortality that make life "nasty brutish and short," constitute the motivating ground of collective life.[13] And yet our discourse dismisses out of hand the value of health when we consider rivals to *Lochner*, or candidates for what West calls "law's deep values" that "complete the truncated analysis critiqued by Unger and his followers."[14] This willful health-blindness is ever more curious, requiring more justification and correspondingly more pushback than we have mustered thus far, particularly when considered in light of Wendy Parmet's sounding of the old and persistent truth, *salus populi est suprema lex*.[15] An embodied justice would indeed counter the neoliberal invisibilization of human costs.[16]

For a right to be "deeply rooted in this Nation's history and traditions," it must be nurtured over time. An obscuring of those roots, a denial of that tradition, works to discourage investment and douse hope.[17] To believe that we have no US health right is a stance that, like Susan Marks's enemy, fatalism, becomes self-fulfilling. We cannot be reminded too often that "social facts are facts only insofar as people regularly reproduce them."[18] If this all sounds circular, how we break that cycle may ring so as well. Yet it is the project of this book. Each chapter contains an invitation to draw a new circle, to bring ourselves back to the reasons for why we come together, both for security and flourishing. Each argument was meant both to reveal ourselves and propose ourselves, potentially whole again in our trust that—and here I quote a Jedediah Britton-Purdy line dwelling in my head throughout these pandemic times—"Americans already are what they have never yet been."[19]

---

[13] *See, e.g.* Robin L. West, "Reconsidering Legalism," 88 *Minn. L. Rev.* 119, 132–5 (2003) (citing Jean Hampton, "Democracy and the Rule of Law," *in* The Rule of Law 13 (Ian Shapiro ed., 1994), and Michael P. Zuckert, "Hobbes, Locke, and the Problem of the Rule of Law," in *The Rule of Law* at 63.).

[14] ROBIN L. WEST, RE-IMAGINING JUSTICE 154 (2003).

[15] WENDY E. PARMET, POPULATIONS. PUBLIC HEALTH AND THE LAW (2009).

[16] Thanks to Michael Thomson and Beth Goldblatt for this phrase, "embodied justice."

[17] *See, e.g.*, Washington v. Glucksberg, 521 U.S. 702 (1997) ("the Court has regularly observed that the Clause specially protects those fundamental rights and liberties which are, objectively, deeply rooted in this Nation's history and tradition").

[18] PAUL STARR, ENTRENCHMENT: WEALTH, POWER, AND THE CONSTITUTION OF DEMOCRATIC SOCIETIES 1 (2019).

[19] Jedediah Britton-Purdy, *What John Rawls Missed*, THE NEW REPUBLIC (October 28, 2019), https://newrepublic.com/article/155294/john-rawls-missed-create-just-society (accessed May 23, 2022).

Index

For the benefit of digital users, indexed terms that span two pages (e.g., 52–53) may, on occasion, appear on only one of those pages.